CONTEMPORARY GALICIAN
CULTURAL STUDIES

WORLD LITERATURES REIMAGINED

MODERN LANGUAGE ASSOCIATION OF AMERICA

Brazilian Narrative Traditions in a Comparative Context
Earl E. Fitz. 2005

Tales of Crossed Destinies:
The Modern Turkish Novel in a Comparative Context
Azade Seyhan. 2008

Contemporary Galician Cultural Studies:
Between the Local and the Global
Ed. Kirsty Hooper and Manuel Puga Moruxa. 2011

CONTEMPORARY GALICIAN CULTURAL STUDIES

BETWEEN THE LOCAL AND THE GLOBAL

Edited by

Kirsty Hooper and
Manuel Puga Moruxa

THE MODERN LANGUAGE ASSOCIATION OF AMERICA

NEW YORK 2011

MLA and the MODERN LANGUAGE ASSOCIATION are trademarks owned by the
Modern Language Association of America. For information about obtaining permission to
reprint material from MLA book publications, send your request by mail (see address
below), e-mail (permissions@mla.org), or fax (646 458-0030).

LIBRARY OF CONGRESS CATALOGING-IN-PUBLICATION DATA

Contemporary Galician cultural studies : between the local and the global / edited by
Kirsty Hooper and Manuel Puga Moruxa.
   p.   cm. — (World literatures reimagined, ISSN 1553-6181 ; 3)
   Includes bibliographical references and index.
   ISBN 978-1-60329-087-6 (alk. paper) —
   ISBN 978-1-60329-088-3 (pbk. : alk. paper)
   1. Galician literature—20th century—History and criticism.   2. Literature and
society—Spain—Galicia (Region)   3. Galicia (Spain)—Intellectual life—20th century.
I. Hooper, Kirsty.   II. Puga Moruxa, Manuel.
   PQ9458.C68 2011
   869.09'9461—dc22   2010045089

World Literatures Reimagined 3
   ISSN 1553-6181

Cover illustration for the paperback edition: *Cathedral of Santiago*, photograph by Xurxo
Lobato, from his series Camino de Santiago. Used with permission of the photographer

Published by The Modern Language Association of America
26 Broadway, New York, New York 10004-1789
www.mla.org

For John Rutherford
Remembering Xoán González-Millán
and Tim McGovern

CONTENTS

World literature: for many years, this concept has been little understood and even less agreed on. Since Goethe's invention of the term
Weltliteratur, in 1827, readers have tended to invest world literature with
both an impossibly ideal character and an inconceivable material scope. For
some, it is a highly selective canon of works that transcend their national
literatures and languages. For others, it is everything—the sum of all the
national literatures considered together. For still others among a spate of recent theorists who have embraced the topic, world literature is the outcome
of a confrontation between received forms and local conditions, a mode
of reading and exchange between works of different times and places, or a
metropolitan construction that ensures the maintenance of categories such
as "major" and "minor" literatures.

Meanwhile, world literature has become increasingly prevalent in departments of literature, as the rubric for a kind of course that—despite its
name—usually reflects local institutional notions of what might be relevant.
While the concept has been undergoing considerable intellectual revision in
recent years, little has changed for teachers or students who seek to expand
their reach.

The series World Literatures Reimagined, sponsored by the MLA's
Publications Committee, seeks to redress this gap by exploring new con-
ceptions of what world literature—or literatures—might mean. Written by
specialists but addressed to a wide audience, books in the series consider
particular literatures in an international context. They seek to develop new
articulations of the connections among literatures and to give a sense of the
ways in which literatures and their cultures might be like and unlike one
another. Among other things, volumes in the series look afresh at works that
might expand or complicate our notions of world literature; make compari-
sons between less well known works and their better-known counterparts;

and deal forthrightly with translation, showing teachers and students what is (and what should be) available in English. A shelf of these volumes should go far to encourage the reimagining of world literatures in our consciousness as well as our classrooms.

Roland Greene
Series Editor

ACKNOWLEDGMENTS

We would like to express our thanks to all the people who helped bring this project, first conceived at the Queen's College, Oxford Centre for Galician Studies in 2002, into being.

First we thank John Rutherford, a wonderful mentor, supporter, and colleague, without whom neither the center nor this project would exist.

María Liñeira, Lourdes Lorenzo García, Helena Miguélez-Carballeira, Gabriel Rei-Doval, Lisa Shaw, and Claire Taylor provided support and encouragement in different ways.

Staff members and readers of the MLA shepherded this project through many different stages. We are especially grateful to Sonia Kane for her wise and gracious counsel during the last seven years.

We are grateful to our contributors, for their unfailing patience and unflagging enthusiasm. We hope they will be as proud of the finished product as we are.

Finally, we dedicate this book to the memory of two beloved and much missed colleagues. Xoán González-Millán was the father of Galician studies in the United States, and we remember him for his outstanding scholarship, his warm encouragement of younger scholars, and his ceaseless advocacy of Galician culture on the world stage. Tim McGovern was one of the freshest voices in the field and, had he lived longer, would have made a great contribution to its development; we remember him for his boundless enthusiasm, his innovative scholarship, and his unstinting friendship.

Introduction:
Galician Geographies

Kirsty Hooper and Manuel Puga Moruxa

If the twenty-first century is to be characterized, as Manuel Castells has argued, by the conflicting trends of globalization and identity, then Galicia provides an ideal location for exploration of the resulting tensions. Located in the extreme northwest of the Iberian Peninsula and to the far west of Europe and bordered on two sides by the Atlantic Ocean, to the south by Portugal, and to the east by the Spanish *autonomías* of Asturias and Castilla-León, Galicia stands at the crossroads between land and sea, Europe and America, the Atlantic north and the Mediterranean south, *hispanidad* (the Spanish-speaking world) and its Portuguese counterpart, *lusofonía*. This peripheral position is colorfully summarized in the name given to Galicia's westernmost point: for the Romans, it was Finis Terrae, the end of the known earth; in Galician it is Fisterra, and until 2002 a version of its name, Finisterre, was familiar to listeners of BBC Radio's daily shipping forecast.[1]

Because of Galicia's ambiguous geographic and cultural position and recent social and political history, what it means to be Galician—the question of *galeguidade* ("Galicianness")—is constantly up for discussion. The end in 1975 of almost four decades of Spanish centralist dictatorship and the subsequent advent of democracy in Spain have opened up a public space for the reconstitution of *galeguismo*, the movement for political and social recognition of Galicia's autonomy. This development has in turn created a space for debating new and old configurations of *galeguidade* in a pluralist context characterized by the possibility of multiple, dynamic, innovative appropriations of existing codes of identity. At the same time, the rise in the 1980s of the new Europe, in which Spain is one of the most enthusiastic participants, has created a new framework for international, interregional, and interlocal relations. Finally, the advent of new technologies and improved transport links during the 1980s and 1990s have, in Galicia as elsewhere, greatly facilitated contact between Galicians at home and in the diaspora communities that are the consequence of Galicia's long history of emigration. *Contemporary Galician Studies: Between the Local and the Global* therefore has a double purpose. We wish to provide a practical guide to this compelling culture and to an increasingly dynamic field of study that remains largely unknown throughout the wider academy. At the same time, we hope to contribute to the development of that field of study by providing the first English-language collection of analyses of Galician culture and identity in the context of the local, national, European, and global changes that have shaped their development decisively since 1975.

Galicia and Galicians: Between the Local and the Global

With a population of less than three million in 2008, Galicia is currently home to about 6% of the Spanish population (this percentage is slightly greater than that of the Basque Country [4.7%]; in comparison, the figure for Catalonia is 16%).[2] Despite the country's small size, however, Galicia and Galicians have had a considerable impact on cultural, social, political, and economic developments not only in Spain but throughout the Hispanic world. Tellingly, although Galicians are only 6% of the Spanish population, the electoral census used for the 2009 Galician elections reveals that they make up some 27% of Spaniards abroad (or at least of Spaniards registered to vote overseas).[3] Galicia has formed part of the Spanish state since its inception, and many of those who have forged what we know as modern Spain were of Galician origin, such as the feminist intellectual Emilia Pardo Bazán (1851–1921), the modernist playwright and novelist Ramón del Valle-Inclán (1866–1936), the Nobel laureate Camilo José Cela (1916–2002), and General Francisco Franco himself (1892–1975). Galicians and their descendants are building an increasingly high profile in contemporary Spanish and global popular culture as well, from the fashion designers Amancio Ortega and Rosalía Mera (founders of the well-known Zara brand), Adolfo Domínguez, and Roberto Verino through sportsmen like the Tour de France winner Óscar Pereiro; musicians like Julio Iglesias, Luz Casal, and Carlos Núñez; and actors like Luis Tosar and Nancho Novo. The question of the extent to which such figures are Galician in any sense other than that Galicia is their place of birth is a vexed one. In literature and culture in particular, the boundaries between Galician and Spanish have long been the subject of heated debate, in part because of the weight given to culture in the absence of Galician national institutions during the nineteenth and much of the twentieth century.

The debate intensified in the decades since the demise of General Franco in 1975. The subsequent advent of democracy reconstituted Spain as a nation of *autonomías,* in which Galicia, along with Catalonia and the Basque Country, has the status of a *nacionalidade histórica* ("historic nationality"). This controversial term was designed to appease both centralists (who sought to maintain the unity of the Spanish nation-state and therefore rejected the existence of other nations within Spain) and the Basque, Catalan, and Galician nationalists who were determined to see their homelands recognized in law. While it provided a temporary solution to this fundamental ideological division, the category of *nacionalidad histórica* is now coming under increasing pressure. The Catalan Statute of Autonomy, revised and approved by referendum in 2006, now controversially includes reference in the preamble (not in the main body of the document) to Catalonia as a nation, bringing it into conflict with the Spanish constitution, which upholds "la indisoluble unidad de la Nación española" ("the indissoluble unity of the Spanish nation" [*Constitución*]). The Spanish government's response has been to recognize the declaratory value of the statute's description of Catalonia as a nation but to award it no legal status. The Bloque Nacionalista Galego (BNG; "Galician Nationalist Bloc"), like its Catalan counterparts, has been campaigning for a change in terminology for some time; in 2005 it proposed significant revisions to the Statute of Autonomy, in which the word *nación* ("nation") is prominent. During the nationalist-socialist coalition administration of 2005–09, a parliamentary commission was established to drive forward these revisions, but the establishment of a new conservative administration following the spring 2009 elections makes progress unlikely for the foreseeable future.

What might appear to be little more than a dry discussion of legal terminology has considerable ramifications for wider debate about Galicia's local and global situation. Galicia's relationship with the rest of the world is complicated: on the one hand, Galicia operates as a full national culture, having its own language, literature, and institutions; on the other, because it remains a part of the Spanish state, its nationhood is disputed and therefore secondary. In consequence, for Galicia as for Spain's other historical nationalities, the relationship with the world beyond the state is fundamentally shaped by, as well as mediated through, the relationship with Spain. This position does not go unquestioned, as artists and thinkers in Galicia, Catalonia, and the Basque Country seek to develop new ways of articulating and experiencing these nations' relationship with the world beyond Spain that reveal the vertical relationship with the state to be as limited as it has been limiting. Scholars such as Stewart King, in his work on postcolonial Catalonia; Joseba Gabilondo, in his rethinking of Basque culture in terms of Gilles Deleuze and Félix Guattari's discussion of minor and major literatures; or José Colmeiro ("Peripheral Visions"), Kirsty Hooper ("New Cartographies"), Burgard Baltrusch ("Galiza e lusofonía") and Helena Miguélez-Carballeira ("Alternative Values") in their debates about the validity of the term *post-national* in the Galician context not only respond to but also critique and reformulate global theoretical frameworks whose application to the Iberian Peninsula has so often been reductive or largely absent.

It is unsurprising that Galicia's political and social development has been closely connected with that of Spain, and it should be equally unsurprising, given Galicia's geographic location, that Galicia has long had strong (albeit seldom formalized) social, cultural, and intellectual ties with Portugal. The two nations share a linguistic origin in the Galician-Portuguese variant of Iberian Romance and a cultural origin in the medieval songbooks—the *Cantigas de Santa María* and the *Cancioneiros da ajuda, da Vaticana,* and *Colocci-Brancuti.* The language of the *Cantigas* and *Cancioneiros, galego-portugués,* as the literary language of the Spanish court, performed the same function in the Iberian Peninsula as Occitan did in France and Italy. Galician and Portuguese took separate paths only after Portuguese independence in the twelfth century, when Portuguese gained in status as a language of state, while the institutionalization in Spain of Castilian reduced Galician (like Aragonese, Asturian, Basque, Catalan, and Leonese) to the status of vernacular. Many of the current arguments for Galician-Portuguese connections are filtered through the linguistic context. Even today, after centuries of Castilian influence, the Galician language is more closely related to Portuguese, so that as John Thompson explains in his essay in this volume, there is a current of thought in Galicia that seeks to reintegrate Galicia with Portugal. Despite the recent, limited success of the *reintegracionistas* in persuading the Real Academia Galega (RAG) to push through orthographic adjustments that make the *normas* ("norms," in the document setting out the official standard form of the Galician language) a stronger reflection of the Portuguese influence, Galician–Portuguese connections have rarely been reflected or, indeed, recognized at the state level, although the new EU zone of Galicia–Norte de Portugal offers recognition at the suprastate level. Nevertheless, there are increasing numbers of initiatives designed to bring the two countries together at a cultural and intellectual level, such as the

GALABRA (galego-luso-afro-brasileiro) research group based at the Universidade de Santiago de Compostela and the *Revista portugaliza*, published online by the Associaçom Galega da Língua (*AGAL*).

Galicia's geographic ambiguity is also reflected in the continuing struggles over where to place Galicia politically, linguistically, and culturally on the world stage. Paradoxically, the Galicianness of Galician-born people and their descendants outside Spain has in the past been less in question. Galicia's long and familiar history as a land of migrants has placed Galicians and their descendants all over the world, although historically the closest connections have been with the Americas (from the sixteenth to the mid–twentieth century) and with northern Europe (from the 1960s onward). In fact, the migratory flow of Galicians to the Americas during the nineteenth and twentieth centuries was so significant that in many Latin American countries—especially Argentina, Colombia, and Uruguay—*Gallegos* ("Galicians") is the common term used to describe all Spaniards (*Diccionario de la lengua* [22nd ed.]). The Galician diaspora, even if we consider those born within only two generations from the homeland, might include figures as well known as the Cuban president Fidel Castro (his surname is almost stereotypically Galician, referring to the ancient fortified villages that dot the Galician landscape), the French-born singer and musician Manu Chao, the Swiss-born racing driver Niki Lauda, Jerry García (lead singer of the Grateful Dead), the caustic United States gossip columnist and blogger Pérez Hilton, and the Hollywood actors Martin Sheen (born Ramón Estévez) and his sons Charlie Sheen and Emilio Estévez. The strong presence of these Galician diaspora communities all over the world, whether individual members strongly identify as Galician or not, reinforces the ambiguity of Galicia's geographic position, as it has since the nineteenth century. In this volume, this topic is developed especially in the essays by Jaine Beswick, Eugenia R. Romero, and Kirsty Hooper.

Despite the long-established connections with Spain and Portugal and the influences of the cultures encountered by Galicians in the diaspora, Galicia's own culture remains distinctive. After a long and difficult history, it is now beginning to emerge as a source of pride rather than shame. The essays in this volume explore the implications of this culture, its past history and its ambiguous position in the present, as Galicians today seek to resituate themselves and their nation in terms of the radically shifting regional and national discursive maps of twenty-first-century Iberia. A central project of this volume is thus to trace, question, and even, perhaps, reshape the boundaries of Galicianness and the debates and practices that have sustained them. Through this project, we hope to contribute to the creation of a position where Galician literature, culture, and identity can be studied on their own terms—that is, not only as an adjunct to Spanish literature, culture, and identity but also as a vital contributor to a global system of cultures that, as Édouard Glissant would have it, is "not prompted solely by the defining of our identities, but by their relation to everything possible as well—the mutual mutations generated by this interplay of relations" (89).

A Brief History of Modern Galician Culture and Identity

In part 1, "Histories," we provide an outline narrative of the development of Galician nationalism and modern Galician literature since the early nineteenth century, to orient readers to the general historical and cultural framework in which the rest of the volume moves as well as to introduce some of the key terms used throughout.[4] The essays, especially those by Lourenzo Fernández Prieto, Antón Figueroa, and María do Cebreiro Rábade Villar, all work in different ways to interpret and analyze this master narrative.

The institutional history of modern Galicia begins with the shift in relations between Spain's center and peripheries that followed the Napoleonic invasion of 1808–13 (Ucelay). Increasing administrative centralization peaked in 1833, with the territorial reforms carried out under the jurisdiction of Isabel II's minister, Javier de Burgos. Under these reforms, the ancient Kingdom of Galicia, which had existed as an administrative unit—if little more—since the Middle Ages was carved up into the four provinces that still make up Galicia today: A Coruña (in Spanish, La Coruña), Lugo, Ourense (Orense), and Pontevedra. The loss of the symbolic unity of the ancient kingdom inspired a political movement during the 1830s and 1840s that was called *provincialismo*, its principal demand being the creation of a single province of Galicia, if not the restoration of the kingdom itself. In April 1846, a small group of soldiers under the direction of General Solís attempted to seize control of the Galician administration but were swiftly defeated by the Spanish army. The ringleaders were executed in the small village of Carral, near A Coruña. The defeat of the Levantamento de Carral ("Carral Uprising") or, as it is increasingly called, the Revolución de 1846 ("1846 Revolution") led to immediate sanctions against the emerging *gale-*

guista political movement. In consequence, the movement's focus switched to the cultural sphere. A decade after Carral, a group of Galician intellectuals, students, and artisans came together at the Banquete de Conxo ("Conxo Banquet"), in the small town of Conxo, near Santiago de Compostela, in a meeting that is generally considered the foundational act of the nineteenth-century Galician cultural revival, known as the Rexurdimento. The Xogos Florais ("Floral Games") that took place at Tui in 1861 and the publication of Rosalía de Castro's first Galician-language collection of poetry, *Cantares gallegos* ("Galician Songs"), in 1863 ushered in the Rexurdimento proper.

The success of the Rexurdimento in the 1860s and 1870s, especially in the fields of Galician-language poetry and of historical, linguistic, and ethnographic scholarship, created a solid basis for the expression of modern Galician culture and identity. It gave rise to the institutionalized narrative that remains dominant today, in which Galicia's ideological development from provincialism to regionalism to nationalism is paralleled by the progressive reclamation of the Galician language, from a peasant vernacular to an elite literary language.

Like any teleological narrative, however, this one is structured as much by what it leaves out as by what it includes. The narrative of progression from vernacular to literary culture and (at least in cultural terms) from messy bilingualism to Galician monolingualism excludes some of the most interesting literary production of the period. New work on the nineteenth century, by scholars like Alex Alonso and Danny Barreto, is beginning to reclaim genres that have not traditionally received a great deal of scholarly attention, such as the press and popular (as opposed to high literary) fiction. Meanwhile, revisionist approaches to the work of Rosalía de Castro, such as the essays in this volume by Rábade Villar and Gabilondo, embrace Castro's bilingualism and her "fractured" Galician, thus seeking to refigure the origins of modern Galician literature in the gaps between languages. From Gabilondo (in this volume), Catherine Davies, and Silvia Bermúdez, among others, we can also see Castro's poetic production as inherently Atlantic, both in its lyrical evocation of the experience of emigration (it is no coincidence that *Cantares gallegos* was published exactly a decade after the Spanish government lifted restrictions on emigration to South America) and in the material circumstances of its production (it is impossible to ignore Castro's heartfelt thanks, in the prologue to *Follas novas* ["New Leaves"], to the Galician expatriate community in Cuba, who had provided essential financial support for her work and its publication).

We can begin to see, then, that from very early on Galician culture transcends geographic, linguistic, and generic boundaries. During the last decades of the nineteenth century and first decades of the twentieth, Spain was changing. Political developments triggered by the 1868 revolution and abdication of Isabel II made the situation much more propitious for an ideology that supported Galicia's emerging cultural identity. The relatively limited aims of the *provincialista* movement of the 1840s gave way to a more ambitious *rexionalista* ("regionalist") agenda, which sought autonomy for Galicia within the Spanish state. The *rexionalista* movement had three principal strands: the liberal strand, based in the northern port city A Coruña and led by Manuel Murguía (husband of Rosalía de Castro); the federal strand, based in the inland city of Lugo and led by Aurelio Ribalta; and the traditionalist strand, led by Alfredo Brañas. *Rexionalismo* was established in Galician politics by the 1880s, a position that was sealed by the publication of works by Murguía and by Brañas, both called *Regionalismo gallego* and both published in 1889 by the foundation of the weekly journal *Revista gallega* ("Galician Review"), which ran from 1895 to 1907. The foundation of the RAG in 1906 and the increasing importance of the agrarian movement embodied in Solidaridad Gallega ("Galician Solidarity"), founded in 1907 on the model of the Catalan Solidaritat Catalana, aimed to broaden the intellectual and social reach of the *galeguista* movement. It is important to note that much of the impetus for the institutional developments that took place during this critical period came from Galicia's overseas communities: the establishment of the RAG and, in 1907, of the Galician flag and anthem were driven ideologically and financially by expats, mostly in Cuba.

With regard to literature, we might consider the *rexionalista* period as bookended by the publication of the first novel in Galician, Marcial Valladares's *Maxina* (1880), and the first novel in Galician written by a woman, Francisca Herrera's *Néveda* (1920). Both texts are sentimental, and most critics have perceived little evolution between them, reading *Maxina* principally for its philological value and *Néveda* as a late imitation of the work of Rosalía de Castro. It is a critical convention to bemoan the relative lack of Galician-language narrative during this period, and it is true that much of the popular cultural production described as Galician is actually in Spanish, such as works in the series Biblioteca de Escritores Gallegos ("Library of Galician Writers," founded 1910), which was based in Madrid. But the linguistic boundaries between Spanish and Galician narrative remain porous during this period, especially in the light of Rábade Villar's and Gabilondo's work on Castro. Even *Maxina* is described, in its subtitle, as a "Conto galego-castelán" ("Galician-Castilian short story"), and it used both languages to reflect the social reality of the time. Conventional literary histories pay little attention to genres other than poetry in this period, allegedly on the grounds of aesthetic quality but really because scholars after the 1950s (possibly even the 1920s) needed to promote a narrative of elite and monolingual cultural production. Little critical attention was therefore paid to fiction, and to cultural landmarks such as the first historical novel, the first female-authored novel, and the first drama, most of which was considered sentimental, anachronistic, and ruralist.

The progressive move toward an institutional focus on elite and monolingual cultural production broadly parallels the ideological shift from *rexionalismo* to full-fledged nationalism that began with the new century but really took hold during its second decade. The foundation of the linguistic societies Irmandades da Fala ("Brotherhoods of the Language") in several Galician cities between 1916 and 1919 and the Asamblea Nacional ("National Assembly") held at Lugo in 1918 laid the groundwork, but it was the publication of Vicente Risco's *Teoría do nacionalismo galego* ("Theory of Galician Nationalism") in 1920 that established nationalism as an important cultural, ideological, and political movement in Galicia.

During the 1920s, Risco and his colleagues Alfonso Rodríguez Castelao (usually known simply as Castelao) and Ramón Otero Pedrayo established the parameters of the modern Galician nation: language, territory, and history. These three intellectuals, known as the Xeración Nós ("Us Generation," after *Nós*, the influential cultural magazine they founded in 1920), are generally considered the founding fathers of modern Galician thought. The cultural manifesto "Máis alá" ("Further Still"), published in 1923 by the avant-garde poet Manoel Antonio, provides an illustration of the shift of worldview necessary to implement Risco's new nationalist ideology, in its violent ejection of Castilian-speaking intellectuals such as Ramón María del Valle-Inclán from Galician literature. The writers of the *Nós* Generation worked hard to situate Galicia in the wider intellectual movement of modernism, producing translations of European works, such as the novels of James Joyce, and developing Galicia's cultural identification with other countries—Ireland in particular. Castelao deserves particular attention for his innovative mixture of visual and textual culture, supported by his theoretical writings on art and humor as a form of resistance. Especially interesting are his series of political cartoons, which develop a critical line begun by Goya, and his *Cousas* ("Things"), which reinterpret the rural as a center of social and political criticism. Although Castelao's work was popular in Galicia, but also—as evidenced by lectures and traveling exhibitions of his art—throughout Spain, the *Nós* Generation and their audience were an elite minority. Most literate Galicians were still happily reading popular fiction, much of it in Spanish.

The advent of the Second Republic in Spain in 1931 gave the Galician nationalists an unprecedented opportunity for political action. Castelao was a founder of the Partido Galeguista ("Galicianist Party") and represented the province of Pontevedra in the Republican government from 1931 to 1933 and in 1936. His special project was the creation of a Galician Statute of Autonomy, but in July 1936, two weeks after he had succeeded in getting it passed by plebiscite, Franco's forces rose up against the Republican government, the civil war broke out, and Galicia fell swiftly to the attacking army. Castelao, caught by chance in Madrid, avoided the fate of many other Galician nationalist politicians and activists who were executed or imprisoned; after the war ended in 1939, he settled in Argentina, where he would play an active part in both the Republican government in exile and the community of Galician exiles. It was also in exile that he completed his political magnum opus, *Sempre en Galiza* (1944; "Forever in Galicia").

The civil war and the subsequent dictatorship marked another important rupture in the history of *galeguismo*, as most of its leaders were silenced, imprisoned, forced into exile, or killed. When in the 1950s and 1960s the dictatorship became rather more permissive, the *galeguista* movement could resume part of its activity through literary and cultural production. Thus, the Editorial Galaxia was founded in 1950, under the leadership of Ramón Piñeiro, the most influential figure of the *galeguistas do interior* ("Galicia-based Galicianists"). Piñeiro and his peers (including the great literary historian Ricardo Carballo Calero), often referred to as the Xeración Galaxia ("Galaxia Generation"), sought to continue the work of the *Nós* Generation in both intellectual and creative terms, especially the *Nós* strategy of situating Galicia as part of an elite European culture. But disagreements soon emerged between this group and the *galeguistas* in exile in America, one of whose most distinguished figures was the artist Luís Seoane (Castelao having died in Buenos Aires in 1950). The Galicians abroad—principally in Argentina, Brazil, and Cuba—remained committed to political activism, whereas those who remained in Galicia, especially the Galaxia group, advocated the sole pursuit of cultural activity, recognizing that political action was impossible under current conditions.

It was not until the mid-1960s that political activity began again, with the foundation of political parties: the Unión do Pobo Galego (UPG; "Galician People's Union") and the Partido Socialista Galego (PSG; "Galician Socialist Party"). These parties of course remained clandestine until the restoration of democracy. In a way, they had to begin from scratch, as their link with the Partido Galeguista of the republic had been practically severed. Their ideological principles were also different, as they now embraced socialism (PSG) or communism (UPG). Understandably in the circumstances, the ability of these parties to enhance the *galeguista* cause, and to construct and expand a discourse of national identity, was limited. The most important achievements of the *galeguista* movement during the "longa noite de pedra" ("long night of stone"), as the poet Celso Emilio Ferreiro described the dictatorship, came from the fields of literature and culture. For example, the trend called Nova Narrativa Galega ("New Galician Narrative"), from the late 1950s to the early 1970s, was influenced by the French *nouveau roman* and practiced by writers like Xosé Luís Méndez Ferrín, María Xosé Queizán, and Carlos Casares.

Galicia's transition to autonomy after the death of Franco in November 1975 was codified with the ratification in December 1980 of the Statute of Autonomy (signed 6 April 1981), followed in October 1981 by the first autonomous elections. The Xunta de Galicia, the Galician government, was established and given certain powers over education, economy, industry, health, the environment, the infrastructure, and agriculture—although as events would constantly prove, it was always ultimately subordinate to the central Spanish government.

It is something of a paradox that Galicia's experience of self-government has throughout most of these years been dominated by nationwide parties like the conservative Partido Popular (PP) and, later, the socialist Partido dos Socialistas de Galicia–Partido Socialista Obrero Español (PSdeG-PSOE), in which Galician nationalism has been relegated to a subordinate position. One reason might be the weakness or precarious character of the Galician national consciousness as a result of the successive failures of the nationalist movement in the past. Another reason might be the organizational problems in which nationalists got embroiled during the formative phase of the establishment of the autonomous community and the consequent difficulties they experienced before being united under a single political banner.

Indeed, it was not until the early 1990s that all the nationalist parties joined forces after the Partido Nacionalista Galego ("Galician Nationalist Party") and Esquerda Galega ("Galician Left") joined the BNG.

The period of autonomy has been dominated by the PP (formerly Alianza Popular) under the strong leadership of Manuel Fraga Iribarne, the former Franco minister who was president of the Xunta for sixteen years (1989–2005). Fraga's government could be characterized as a peculiar mixture of authoritarianism, through the establishment of a dense web of power that controlled all the institutions of the community (including the media), and a right-wing populism based on the constant invocation of Galician rural culture. Fraga appropriated the legacy of *galeguismo* in its regionalist form (his main reference was Alfredo Brañas) but explicitly rejected and fiercely fought Galician nationalism. Just as Fraga's rule over Galicia began to look as if it would never end, the wreckage of the *Prestige* oil tanker in 2002, which covered the whole Galician coast with fuel, provoked an unprecedented mobilization of Galician civil society as a reaction to the disastrous management of the ecological crisis by both the Xunta and the central government. It is this mobilization, organized and led mainly by intellectuals and artists under the banner of *nunca máis* ("never again"), that eventually led to the downfall of the Fraga government in the 2005 Galician election, when it was replaced by a socialist-led coalition of socialists (PSdeG) and nationalists (BNG). This coalition held office for only one term; a shock election victory in March 2009 brought the PP back into power, a result that will undoubtedly have serious implications for the continued progress of the nationalist movement and for the relationship between Galicia and the Spanish state.

In the realm of culture, a key term throughout these years has been the concept of *normalización* ("normalization"), used most notably in the field of language, after Galician was given official status for the first time alongside Spanish both in the Statute of Autonomy and the Lei de Normalización Lingüística ("Language Normalization Act") of 1983. Thanks to this act, Galician was introduced into the school curriculum progressively, first as a subject (Galician language and literature) and later, partially, as a vehicular language for the study of a range of academic subjects. Galician, defined in the statute as the "lingua propia de Galicia" (*O Estatuto* [art. 5]; "Galicia's own language"), has been progressively adopted by the Xunta administration and nowadays is the dominant language used in the Galician parliament. Normalization has featured prominently in most other cultural fields, from literature and cinema to pop music and the fine arts, and it is discussed and analyzed from different points of view in most contributions to this volume.

Rationale and Organization

Our intention is to present to the widest possible readership the principal debates and issues shaping contemporary Galician culture. We hope to provide a forum where the specificities of the Galician situation combine with wider critical debate, thus providing new perspectives on both the local and the global. The essays in this volume respond to Galicia's changing context, moving Galician culture outside the limited, parochial, and always mediated borders of a vertical association with the Spanish nation-state and onto a global stage. They seek to place Galician culture in an international context, in terms of a global culture that is increasingly characterized by horizontal relations among regions, discourses, social movements, and individuals as well as among nation-states and their national literatures. A crucial element of the collection is the participation of scholars (some are also practitioners) from both the Galician and the anglophone academy. Intellectual exchange between scholars working within and beyond Galicia has not always been straightforward for a variety of reasons, some shared with the Spanish academy, others specific to Galicia as a minority—some would say a *minorizada* ("minorized")—culture without state support. But thanks to the efforts of pioneers in the field—notably John Rutherford in the United Kingdom and the late Xoán González-Millán in the United States—spaces have begun to emerge where scholars from different backgrounds can come together for debate and discussion. We hope that this volume will continue the process begun by Rutherford and González-Millán, to whom our project is dedicated.

The fifteen contributions that make up the volume come from scholars based in Galicia, the United Kingdom, the United States, and New Zealand. Each represents the very best of its particular approach to Galician studies. That the reader will find diverse opinions and a wide range of approaches we consider a positive thing. Aware that the field of cultural studies, which has informed our own scholarly work, has so far been a largely Anglo-American phenomenon, we want not to import its objects and methodologies wholesale but to use it as a starting point to open up a provocative dialogue that addresses pressing geographic and cultural issues with sensitivity. For this reason, we did not give a critical framework for contributors to follow, nor did we limit contributions to those taking up particular positions, either practical or theoretical, with regard to the object of study. We neither limited nor prescribed the subjects on which our contributors could write. In this way, we hoped, a picture would emerge of the trends developing in current research and practice in the field.

Two genres are conspicuous by their absence: there is no essay devoted to Galician music (although music is included in the essays by Romero and by Colmeiro) or to theater (although Bermúdez discusses performance more generally). This is not to say that there is not innovative practice or research in both areas; simply, most of our material lies in other areas.[5] We hope that this collection, while never intended to be a comprehensive survey of Galician cultural and literary practice, provides a strong sense of where innovative practice and research are taking place and, perhaps more important, a stimulus to further research.

The volume is divided into three parts: "Histories," "Identities," and "Cultural Practices." Part 1 focuses on the different interpretative frameworks Galician scholars and practitioners have used to make sense of their experiences. Part 2 shifts to the theorization of Galicianness—whether through language, emigration, or sexuality. The essays in part 3 pick up on many of these overarching questions, formulating them through attention to case studies of specific cultural practices—from the revisiting of Galicia's cultural heritage, through the visual, avant-garde, or performance-based re-imagining of poetry, the canonical genre par excellence, to the emergence of less established genres such as narrative, television, and cinema. There is overlap between the essays in each part, as the same questions arise again and again.

What emerges from the collection as a whole is a view of culture, understood in the broadest sense as the world of both practices and representation, as a privileged site for the working-out of issues of identity. Cultural media from novels to rock music, performance poetry to newspapers, sculpture to television advertising, offer a window on the various ways in which Galicians today try to make sense of *galeguidade*, of what it means to be Galician, as much in a global as in an individual, Hispanic, or Iberian context. All the essays are acutely aware of the way that cultural practitioners, from film directors to journalists to novelists to *gaiteiros* ("bagpipers"), bridge the gap between the public and private spheres. In different ways, they explore how artists and writers situate themselves with regard to existing maps of Galician culture, from those who place themselves unambiguously at the service of a conventional national discourse, adopting a utilitarian approach to cultural creation, to those who claim to speak only for themselves, advocating a conception of culture that is individualist and inherently autonomous of political ideology.

Galician culture provides a special opportunity to explore such processes, as the lack of a well-established national discourse (Galician or Spanish) opens up a space to define and create identity in various directions. That the picture becomes complex as the national question intersects with issues of class, gender, and sexuality has important consequences in the cultural field. Since identity is not fixed in taken-for-granted forms, Galician artists are forced to become more self-aware. There are a great number of public and private debates about what it means to be a Galician artist and about the implications for artists of locating themselves in the Galician literary and cultural scenes (as opposed to placing themselves in the Spanish tradition).[6] Thus Galicia is an ideal location for exploring central issues of contemporary cultural debate. These questions are raised again and again in our volume: How and by whom is culture validated? To what extent is cultural production mediated by the local and the global? What is the role of ethnic and national stereotypes in global markets? What is the relation between language and cultural production? How far can and should ideology inform cultural production? And what place is there for Galicia in the brave new world of the twenty-first century?

The reader will notice occasional spelling variations between essays in words such as Galiza/Galicia and between names such as Manoel Antonio / Manuel Antonio. They reflect differing usage in the field, and we have respected each author's preference for particular options. For a comprehensive account of the background to this variation, see John Patrick Thompson's essay in this volume. On a similar note, while the writer Rosalía de Castro has traditionally been referred to by her first name in Galician literary studies, there is a move among some critics to refer to her by surname in line with standard practice for other writers. The reader will find examples of both practices in this book.

Notes

1. The area formerly known to listeners as Finisterre has now been renamed Fitzroy, to avoid confusion with Galicia's Fisterra point.

2. The Galician population in 2008 was 2,784,169 (see the Web site for Instituto Galego de Estatística); the Catalan population in 2008 was 7,364,078 (see the Web site for l'Institut d'Estadistica de Catalunya); and the Basque population in 2007 was 2,124,200 (see the Web site for Euskal Estatistika Erakundea).

3. According to *Oficina del Censo Electoral*, just over 334,000 Galicians are registered to vote overseas, out of 1.2 million Spaniards.

4. For a comprehensive and accessible account of Galician history, see Gemie, which at the time of this writing is the only English-language history of Galicia available.

5. For a bibliography on Galician music, we refer readers to the essays collected in the recent special issue of the *Journal of Spanish Cultural Studies* on Spanish popular music (esp. Colmeiro, "Smells"; Hooper, "Many Faces").

6. See, for example, the interviews with key Galician figures in Hooper ("Forum") and the diverse responses there to the question of how a Galician writer should be defined.

PART 1

HISTORIES

Introduction to Part 1

The writing of history has long been a powerful tool in identity construction. The national histories of Europe that were written in the nineteenth century to legitimize the origin myths of peoples newly conscious of the potential of national organization continue to shape our understanding of who we are and where we come from. These histories, inspiring and empowering as they have so often been, are not objective records of the development of a people but contingent, selective, and exclusionary narratives constructed to fit the purpose of a particular group at a particular time. This postmodern idea is not as universally accepted as those of us working in Anglo-American cultural studies might assume. For emerging nations and other cultural groups whose experiences have not always been included, or even acknowledged, by the writers of the dominant histories, the celebratory, teleological model continues to exert a powerful attraction.

In Galicia, the importance of history and literary history in particular remains essential in the legitimization of an identity that considers itself besieged on many fronts. The history of Galicia has been undergoing refinement since the middle of the nineteenth century, when the liberal, regionalist intellectuals Manuel Murguía and Benito Vicetto (1824–78) published their monumental studies, both titled *Historia de Galicia*, in 1865 and 1863–73, respectively. These were not the first national histories in the modern sense—José Verea y Aguiar published one in Ferrol in 1838, and Leopoldo Martínez de Padín published another in Madrid in 1849—but they were the first written explicitly as support for the growing *galeguista* movement. Literary history too has had a crucial role to play: in the absence, through much of the nineteenth and twentieth centuries, of institutional space for public discussion about Galicia and its future, the cultural space became even more important. The first history of Galician literature, by Augusto Besada, was not published until 1887, and only the first volume was ever completed, but even this truncated project succeeded in codifying for the first time the importance of a Galician literature as differentiated from Spanish literature. Subsequent histories of literature, from Eugenio Carré Aldao's monumental *Literatura gallega* (1903; revised 1911) to Benito Varela Jácome's *Historia de la literatura gallega* (1951) to Ricardo Carballo Calero's *Historia da literatura galega contemporánea* (1974), have gradually refined the borders and characteristics of Galician literature and history—and, through them, of Galician identity—until today the subject is well established as an academic discipline.

The four essays in part 1 explore the benefits and limitations of the theory and practice of Galician national and literary history that have developed from the works of Vicetto, Murguía, Besada, Carré Aldao, and Carballo Calero. Implicitly or explicitly, they address the conflict between traditional assumptions of historical objectivity and universality and approaches, more recent, that recognize how power differentials create social, political, and economic inequalities, brought to bear not only on Galicia itself but also on the marginalized voices within its borders. Galician history, like so many others, has conventionally been narrated as a triumphalist and teleological vindication of a Romantic myth of origins, as the steady advance of a people toward full consciousness, which is symbolized by the recovery of a pure language. Lourenzo Fernández Prieto, Antón Figueroa, María do Cebreiro Rábade Villar, and Joseba Gabilondo show that this narrative is characterized by partiality, shaped by elisions and exclusions, and thus open to varying interpretations. Rábade Villar argues that fragmentation and discontinuity are characteristic of Galician history and should be embraced for their potential rather than swept under the carpet.

The two essays that open the volume are by established Galician thinkers whose work has hitherto been unavailable in English. Fernández Prieto, a historian of contemporary Galicia, provides an overview of historical studies in Galicia today, showing how even the popular understanding of Galicia's past is being transformed as historians revisit the elements of Galician history that have been taken as foundational and reevaluate the narrative that has conventionally been built on them. He begins by outlining what he calls the "myth of backwardness"—social, political, economic, and cultural backwardness—that has shaped both Galicia's self-image and the way Galicia has been seen both in the rest of Spain and further afield. The endurance of this myth he attributes to the Franco dictatorship's appropriation not only of history as knowledge of the past but also of memory as an agent beyond the private sphere.

Fernández Prieto proposes that until recently there was no real history of Galicia, because it was either subsumed into Spanish history or dismissed by the myth of Galician backwardness. He shows how recent research makes this myth untenable. Challenging the long-standing focus, even by *galeguistas*, on Galicia's Celtic heritage or medieval apogee, he points to Galicia's recent seafaring and agricultural achievements. By revisiting Galician history not from an externally imposed concept of progress but from a Galicia-centered perspective, contemporary historians have demonstrated that Galicia did in fact undergo industrial development during the nineteenth century but on a local scale that was not necessarily recognized on the national level: the canning industry and the development of unique agrosystems are two telling examples.

Figueroa is a literary theorist whose works *Diglosia e texto* (1988; "Diglossia and Text") and *Nación, literatura, sociedade* (2001; "Nation, Literature, Society"), along with those of his colleague Xoán González-Millán, laid the foundations for the introduction of sociologically based theory, particularly the work of Pierre Bourdieu, into Galician studies. He employs Bourdieu's concept of field to explain the complex network of relations that makes up Galician culture. He revisits the role of the writer and the interaction between art and other fields, particularly politics, from the threshold of the twenty-first century. Figueroa's focus on the writer and individual agents in the process of cultural formation is especially welcome at a time when the rapid expansion of the Galician publishing system is giving space to more and more authors, and thus to a greater range of voices, than ever before. Long-standing assumptions about the political responsibility of the writer in Galicia are therefore coming into question. The writer's traditional role as the voice of the culturally disenfranchised Galician people has been diminishing since autonomy in 1981, although certain writers—perhaps most notably Manuel Rivas and Suso de Toro, both novelists and journalists—continue to perform that function.

That Galicia's new autonomy has changed the relation between culture and politics does not mean the connection is broken. The connection is now complicated by the addition of the economic field, for the Galician government has invested a great deal of its budget in the promotion and support of culture at all levels, from publication subsidies and literary prizes to the creation of literary journals and the development of university departments. More writers are now able to make a living from their writing—although, as Figueroa points out, the discourse of national commitment acts as a kind of concealing umbrella, enabling cultural agents to privilege pure commitment (often expressed as a pure aesthetics) over the dirty business of money. Different systems for valorizing culture are in play, some heteronomous and others autonomous, but this variety remains largely unacknowledged in public discourse and especially in the theory and practice of culture planning. The latent networks of economic, political, and cultural connections that have been developing since 1981 thus require close attention and analysis if a descent into endogamy is to be avoided. Figueroa does not advocate a naive attempt to transcend these networks; he argues, rather, that they be approached with open eyes. He sees great promise in newer forms of cultural production, such as architecture and fashion, which have not been naturalized in the same way as literature. (The question of the renewal of cultural forms is taken up in part 3 by María Reimóndez, Hooper, and Bermúdez.)

Rábade Villar and Gabilondo both build on the groundwork laid by Fernández Prieto and Figueroa to propose novel approaches to Galicia's foundational histories. Rábade Villar picks up on the question of legitimization discussed by Figueroa to argue that the traditional justification of Galician cultural history through the invocation of aesthetic quality, or what she calls "positivist and stylistic methods," is no longer viable and in fact often quite naive. She proposes that the connection between literature and politics that has shaped much Anglo-French criticism since the 1970s needs to be embraced as the heart of Galician studies rather than seen as an irrelevance or a betrayal (or, in Figueroa's terms, subsumed beneath the umbrella of pure aesthetics and pure commitment). The roots of Galician literature are to be found in the loss of political power and the conscious decision of Galicia's early writers to "make virtue from political necessity" and to employ what Emily Apter has called the "language of damaged experience" (149). This is an act not of resignation but of defiance—a distinction essential to the future of Galician culture, given the continued influence of cultural planning, because a culture planned around resignation to (and avoidance of) its fragmentations, ruptures, and discontinuities will have a future very different from one that makes them a productive site for resistance.

Rábade Villar sees the poet Rosalía de Castro (1837–85) as the paradigmatic example of a writer consciously choosing a language of rupture, looking on a micro level at the linguistic fluctuations in Castro's poetry that have often been dismissed as the results of naïveté or lack of education. Castro's influence on the development of Galician nationalism has been such, since her early death in 1885, that she and her works—particularly the poetry collections *Cantares gallegos* (1863) and *Follas novas* (1881)—are often conflated with Galicia. Accepting Castro's linguistic fluctuations as a conscious choice rather than dismissing them as primitive or a sign of ignorance is essential to understanding Galicia's cultural development.

Gabilondo examines the paradox of Castro's linguistic fluctuations on a macro level. He considers her Spanish-language narrative, published during the same period as her Galician-language poetry, as a means of deconstructing the conflation of poet, language, and nation. Pointing to the failure of existing Spanish literary histories to adequately account for the place of non-Spanish language in the cultures of the Peninsula, he proposes a postnational approach to circumvent the problem of languages that do not coincide as neatly with national borders as literary historians have generally assumed.

Castro is an ideal author with which to begin this project, because of the separation, in scholarly literature, between what Gabilondo calls her geopolitical positioning, as the symbol of Galician nationalism, but also as a Galician who migrated to Madrid and whose works were financed by the Galician community in Cuba, and her biopolitical positioning as a woman. She and her works are the embodiment of the feminist, postnationalist critique that he believes is the only way to bridge the theoretical chasm between the geopolitical and the biopolitical. Despite her symbolic position at the heart of the formulation of modern Galician identity, Castro chose to exile herself from Galician literature toward the end of her life, publishing her third and final collection of poetry in Spanish. For Gabilondo, her decision is the foundational act of modern, monolingual Galician literature, while her subsequent separation from that literature makes her the first in a long line of women writers, many of them bilingual, for whom no place in the Galician canon can be found.

Gabilondo's essay, like those of Rábade Villar and, from a different perspective, Figueroa, traces the fault lines running through the traditional concept of Galician (national) literature, in particular those that mark Galicianness: language, culture, and territory. These fault lines are of concern to scholars not only of Galicia but of all cultures, dominant and emerging. These essays are less about the historical events that have taken place in Galicia than about the uses that have been made of them. As Rábade Villar points out in her meditation on the role of critics and historians in an emerging culture, they not only are analyzing their object but also are implicated in it.

Interpreting Galician History: The Recent Construction of an Unknown Past

Lourenzo Fernández Prieto

This essay offers an overview of different interpretations of Galician history in the light of current Galician historiographical scholarship, which looks at methodological problems and debates in current research instead of focusing on specific stages in the construction of Galicia's history. I highlight the key images through which the past is currently explained, emphasizing that one of the principal objectives of recent historiography (albeit one that is not always explicitly stated) is the revision of some of our most long-standing assumptions. Fresh interpretations of Galician history are beginning to replace the familiar ones, which were characterized by commonplaces traditionally neither defined nor explained, much less exposed to doubt or criticism. Research into new areas of both the recent and distant past is producing results that are often very different from those we might expect. Through methodical historical scholarship, revisionist scholars are developing a deeper knowledge that turns some established historical commonplaces on their head, demonstrating how Galicia's past is in many respects entirely different from the one we thought we knew. One of the most influential commonplaces has been the theme of backwardness, fundamental to so many interpretations of Galician history and forming part of both Galicians' collective memory and their deepest historical consciousness.

I begin by considering the object of study itself, recent histories of Galicia and their role in broader interpretations of history, and I investigate some of the limitations of the territorial frameworks that have dominated both revisionist and traditional historical models. Then I address the central trends in current historical interpretations of Galicia, in the light of the questioning, and even rejecting, of the myth of backwardness, which I consider the principal structuring axis of contemporary historiography in recent decades.

The Methodological Framework of Galician History

The political, cultural, and intellectual rupture of 1936 meant that until very recently Galician history as such did not exist, and those historical studies that were published were characterized by minimal professional rigor. When we leave to one side the histories of Galicia written by the earliest Galician historians such as Benito Vicetto and Manuel Murguía and take into account the break caused by the civil war, it is only in the late twentieth century that Galicia has been presented as a well-defined object of historiographical study. During the dictatorship only the history of Spain (and preferably that of the pre-nineteenth-century empire) was considered an appropriate subject for historians. The first history of Galicia published after the dictatorship, by the AN-PG (1979; Asamblea Nacional–Popular Galega), was promoted by the political nationalist movement and comprised a series of contributions by young but already recognized specialists who approached history chronologically (Barreiro et al.). The following year another *Historia de Galiza*, sponsored by the recently established bank Caixa Galicia, brought together essays by six academic specialists (Bermejo et al., *Historia*).[1] A few years later, the first single-authored history of Galicia since the end of the dictatorship was published (Villares, *Historia*), followed by several more, their numbers increasing through the 1980s and 1990s.[2] During the transition to democracy (1975–82), the history of Galicia was essentially a history of *galeguismo*: the account of a political project that has never been dominant but had considerable influence. But the history of *galeguismo* is not the same as the history of Galicia, and since the 1980s an economic and social history has also begun to emerge.

Because the space chosen for historical analysis is never neutral, the definition of a framework for study is of paramount importance.[3] For historical analysis to be effective, it must be located in a particular territory. In practice, however, the choice of territorial boundaries is usually ideologically rather than methodologically motivated, given the nature of history as an instrument of legitimization. Historians seem condemned to become involved in the political and social struggles over the legitimacy of their object of study. Inevitably they must choose which side they are on. These legitimizing and choosing of sides are sometimes enacted unconsciously by the historian. The ideology that historians attempt to transcend tends to show through regardless. By default, the dominant ideology (i.e., the ideology that is able to achieve the greatest degree of social consensus) always influences historical discourse, so that the development of an autonomous Galician political space has led to a focus, often automatic, on Galicia. Left unexamined, this conflation of political and scholarly boundaries may suppress the diversity brought to historical research by attention to different levels of socioeconomic, political, and cultural development. The acritical and achronic acceptance of the borders of the current territory of Galicia as the ultimate, undifferentiated borders of historical analysis can lead to errors just as grave as those resulting from a similarly unquestioning recourse to Spanish state borders: remember the Spanish historical atlas published by the Franco regime, on which the Roman roads ended at the Portuguese border.

Historians can choose to situate their research in different contexts: global, intercontinental (Europe-America), continental, subcontinental (the Balkans, East Asia), interstate, national or state, regional or local, but the main point of reference is almost always a space defined from the present. This role can be taken by the nation-state or by interstate entities like the EU. In the last few decades, for both political and methodological reasons, historians have helped break down the concept of space that has traditionally underpinned historical research. The renewal of historiography since the 1970s through the influence of the French *Annales* school has led to a search for natural territorial units on which to base historical research. In comparison to these natural units, the state framework has been seen by most social and economic historians as an uncomfortable, distorting corset, pulling together realities that are too different. The emphasis on nonstate or substate units, together with the creation of the Spanish autonomous communities as part of the transition from dictatorship to democracy, has been a crucial factor in the development of a Galician framework for historical research.

The task of situating Galician history in universal history and the struggle to endow it with historiographical legitimacy have been more difficult and more controversial than might appear today, and the process is still far from complete. In the past, Galician history was considered simply local history, concerned with minor matters; furthermore it tended to be practiced by amateur historians working outside academia.[4] Unlike history based on state borders (history with a capital H), which politicians and editors alike have considered to be the most suitable basis for constructing the past, local history has been of little general interest. The revisionist historians did much to break down the boundaries between it and so-called universal history.[5] Furthermore, the establishment of the autonomous communities and the recovery of Galician as an educated language have created a political and editorial context within which the history—and History—of Galicia can continue to grow.

What Would We Tell a Stranger about Galicia and Its History?

Let me provide a basic outline of the story we might tell a stranger about the history of Galicia, based on the historical work that is currently being undertaken (I bracket off earlier stories of the nation, of which this stranger is ignorant). The story is Galicia as a collective historical subject.

Backwardness and collective memory are principal themes of current historiographical research in Galicia, and they have recently been conceptualized as two sides of the same coin: ignorance not only of our recent past but also of what Galicia was in the last two centuries. Galicians who have lived in the present democracy believe our past to be one of social, political, economic, and cultural backwardness; they are convinced, in other words, that we come from a country dominated by misery and poverty. This concept of backwardness was constructed in the 1960s by the post-civil-war generation; Xosé Manuel Beiras's *O atraso económico de Galicia* (1973; "The Economic Backwardness of Galicia") is its quintessential expression. The development of the concept by researchers in the social sciences was based on two fundamental experiences of the postwar period: the forgetting of what preceded the Republican springtime, a past shattered in 1936, and the burden of Galicia's impoverished agricultural community, a community identified as the source of the backwardness. The cultural break caused by the civil war led to Europe's longest postwar period—the almost two decades between 1939 and 1956—eradicating actual memories and replacing them with a collective memory based in practice on the suppression of the past. History as knowledge of the past, of a past different from the present, was expropriated by the dictatorship. Individual and family memories were silenced and pushed into the private sphere.

The development of modern history scholarship in Galicia engaged the power of the past to shape the present. Of course, the aspects of history studied at any given period (in this case the last quarter of a century) reflect the concerns of that period. The choices the historians made clearly reflect the concerns arising from the transition to democracy and autonomy:

> The history of the countryside and of the peasants as active, collective subjects of the rural world occupies a primary place. Research has been done on the system of land ownership, the unique nature of common land, the history of forestation, agrarianism as a form of social organization, and technological change as a problem.

> Political history is difficult to write in a stateless nation, and so there is a great deal of writing on nationalism as a nation-building project. Research has been done into its organizations, its ideological discourses, and the ideologues themselves.

> Industrial history began with explanations of deindustrialization in the nineteenth century. Later it moved into discussion of the expansion of the fishing and canning trades as evidence of a process of industrialization based, since the beginning of the twentieth century, on the maritime-and-fishing complex.

> The history of emigration and of its negative influence—for example, on Galicia's demographic makeup—has turned in recent years to the discovery of its positive aspects, for example, the returning migrants and the networks of Galician communities around the world.

> The history of the civil war, of the subsequent repression by and then resistance to the Franco regime, has recently opened up thanks to the new tools of oral history and to growing interest in a past that was expunged.

There are other fields or lines of research, such as the history of the labor movement, but they are covered by the above list.

What does the research reveal about the most pressing issues facing Galicia in the early years of the twenty-first century? An analysis of what historians have done provides a useful window onto many of the factors that shape Galician identity today. Historiographical research, both current and past, has identified Galicia variously as

> a territory delimited by its geography, summarized in the Roman view of Galicia as the end of the (Atlantic) world—note the Galician place-name Fisterra ("world's end")

an ancient territory culturally and materially defined during the Iron
Age and the Roman period, which the Swabians turned into a medieval kingdom. It lost this status on the emergence of the kingdoms
of Portugal and Castile, which divided it between them.

an agrarian and, until recently, predominantly rural country

a society defined in the modern period by emigration

a nation whose consciousness is defined by culture, language, and the
collective will to political construction

a nation with a recent history conditioned by the civil war and a long
postwar period

Galicia is home to almost three million inhabitants located in 313 local
councils, 3,500 parishes, 7 cities, and 30 large towns in 30 local districts.
As a territory, it has historically combined the advantages and disadvantages
of its position in the far northwest of the Iberian Peninsula. Although its
territory and political borders have never coincided, it has from ancient
times been a highly populated space and, since Roman times, clearly defined
and individually named. A *galeguista* view of Galicia's territorial history has
developed in recent years in opposition to the dominant Castilianist view,
constructed by the Spanish historical school according to the logic of the
Spanish state. This view, based on the argument that the borders of present-
day Galicia were defined, albeit briefly, during the reign of Sancha of León
(1037–85) and under King García of Galicia and Portugal (1065–72), draws
on the findings of the Santiago-based medievalist school (e.g., López Carreira; C. Nogueira, *A memoria*).

Furthermore, historians are beginning to consider Galicia's historical
connections with other seafaring nations, especially England and Ireland,
which share its geographic distance from mainland Europe. Both islands,
England and Ireland developed in very different ways, one becoming central
to Europe, the other remaining peripheral. That Galicia has occupied both
a central and a peripheral position with regard to Europe and the world
means that historians can look to both England and Ireland for historical
models. For example, the megalithic culture of Galicia in the third mil-
lennium BC has much in common with the other cultures of the Atlantic
rim, and there has been speculation about maritime contacts, both mentioned in ancient legends and evident from archaeological research. Until
the Counter-Reformation, Galicia was open to the European Atlantic, as

the medieval maritime trade routes studied by Darlene Abreu-Ferreira and Alain Huetz de Lemps, together with Galician participation in the Portuguese and Castilian discoveries, reveal. This relationship was cut off by the Habsburgs, with whom the only encounters were military: Drake in Coruña (1589) or the Spanish Armada, which sailed out of Galicia. From the end of the ancien régime, in the nineteenth century (and also partly during the eighteenth century), maritime trade relations were recovered in three ways: through transoceanic migration; through the linen and wheat trade with the Baltic; and, from the middle of the nineteenth century, through the export of cattle to England. Nevertheless, in the modern era Galicia would become increasingly peripheral to both European and peninsular politics.

The importance of the sea in Galicia's development has been unquestionable, but it was through research into Galicia's rural past, from the eighteenth century until the civil war, that we began to challenge the story of age-old economic backwardness. According to the conventional version of history, Galicia was defined (and defines itself) as a primarily rural space, and of course rural is closely associated with backwardness for many contemporary urban thinkers. Research by historians of rural Galicia has contributed a great deal of evidence to show that profound transformations indeed took place in the rural space. For example, historians can now distinguish the old threshing machines we personally remember from the Roman plow that symbolized the technological stagnation of Galician agriculture and reinterpret them as evidence of modernization, together with hybrid crops, the creation of the Galician blond breed of cattle, and other technological innovations. Agrarianism began to be seen as a social phenomenon. It was an instrument in the struggle for the land and eventually led to the granting of land to the peasants, the construction of a modern civil society in the countryside, the participation of the peasants in the political system, and their successful participation in the market as both buyers and sellers. This revisionist view of agrarianism counters the traditional interpretation of the struggle as the desperate expression of a few rebels who defied guardsmen and local landowners.[6] Going further back, the introduction of corn and the potato took on new significance as evidence of the sophisticated production methods of Galician agrosystems.

The sea and the countryside were the principal economic drivers until 1970. The great agricultural improvements of the eighteenth century were characterized by the introduction of corn and the potato and later the turnip, which led to population growth and an increase in the strength of the peasantry, who controlled the means of production and substantially improved their social and economic standing despite the considerable *foros* ("rents") they had to pay their noble and religious masters. Both Galicia's rural manor houses and the baroque Praza do Obradoiro ("Artisan Square") in Santiago de Compostela symbolize the wealth garnered from these *foros*, in the same way as the increasingly grand construction of *hórreos*, the traditional Galician grain stores, represents the peasants' growing surplus income after the end of the eighteenth century. This agricultural revolution spread from the Atlantic coast inland until well into the nineteenth century, eliminating the tradition of letting land lie fallow and generating an intensive agriculture capable of supporting an increased population. Thanks to advances in cattle production in the second half of the nineteenth century, Galicia began to trade with England and Portugal, exporting significant quantities in the 1880s and placing Galician production in an international market before the arrival of the railway.[7]

In the urban world too, which traditionally played a small part in Galician collective memory, the image of backwardness has begun to be undermined by historical research. The often lamented absence of industrialization has been contradicted at last by a number of detailed scholarly monographs. Scholars uncovered a unique maritime complex, where the tinning of fish was pioneered from the end of the nineteenth century, and the development of shipyards and access to distant fishing grounds from the 1920s (Carmona and Nadal). Similarly, new knowledge about urban businesses, utility companies, and banks has given a new significance to the role of Galician industry in the first third of the twentieth century. Furthermore, we have uncovered the modernizing role of emigrants in such social developments as lay education, the construction of democracy, the labor movement, and the development of sport (Míguez Macho; Domínguez Almansa). The increase in population was accompanied not by any significant increase in urban and industrial employment but rather by deindustrialization (Carmona). In the early nineteenth century, linen, conserves, the salting industries, and so on did not succeed in adapting to the first wave of industrialization and declined progressively as a result of competition from European (French and English) industry first and later from Catalan industry. This is the origin of the backwardness that was believed to mark not only the means of production but also the collective consciousness. Looms, for example, are no more than an ethnographic and tourist curiosity today (like Camariñas lace), but they are evidence of a strong tradition, which remains present in Galician surnames such as Liñeira and Liñares, which come from the Galician and Spanish word *lino*, meaning "linen or flax."

Agrarianism had a huge influence in Galicia and played a part in three of the most significant processes leading to social and agricultural change: the repeal of the *foros* in 1926, which consolidated the social and economic position of the peasants as they became owners of their own land; improvements in production introduced by the peasants and encouraged by state bodies; the organization of civil society and the political predominance of the countryside, which continues in symbolic form today. Galicia is a land of peasants not only in cultural terms but also through the physical and social memory of agrarianism. Agrarian charities and schools were established at the end of the eighteenth century; the *fidalguía* ("petty nobility") took the place of the Galician nobility; the church lost its economic power with the seizure and sale of its property during the same period; and from the end of the nineteenth century the repeal of the *foros* and subsequent disentailment of land allowed the peasants to displace the petty nobility. Hence the proliferation of abandoned manor houses, which were opened to the public only in August 2009. From the end of the nineteenth century, the displaced petty nobility sought a new source of revenue and found it in the military, higher education, the judiciary, and politics.

The canning industry and many other maritime activities after 1880 continued the development of an Atlantic industrialization linked to the ports of Vigo and Ferrol, which had its roots in the construction of the naval arsenal in Ferrol in the eighteenth century. This industrialization affected industries based around shipyards (metal, printing, wood) and fishing and related industries, from the manufacture of the *traíñas* ("nets for sardine fishing") to the more recent construction of enormous fish-freezing ships. This sector acted as the driving force of industry as a whole, though truncated by periodic sardine-shortage crises such as that of 1924–25. One of the symbols of Galicia's current industrial modernity, an example of an innovative business, is Zeltia Agraria (and its affiliated companies, such as Pharmamar), whose origins bring together land and sea. The organized workers' movement, particularly the Confederación Nacional de Trabajo (CNT; "National Labor Confederation") and the Unión General de Trabajadores (UGT; "General Workers' Union"), also has a strong base in Galicia's Atlantic cities, but its ideological and organizational influence is limited to towns and cities. After the civil war, and especially since the 1950s, a number of other industries developed: Citroën, Alúmina, Endesa in the town of As Pontes, and, above all, hydroelectric production (FENOSA; Fuerza Eléctrica de Noroeste S. A.). The mining industry also expanded beyond its long-standing origins (granite, stone, wolfram). More recently, fashion—both designer (Domínguez, Verino) and mass-produced (Zara-Inditex)—appears to have risen from a vacuum, because it was not promoted by any of the public authorities when it first emerged. But there was already in place a commercial tradition based on a wide internal network and a strong internal demand, a tradition—never lost—of textile production (specifically linen). There was also a universal vision of distribution that fits logically in a land of emigrants.

A Land of Emigrants

During the Franco dictatorship, the institutional view of Galicia was, demographically, a land of poverty-stricken emigrants streaming abroad in order to live. Economically, it was considered a land of irreversible agricultural backwardness, lost in the mists of time. Culturally, it was considered a land of ignorant peasants who insisted on speaking in dialect because that was all they knew and they had too little education for anything else. Anthropologically, Galicia was seen as a land of witchcraft and of the *morriña* ("homesickness") of weeping emigrants, just as it was for the Castilians back in the seventeenth century. Politically, Galicians were seen as those who fought Franco's war and were his countrymen.

While it has been traditional to interpret Galicia's history of emigration in terms of drama and underdevelopment, historians are beginning to look beyond the obvious conclusion that the emigration was a demographic disaster and even beyond the sentimental construct of *morriña*. The phenomenon has largely been studied from a quantitative point of view. In the 1787 Census of Spain, carried out by the Conde de Floridablanca, Galicia was home to 13% of the Spanish population. In the most recent census in 2008, the proportion was just above 6%. This loss of population is due principally to emigration: between 1860 and 1970, more than 2.3 million people left Galicia; 1.2 million (or one in four of those born in Galicia in this period) never returned. Today, more than 1.3 million people born in Galicia live abroad.

As we now know, there have been several different waves of emigration, each with its own causes and characteristics, despite the continuous outflow. The most recent, in the second half of the twentieth century, was the worst, both in the conditions that triggered it and its effects. Between 1900 and 1930, the natural increase of population fell by 60%, but there was also significant overseas seasonal migration. Those going to South America were aided, first, by the existence of a similar language (Spanish or Portuguese) and, second, by the networks of relatives and Galician-organized parish societies and centers that had existed since the nineteenth century. After the civil war, between 1945 and 1979, the natural increase of population fell by 90%, and migrants went principally to other parts of Europe, where there were no existing networks and, unlike in South America, no shared language. People were forced out by the state's destruction of the foundations of the agricultural economy and its promotion of rural depopulation. This wave of emigration, still fresh in memory, is more dramatic than earlier waves and has obscured the positive aspects, of the pre-civil-war emigration experience.

The recovery of those positive aspects, after decades when historians focused exclusively on the negative impact of returning migrants, can be seen in research on the parish schools set up by emigrants, the cultural and social foundations of *indianos* ("returning migrants") for example in Cee, Betanzos, and Ribadeo; on the creation by emigrants of rural associations and societies; and on the emigrants' contribution to the construction of a civil society and to the introduction of innovative knowledge and practices. Returning emigrants provided resources, both material (investment, buildings) and abstract (knowledge, cultural customs). This new reading of emigration demonstrates, for example, that remittances from Galician emigrants in a single year in the 1920s would have been sufficient to purchase the twenty largest Galician businesses of the time.

Historians are now beginning to argue that the story of Galician emigration since the nineteenth century in fact demonstrates Galicia's integration into modernity. Galicia's agricultural system was capable of producing a large population but lacked the industrial sectors that would have created sufficient employment to support it. Galician rural society created complex networks and chains of emigrants who called on neighbors and relatives to emigrate, either for a short period, to see the world, or permanently. The civil association of emigrants in their host cities is a modern form of emigration shared with other European societies. Galician migration was not, as in Ireland, a result of hunger or the product of a great crisis, although there were smaller crises that led to smaller waves of migration. To emigrate, a Galician needed access to financial resources that most people in other southern European countries lacked. American cities such as Buenos Aires, Havana, Montevideo, Rio de Janeiro, and New York were the largest Galician cities, in terms of numbers, between 1850 and 1950, with more Galician residents than Lisbon or even Madrid. In those cities, Galician migrants learned about social, technological, cultural, and intellectual modernity.

A Land with a Self-Conscious Identity: *Galeguismo*, Language, and Culture

The first questioning of Galicia's exclusion from history came from Galicians' realization that *galeguismo*, for so long dismissed as simply a sentimental or literary phenomenon, was in fact an ideological phenomenon and Galician nationalism a political instrument. The detailed study of the development of *galeguismo* that followed became a means of reevaluating the culture and language that marked Galicia as distinct and also of reconstructing both the idea and the Republican reality of autonomy, which can be considered the political expression of Galicia's cultural and linguistic difference. But the history of *galeguismo*, though it signaled an element of positive identification, was not sufficient to remove the shadow of backwardness that dominated Galicia's collective consciousness. New research into the *galeguista* project was easily integrated into the narrative of underdevelopment, since a failed project inevitably creates a perception of backwardness. But scholars today are showing how in fact the appearance in Galicia of a unique and differentiated consciousness coincided exactly with a double world revolution, the construction of a state and of a market.

This consciousness was always either cultural or political. In the nineteenth century, history was more important than language as a marker of identity, and there were many different views regarding the relationship of Galicia with Spain. At the same time, identity was always connected to the economic problems resulting from Galicia's infrastructural marginalization from the state, ever since Antolín Faraldo spoke in 1846 of "Galicia colonia da Corte" ("Galicia, a colony of Madrid"). The dominant ideological positions have always been progressive, in both popular and populist senses, although the peasants (Galician speakers) have been considered the privileged bearers of the national essence. The political and cultural construction of the nation gradually came together over two centuries, and since the beginning of the twentieth century, Galician emigrants have had a great influence over it. We might say that travel contributed to the construction of the nation, as

Galicians acquired a sense of self-consciousness through contact with other national identities.

Political nationalism emerged as early as 1846, with a generation of progressive students and intellectuals. Faraldo, Neira de Mosquera, and Pío Rodríguez Terrazo, among others, created *provincialismo* ("provincialism") as a vindication of Galicia in the face of the reactionary nature of Spanish government under Isabel II. Political nationalism took on a reformist and also federal orientation from 1868 (the year of the revolution that overthrew Isabel II) until the end of the nineteenth century, when it became known as *rexionalismo* ("regionalism"), which achieved a high level of theoretical sophistication but had little political influence. There was a conservative strand of regionalism led by Alfredo Brañas, which opposed both centralism and liberalism and sought to restore the ancien régime, but in the end the liberal (or progressivist) strand led by Manuel Murguía, inspired by German Romantic notions of the nation, dominated. At the dawn of the twentieth century, the principal national institutions and symbols were established, initially in the emigrant communities, especially Havana: the Academia Gallega (later Real Academia Galega) was established in 1906, the Galician national anthem in 1907, and the Galician flag in 1909.

The foundation of the Irmandades da Fala ("Brotherhoods of the Language") in 1916 represents the articulation of a political nationalism that was part of the formation of new European nations in the aftermath of World War I. It was supported by a political theory of nationalism formulated by Vicente Risco, among others, and also by an economic nationalism that was to be based on Galicia's strengths, encapsulated in the works of Lois Peña Novo and Alexandre Bóveda. The Partido Galeguista (PG; "Galicianist Party"), founded in 1931, and the Organización Republicana Gallega Autónoma (ORGA; "Autonomous Galician Republican Organization"), created in 1929, both had political influence. During the Second Spanish Republic (1931–36), they promoted Galicia's first Estatuto de Autonomía ("Statute of Autonomy"), which was approved by referendum in June 1936 and gained parliamentary status (albeit through a parliament already in exile) at the Cortes de Montserrat in February 1938, at the height of the civil war. The principal political protagonists during this period were Alfonso Castelao, writer, artist, and founder of the PG; Antonio Villar Ponte, writer, journalist, and founder of ORGA; and Ramón Suárez Picallo, emigrant, journalist, and playwright who was involved in both ORGA and the PG.

The sociopolitical Galicianist movement was divided and fragmented

as a result of the war and the postwar exile of many *galeguistas*. During
the 1950s, the Galician movement in Galicia limited itself to the cultural
sphere. Gradually, a new generation returned to political nationalism during
the 1960s. This new nationalism was inspired by the new left, the Cuban
revolution, and Third World liberation movements. It took three forms: the
Partido Socialista Galego (PSG; "Galician Socialist Party"); Unión do Povo
Galego (UPG; "Galician People's Union"); Galicia Socialista (GS; "Socialist
Galicia"). From the early 1970s, the new nationalism was closely linked to
the new urban labor movement.

Cultural *galeguismo* was represented in the nineteenth century by historians such as Benito Vicetto and Manuel Murguía and poets such as Rosalía de
Castro, Eduardo Pondal, and Manuel Curros Enríquez. Its main expression
was the Rexurdimento, which echoed a surge in nationalist consciousness
across Europe, from Ireland to Russia. The minimal political influence of the
turn-of-the-century *rexionalista* movement contrasts strongly with the great
cultural influence of *galeguismo*, connected with the recuperation and recast-
ing of culture, music, and popular (rural) dance as specifically Galician. The
proliferation of choirs, dance groups, and music groups, which also constituted a new social network, was a key factor in the creation of an apparently
homogeneous, hegemonic popular culture in the cities and large towns. All
levels of society thought of this culture as uniquely Galician. The culture of
the *muiñeira* and "The Rianxeira," both musical and dance forms, had un-
deniably rural roots—in contrast, for example, with the culture of Catalonia.

After the foundation of the Academia Gallega in 1906, the literary
language was developed through wider usage in public life generally; this
process intensified in the 1920s. Galician became a language of learning
with the creation of the Seminario de Estudos Galegos ("Galician Studies
Seminar") at the Universidade de Santiago de Compostela in 1923. Galician could now no longer be considered simply a language of the poor; it
was also the language of intellectuals. A whole university generation used
it, even writers, such as Wenceslao Fernández Flórez and Gonzalo Torrente
Ballester, who would ultimately abandon it in the 1960s. The advent of the
Second Republic saw the focus of the *galeguista* movement shift to politics at
the expense of culture. After the Galician political movement was destroyed
in the war and persecuted under Franco, there was a return to culture with
the Galaxia Generation of the 1950s. In the last years of the Franco dictatorship and during the transition to democracy, cultural and literary nationalism intensified with the advent of new writers and poets and a wave of

popular music that considered itself Celtic, which paralleled a Celtic trend in the Anglo-Saxon world.

A Society Marked by the Civil War and the Postwar Period

Galicia's experience of the civil war and postwar period can be summarized as fifteen days of war, fifteen years of exile, and twenty years of aftermath. In Galicia, Franco's coup swiftly triumphed. There was no war fought on official fronts, but the guerrilla war lasted from 1939 until the 1950s. The repression was brutal because Galicia was fundamentally Republican; there was no great civil support for the military coup, but neither was there the possibility of escape. Repression took the form of cleansing and terror designed to impose the new order; it had dramatic effects, as we are beginning to learn from recent research.[8] Francoism thus began earlier and lasted longer in Galicia than it did elsewhere. The repression, carried out systematically, meant the dismantling of the civil society that had been created during the previous forty years and of the political pluralism that had existed since the nineteenth century. Under Franco's regime, submission was the only guarantee of survival and of social participation; people had to break with previous dynamics, especially in the countryside. Ana Cabana and Daniel Lanero have both shown that resistance soon turned into accommodation, along with the establishment of a Francoist ideology based on the memory of hunger and fear, on repression, and on frequent coercion. It is not easy to create a nonrural civil society to replace what was destroyed.[9] The Galicia of that long postwar period is an overpopulated countryside (both urban development and the traditional forms of emigration overseas had been cut off) full of starvation. That the experience of Francoism has survived in collective memory to today, albeit fragmented by a mixture of terror and amnesia, testifies to the continued impact of the war on Galicia.[10]

Galician historiography has been revisiting and redefining a past that is becoming more and more different from the past conventionally depicted. Twenty-five years of research have provided a solid challenge to the ahistorical mind-set that previously dominated, revealing above all a recent past that is largely unknown. As so often happens in countries with a hidden, uncomfortable past, Galicians knew more about the *castros*, the ancient Celtic hill forts, than about their own grandparents, more about Juan Álvarez Mendizábal's expropriation of church land than about twentieth-century agrarianism. They lacked a coherent interpretation of the material relics and memorials that contradicted the undifferentiated backwardness in which they imagined they had been mired since the beginning of time. The efforts of historians to reinterpret key events, figures, and themes in ever more nuanced ways have addressed these issues. Even so, Galicians have not yet succeeded in erasing the familiar image of Galicia—not to mention Galicia's self-image—as a land of cheap shellfish, a place to build a second home in a picturesque and undeveloped rural environment. But the future is likely to bring change, and Galicians' vision of the past will have a part to play in that change. Everything in its time.

Notes

This essay was translated from Galician by Kirsty Hooper and Manuel Puga Moruxa.

1. The volume was reissued by Tambre in 1996 in an updated and extended version, including two new authors (Vázquez Varela et al.). It is one of the first general histories to take Francoism as a period in its own right. The AN-PG history published in 1979 includes Francoism only in a brief appendix, while the Caixa history (1980), includes it in a section on social and economic change in the second half of the twentieth century.

2. Two recent anthologies that contain up-to-date studies of contemporary Galicia are Constenla and Domínguez; Juana and Prada, *Historia*.

3. The following discussion appears in my "Os espacios do cambio."

4. Local history is typically an amateur enterprise. Its dismissal has been vigorously questioned, in theory and in practice, throughout the Spanish state.

5. A universal history is extremely difficult to construct, from Voltaire to Fukuyama, via Hegel and Marx.

6. Soto leaves few doubts about agricultural developments during the contemporary period and the risk of agricultural setback due to the war and subsequent dictatorship.

7. Galician exports during the 1880s, were equal to 90% of the total cattle that went from Denmark to the United Kingdom.

8. Juana and Prada bring together the latest research on the subject (*Lo que han hecho*). Lanero Taboas discusses the repression in the Arzúa area. See also the work done in the past year by my interuniversity research team Nomes e Voces (*Nomes*; "Names and Voices").

9. Cabana, like Lanero Taboas, reveals the social and political history of the hitherto historiographically unstudied Franco period.

10. On the memory of the war, see Fernández Prieto, "Memoria."

National Literature and the Literary Field

Antón Figueroa

Any national legitimization project, whether completely or only partially successful, is a social process that commits an entire group to the search for internal and external recognition. As a political process, it is also epic, insofar as it seeks the support of the group regarding the nature of the project. The specific procedures for such projects vary a great deal, as do their pace and results. Popular acquiescence is sought through the political use of all sorts of rationales: historical, geographic, ethnic, artistic, and so on. In consequence, knowledge, especially in the arts and humanities, is put at the service of the common project. In Galicia, for example, the mid-nineteenth-century revival known as the Rexurdimento is usually associated with cultural forms, especially poetry. However, the term (like Risorgimento in Italy and Renaixença in Catalonia) in fact refers to a movement that was initially political rather than cultural; the renewal of the Galician language, literature, and other forms of artistic activity were part of the political project to reclaim a national status for Galicia.

Artistic activity and political or economic activity in Galicia have thus been firmly entwined since the mid-nineteenth century, and I have found Pierre Bourdieu's idea of an (artistic) literary field very useful in understanding and explaining their tangled relation. Bourdieu defines the concept:

> The literary field is a force field acting upon all who enter it, and acting in a differential manner according to the position they occupy there (whether, to take the points furthest removed from each other, that of a writer of hit plays or that of an avant-garde poet), and at the same time it is a field of competitive struggles which tend to conserve or transform this force field. (*Rules* 232)

For Bourdieu, a field is a network of relations in play around unevenly distributed types of capital (which might be political, scientific, academic, artistic, literary, or religious), and each field prescribes its own values and rules. His concept of *habitus*, developed from the Aristotelian-Thomist concept of the same name (*Choses* 20–21), explains the mechanisms of internalization, of the acquisition of social rules by social actors. *Habitus* is an unconscious incorporation that constrains action in the social world, the concrete strategy that is most suitable at any given moment. The literary and cultural fields, like any other, are constrained by the fields that surround them, especially the economic and political fields. The literary field is therefore shaped by two hierarchical principles of organization: an autonomous principle of internal hierarchization, which is based on pure literary factors, and a heteronomous principle of external hierarchization, which tends to be organized around interests outside the field—that is, with interests that mirror those of the economic or political fields ("Champ" 7).

Artistic Autonomy and the Formation of the Modern Nation

Bourdieu's notion of a field with these two hierarchical principles of organization can help explain the interaction between the political and artistic fields that is so characteristic of processes of nation building in modernity. For this reason, certain nineteenth- and twentieth-century European artists (composers such as Manuel de Falla, Jean Sibelius, Bedřich Smetana, and the Russian Five) are given the political label nationalist, which carries no pejorative sense. *Nationalist* clearly indicates the dialectic that conditions the artistic fields, which on the one hand are autonomous, a field in their own right, and on the other, heteronomous—that is, subject to the rule of politics.

The interaction between politics and art is especially important when we talk about the emergence of the Galician literary sphere in the late nineteenth and early twentieth centuries, for two very different reasons. In the first place, print products in this era, although less widely available than they are today, had a much greater importance and symbolic authority thanks to their almost exclusive hold (shared with oral literature) over the diffusion of ideas and stories. The second reason is that the new political responsibility of the literary field introduced heteronomous factors into it—that is, factors that increased its dependence on the political field—at the very moment when European literatures were being configured as autonomous and authors as liberated from monarchical power, from patronage, and from mercenary obligations. In the literatures that emerge during this period, including those of stateless nations such as the Galician, Catalan, and Basque, authors are still conditioned by a national duty that seems impossible to avoid, at least until the nation achieves the recognition it desires. In Galicia, it is evident that authors will not achieve full autonomy, and literature will never achieve the long-desired normalization, until the literary field is liberated from external political responsibilities.

I recognize that artistic autonomy is never absolute. Art always contributes to the internal construction of the nation, simultaneously bringing it into existence and obtaining external recognition for it. Consider how in his films Luchino Visconti contributed both to the internal construction of the Italian nation and to its international recognition: his cinema was recognized, both in Italy and elsewhere, as Italian. And yet the political functions that he performed cannot be likened to those of Alessandro Manzoni's poetry or Giuseppe Verdi's music during the nineteenth-century Risorgimento that underpinned the process of Italian unification, because the political responsibility of art was greater during the nation-building process. The Italian unification was successful, and by the beginning of the twentieth century, Italian artists could begin to free themselves from their epic functions.

The political functions of the literary sphere now, at the beginning of the twenty-first century, are different in the literatures of England and France, which were recognized well before the nineteenth century, or in the literature of Italy, which was successfully normalized in the nineteenth century, from the political functions of literature in communities that continue to struggle for political recognition. These aspire in various ways to have their identity recognized. Galicia's artistic processes carry a social charge that plays out as a clash between the autonomy that is indispensable for the survival of art and the political action that is equally necessary for the existence of the group.

Autonomy in a literary field does not mean the bourgeois notion of art for art's sake, which is indifferent to social issues. Rather, it refers to the way the literary institution provides the means to obtain symbolic power and social recognition internally, within itself, so that it does not depend on external factors to obtain them. Artistic autonomy has nothing to do with the personal political choices of the agents (artists, writers, filmmakers) or with the themes of their work. Writers, precisely because of the recognition achieved in the field, can make their political choices, even explicitly in their texts, without losing autonomy. The following example of Émile Zola is revealing:

La thèse de la coïncidence progressive de l'autonomie de l'institution et de l'autonomie des contenus part d'une vision téléologique peu convaincante. Zola intervint ainsi dans les affaires politiques à un moment d'autonomisation très grande du champ et c'est du fait de autonomie et du prestige acquis à l'intérieur du champ qu'il pouvait se permettre d'intervenir. (Jurt 99)

The thesis that the autonomy of the institution and the autonomy of the contents progressively coincide stems from a rather unconvincing teleological point of view. Zola intervened in politics at a moment of great autonomization in the field, and it is precisely thanks to the autonomy and prestige he had already gained within the field that he was able to allow himself to intervene. (my trans.)

While art is subject to intense political pressure at the beginning of any national process, I would argue that the drive toward autonomy appears in some form from the earliest moment. I recall a text by Jesús Bal y Gay, a Galician composer and musicologist in the 1920s who forcefully criticized movements that privileged the (political) use of folklore, because he saw them constantly collapse into stereotypes. Bal y Gay criticized composers as emblematic as Xoán Montes (1840–99), José Castro González ("Chané"; 1856–1917), and Pascual Veiga (1842–1906), to reclaim the autonomy of music as an art form that could take up its own positions and, what is more, renew itself:

Uns cantos músicos sinxelos e vountosos, sintíronse obrigados a poñer en música os versos dos poetas mais nosos. Ise feito, no século XIX, non poiderá ser esquencido *xa* dos músicos galegos que veñan no futuro. Os cimentos, non, o vieiro da nos música moderna está *xa* aberto.

Mais non vaia a creerse isto que eu digo nun senso de loubanza pra a música que iles fixeron. A súa música, hoxe, cando o arte musical ten un caris cada día mais depuradamente inteleitual e cando a sensibilidade afínase ao mesmo tempo que se adequiren mais firmes coñecimentos téinicos, a súa música non debe terse como modelo para as xenerazóns seguintes—no que se di musical. . . .

Por qué non abrangueron as súas obras a eternidade, é cousa que arestora parécenos nidia dabondo. No arte é preciso erguer moito a puntería para que a frecha trema no blanco. Todo canto coidado teñamos de afiar o *métier*, de ollar i escudrinar os mais outos exemplos será pouco. (2)

A small number of eager and simple composers felt themselves obliged to set to music the verses of the poets who are most dear to us. This endeavor, back in the nineteenth century, should not be forgotten by the Galician composers to come. The foundations, no, the path of our modern music has now been opened up.

But do not take what I am saying simply as praise for the music they made. Their music, today, when the art of music is daily becoming more purely intellectual and when our sensibility is refined as we acquire stronger technical knowledge, their music should not be taken as a model for future generations—as what we might consider *musical*.

The reason their works did not achieve immortality now seems perfectly clear to us. In art it is necessary to raise your aim high so that the arrow hits the target. However much care we might take to sharpen the metier, to consider and scrutinize the most perfect examples, it will not be enough.   (my trans.)

Bal y Gay, more ambitious in spirit than his contemporaries, was obviously claiming the metier, artistic autonomy, and thus a more universal profile for his art.

It is interesting that Xosé Luis Méndez Ferrín, perhaps the most widely known writer in Galicia today (and very politically committed), should say, sixty years after Bal y Gay:

> O escritor galego, como tódolos escritores, habita a función poética e non ten obrigas que o aten á representación de nocións. O seu compromiso é coa mensaxe e coa forma da mensaxe. A súa tarefa, o combate cruento pola expresión distinta, o que equivale ao sabotaxe permanente do idioma, á predación dos seus recursos infinitos. Asín se realiza o escritor a asín consolida avances sociais indestructíbeis.   (qtd. in Angueira Viturro 524)[1]

> A Galician writer, like any writer, dwells in the poetic function of language and has no obligation simply to represent ideas. The writer's commitment is to the message and the form of the message. The writer's task is the bloody struggle for distinct expression, which is the same as the permanent sabotage of the language, the plundering of its infinite resources. That is how a writer is made, and that is how indestructible social advances are consolidated.
> (my trans.)

What Bal y Gay and Méndez Ferrín are doing is simple: they are claiming autonomy for Galicia's musical and literary fields. The problem is not that Galician writers or artists adopt political positions in public; that particular political choices appear in their texts; or that, like politicians, they speak in the name of the people. The problem is that in Galicia, these fields are configured in such a way that writers are forced to position themselves according to the political choices they make, that the literary field values external elements over internal. Texts must focus on certain subjects in order to be valued. Political position may make up for artistic failure. Political heteronomy may allow failed artists to reinvent themselves as cursed artists. Even if the literary field were to have sufficient autonomy, writers' political choices do not in the end weaken institutional autonomy. On the contrary, certain political choices can even reinforce the autonomy of the field.

Even if there are substantial differences between the initial moments of national affirmation, such as the Rexurdimento and the normalized period, we should recognize that these processes are constantly evolving toward greater autonomy for the respective fields. Generally the political function of the literary world diminishes as the political field begins to constitute itself with specialized agents—that is, with professional politicians. This development also increases the literary field's autonomy and thus brings about a change in the relevance of the author and the functions of his work. In Galicia, the literary work of the artist and writer Alfonso Rodríguez Castelao (1886–1950), well established in the literary canon, cannot be separated from his official, public role as a member of the Spanish parliament and, later, as president of the Galician Republican government in exile. Castelao's literary achievement is much more conditioned by his political role than that of any of today's established authors, even one as politically committed as Manuel Rivas (b. 1957), who became one of the leaders of the Nunca Máis pressure group in response to the sinking of the oil tanker *Prestige* in 2002.

The shift toward artistic autonomy in Galicia was heavily conditioned by political events, such as the Francoist uprising in Spain in 1936, which reduced the so-called peripheral cultures, including Galician, to silence or exile. The recovery of democratic institutions after Franco's death in 1975 produced a literary recovery whose aim was greater autonomy for the literary field. Looking closely at this literary recovery, we can see, despite everything, the persistence of social habits that were present at the beginning of the process. The urgently felt collective interest continues to shape artistic communication. It introduces into society not only modes of literary production but also norms of writing and reading, images of the writer, themes, literary-political values, and certain inertias and constants that are linked to its political origins and still color what appears to be straightforward artistic communication.

Between Politics and Art: The Recovery of a Galician National Literature

At the beginning of the Galician process of recovery in the mid–nineteenth century, many of the arguments used by protonationalist or regionalist politicians were historical. Thinkers such as Manuel Murguía, Alfredo Brañas, and Benito Vicetto evoked a Galician past with a personality of its own—the ancient Swabian kingdom (411–585) or the medieval Kingdom of Galicia with its prestigious Galician-Portuguese language, its intense and celebrated literary and musical life in the *cantigas* songbooks, and its emblematic figures like the Mariscal Pardo de Cela, murdered in 1483 on the orders of the Catholic monarchs Fernando and Isabel. Scholars like Murguía and Vicetto were attempting to rewrite the history of Galicia that had been excised from Spain's official history. The conflict between Galician and Spanish historical discourses continues even today. By the end of the nineteenth century, at the height of the Rexurdimento, what had begun as a historicist argument evolved along ethnic lines, focusing on the distinct nature of the Galician people rather than on their history.

The ethnicist position was fully developed in the 1920s by the group of writers and intellectuals known as the Xeración Nós (1920–36; "Us Generation"), the first to define Galicia as a nation rather than a region. For writers such as Castelao, Vicente Risco, and Ramón Otero Pedrayo, the nation was linked to the idea of a people that possesses a soul and is located in a territory. The differences between cultures are explained because they belong to peoples who have different souls. Thus Otero Pedrayo argues for the idea of two different souls in Europe: the Mediterranean soul of the Provencal poets, with their belief in the classical concept of destiny, and the Atlantic soul of the bards, Romantic, Celtic, believers in *saudade* ("painful longing") and free will: "eu non comprendo un celta protestante" ("I do not understand a Protestant Celt"), writes Otero (127). Halfway between the ethnicist argument and historical discourse, we find the use of myths regarding Galicia's most remote, even prehistoric ancestors, to justify the unique soul of the people. In this way, the Celts, according to Galician historiography based on archaeology and some toponyms, would be the original inhabitants of the *castros* ("ancient hill forts"), a notion that is controversial and disputed by historians today.

The concepts of *pobo* ("people"), *alma* ("soul"), and *terra* ("land") that underpin the *Nós* Generation's vision of Galician identity are closely connected with another fundamental place of the theorized Galician nation: the rural space, embodied in the folklore that is thought to retain the essence of the people's enduring soul. During the 1920s and 1930s, the functions of art in the construction of the nation begin to manifest themselves clearly, as scholars and artists start to gather folkloric elements from oral literature, music, ethnography, and so on. The rural world thus became a source for every kind of story, and these stories fulfilled the political and rhetorical function of legitimizing the nation.

In the mid–twentieth century, the essentialist argument began to disappear from theorizations of Galician nationalism, as the interpretation of Galicia's history and culture as Celtic, which had been a differentiating strategy of Rexurdimento writers such as Eduardo Pondal, increasingly came into question. This is not to say that the initial reasons and arguments for the Celtic position are not still present in both literary and political praxis. There is a certain essentialism in every nation, which is experienced as something obvious, as common sense, as a conviction held by every citizen. In Galicia, this essentialism is even more evident. Researchers who study these processes must try to place themselves to one side of the established wisdom to observe them simply as praxis. We should not pass judgment on the historical, linguistic, or folkloric arguments used in the past from the point of view of our present; we should judge them, rather, by their collective political, cultural, and literary results. There is no point in simply dismissing essentialism, as some who oppose it do, by claiming that the reasoning employed will later turn out to be false: the deeper truth of that reasoning lies in its still-relevant political and artistic potential.

The restoration of democratic institutions in Spain after 1975 marked a turning point in this intense dynamic. Writers and other artistic agents, now free of heteronomous political obligations, which were assumed by professional politicians, began to liberate themselves from their historical role as receptacles and interpreters of the national memory. They liberated themselves, too, from the almost exclusive responsibility for teaching the nation's cultural memory. During the 1970s and 1980s, Galician writers and artists became aware of the need for autonomy and new repertoires. Autochthonous motifs and the rural world were no longer seen as the only instruments or conditions for canonization and production, and artists and writers became increasingly free in their choice of themes and forms. Artistic fields took shape, each developing its own internal characteristics, and competition between artists replaced the earlier cooperation in the pursuit of a common project. The emerging literary field was characterized by more purely literary strategies. Artists and writers were lured by economic gain and public recognition, temptations that had usually been absent in the prophetic era. Now, at the start of the twenty-first century, the old tendencies may not have disappeared completely, but they have lost their central role in the legitimization of writers and texts.

Artistic sectors evolve each according to its own dynamics. In Galicia, architecture, painting, music, literature, and fashion have followed different paths and reached very different levels of development. I believe that the role each field played at the outset influenced its future. Perhaps the possibilities for innovation were greater for those arts that had no political role during the Rexurdimento, since they started from scratch. Whereas literature, politically committed at the beginning of the process, then had to deal with the persistence of literary habits established as tradition, which always affects the present. Galician fashion, perhaps because it started from scratch, was not drawn into folklore or ritual, and modern Galician architecture has hardly ever turned to tradition as a creative norm. In music, although the recourse to Celtism and folklore still plays an important part, the means of expression has diversified. But political considerations can still affect the artist. On Galician radio, Abe Rábade, a young musician who had achieved public recognition as a jazz performer and composer, was interviewed. During the interview, somebody felt obliged to justify the music by saying that it was Galician, which reflects the weight that repertoires from the past carry.

Knowledge and art in Galicia have generally gained greater autonomy from national political obligations, especially in the last quarter of the twentieth century. Yet traditional beliefs and habits are still widespread at the social level. Scholars may be even more objective, writers and artists even more independent, but past viewpoints persist in society, especially given their political profitability and effectiveness. Artistic works may be more autonomous, but readers and viewers continue to apply old norms of interpretation. It is true that the recourse to folklore or to the past and its artistic utilization helped form Galician identity. It is also true that this approach, applied to aesthetic forms, can help destroy that same identity. The imposition of politics on art may result in the loss of art's autonomy and capacity for renewal. In Galicia, there will be little potential for cultural fields to become autonomous as long as art continues to play this national, political-pedagogical role. The image of the writer or artist as politician, prophet, and pedagogue is still pertinent, and it continues to develop today in parallel with the image of the militant reader.

This political heteronomy does not function in the same way as the economic heteronomy described by Bourdieu ("Champ" 6; *Règles* 300). Economic heteronomy, which can affect not only sectors of the literary field but also its agents, becomes a temptation at the end of the creative process: writers, once they have acquired symbolic power, can be tempted by economic interests. In contrast, political heteronomy, at least in Galician literature, seems to work differently on both field and agent. The literary field is politically committed from the start, so that political heteronomy appears at the start of the creative process and tends to diminish toward the end. It diminishes for writers as they become established in the field. Note also that writers do not experience political commitment as a liability or obstacle to their work. In fact, it can be a liberating project, as the literary field emerges as a heterodoxy in relation to the Spanish political field. At the same time, the literary can stand aloof from the nation. The influence of politics over the autonomy of the literary field is therefore complex. Even as its general tendency is to disappear, its effects persist in the form of repertoire or *habitus*.

The political function that has shaped Galician literature since the beginning continues to influence it and to create anomalies in its functioning. An examination of literary practice in Galicia reveals many examples where the literary field seems autonomous. We find a restricted field of production composed of writers who are not subject to economic influence, because they have another profession that supports them. Even such literary celebrities today as Xosé Luís Méndez Ferrín and María Xosé Queizán continue to work as schoolteachers. At the same time, we can clearly see the shift from a restricted field of production to the field of mass production. Commercial gain is still considered a sign of normalization, can still be interpreted in political terms (working for the cause), an interpretation that tends not to perceive the dialectic between the subfield of restricted production and the subfield of mass production. Economic gain or celebrity, which writers such as Suso de Toro and Manuel Rivas have achieved, is not perceived as a paradox with the militant's characteristic indifference toward material success: the umbrella of the nation, in Galicia, can be invoked to cover and conceal any contradiction between creating art and making money.

When writers who are trying to achieve noncommercial, symbolic power accuse other writers who use external means to establish themselves (the Spanish media, for example) of playing with two decks, the latter defend themselves vigorously. Both groups of writers appeal to the general need to complete the process of normalization. Their position is ambiguous: from the artistic point of view, to situate themselves in the field of mass production may mean a loss of symbolic power, but this power is recoverable if they justify themselves by claiming to perform a politically orthodox and even engagé function. The loss of symbolic power is offset by the profit of a renewed political legitimacy. This dialectic is easily observable when writers are appreciated by the most politicized sectors, which are concerned with the task of normalization, while simultaneously censured by the most autonomous sectors of the field.

When we talk of normalization, we presuppose an essential difference from the other, the outsider, who is what is ultimately imagined to be normal. The striving to erase the difference produces a certain mimeticism, which leads to the application of legitimized theoretical models (textbook examples, so to speak) from other supposedly normal literatures in order to outline a program of action. What I mean is that literary theory, to a certain extent, becomes a blueprint or guide to practice, and so the theorist or critic appears to have a normative authority and great symbolic power over writers. People tend to use whatever instruments of analysis are available, not to explain literary practice but to serve the development of normalization, which then consists of governing production instead of creating conditions of production that would authenticate a possible literary politics. A global discourse then emerges in the literary field, based on suppositions that are, in the end, equally political. This work restrains the spontaneity of practice, encouraging imitation.

To give an example, if this discourse imagines a model series of literary genres (literary novels, detective stories, penny dreadfuls, erotic novels, etc.), that model becomes a basis for what ought to exist. But it is absurd to plan the confluence of orthodoxy and heterodoxy, of the dominant and the dominated. This mimetic process tends to destroy the dynamic proper to any field and demands an artistic price that possibly the planners themselves are unaware of, given that their own practice deprives them of the necessary distance to observe the process. I think of such planning as a kind of culture or *habitus* that is introduced into the literary field and that its agents have incorporated as a heteronomous element that is ultimately political. But there exists no official, systematic form of culture planning in Galicia.

I return to the current urgency of the Galician literary field, created by a civil war that silenced, murdered, persecuted, or exiled most of Galicia's cultural agents, to the recuperation of civil liberties after Francoism that turned writers in varying degrees and different ways into committed figures. Even now, after the literary field has managed to gain greater autonomy under a recognized (if fragile) political autonomy, the image of the writer maintains a double character: heterodox and prophetic image compared with what is perceived as Spanish cultural orthodoxy, orthodox and pedagogical in relation to the Galician national project. Writers still play a political role in that they speak in the name of the people; as the people's representatives, they are often driven to take political positions. We saw this in 2002, after the sinking of the oil tanker *Prestige*, when the best-known Galician writers, such as Rivas and Toro, organized and led the popular demonstrations along with other artists, among them Rafa Villar, Luis Tosar, and Uxía Senlle. This commitment to represent reappears especially when it is perceived that the political powers are not doing their job. Although contemporary Galician writers realize that tradition, folklore, and rural themes no longer automatically bring recognition, they must bow to subtle but incontestable national imperatives if they wish to obtain or preserve public recognition and social legitimization.

This politicization of cultural processes, the result of the responsibility that artists and all intellectuals feel toward Galician culture, prompts certain habits, such as a resistance to specialization. The nationalist education trade union organizes literary courses for its members, and politicians commonly speak with authority on cultural, historical, and philological topics. At the same time, many members of the academic world, having achieved renown in the cultural sphere, consider it natural that they be given political posts. Such posts were given particularly during the last change of government, in 2005. Sometimes writers and artists try to exploit political positions to obtain prestige (which is heteronomous, after all)—just as can happen in the academic world.

I have shown how the circumstances in which the Galician literary field emerged have conditioned its present state. The field originated as an identity politics movement, which had an epic character, because it tried to mobilize a whole group. This political-cultural group that emerged in the nineteenth century developed gradually until the Spanish Civil War (1936–39). In the period 1920–36, we see the emergence of a purely literary field, complete with internal competition, of which Manuel Antonio's manifesto "¡Máis alá!" (1922; "Further Still!") (Manuel Antonio and Cebreiro) is a good example. This dynamic, silenced or condemned to survive in exile during the dictatorship, took an important step forward with the restoration of democracy in 1975. The official establishment of political power by the Spanish Constitution of 1978 and, a couple of years later, the establishment of the Autonomous Community of Galicia with its own political institutions created new possibilities. Politicians are increasingly differentiated from belletrists and artists, who are now liberated from many extraliterary or extra-artistic functions. This situation has in turn created new problems. The status of Galicia as a minority language or culture that must be defended justifies the intervention of politicians (of any party) in the cultural field. Political authorities do not always have the necessary vision or discipline to limit themselves, in their decisions, to nurture the development of artistic fields. For their part, the artistic fields, still unaccustomed to creative freedom, are too dependent on external authorities. Nevertheless, it is possible now to see how at the very root of the process there appears, however weakly, a desire for artistic autonomy.

Galician literature gives the impression of still being part of an unfinished, fragile process. Habits outlive their causes, and these causes have not disappeared completely, because Galician culture continues to struggle for survival. The linguistic situation is still insecure. Even if the initial ideology has changed, even if the essentialist ideas that served the affirmation of Galician identity in the nineteenth century are no longer as evident in public discourse, they persist in popular culture today, in readers and in reading habits. It is the same with the foundational myths of Galician nationalism. The humanities and humanist discourses in Galicia remain committed to the Galician nationalist process. Readers of this essay can see for themselves how even academic discourse, without trying, remains engagé. Galician literature, like other so-called minor, minority, or minoritized literatures, thus finds itself faced with a dialectic between the autonomy of the literary field (albeit relative), which is indispensable for its artistic survival, and the political action that is equally necessary to establish, restore, and maintain it.

Notes

This essay was translated from Galician by Kirsty Hooper and Manuel Puga Moruxa.

1. The quotation is taken from an unpublished recording of Méndez Ferrín at the I Congreso de Escritores Galegos, which took place in Poio in 1981.

Further Reading

Figueroa, Antón. *Nacion, literatura, identidade.* Vigo: Xerais, 2001. Print.

Figueroa, Antón, and Xoán González-Millán. *Communication littéraire et culture en Galice.* Paris: L'Harmattan, 1997. Print.

Gondar Portasany, Marcial. *Crítica da razón galega.* 2nd ed. Vigo: A Nosa Terra, 1995. Print.

González-Millán, Xoán. "Do nacionalismo literario á literatura nacional: Hipóteses de traballo para un estudio institucional da literatura galega." *Anuario de estudios literarios galegos 1994* (1995): 67–81. Print.

———. *Literatura e sociedade en Galicia, 1975–1990.* Vigo: Xerais, 1994. Print.

———. *A narrativa galega actual, 1975–1984: Unha historia social.* Vigo: Xerais, 1996. Print.

———. *Resistencia cultural e diferencia histórica, a experiencia da subalternidade.* Santiago: Sotelo Blanco, 2000. Print.

Cultural History and Resistance: The Articulation of Modern Galician Literature

María do Cebreiro Rábade Villar

> Notre héritage n'est précédé d'aucun testament.
> —René Char

> Our inheritance was left to us by no document.

Literary Criticism in Galicia

In this essay I explore some of the most sensitive areas of contemporary Galician literary studies, in the belief that intellectual debate, especially if it does not avoid uncomfortable questions, can strengthen the social reality on which it is projected. The relation between literature and testimony, the transposition of linguistic conflict onto literature, the connection between language and revolution, the place from which one writes, and the risks of oversubjecting literature to planning and nationalization are some of the forms taken by the relation between literature and politics—or rather, perhaps, between culture and power—in Galicia. In this context, they cannot be considered accidental or coincidental; they are at the very heart of theoretical discussion.

A tradition, albeit limited, of looking critically at the history of modern Galician literature has existed since the last quarter of the twentieth century, when different theorists began to take Galician literature as a subject, a problem, and a cause. Works such as Antón Figueroa's *Diglosia e texto* (1988; "Diglossia and Text"), whose very title alludes to conflict, or Xoán González-Millán's *Literatura e sociedade en Galicia* (1994; "Literature and Society in Galicia") were pioneering in this area. The application of their analytic tools to the discipline of Galician literary studies has, in practice, enabled longstanding positivist or stylistic methods to be complemented (if not always replaced) by readings that are more attentive to the interactions among culture, history, and society.

Little of what has followed, in terms of Galician literary criticism and theory, can be understood without taking these precedents into account. Without making claims to exhaustiveness, I would draw attention to three major tendencies in current Galician literary studies: feminist studies, sociological studies, and historiographical studies. Helena González, of the Universitat de Barcelona, is the researcher who has paid most attention to the methodological renewal of feminist literary criticism, with works on female-authored Galician poetry, such as the recent *Elas e o paraugas totalizador* (2005; "Women and the Totalizing Umbrella"). Sociological studies, based on Pierre Bourdieu's theory of literary fields and Itamar Even-Zohar's polysystem theory, applied to the Galician-Luso-African-Brazilian system, underpin the approach of the Galabra group, linked to the Universidade de Santiago de Compostela (e.g., see the work of Elías Torres). An approach concerned with the social functions of literature, which is in many ways close to cultural studies, can be seen in the work of some of the researchers included in the special Galician issue of the *Journal of Spanish Cultural Studies* (Hooper, *New Spaces*). Finally, historiographical concerns underpin Dolores Vilavedra's attempt to rearticulate the periodization of modern Galician literature, not only in the multivolume *Diccionario da literatura galega* ("Dictionary of Galician Literature") that she edited between 1995 and 2004 but also in her *Historia da literatura galega* (1999; "History of Galician Literature"). The intersection between literary theory and historiography is one of the focuses of Arturo Casas's work, from his reflections on the concept of "literary generation" ("A cuestión") to his critical approach to the integration of Galician literature in that of the Iberian Peninsula as a whole ("Problemas," "Sistema").

Despite their evident potential, these fertile approaches cannot at the moment be said to have resulted in a new model of criticism, precisely because of some of the factors outlined by Figueroa and González-Millán. The subordination of Galician literature to other social fields and the absence of a university system that makes Galicia a true center of academic study are just two of the many symptoms of this insufficiency. Nevertheless, Figueroa's and González-Millán's essays in the 1980s and early 1990s certainly provided the basis of a promising line of research, demonstrating that it was possible to approach Galician literature in a way that was both rigorous and radical.

It is worth stressing, if at risk of tautology, that works such as *Diglosia e texto* and *Literatura e sociedade en Galicia* were written on the assumption that there existed a social space in which they could circulate and be discussed. A feature of works that stimulate further thought is that they do not underestimate their audience. Galician literary critics must be highly optimistic to assume that they have an audience; that Galicia (also) exists—a less optimistic version of this statement would replace *also* by *still*; that a Galician literature exists to be recounted (to children and to adults); and that it is worth the effort to generate criticism of that literature. Since, as we know, the world is not at present hospitable to statements that suppose a certain degree of intellectual complexity, to be a critic of Galician literature is not only an act of will but also an act of trust.

Where There's a Loss, There's a Response: Galician Literature and Testimony

An important field of literary research at the moment sees the concepts of catastrophe and testimony as a stimulus for historical and literary reflection. Inevitably, this kind of research can make the chronicle, and every other method of recording events more or less in real time, one of the most privileged genres of analysis.[1] Galician literature advocates extensive use of the term *testemuñal* ("testimonial"), extending the meaning of *testimony* beyond that of the court record to include a corpus of texts that, deliberately or not, has made resistance one of its raisons d'être.

Since the Rexurdimento, Galician literature has confronted the problem of social fracture and historical discontinuity and in some cases paradoxically turned these conditions into stimuli for its own construction and survival. For this very reason, it is worth pausing on the concept of loss, focusing especially on its aporetic character. Freudian theory of melancholia has long seen in loss the a posteriori construction of an object of pain, and Jacques Derrida, deconstructing Freud, underlines the active character of any loss when he compares the function of memory with the structure of the archive. Modern Galician literature is critical by definition, first emerging in response to a literary vacuum, which the relatively late discovery of the Galician-Portuguese *cancioneiros* ("songbooks") helped define as restoration of a loss. Even today, the attraction of mechanisms associated with continuity and discontinuity, loss and recovery, forgetting and remembering, allows us to see the socioliterary uses of a concept such as historical memory, so current in the peninsular context through its association with the acts of reparation to the victims of Francoism.

Literature took on a function that we might call supplementary, because sociopolitical factors impeded the development of other public means of expression and articulation. It was literature that at many points in history led the production of an autonomous and dissenting way of thinking. The strong connection between literature and the production and circulation of ideas in the Galician social space has not yet been sufficiently explored. The belief that literature is a specific type of thought—to be more precise, a divergent type of thought—is a historical achievement of European Romanticism and its theory of the poetic imagination as a revolutionary intellectual force. European Romanticism alone is the aesthetic and ideological context of the Galician Rexurdimento. Since the twentieth century, of course, with temporal variations that depend, among other factors, on the degree of industrialization achieved, Western societies have been undergoing a process in which works of art, including literature, largely lose their role as vehicles for ideology as they come to be considered commodities and culture a leisure activity.

Robert Weimann describes this process in his explanation of the expression *cultural capital*:

> "Cultural capital" is not exactly an inviting phrase, but as a provocative metaphor it may well be taken to suggest that the present space of cultural activity is much less autonomous, much less a derivative of a nucleus of creativity in the fine arts, than seemed to be the case in the circumstances of an earlier, "classical" phase of industrialized society. (221)

Problems begin when we try to apply the expression *industrialized society* literally to contemporary Galicia, or any other society whose degree of incorporation in modernity differs from what we have come to consider the norm. In his foundational "Etnopoética para unha literatura periférica" ("Ethnopoetics for a Peripheral Literature"), first published in 1988, González-Millán examines the implicit assumptions of the *deber-ser* ("ideal condition") of a literary system and defends the need to question inherited patterns to produce models of understanding suitable for the phenomenon he is trying to describe. Today we would call the project something different— something that escapes the essentialist echoes of the term *etnia* ("ethnic group")—but most of González-Millán's objectives are still entirely pertinent. A project such as this would try to confront questions like the different meanings of the term *cultural capital* for Galicia. Or, putting it another way by returning to Bourdieu's theory of social field (*Règles*), it would try to

clarify the connections, as unstable as they are inevitable, between the Galician literary field and the fields of economic and political power.

Since the second half of the nineteenth century, a good deal of the differential energy in the production of literary works has come from political
conflict. We should thus reconsider the idea that the production of literature from a subaltern position constitutes an obstacle to the development of
a literary field. The epic character of a literature, understood as its deliberate
inscription in a context of urgency and its will to intervene in that context,
does not necessarily reduce its expressive potential. It is a fact, verified in
the recent poetry of authors such as Derek Walcott or Seamus Heaney, that
there are authors who make literary virtue out of political necessity. That
Rosalía de Castro's *Cantares gallegos* (1863; "Galician Songs") is literature
written with the purpose of enhancing a political cause does not reduce its
literary worth; on the contrary, it increases its value as a foundational text—
value being understood here, in the empirical sense, as being socially assigned and not an intrinsic quality. That this literary value was not assigned
by society to other recent authors (such as the social poets of the 1970s) does
not invalidate this consideration.[2]

In fact, as a result of what Hegel would call "cunning of reason," the
subaltern situation from which Galicia suffered as a result of the failed
nineteenth-century revolutions of 1846 and 1868 was a significant factor in
the development of an independent Galician literature. The idea of loss of political power goes a long way toward explaining the poetic projects of Rosalía
de Castro, Manuel Curros Enríquez, and Eduardo Pondal. At the beginning
of the twentieth century, the articulation of a specific prewar avant-garde in
Manuel Antonio's manifesto "¡Máis alá!" (1922; "Further Still!") (Manuel
Antonio and Cebreiro) makes it impossible to distinguish between poetics
and politics. We can still see its effects in the second half of the twentieth century, in the national allegories of the authors of the Nova Narrativa Galega
("New Galician Narrative") in the 1960s.[3] The historical discontinuity that
has so often been noticed in Galician cultural discourse was translated, periodically, into a determined effort to assert the right to exist, in the implicit
belief that an established literature could contribute to the legitimization of
space and be an active response to the pressure of the hegemonic authorities.

The relation between literature and testimony is complex in any cultural environment and takes on particular inflections in each. I am using
testimony here in a way slightly different from its most common critical usage, which links the term to memory of the Holocaust and to Latin Ameri-

can chronicles of the military dictatorships of the twentieth century. The Galician cultural experience, while apparently distant from these contexts, suggests new possibilities for understanding the concept. For example, how far can a national literature represent itself historically as a testimony of resistance to linguistic or cultural disappearance? If we consider testimony as a privileged form of expression capable of transmitting things according to its own version of truth,[4] can literature serve as a testimony? And, if it can, as a testimony to what truth? A question such as this takes on full meaning only when we ask it in relation to specific historical and cultural situations, in which it is difficult to separate fact from narrative. Since literature nowadays tends to be identified with fiction, owing to a tradition of thought that is not as ancient as it may appear, we might be tempted to reply that facts and stories are two entirely different things.[5]

In contrast, contemporary philosophy repeatedly shows the mutual implication, if not indistinction, between the domain of what happens and the domain of what is described, and it does not seem easy to move beyond such considerations to return literary studies to the age of innocent positivism and hedonistic stylistics. But the impossibility of returning to former paradigms again exemplifies Hegel's "cunning of reason." Whereas postmodern relativism would argue that there are only stories, situations like Galicia's confirm that stories, literally, construct cultures. By stories I do not mean simply testimonial or committed literature but literature as testimony and writing as commitment. Although the relation between literature and truth is not necessarily a one-to-one correspondence, we can continue to speak of Galicia as a social and political reality precisely because of the existence of a Galician literature. Conversely, that we can recognize a political and social reality with the name of Galicia invites us to ask which literary forms should be associated with that name. It may be that the complexity of Galicia's situation today has not yet found a reflection in the literary models that have developed to describe it.

Writing in the Open Wound: Standard Spelling and Minor Literature

In a study of the relation between translation studies and comparative literature, Emily Apter devotes an interesting chapter to what she calls, paraphrasing Walter Benjamin, the "language of damaged experience" (149–59). She studies how different contemporary writers deliberately use linguistic forms such as dialects, pidgins, and patois to reflect colonial or class conflicts and thus to abolish, through textual contamination, the supposition that the standard form is the zero point of language. More broadly, Apter's hypothesis can also help us understand the literary use of languages in which, as with Galician, the problem of standard spelling (*norma ortográfica*) has become crucial, carrying political connotations. Her discussion of the representation of damaged experience through language can shed light on the models of written Galician underpinning different literary projects. Phenomena such as diglossia and language conflict have become topics in disciplines such as the social history of language or sociolinguistics. Less attention has been paid to how ideas about language have historically affected the works of writers in Galicia. I am not referring to the well-known problematic of the role of Castilian-language literature produced by Galician-born writers, a subject that needs to be studied from a nonessentialist perspective, where the "language criterion" for defining a national literature[6] is taken not as the norm but as the result of a pact that generates what Bourdieu would call cross-field effects.[7]

We need a form of analysis that can determine the value of the literary, social, and political meanings of linguistic choices made by authors, because language and orthographic standards have been inadequate criteria in the context of the articulation of Galician literature ever since the Rexurdimento. Consider the lack of a linguistic criterion for the definition of the literary field; consider the recent debates about the form the standard language should take; and consider the anxiety over linguistic purity that has displayed such a range of symptoms. An illustration of this last phenomenon is the reception of Rosalía de Castro's work, given its emblematic, foundational nature. The following passage from Ricardo Carballo Calero's prologue to his Castilian-language edition of Rosalía's *Cantares gallegos* (1863) is particularly interesting:

> El idioma que tenían a su disposición los iniciadores del Renacimiento romántico (que no conocían los textos medievales) era una lengua dialectal empobrecida, muy erosionada por la lengua oficial y fragmentada en variedades comarcales. En esta lengua, la de los cantares o modismos que comenta, escribió Rosalía. Es una lengua viva, pero no pura, muy influida por el castellano. Su léxico es vacilante, así como su morfología y su fonética. (27–28)

> The language the instigators of the Romantic renaissance had at their disposal—for they were not aware of the medieval [Galician-language]

texts—was an impoverished dialectal language, seriously eroded by the official language and fragmented into local varieties. It is in this language, the language of the popular songs or sayings she describes, that Rosalía wrote. It is a living language but not a pure one, strongly influenced by Castilian. Its vocabulary fluctuates, as do its morphology and phonetics.

Here, clearly formulated, are the greatest fears of this ideology of linguistic purity: fragmentation, identified with the use of dialectal forms, and contamination, identified with the pressure from Castilian. Because Carballo Calero is addressing his readers in Castilian, his introduction to Rosalía's work can at times sound like an apology or at least a justification.

Similarly, when Ernesto Guerra da Cal presents Rosalía de Castro's work to a Portuguese audience, he refers to phenomena such as the use, in the same poem, of different forms of a particular linguistic term, explaining it as a result of the poet's lack of education:

> Rosalia é, portanto um escritor "bilingüe." E pomos esse adjectivo entre aspas, porque no caso dela tem um sentido "sui generis." Efectivamente, não se trata aqui dum escritor que por nascimento, residência, ou escolarização chega a dominar duas línguas e a manejá-las com igual controlo e espontaneidade. Rosalia faz poesia em duas línguas. Uma delas, a galega é a materna, a que mamou com o leite de mulher anónima que lhe deu o peito na aldeia; língua essa que com certeza usou com total exclusividade durante a sua infância e adolescência. Mas essa língua era uma fala-dialecto, de comunicação puramente rural, camponesa, degradado resíduo silvestre, agráfico, da língua palaciana do antigo Reino da Galiza, outrora usada para trovar por Afonso X, Rei da Castela e o seu neto D. Dinis, Rei de Portugal. A outra era o castelhano, a língua oficial da Espanha, que ela rudimentariamente aprenderia na escola primária . . . e nos vagos estudos secundários que se diz ter recebido em Santiago. . . . Nesse plurissecular e peculiar "bilingüismo" formou-se Rosalia. Num galego dialectal, sem faixa culta, bastardizado pela agressão quotidiana do "acrolecto" "espanhol." E num castelhano desprovido da base nutrícia do humus vivificante do seu próprio substrato de base popular; que por ser duma língua e uma cultura diferentes, era por sua vez agente de erosão do idioma dominador. Ambos igualmente "incompletos." Nessa área cinzenta, de choque, de engalfinhamento e corrupção glotológica, há que situar Rosalia. (xix–xx)

Rosalía is thus a "bilingual" writer. And I put the adjective in inverted commas, because it has a particular meaning in the case of this writer. This is not a writer who came to know two languages through birth, residence, or education and to use them with equal command and spontaneity. Rosalía writes verse in two languages. One of them, Galician, is her mother tongue, the one she drew with the milk of the anonymous woman who suckled her in the village; she surely used this language almost exclusively in childhood and adolescence. But this language was a dialectal tongue, used only in rural areas, by peasants, a degraded sylvan residue, never written down, descended from the court language of the ancient Kingdom of Galicia and later used by the troubadours of Alfonso X of Castile and his grandson Don Dinis of Portugal. The other language was Castilian, the official language of Spain, which she must have learned the rudiments of at primary school . . . and in the vague secondary education they say she received in Santiago. . . . Rosalía grew up with that peculiar form of bilingualism. With a dialectal form, lacking an educated variety, bastardized by continual aggression from Spanish. And with a form of Castilian that lacked the lively layer of popular use, which, coming from a different language and culture, in turn contributed to the erosion of the dominant language. Both languages were equally "incomplete." In that gray area, of clashes and arguments and linguistic corruption, that is where we must place Rosalía.

The inverted commas or quotation marks—written representation of a twinge of conscience, and therefore of distance, with respect to what is being said—barely conceal the linguistic prejudice that equates correctness with purity and literary competence with literacy. Leaving to one side the validity of a judgment that denies Rosalía was fully literate,[8] I point to the essentialism that underlies the identification of Galician as the natural language of the peasants, as seen in the metaphor of language transmitted through milk.

Taking up some of the ideas of Gilles Deleuze and Félix Guattari about the subversive potential of what they called minor literature—not necessarily identifiable with Galician literature as a whole—today it seems more appropriate to understand certain literary events as deliberate decisions rather than as accidents. In an author as aware as Rosalía, it does not seem likely that the linguistic fluctuations are the result of negligence or ignorance. In fact, as we can clearly see from her statements in her prologue to *Cantares gallegos*, she chose to write in a damaged language in order to represent a damaged experience. The hesitations and fluctuations in the spellings she chooses are not the consequences of that decision but formal ways of representing a rupture in the order of reality.[9]

The playwright Harold Pinter said that Shakespeare wrote through an open wound and that, thanks to him, "We tell when it ceases to beat and tell it at the highest peak of fever" (5). The strategy Pinter attributes to Shakespeare is behind the conscious work of some of the authors who have made the decision to belong, since the Rexurdimento, to the matrix of Galician literature.[10] They are authors who write "through the open wound," who tell the wound "at the highest peak of fever." For Rosalía de Castro, founder of modern Galician literature, to write through the open wound was to find herself in an aporetic situation: the paradox of being able to write in a language she did not know how to write.

The Language of Rupture: Galician Literature and Revolution

The historical circumstances that accompanied the production and circulation of Galician culture since the Rexurdimento make it necessary to reflect on the relation between literature and politics. The problems and challenges of this relation begin with the so-called Generation of the Conxo Banquet, made up of workers, politicians, and students who, in 1856, tried to continue the provincialist revolution led by General Miguel Solís in April 1846 (and swiftly repressed by the central government) and have continued ever since in a range of forms. This conflation of political action and cultural practice emerged again with particular intensity in the Irmandades da Fala ("Brotherhood of the Language"), which shaped the early years of nationalism in 1916 and, after the civil war, in the anti-Franco resistance movements. One of the constant features of Galician cultural history is the polarity between so-called political nationalism and cultural nationalism. This tension would reach a peak of visibility in the foundation and development of the Galaxia group of writers and intellectuals who, from the 1950s, defended a strictly cultural—or even symbolic—understanding of Galicianist claims. Against them were the emerging, left-wing political organizations that considered the cultural route inadequate as a means for realizing a series of objectives and demands; these organizations were often guided by aspirations of independence.[11]

To wonder about the links between language and revolution is equivalent to wondering about the links between catastrophe and testimony. Does testimony always come a posteriori? What is the chronological relation between war and war reporting? "There is no document of culture which is not at the same time a document of barbarism," said Walter Benjamin (392), but what we have to clarify now is the distance between barbarism and culture, between the negation of a culture and that culture's assertion of itself. Rosalía de Castro knew that all her choices required a justification.

For that reason, her writing is full of prologues, and those prologues are eloquent. Decades later, the avant-garde poet Manuel Antonio chose the manifesto, a highly argumentative genre, to claim the same right, in "¡Máis alá!" By the time Galician literature reached Manuel Antonio, it was already a cultural discourse, and so he could beat against it with force.[12]

Ultimately, and as a clear example of the imbalance between poetic practice and critical consciousness, Galician literary historiography has been articulated around formal events, concealing the political relevance that, intentionally or unintentionally, cultural practice has always had. The Floral Games that took place in Galicia in 1861, conventionally taken as the *terminus post quem* of the Rexurdimento, were poetic contests imported from a literary fashion practiced in Catalunya and Provence. They may also be understood through events whose political character, clearly not entirely absent from the organization of the Floral Games, is expressed more forcefully.[13]

Historians such as Xusto Beramendi have recently highlighted the decisive importance of the failed revolution of 1846—the Levantamento de Carral ("Carral Uprising")—in Galician political thought. Similarly, a great effort of historical imagination would be needed to conceive how revolutionary ideas were fundamental to the Generation of the Conxo Banquet, so as to situate there the true beginnings of contemporary cultural discourse. I am referring as much to the strategies of political action as to the cultural projects that attempted to create an emancipated Galician culture. The conditions for the construction of a modern literature, understood as a means of resistance to the dominant order, were already present at the Conxo Banquet. For as several studies of the French Revolution have shown, the problem of representation, which every national literature must confront, is one of the central questions in revolutionary theory and praxis (Paulson; Hunt). Every revolution takes place beneath the shadow of what never happened, and in Galicia the never happened is also the literary possibility of witnessing a differentiated identity.[14]

Literary Positions: The Discourse of Resignation and the Discourse of Promise

Literary discourse has responded in two diametrically opposed ways to the successive historical fractures that modern Galician culture underwent. One response was what we might call a discourse of resignation. In the political sense, it is revealed as a desire to reach agreement; in the epistemological sense, as convergence with the dominant *doxa*. The literary projects we might assign to this model tend to be focused on an Arcadian past, to be based on a myth of origins and driven by an attempt at imaginary evasion of the historical present. One of the most interesting effects of this model is the way that the devices of fantastic and comic literature—and even certain methods of the avant-garde—have linked up with ideologically reactionary forms. It might be productive to examine, in this light, the futurism of Vicente Risco and of Eugenio Montes in pre–civil war poetry, but also the use of classical and Arthurian myth in the narrative of Álvaro Cunqueiro. In the same way we might interpret the recovery by the Galaxia group of the particular form of philosophical idealism that the Portuguese poet Teixeira de Pascoaes called *saudosismo*. For Ramón Piñeiro, one of the group's most influential thinkers, *saudade* ("nostalgia") was a defining characteristic of the Galician soul. It is easy to criticize Piñeiro's interpretation of Rosalía de Castro's work as a compensatory movement that tries to resolve, through ontological characterization, the possibility of Galicia's being recognized as a political entity.[15] The conversion of Rosalía into the *prima causa* of Galicia's emergence as a people is telling, in an analysis that rejects sociohistorical elements to affirm the essentialist identification between Rosalía and the Galician nation.[16]

On the one hand, Piñeiro resorts to an argument that is often tautological ("Que saudade e lirismo teñen moito que ver entre si é cousa que non precisa afirmación" ["A saudade" 116; "It does not need to be said that *saudade* and lyricism have a great deal in common"]) and inclined toward what the New Criticism called the intentional fallacy ("Coa súa inmensa capacidade de amor, Rosalía identificouse *moralmente* co seu pobo e *sentimentalmente* co seu país" [105; "With her immense capacity for love, Rosalía identified *morally* with her people and *sentimentally* with her country"]). On the other hand, he seems to suggest that Galician national identity could have emerged spontaneously; he imbues a transcendental and even mystical meaning to the metonymy that equated Rosalía with Galicia:

> Rosalía fundiuse moralmente co seu pobo e fundiuse sentimentalmente coa súa terra. Por esta dobre fusión, púidonos dar e darlle ó mundo a primeira imaxe espiritual de Galicia. Hai, de certo, unha Galicia rosaliana, unha imaxe rosaliana de Galicia, que é, ata os nosos días, mesmo a que acadou maior vixencia dentro e fóra da nosa terra. A visión que Rosalía tivera de Galicia (máis ben tristeira no tocante ó reino das cousas humanas e profundamente exaltada no sentimento da paisaxe) foi a que pasou a caracterizar a imaxe que

de Galicia se ten modernamente. Despois de Rosalía, propios e alleos viron a Galicia de maneira distinta a como a viran antes. O seu espírito, ó realizar a síntese, a unidade de terra e pobo, incorporouse de maneira activa e perenne ó conxunto da realidade galega e fíxose sustancia súa.   (107)

Rosalía was fused morally with her people and sentimentally with her country. Through this double fusion, she was able to give us, and give the world, the first spiritual image of Galicia. There exists, surely, a Rosalian Galicia, a Rosalian image of Galicia, which even today is the one that has become best known within and beyond our homeland. Rosalía's vision of Galicia—a sad vision with regard to human things and a profoundly ecstatic feeling toward the landscape—has come to characterize Galicia's modern-day image. After Rosalía, Galicians and others saw Galicia differently. Her spirit, bringing together land and people, has been incorporated actively and permanently into Galician reality and become consubstantial with it.

The second response to historical discontinuity could be termed the discourse of promise, which finds its political transposition in the will to rupture and which, from the epistemological point of view, is translated into a detour from hegemonic thought. The literary works shaped by this model look to the future, sometimes even in a literal, grammatical sense. Note the repeated use of the future tense in the poems in Manuel Antonio's *De catro a catro* ("From Four [o'Clock] to Four [o'Clock]."[17] Compared with certain prewar avant-garde futurisms (Marinetti in Italy; Montes and Risco in Galicia), the future tense I refer to here is not apocalyptic but advocates openness to what is radically new—just as in Vladimir Mayakovsky. But that time of promise precedes the avant-garde. It was already evident in the first line of the first poem of Rosalía's *Cantares gallegos* in 1863, where a female figure is given the order "Has de cantar" (31; "Sing you will").

This opposition between a discourse of resignation and a discourse of promise could also have been expressed in the terms used by Walter Benjamin when he contrasted the concepts of "archaic image" and "dialectical image" (Missac 138). For Benjamin, the dialectic image carries the revolutionary content (the *Jetztzeit* ["the now"] is the time the author identifies with the historicity of the revolution), whereas the archaic image alludes to the archetypes of mythical time. This is an interesting distinction, considering that it was such revolutionary historicity that inspired in the 1960s many of the writers of the so-called Nova Narrativa Galega ("New Galician Narrative").

Taking up a formula from Lucien Goldmann, Raymond Trousson claims that "dans le genre utopique, l'éthique de l'écrivain devient le problème esthétique de l'oeuvre" (372; "in the utopian genre, the ethics of the writer become the aesthetic problem of the work"). In the short stories of the Nova Narrativa Galega, the political position of the writer did indeed become the true aesthetic problem of the work—especially in Xosé Luís Méndez Ferrín's *Retorno a Tagen Ata* (1971; "Return to Tagen Ata"), which can be read in the light of Fredric Jameson's concept of national allegory as developed in the context of subaltern literatures. Few notions question the separation of fantastic literature and historical referent as strongly as that of national allegory.

Literary works that come under the utopian genre belong to the discourse of promise; as a result, their meaning could not be more different from *saudade*. Thierry Paquot talks about what he calls political indifference, connecting the loss of space for utopia with nostalgia in the modern industrialization process:

> Avec la fin de l'industrialisme et la suprématie des techniques de communication, l'utopie a perdu la nature de sa révolte, la clef de son songe. Elle appartient à un temps révolu. Elle date. Et une utopie qui date se nomme *nostalgie*. (67)

> With the end of industrialism and the supremacy of mass media, utopia has lost its revolutionary character, the key to its dream. It belongs to a revolted time. It becomes dated. And a utopia that becomes dated is called *nostalgia*.

Literature produced from the cultural peripheries confirms that utopia is not a completely dead end. In what Jameson termed "the era of multinational capitalism" ("Third-World Literature"), the literary discourses of promise became as distanced from assimilation as from nostalgia and show that resistance is not simply a means of asserting one's identity but also a mechanism for questioning global logics.

Literary Production and Repertoire Planning: Culture as Resistance to Market Forces

In a study of the relation between translation and cultural planning, Gideon Toury defines the central concept of his work in the following terms:

> PLANNING would consist in any act of (more or less deliberate) interven-
> tion in a current state of affairs within a social group, i.e. making decisions for
> others to follow; whether the impetus for intervening originates within the
> group itself or outside of it.

Defined in this way, cultural planning is one of the most visible processes
in contemporary Galician culture, especially in the period since the ratification of the Statute of Autonomy in 1981. The need to introduce repertoires
that respond, among other things, to the demands of an education system
that includes learning about Galician literature conditions the decisions of
publishing houses and other participants in the process. Toury goes on to
observe that planning can be a means for cultures to "[fill] a void which *has*
been noticed." Even where there is an undoubted relation between power
struggles and planning, he categorically rejects the notion that such a consideration should serve as a point of departure for a revision of the planning
process, in accordance with the attempts at axiological neutrality that are
so characteristic of polysystem theory. Meanwhile, somebody must take up
the task of evaluating the meaning of literary planning in Galicia, even at
the cost of breaking with the protocols of scientific objectivity. For example, it would be worthwhile to look at how the Galician publishing system
has dealt with the absence of certain literary genres during the last thirty
years.

Attempts at planning are necessary, even inevitable, in the development of any cultural field, especially for an emerging culture. But there is
evidence that the results of these attempts were not anticipated by the agents
who implemented them. With regard to translation, considered a paradigmatic example of the planning process, it is easy to see the process as atom-
izing and even ad hoc, oscillating between the collections of great classics
that were preferred in the 1980s, both in the children's and adult markets,
and the current rush to translate certain contemporary authors into Galician before they are translated into other, neighboring Romance languages,
as we have seen in the cases of Paul Auster, Amélie Nothomb, and Bernardo
Atxaga. Also noticeable, since the second half of the 1990s, is the contrast
between the emergence of a significant number of Galician women writers
of poetry, narrative, theater, and essay and the media's continued treatment
of them as exceptional.[18] I would also cite the relative failure of the promotion of certain genres, such as erotic short story and crime fiction, during
the 1980s. Fifteen years later, the relative isolation of a writer like Diego

Ameixeiras, who works at the limits of genre fiction, demonstrates the difficulty of imposing choices from above.

Fully normalized markets have no need of agents to recommend what they judge to be most appropriate. A liberal would consider this situation fortunate; a Marxist, unfortunate. Nowadays, both would be able to claim that in normal literary cultures it is literary capital that does the work of selection. At a moment when in France there is much talk of cultural exceptionalism to promote greater state control for the protection of its national culture, as a counter to the overwhelming pressure of globalization, it is ironic that Galician cultural agents are worrying about the gaps in the Galician market and the weakness of the modern book industry. Should we call for the return of an Arcadian concept of literature, where researchers can devote themselves freely to the discussion of the most refined aesthetic topics, their backs turned to the undeniable influence of the market, the media, and other nonaesthetic factors on the circulation of literary works? Quite the contrary: analysis of Galician literature should not merely recognize the existence of the concrete conditions of its emergence but also act consequently. This is precisely where the asepsis recommended by Toury does not seem adequate to me. Critics, whether they like it or not, are participants too.

The participation or connivance of critics in the current state of global culture is borne witness to by Hans Ulrich Gumbrecht: "There is no position outside the market that allows the participants to determine its internal mechanisms. Nor is there a position for us outside the streams of cultural capital" (262). Formulated here with singular clarity is one of the most disturbing ideological consequences of globalization, that it is impossible to resist market forces. But we must focus on those cultural forms that work against the logic of assimilation; resist pessimism, all but endemic in the cultural sphere; and combat cynicism, which is one of its most sterile forms. Gumbrecht observes:

> Positions "on the margins" have of late become an object of the humanists' desire. I am not primarily referring here to geographical, social, cultural, and political margins. Rather, I want to point to an epistemological situation that marks a lack. It is the lack of a standpoint for an observer outside the object of his observation; in other words, the lack of a standpoint providing that very distance from an object that used to carry the promise of "objectivity." (249)

Between the decision to avoid passing judgment, advocated by Toury, and the impossibility of maintaining distance from the object of study, expressed by Gumbrecht, there are more similarities than differences. Toury and Gumbrecht share a pessimism about culture's ability to have an impact on its environment. Gumbrecht's urgency to clarify that his defense of the margins does not mean positioning himself on the geographic, social, cultural, or political periphery is unsettling, to say the least. Epistemology, when it is formulated from a nonplace, inevitably becomes ideology. On the other hand, literary studies that focus on Galicia often cannot—nor do they want to—avoid locating themselves on a geographic, social, cultural, or political periphery. Their objective is to locate themselves in a way that is not resigned but defiant. Cultural pessimism is the opposite of criticism.

The fractures running through modern Galician cultural history have become an important source of cultural energy for all those writers who have made the language of rupture a site of resistance. From Rosalía de Castro to Xosé Luís Méndez Ferrín, literary representations of this rupture have impeded separation of the cultural and political spheres, inviting us to try out more subtle and comprehensive ways of connecting the two. We could say that the most active Galician culture emerges as a response, whether immediate or not, to great crises. The *provincialista* response to Solís's revolutionary movement of April 1846 emerges a decade later, in the Generation of the Conxo Banquet, the true origin of the Rexurdimento. It reemerges time and again in the twentieth century. Consider the dialogue—not, of course, without tension—between the *Nós* Generation and the avant-garde during the 1920s or the fissure between the *culturalismo* of the Galaxia Generation and the political activities of the *galeguistas* in exile during the Franco dictatorship. On the threshold of the twenty-first century, the influence of protest movements led from virtual space, by groups such as Redes Escarlata ("Scarlet Webs"), is enormous.

Despite all the rhetoric that celebrates interliterary dialogue as an enriching phenomenon, the truth is that cultural history has frequently allied itself with the will to domination, whether in the form of occupation, colonialism, imperialism, or any of the other movements we have long been familiar with and can imagine well into the future. Both literature and the study of literature can do little but reflect this human fact. When writers and critics try to escape the historical reality of domination by constructing cultural discourses, under the surface of normalization realities lie concealed that ought to be revealed. In a famous passage from the *Economic and Philosophical Manuscripts of 1844*, Karl Marx observed that the formation of the five senses was a result of universal history (141). In the light of this recognition of the contingent character even of that which we believe to be least contingent, we should ask ourselves about the sixth sense that made possible the historical expression of a more or less independent literature in adversity.

Criticism may not always be the place for testimony, but it can help emphasize all the projects of conscious writing that have made Galicia a utopian place—even when *utopia* seems not to fit with the *doxa* and aesthetics of the times. In other words, just because loss of identity can be transformed into a cultural motor does not mean we should justify the pressures that prompted the transformation. Independence is precious, more so in life than in literature. But, since we know that domination exists, cultural theory should bring together the lines of meaning that make intelligible how the cultural periphery—which tends to coincide with the economic periphery—has responded to historic inequality.

I have tried to show that Galician literature has always been a site of conflict, a territory where battles have been waged, and remain to be waged, over the terms in which we should define that faraway land called Galicia.

Notes

This essay, translated from Galician by Kirsty Hooper and Manuel Puga Moruxa, is indebted to the project Toward a Comparative History of Iberian Literatures, directed by Fernando Cabo Aseguinolaza.

1. For a comprehensive example of this type of analysis, see the work edited by Márcio Seligmann-Silva, following thinkers such as Walter Benjamin or, more recently, Jacques Rancière.

2. I am thinking, for example, of the Novísimos ("the Newest") anthologized by María Victoria Moreno, imitators of the realist aesthetic developed by authors such as Celso Emilio Ferreiro in the 1960s.

3. Renewal of literary themes and techniques began in the 1960s with the narratives of Xosé Luís Méndez Ferrín, María Xosé Queizán, Xohana Torres, and Gonzalo Rodríguez Mourullo. For the concept of national allegory, see Jameson, "Third-World Literature."

4. This is the definition of *testimony* given by Rancière (177).

5. As an illustration of the complex relation between poetry and politics, see how Rancière responds when his interviewer asks him about Paul Celan's resistance to making a direct link between literature and testimony: "É preciso, creio, resistir a uma certa mística do poema como testemunho sobre o indizível. Na apreciação de Celan, e geralmente na da literatura relativa ao genocídio, há, em minha opinião,

uma hipérbole do indizível. . . . Tudo o que se diz é dizível. E o indizível é sempre o indizível de uma linguagem, aquilo a que se refere mas também aquilo a que dá ritmo e cor" (182; "It is necessary, I think, to resist a certain mystique of the poem as testimony of the unsayable. In criticism of Celan and more generally of literature on genocide, there is, in my opinion, a hyperbole of the unsayable. . . . Everything that is said is sayable. And the unsayable is always unsayable in a particular language, that to which it refers, but also that which gives it rhythm and color" [my trans.]).

6. According to what Carballo Calero calls "criterio lingüístico" ("language criterion"), Galician literature would be defined as all texts written in Galician (*Historia* 274–75). As the critic himself admits, the retrospective application of this parameter to certain periods of Galician literary history is problematic. We need only look at a text as foundational for literary nationalism as Eugenio Carré Aldao's *Literatura gallega* (1911), whose anthological appendices are a clear example of the foundation of national literariness on nonlanguage grounds.

7. One possibility would be to pay attention to the differences in the internal reception of literary corpora as different as Manuel Murguía's political thought; Valle-Inclán's theater; Manuel Rivas's and Suso de Toro's journalism; and the narrative of Luisa Castro, Alvaro Cunqueiro, and Torrente Ballester—all written in Spanish but provoking responses that depend on factors more complex and socially conditioned than the choice of a written code.

8. Guerra da Cal emphasizes this view when he adds, "A cultura de Rosalia deveu ser pobre e tardia. As suas leituras literárias provavelmente começariam a partir da sua relação com Murguia. Os poucos autógrafos dela que sobreviveram estão eivados de faltas ortográficas que manifestam um nível de domínio apenas semi-letrado do espanhol" (xxn9; "Rosalia's education must have been poor and late. Her literary readings probably began with her relationship with Murguía. Her few surviving manuscripts are full of spelling errors that betray a barely semiliterate command of Spanish").

9. In this light, it is not unexpected that in the manifesto "¡Máis alá!," which is the first great rupture in Galician literary discourse after Rosalía, Manuel Antonio explicitly rejects any attempt to standardize the Galician language (Manuel Antonio and Cebreiro).

10. I use *matrix* to highlight the conventional, conditional nature of the term *Galician literature*, a term that gains in meaning through the conscious determination with which it has been used since the Rexurdimento. To define oneself as a Galician author demands a rhetorical force, as shown in the prologue where Rosalía renounces Galician as a literary language or, more positively, in Manuel Antonio's "¡Máis alá!"

11. Fredric Jameson's description of the "'protopolitical' impulses in high modernism" is singularly applicable to the strategies of the Grupo Galaxia during the 1950s: "the 'Utopian' substitution of cultural politics for politics proper, the vocation to transform the world by transforming its forms, space or language" ("Politics" 61).

12. Since Marx and Engels's *Communist Manifesto*, we know that "to manifest" means

to reveal or display what has been latent or spectral. But we can manifest only what the environment authorizes us to say, even at the risk of violating the environment. To put it another way, we can manifest only those truths that the environment can bear.

13. The Floral Games in A Coruña were driven by the returned emigrant José Pascual López Cortón, who would later sponsor the publication of the *Álbum de la caridad*. The volume collects the prizewinning poems from the 1861 competition as well as a "mosaico poético de nuestros vates gallegos contemporáneos" ("poetic mosaic of our contemporary Galician bards") compiled by the brothers Antonio and Francisco María de la Iglesia. It includes the work of up to forty Galician-language poets, including Rosalía de Castro and Eduardo Pondal.

14. Lynn Hunt observes, "French revolutionaries did not just seek another representation or authority, a replacement for the King, but rather came to question the very act of representation itself" (88).

15. In an openly apologetic tone, Piñeiro outlined in a brief essay the differentiation of culturalism from political action, which at the time meant the strategic opposition between the *galeguismo* of the Buenos Aires–based Galician exiles and the intellectuals who had remained in Galicia. The defensive tone of the essay is noticeable from the start ("Cultura" 377).

16. The essay "A saudade en Rosalía," originally published in 1952, was republished with other texts in the volume *Filosofía da saudade*, which I cite from hereafter.

17. The book begins in the future tense: "Encheremos as velas / coa luz náufraga da madrugada" "We will fill the sails / with the shipwrecked light of the early morning" (16 ["Intencións"]).

18. Kirsty Hooper has analyzed the problem of historical discontinuity of Galician women's writing, evident in fiction, theater, essay, and poetry ("Girl"). Helena González refers to the problems of the apparent visibility of women in the literary market and in the media ("Subxectividades").

Toward a Postnational History of Galician Literature: Rereading Rosalía de Castro's Narrative as Atlantic Modernism

Joseba Gabilondo

In memoriam Xoán González-Millán

Postnational Literary History in Spain

Spain is undergoing a new neoimperialist expansion toward both Latin America and the peripheral nationalities of the state. This move is culturally legitimized, among other discourses, by the ideology of the universality of the Spanish language. The speech delivered by King Juan Carlos I of Spain at the Cervantes Prize in 2001 is a good index of the cultural policies of the Spanish state. It is no accident or isolated incident, as José del Valle and Luis Gabriel-Stheeman clearly show in their groundbreaking work. When the king states that

> nunca fue la nuestra lengua de imposición, sino de encuentro; a nadie se le obligó nunca a hablar en castellano: fueron los pueblos más diversos quienes hicieron suyo por voluntad libérrima, el idioma de Cervantes.
> ("Premio Cervantes")

> ours was never an imposed language, but rather an encountered one; nobody was ever obliged to speak Castilian: it was the most diverse peoples who, out of their own free will, made the language of Cervantes their own.

it is clear that the Spanish state is refashioning the old imperialist discourse of *hispanidad* in new global terms (del Valle and Gabriel-Stheeman 229).

In this context, the debates about the different languages and literatures of Spain about what constitutes Galician, Basque, Catalan, or Asturian literature acquire a special importance. Are these peripheral literatures constituted by the historical languages of each region (Galician, Basque, Catalan, Asturian . . .) or by the languages used by their inhabitants (Spanish and other migrant/diasporic, languages such as Portuguese, French, Arabic, English, et cetera in addition to the historical languages)? If posed as an either-or alternative, this discussion produces a dangerous reduction of a larger problem that must be understood in its historical complexity. In short, the ahistorical reduction of the either-or alternative is ultimately a question about the state language: is Spanish a language of Galician literature (and other peripheral literatures)?

The above question about the state language must be treated as reductivist and fetishistic: it constitutes a reduction of a historical problem-trauma to its symptom. The trauma is the global limit to state expansion, whereas the symptom is precisely the historical persistence of peripheral languages as ultimate "sign" of the failure of state expansion. This trauma can be approached in a historical and nonsymptomatic way, if we avoid state fantasies of expansion and neoimperialism. A more historical approach would require posing the following question: Is Galician (or any other peripheral language) part of Spanish literature? To this day, no history of Spanish literature has answered this question in a politically and theoretically meaningful way. Every attempt to account for "peripheral literatures" in the context of the Spanish state and its culture has been reduced to the logic of the "reservation-ghetto"—or in more philosophical terms, via Jacques Derrida—to the logic of the *différance*, which, as we know, is the constitutive element of any identitary presence and logos (in this case, the Spanish state's logos). In short, the question leads to a historical analysis of what the Spanish state is, to an anamnesis of its political and historical legitimation. However, this question is too traumatic to yield symptoms or fantasies; it is not even raised.

Only the question of peripheral literatures raises all kinds of fantasies (and ideologies), since it is centered on the issue of the other. As psychoanalysis explains, it is the fantasy of the other, what the other is and is not, that keeps the self (the Spanish state) from disintegrating—hence the symptomatic and libidinal nature of the other. Everybody wants to discuss that question, the question of the other, in order ultimately to dismiss it. Similarly, there is little discussion in the peripheries about what Spanish literature is. This question does not give rise to any fantasies/ideologies in the peripheries either, since it is well understood that this line of inquiry always reverts back to the issue of the periphery as other although it does not have to.

Francisco Rico's canonical collection of essays on contemporary Spanish literature written in Castilian is a good example of a nationalist approach to the above supplemental logic: *Historia y crítica de la literatura* española: *Los nuevos nombres, 1975–1990* ("History and Criticism of *Spanish* Literature: The New Names"; my emphasis). The opening study, written by the editor of the collection, Darío Villanueva, refers to the conflict that arises in each Spanish peripheral nationality between its own historical language and Castilian. Villanueva concludes that it is

> un conflicto de lenguas que, entreverado de política, tiende a provocar una dialéctica entre dos culturas, la vernácula y *la mal llamada "castellana,"* sobre el supuesto de que no cabe punto de equilibrio, sino que una deberá erradicar a la otra.   (15; my emphasis)

> a conflict of languages that, entangled in politics, tends to provoke a dialectic between two cultures, the vernacular and the *ill-labeled "Castilian,"* about the supposition that there is no place for balance and that one will have to uproot the other.

The collection goes on to study exclusively literature written in Castilian as "Spanish" and, conversely, to "uproot" from the volume—and from the Spanish state—the peripheral literatures not written in Castilian. In short, the issue of multilingualism is raised to legitimize-universalize Spanish in the national peripheries and not the other way around.

The reason is the supplemental logic of Spanish nationalist ideology. Villanueva never discusses the presence of peripheral literatures in Spanish literature, since Spanish literature written in Spanish is *the* only literature of the state. He erases the trace of peripheral languages in Spain and turns them into the supplement, the constitutive element, of Spanish literature. Yet, the necessary supplement remains outside his discourse—outside the Spanish state—and, therefore, it becomes the constitutive and founding basis for the existence of a monolingual "Spanish literature"—and thus a "Spanish nation." Literary ideologies such as Villanueva's must be denounced as Spanish nationalism, in its most essentialist and traditional sense, because every Spanish discourse on this issue claims to have overcome the historical "disease" of nationalism and legitimizes itself precisely as nonnationalist (Habermas; Savater; Aranzadi, Juaristi, and Unzueta).

To the reductive nationalist question of whether Spanish is a language of Galician (Basque, Catalan, Asturian, etc.) literature, the only meaningful political, philosophical, and psychoanalytic answer is no. To a symptomatic question, only a fantastic answer is possible. This answer, in its radical negativity, shatters the fantasy of the Spanish other; it highlights the fact that the Spanish language is a symptom of Spain's new neoimperialist expansionism. The fantastic yet shattering "no" is a reflective answer that refuses to allow the Galician language to be relegated the status of Spanish supplement or other. Note that the question has already established that Galician is not part of Spanish literature; Spanish literature needs the Galician language as other to continue to establish an impossible self-identity.

This fantastic and symptomatic impasse requires that the problem be readdressed in a broader historical fashion, so that a new historicization helps us understand both the symbolic order (the historical conditions) and the historical trauma (the historical violence) that produced this symptomatic question and its fantasies. The impasse requires that we rethink historically the problem of Spanish *and* Galician (Basque, Catalan, Asturian, etc.) literatures and cultures. Feminism is one of the privileged discourses from which we can address this problem in its historical complexity. From a feminist point of view, we can rethink *the geopolitical from the biopolitical*— that is, from what feminist standpoint theory calls a "situated knowledge" (Harding; Haraway). Problems in which the geographic nature of politics (geopolitics) is emphasized—nationalism, colonialism-imperialism, migration, class, et cetera—can be rethought through questions in which the biological nature of politics (biopolitics) is emphasized: gender, sex, race, et cetera. Only a feminist postnationalist critique allows us to bridge the chasm between geopolitics and biopolitics, so that we historicize from this chasm by opening it up, rather than closing it, to history.

The Spanish understanding of literature and, more broadly, the different European elaborations of national literary traditions remain deeply rooted in the Herderian-Fichtean-Schlegelian ideology of the imperialist nation-state. For this ideology, the cultural-historical nexus between language and nation is ontological; and it is the raison d'être of any imperialist *mission civilisatrice*. Even the recent refashioning of the main postimperialist European literatures with the addition of -*phone* (anglophone, francophone, etc.) to encompass postcolonial territories responds, among other reasons, to a globalized refashioning of the same Romantic model, in which the bygone empire ultimately reconstitutes itself as the literary ghost of its shattered "civilization." The fact that nobody other than old-fashioned theorists of Hispanism would ever venture to make a similar case for hispanophone literatures—thus reclaiming Latin American literature as a "postimperialist Spanish literature"—is a clear sign that although nationalist ideology continues to define the (postimperialist) nation-state in hegemonic Europe, Spain's nonhegemonic position may allow the problem to be seen in its nationalist and postimperialist complexity.

Literary histories can no longer be thought of in nationalist terms, especially in Spanish-Castilian, French (francophone), and English (anglophone) literatures—all traditions with an imperialist history. For geopolitical minority literatures such as those on the periphery of the Spanish state, the question is not whether to defend a national literary ideology but whether to uphold a strategically essentialist position of exclusivity or, instead, rethink Galician (Basque, Catalan, Asturian, etc.) literature in a new way, in postnationalist terms, without falling into a symptomatic trap.

Galician Literature: A Feminist Postnational Approach

In the case of Galician literature, Kirsty Hooper has already addressed the issue of the *fin de século* ("fin de siècle") and how this period has been rewritten retrospectively in nationalist terms since the 1950s, so that Galician literature is reduced to literature written in Galician. This historical reduction yields a period characterized by the organic metaphors of weakness, decadence, and so on, so that it becomes a transitional period between the Rexurdimento and the period of Irmandades da Fala (1916–36) or Xeración Nós (Tarrío Varela, *Literatura gallega* 92–146). Hooper notes one of the most important effects of the nationalization of fin de siècle literature, the removal of women from the canon:

> When we look at the available literature on Galicia's female authors, it is indubitable that if a "distinctive history" of women's writing ever existed in Galicia, then it has been lost. . . . The history of women's narrative that is left to us is a disrupted, fragmented one that jumps forty years from Rosalía's prologues to *Cantares gallegos* (1863) and *Follas novas* (1880) to the first female-authored novel in Galician, *Néveda: Historia dunha dobre seducción* (1920) by Francisca Herrera Garrido (1869–1950). Does this mean that for forty years, there were no Galician women writers?   ("Girl" 103–04)

Hooper goes on to argue, "It is no coincidence that these years of women's apparent silence, which take in the *fin de século*, are the crucial formative years of modern Galician identity" (105).

By analyzing the work of Rosalía de Castro (1837–85) from a feminist and biopolitical point of view, I extend Hooper's analysis to the period of Rexurdimento and make this analysis constitutive of the entire nationalist enterprise of creating a monolingual literary tradition, an enterprise that runs from the historiographical work of Ricardo Carballo Calero in the 1950s to today. Although at first it appears that the Galician canon is established precisely by placing Castro at its center ("Rosalía, the mother of Galician literature"), I propose that her eviction from Galician literature is the founding act of nationalist Galician literary historiography and its canon. My purpose is to compensate for the shortcomings that cultural studies has brought to feminist studies. As Lou Charnon-Deutsch concludes for all Spanish literatures, "the move in the most recent decade from feminist literary criticism to gender studies to cultural studies and now post-colonial studies has left the pre-twentieth-century Spanish canon largely intact" (137).

The goal of this historical analysis is to highlight the limitations of a nationalist understating of Galician literature, on the one hand, and to claim the need for a new postnationalist approach, on the other. My analysis suggests a different answer, a feminist, postnationalist alternative, to the question of what constitutes Galician literature, without falling into the fetishist and imperialist question of whether Spanish is also a Galician literary language. As Hooper proposes, "we might argue that a key role of Galician Studies is, paradoxically, to examine and contest national boundaries and borders" ("New Cartographies" 125). Thus, I highlight the exemplary and privileged location that Galician literary studies occupies in advancing a feminist-postnational theory of literary history, so that the latter is extended to the rest of the literatures of the Spanish state—as well as France, Portugal, Latin America, and other "peripheral" (Galician, Basque, etc.) diasporas in the Americas and Europe.

Rosalía de Castro: Galician Nationalism and Atlantic Modernism

Rosalía de Castro's connection with Galician nationalism has always been examined from the point of view of her poetry. Yet, here I examine it through her narrative, which is mostly written in Spanish, to understand the instability of her position in Galician nationalism. Ultimately, she exiles herself from Galician language and culture as a reaction to the opposition her journalistic writings encounter among Galician nationalist circles. As a result of her exile, Castro finds refuge in the Castilian language, in which she publishes her last poetic work, *En las orillas del Sar* (1884; "On the Banks of the Saar"). The same exilic experience leads her to develop a new form of writing: modernism. Thus, this final modernist, exilic, Spanish position is not nationalistically Spanish but rather Atlantic.[1] Through this reading of Castro's work, I propose a new mapping of the relations between literature, gender, and nationalism at the inception of Galician literature, which will have many consequences for the way we approach Galician studies today.

The central but seldom discussed conflict between Castro and Galician nationalism,[2] what Cristina Moreiras-Menor calls "the secret" ("El secreto" 322), is central to understanding her literature. The conflict becomes public through a series of articles published by Castro in a Madrid newspaper, *El lunes del imparcial*, in 1880. These articles, known as "Costumbres gallegas" ("Galician Customs"), were published after Castro's two foundational po- etry books in Galician—that is, after she becomes the central figure of the literary imagination of Galician nationalism.

In the last article, Castro presents an old Galician custom:

> Entre algunas gentes tiénese allí por obra caritativa y meritoria el que, si algún marino que permaneció por largo tiempo sin tocar a tierra, llega a desem- barcar en un paraje donde toda mujer es honrada, la esposa, hija o hermana pertenecientes a la familia en cuya casa el forastero haya de encontrar albergue, le permita por espacio de una noche ocupar un lugar en su mismo lecho. El marino puede alejarse después sin creerse en nada ligado a la que, cumpliendo a su manera un acto humanitario, se sacrificó a tal extremo por llevar a cabo los deberes de la hospitalidad. (*Obras* 2: 660)

> Some people there consider it a meritorious act of charity if, when a sailor who has been at sea for a long period of time disembarks at a place where all women are honorable, the wife, daughter, or sister of the house where the stranger seeks shelter allows him to share her bed for a single night. The sailor can leave afterward without considering himself at all tied to the woman who, performing a humanitarian act in her own way, sacrificed herself so greatly to carry out the duties of hospitality.

Nationalist Galician intellectuals interpret this article as Castro's betrayal of a secret of the Galician "nation." As Moreiras explains, the article

> tuvo como consecuencia el enfrentamiento público entre la intelligentsia ga- llega y la poeta, quien fue acusada por los primeros de haber traicionado a su comunidad revelando sus secretos. (322)

led to a public confrontation between the Galician intelligentsia and the poet, who was accused by them of having betrayed her community by revealing its secrets.

As the note inserted by Castro's husband, Manuel Murguía, at the end of the article states, Castro feels hurt by "los insultos que con tal motivo se me han dirigido" (2: 661; "the insults they have cast at me because of it"). A year later, Castro's self-imposed exile from Galician culture and society is made clear in a letter written to her husband. In response to Murguía's message that an editor is interested in publishing another book of her poetry in Galician, Castro replies:

> Me extraña que insistas todavía en que escriba un nuevo tomo de versos en dialecto gallego . . . ni por tres, ni por seis ni por nueve mil reales volveré a escribir nada en nuestro dialecto, ni acaso tampoco a ocuparme de nada que a nuestro país encierra. Con lo cual no perderá nada, pero yo perderé mucho menos todavía.
>
> Se atreven a decir que es fuerza que me rehabilite ante Galicia. ¿Rehabilitarme de qué? ¿De haber hecho todo lo que en mí cupo por su engrandecimiento?
>
> (608)

> I'm surprised you are still insisting I write a new book of poetry in Galician . . . not for three, or six, or nine thousand reals will I go back to writing in our language, nor will I continue to worry about what happens in our country. They won't lose anything, but I will lose much less.
>
> They dare to say I ought to rehabilitate myself in front of Galicia. Rehabilitate myself for what? For having done everything I could to promote it?

Moreiras interprets this exile as an abject positioning where the distance between the subject and the object/other collapses, more, as a double abject position, in which Castro's ego takes simultaneously the place of two others: the Galician other of Spanish nationalism and the emigrating other of Galician nationalism. Moreiras states:

> [E]l gesto de negación rosaliano abre, en el contexto del nacionalismo, la posibilidad de pensar lo propio desde una posición abyecta que constituye un nuevo espacio donde el "yo" nacional incorpora al "otro" variando así, aunque no invirtiendo, su relación de dependencia y subalternidad. (333)

> Rosalía's negation opens, in the context of nationalism, the possibility of thinking about oneself from an abject position that constitutes a new space where the national "I" incorporates the "other," thus varying, although not inverting, the relation of dependency and subalternity.

She concludes that Castro's double abject position places her outside Galician nationalism and inside the subaltern, nonnationalist history of Galician reality, emigration:

> Rosalía, desde su localización dos veces abyecta, dos veces en el margen, se está situando en el mismo lugar que ocupan esos emigrantes gallegos por los que su poesía siente tanta morriña.   (338)

> Rosalía, from her doubly abject position, doubly marginalized, is locating herself in the same place as those Galician emigrants for whom her poetry feels such nostalgia.

Catherine Davies situates Castro's exile in the new conservative turn that both Spanish and Galician nationalism take after the failure of the liberal revolution of 1868–72:

> Aqui é onde hai que busca-las raíces do pesimismo na obra posterior de Rosalía; na súa situación insostible en España e Galicia.   ("A ideoloxía" 305)

> This is where we must seek the roots of the pessimism of Rosalía's later works; in her unbearable situation in Spain and Galicia.

Xavier Castro connects Castro's exile to her being orphaned, which, after the 1880s, also extends to a lack of "nation" (90). Furthermore, as early as 1864, one of Castro's articles, "El codio," had created a similar scandal: two hundred seminarians vandalized the print shop where the article was going to be published (Davies, "Rosalía de Castro's Later Poetry" 611; Mayoral, *Rosalía* 30). Therefore the conflict between Castro and conservative Galician society begins early on, but takes the form of modernist self-exile only in the 1880s.

Castro's traumatic self-exile from Galician into Spanish, from nationalism into modernism, assumes a different shape when her entire written corpus is examined, since most of her narrative is written in Spanish and, therefore, remains outside the literary imagination of Galician nationalism. Her narrative is located precisely in the exilic space that Galician subaltern emigration opens up—a conflictive space, since her shift to Spanish could be interpreted, in Joyce Tolliver's words, as "choosing 'the oppressor's language'" (33). Once Castro's entire written corpus is examined, the abject positioning of her poetry is implemented by the narrative return of the repressed exilic-migrant Galician other. In Castro's narrative, one finds a patriarchal, sadistic, Atlantic position that heralds both the modernism hailing from Latin America (Rubén Darío) and the new intellectual discourse elaborated after the events of 1898 by the Generation of 98. This position is present in her earliest novel, *La hija del mar* (1859; "The Daughter of the Sea"), and therefore predates her Galician nationalist writing. She formulates it in its most critical-radical way in 1867, with *El caballero de las botas azules* ("The Gentleman with the Blue Boots"). Her last novel, *El primer loco* (1881; "The First Madman"), written after the liberal revolution, confirms, although without the same radical tones, the position formulated in *El caballero*.

Castro's narrative position, which I will label "Atlantic" for brevity's sake, must therefore be approached as independent of or separate from her conflict with nationalism. It precedes her nationalist Galician writing and also heralds her later criticism of Galician nationalism. This Atlantic positioning allegorically announces the reception her work will have across the Atlantic at the end of her life. As Davies states:

> [F]rom the 1860s on, Castro did not find a place within a peninsular literary network . . . her isolation increased thereafter. As has been amply documented, the only attention paid to Castro in the 1870s and 1880s (following the second edition of *Cantares gallegos*) was that of the Galician diaspora in Cuba and Argentina.   ("Rosalía de Castro: Cultural Isolation" 181)

Moreover, the twenty poems that form the basis of *En las orillas del Sar* were originally published in Argentina (182). Castro's own discursive Atlantic positioning, as articulated by her novels, heralds the critical journey her work will make from Galicia to the Americas, then back to Spain. Davies reminds us, "Castro was admitted much later into the Spanish literary canon on the basis of her reputation as a popular Galician poet acquired in the former Spanish colonies, among the mostly male Galician diaspora" (182). In this respect, Castro's famous poem "Estranxeira na súa patria" (*Obras* 2: 311; "A Stranger in My Own Land") summarizes her condition.[3]

Castro's Narrative: A Biopolitical and Geopolitical Analysis

Castro wrote five narrative works, most of which can be considered novels: *La hija del mar* (1859), *Flavio* (1861), *Ruinas* (1864), *El caballero de las botas azules* (1867), and *El primer loco* (1881). She also wrote shorter narrative articles: "Lieders" (1858), "El cadiceño" (1863; "The Gaditan"), "Conto gallego" (1864; "Galician Story"), "Las literatas" (1866; "The Literatae"), "Costumbres gallegas" (1880; "Galician Customs"; also known as "El domingo de ramos"; "Easter Sunday"), and "Padrón y las inundaciones" (1881; "Padrón and the Floods"). All her narratives, with the exception of "Conto gallego," are in Spanish. An Atlantic discursive structure is characteristic of them all, but it is complex and calls for a separate biopolitical and geopolitical analysis.

Biopolitically, the Atlantic discursive structure of her work is organized around a sadistic father figure and position that sets Castro's writing apart from most of her contemporary peers, both ideologically and discursively. It is precisely this position that allows her to articulate a modernist discourse in her late narrative. Since this figure changes radically throughout Castro's narrative career, it is important to examine its earliest formulation. In her first novel, *La hija del mar*, the tyrannical father, Alberto Ansot, is derived from Romantic and gothic literature---as well as from *folletín* or serialized literature. However, Castro's discursive elaboration is not Romantic. On the one hand, one of the female figures, the adoptive mother, Teresa, is entangled in a masochistic relationship with Ansot; both are punished and vanish from the narrative at the end of the novel. Elena Sánchez Mora, following Sandra Gilbert and Susan Gubar's criticism, points out that the mother and father are not simple mimetic representations of a gendered real world but rather projections and introjections of the authorial anxiety experienced by women writers in the nineteenth century (253). Isabel Estrada, following Anne Williams, notes that this ambivalence is also found in feminist gothic literature (84). On the other hand, a third character appears, the young Esperanza, Teresa's adoptive daughter, who is caught in the middle of the sadomasochistic parental scenario and, as a result, also dies.[4] Ultimately, the nuclear family, in Romantic or gothic disguise, is exorcised through a narrative of sadomasochism that works as a denunciation of the father's seduction of the daughter—later legitimized by psychoanalysis. As Susan Kirkpatrick concludes, "In Esperanza, then, Castro explores the possibility of a pre-Oedipal desire for reunion with the mother as an alternative to subjection to the sexual law of the father" ("Fantasy" 79).

The geopolitical dimension of this sadomasochist formation is important as well. Beginning with *La hija del mar*, and only excepting *El caballero*, the masochist woman desiring the sadistic father is always bound to Galicia (in *El caballero*, the masochist female position is occupied by a group of women located in Madrid). In other words, the masochist woman, often a mother, lives on the periphery of Spanish nationalism and, more specifically, in the rural and subaltern Galician countryside or coast—the space that Galician nationalism later reclaims for the foundation of its ideology. This landscape is also present in Castro's poetry ("As torres de oeste" ["Towers of the West"], "Ca pena o lombo" ["With Sorrow on Her Back"] [*Obras* 2: 430, 437]).[5]

The sadistic father figure in all Castro's novels is related to a (post)colonial,[6] Atlantic geography. In *La hija del mar*, he comes from the Americas;[7] in *Ruinas*, the inheritance that empowers the protagonist comes from the Americas; in *El primer loco*, the husband of the female protagonist is North American. Finally, in *El caballero*, the introductory dialogue between the "*caballero*-to-be" and the muse centers on the before and after of his voyage to the Americas:

> [C]on solo cinco mil reales, ¡incomprensible maravilla!, diste la vuelta al mundo, reposando después, allende los mares, sobre una tierra virgen, en las Antillas, en fin, en donde los afortunados refrescan la frente abrasada por el calor del clima, en ríos que corren sobre cauces de oro. Cuando después, perfectamente conocedor de la política, de la estética, de la fisiología, de la mineralogía y de las costumbres extranjeras, te devolviste generosamente a la patria. . . . (2: 11)

> With only five thousand reals—incomprehensible marvel!—you went around the world, settling overseas, on virgin soil, in the Antilles, where the fortunate refresh their brows burned by the heat of the climate, in rivers that run over golden channels. When later, perfectly familiar with politics, aesthetics, physiology, mineralogy, and foreign customs, you generously returned yourself to the fatherland. . . .

When the "*caballero*-to-be" comes back and acquires all the power and wealth that his (post)colonial return allows him, he seeks the glory of artistic fame and thus, at the beginning of the novel, summons the muse to help him. The muse sends him back outside the Spanish territory; the protagonist returns for a second time as the "caballero de las botas azules" or "duque de la Gloria" ("gentleman with blue boots" or "Duke of Glory") in full possession of a new wealth that resists commodification (the boots) and signifies not only the colonial Spanish Atlantic but also the broader European colonial field of the Orient: the boots were made on the banks of the Jordan river (2: 36).

Flavio is Castro's only novel in which the geopolitical origins of the sadistic father are not mentioned. The woman-mother bound to Galicia and the (post)colonial father hailing from the Americas complement the Atlantic geography of Castro's narrative. Whereas the father is endowed with (post)colonial mobility and transcendence, the masochistic woman is bound to a subaltern Galician geography that does not respond to the geopolitics of Spanish and/or Galician nationalisms. She is marginal even to the small villages or towns in which she lives. Therefore she does not participate in any nationalist project of imagining the community (Anderson); she remains on the (Atlantic) margin. In other words, the fatherly figure and the masochist woman are defined not by a national order but by a (post)imperialist-colonial one. Both belong to the nonnationalist Hispanic Atlantic, a space that resists Spain's and Galicia's nationalist political and cultural order and, rather, reflects a more historical Galician geography of Atlantic migration.

This geobiopolitical organization of Castro's narrative also has an economic dimension. Aurea Fernández Rodríguez observes, "[O]s vicios, a avaricia, o afán de lucro e a falta de caridade aparecen a miúdo e preocupadamente reflexados nos textos desta alma sensible que nos revela Rosalía de Castro" (413; "Vices, avarice, the desire for money, and lack of charity appear frequently and worryingly reflected in the texts of this sensitive soul revealed to us by Rosalía de Castro"). Unlike in her poetry, Castro depicts wealthy characters such as Don Braulio in *Ruinas* or the Duque de la Gloria in *El caballero*, but their wealth becomes a more privileged way to continue to criticize the middle class, the high bourgeoisie, and the aristocracy. In her analysis of *Ruinas*, María José Alonso Seoane points out that the novel "se anticipa a *El Caballero de las botas azules* en la actitud irónica, burlona" (425; "anticipates *El Caballero* in its ironic, mocking attitude"). The projective and introjective dynamic I have discussed in relation to gender and the family in Castro's novels can be expanded to social class. Castro's economic criticism remains identified with the migrant subaltern Galician classes in both her novels and her poetry. But this identification (intro-projection) takes a fantastic shape in her novels and thus mobilizes aristocratic characters. Olga Rivera concludes:

> La identificación de Rosalía con los pobres no sólo determina la ideología de clase favorecida en *Ruinas*. Constituye una actitud altamente visible y reiterada en toda su producción literaria, tanto poética como narrativa.   (477)

> The identification of Rosalía with the poor not only determines the favored class ideology in *Ruinas*. It constitutes a highly visible attitude reiterated throughout her literary production, both poetic and narrative.

Nationalist Realism and Antiliterary Modernism

The nonnationalist, Atlantic nature of both fatherly and female characters can also be detected at the level of the literary genres that Castro simultaneously utilizes and criticizes. Castro's novels do not simply capture two different geopolitical formations (the national and the postcolonial-postimperial) and two different biopolitical articulations (sadist father and masochist female) but also two different types of discourse. From the geobiopolitical break I analyzed in Castro's novels, one can view in a very different light the discursive heterogeneity of her novels, which, so far, most critics have considered a sign of literary immaturity or of realist inability. To the nationalist critic who seeks the objective effect of the realist national allegory, Castro's narrative lacks "order" and "homogeneity" ("non está ben articulada" [Davies, *Rosalía* 282; "it isn't well articulated"]; see also Mayoral, "La voz"). Even Ana Rodriguez-Fischer, one of the editors of *El caballero*, cannot escape the retrohistorical effect of reducing two discursive orders to a single one, which she then dismisses as lacking discursive homogeneity and realist consistency—the characteristics of nationalist realism:

> Así, puede hablarse de "obra abierta" o de "estructura suelta" atendiendo a la peculiar dinámica interna que entre sí mantienen las distintas escenas o núcleos narrativos; *un tanto inconexos y desarticulados*, sin otra unión que la figura del protagonista . . . Posiblemente sea esta *fallida articulación* de los episodios novelescos lo que más aleja a *El caballero* . . . de la novela realista, sobre todo si consideramos que el nexo de unión—el héroe—es de muy otra naturaleza y pertenece, por completo, al plano de lo mágico–maravilloso.
> (Introduction 51; my emphasis)

> Thus we can speak of "open work" or "free structure," looking at the peculiar internal dynamic that the different scenes or narrative nuclei have between them; *rather unconnected and inarticulate*, with no other connection than the figure of the protagonist. . . . Perhaps this *failed articulation* of the novelistic episodes is what most distances *El caballero* . . . from the realist novel, especially if we consider that the nexus point—the hero—is very different in nature and belongs completely to the plane of magical realism.

Against this perception of failure, Enrique Miralles is one of the first critics to argue that the novel works as an antinovel (458–60). Several critics have also analyzed its initial references to Cervantes and, as a result, concluded that Castro deploys a Cervantine strategy of criticizing the existing literature, the *folletín* ("serialized novel"), in order to create a new "caballero de la triste figura" ("knight of the sad countenance," Don Quixote), the "caballero de las botas azules" (Fernández Pérez San Julián 476). At a time when "the serialized novel reigned supreme" (Kirkpatrick, "Fantasy" 79), Castro writes an antiserialized novel. It is founded on a double literature that appropriates the codes of the serialized novel, on the one hand, and criticizes them, on the other.

This critique is thematized in the modernist idea of the "book of books," which the Duque de la Gloria distributes among his guests after buying and burning all the books shelved in the Madrid bookstores—including *El caballero*.[8] In this respect, *El caballero* is a forerunner of the other great modernist account of the destruction of all knowledge: Gustave Flaubert's *Bouvard et Pécuchet* (1881). Wadda C. Ríos-Font even claims that *El caballero* is a foundational novel that inaugurates a new form of literature: "[F]rom a context of destruction [Castro] builds a new relationship between author and audience" (188). This new form of literature is modernism: the novel is structured as resisting the literary, reading, and marketing conventions of the time. As Ríos-Font adds, the final goal of this resistance is to create a new (bourgeois) literary consciousness: "[Castro] pushes readers away from the novel's illusion, forcing them to think about its textual nature and their own role in regard to that nature" (194). This modernist strategy is not limited to *El caballero*; Deanna Johnson-Hoffman finds the same structure in *Flavio* (153–61).[9]

Castro's poetry too can now be interpreted in the light of her modernist narrative as a form of Atlantic exile from Galician nationalism, whereby the refashioning of poetic metrics echoes her modernist experiments with narrative. As many critics have noted, her poetry shifts from a more popular and oral register—which is ultimately a polyphony of subaltern Galician voices—to a more individual and modernist one, similar to that of the late Gustavo Adolfo Bécquer (Albornoz) or of the future Rubén Darío (Pérez Botero), while also anticipating free verse (Paraíso). This modernist shift has been neglected by nationalist critics. As a result, Castro's early poetry in Galician has been singled out as sign of her nationalist identity. Yet, given her modernist shift, and as Davies argues, one must conclude:

> O mesmo desapego á sociedade e ás súas convencións literarias, tanto galegas como españolas, levouna ós experimentos formais e á linguaxe hermética e simbólica na súa poesía. Creou así a súa propia realidade inconformista.
> ("A ideoloxía" 305–06)[10]

The same indifference to society and its literary conventions, both Galician and Spanish, led her to formal experimentation and hermetic, symbolic language in her poetry. Thus she created her own nonconformist reality.

This nonconformist reality is modernism, which she first articulates in her novels, anticipating the work of other modernist women after 1898 (Kirkpatrick, *Mujer*).

Father Figures and Atlantic, Modernist Dandies

Although several critics have noticed the excessive—and uncanny—nature of the father figure in *El caballero,* it is important to underscore that the same characteristic applies to all the father figures in Castro's narrative. They cannot be contained in a nationalist discourse centered on the bourgeois ideal of femininity—the angel of the house—and the private sphere. Yet, these fatherly figures mark their exteriority by violently attacking the bourgeois national order. Psychoanalytically speaking, the father figure oscillates between the Real and the symbolic in Castro's writing: a radical difference disrupts the (national) symbolic order of the novel with violence while also asserting its law. That is, the father's violence belongs to the Real; it comes from outside the symbolic order and cannot be contained by it. It is not a coincidence that this position is Atlantic, postcolonial-imperialist, migrant, and modernist. The Atlantic is the site that enables the return of the repressed, which questions and threatens both the Galician and Spanish nationalist orders.

The absence of Castro's biological father—as well as the patriarchal presence of her husband, Murguía—has been mentioned by critics as central to the articulation of what I call Castro's fatherly Atlantic figure (Mayoral, *La poesía* 131–32). But, that figure is a condensation, in the psychoanalytic sense of the word, of several patriarchal regimes in which the absent biological father is simply one element, rather than the sole (biogenetic) explanation. The nationalist inability to contain the father explains the female desire for this sadistic figure in most of Castro's novels. In his violence, the father represents the possibility of transcending the Spanish-Galician national order. At the same time, the fact that the father figure disappears or dies at the end signifies that it is not the father per se but his disruptive and Real violence, the nonnationalist space opened by him, that the female characters desire.

Although a detailed analysis of the fatherly Atlantic position in Castro's novels exceeds the scope of this essay, I would like to sketch out how it develops in her narrative. Castro ends up identifying with the father as a way to occupy a sadistic, intellectual, modernist, Atlantic position. In *La hija del mar*, the father figure (Ansot) is utterly colonial and sadistic ("pirata del África" [1: 179; "pirate from Africa"]), while the female protagonists, young and old, are masochistic. Furthermore, the father is a separate character from the innocent male lover (Fausto) of the young female protagonist (Teresa). In *Flavio* and *Ruinas*, the young male lover occupies the position of father figure and becomes the central figure of the narrative (resp., Ricardo and Montenegro). In both cases, this hybridization of positions (young male lover and father) accompanies a more sadistic representation of the young female protagonist: she becomes more superficial, capricious, and stubborn (resp., Mara and Marcelina). As Sánchez Mora points out, Mara initiates the sadistic cycle in *Flavio*, which turns the innocent young lover Flavio into a sadistic figure at the end of the novel (254). Unlike in *La hija del mar*, the suicide of the seduced young Rosa becomes a secondary plot in *Flavio* (Varela Jácome, "El discurso" 396). In these two novels, both male and female protagonists hybridize into sadistic characters that can alternatively occupy the father position. As Benito Varela Jácome notes, the narrative structure of *Flavio* reverses the Romantic tropes on which it is based, yielding a sort of "*deconstrucción* compleja" (397; "complex *deconstruction*").

The centralization of the sadistic father position takes place alongside the marginalization of the Romantic nuclear family structure, as well as of the nationalist middle and upper classes. Ironically, the representatives of the bourgeois nuclear family structure, both men and women, become the masochist subjects of Castro's late narratives. From the older female protagonist of *La hija del mar*, Teresa, to the aristocratic women and men of *El caballero*, a genealogy of masochist characters occupies the domestic space of the bourgeois ideal of "the angel of the house." Most are women, but male characters too develop a masochistic relationship with the father figure. This other masochistic hybridization parallels the sadistic.

The marginalization of the masochistic, domestic, and national space allows Castro to occupy a discursive position that is outside the political and sexual order of both Spanish and Galician nationalisms. As a result, the invocation and recuperation of the lost father help her articulate an exilic, uncanny position, from which to gain a critical distance and transcend her contemporary cultural, nationalist historical context. To my knowledge, only Kirkpatrick, although from a different perspective, has understood the centrality and importance of the continuity of the father figure in Castro's narrative ("Fantasy" 83–86). It is precisely this exilic, uncanny, and yet fatherly position that allows Castro to develop an intellectual discourse and position proper to modernism. More specifically, the androgynous, Atlantic figure of the dandy present in *El caballero* already announces the intellectual critique that the Generation of 98 develops at the turn of the century. At the same time, the fashion-centered discourse of the novel also heralds, in its fetishistic choice of color and wardrobe—the magic blue boots—the arrival of Latin American modernism, via Darío's *Azul.*

Castro's *El caballero* and its protagonist, the Duque de la Gloria, embody and represent, in their ironic and intellectual discourse, the figure of an Atlantic, intellectual, androgynous dandy: the subject of modernism. The dandy's position can also be defined as one of bodily exile.[11] Castro's own narrative dandyism responds to the "unspecifiable 'beyond'" that defines modernism and its critique of bourgeois, nationalist culture, both Spanish and Galician (Feldman 7). Charnon-Deutsch has noted the centrality of the bourgeois subjectivity that *El caballero* constructs through its modernist resistance to bourgeois desire:

> [T]he symbolic complexity of the [*caballero's*] boots demonstrates Castro's awareness of both the economic and noneconomic (sexual, cultural) processes involved in the working of desire; both are constituent factors in the determination of subjectivity. (133)

As Kirkpatrick concludes, the dandy is the privileged modernist subject of bourgeois critique, because "in eliciting seduction fantasies and then subjecting them to critique, he [the *caballero*] also registers the instability of the gendered positions within them" ("Fantasy" 89).[12] The tradition among Spanish women writers of fetishizing public male bodies and fashion—from the bullfighter in Fernán Caballero's *La gaviota* to Carmen de Burgos's queer characters—is inscribed in an intellectual discourse. This tradition mobilizes patriarchy and its public position in order to perform, on its body, a feminist intellectual critique of modernity and its political, economic, and sexual order. The fact that most of the time the patriarchal figure is dismissed or eliminated from the narrative at the end underscores the importance of its female performance, not the figure itself. Kirkpatrick clearly defines the feminist project of Castro's narrative, and especially of *El caballero*, when she states, "[T]he Duke [of Gloria] attempts to teach women to be resistant readers, to read critically the fantasies scripted for them" ("Fantasy" 88).

It is important to emphasize that the exilic abject position Castro achieves in her poetry, the one that makes her shift from Galician to Spanish in *A las orillas de Sar*, has already taken place in her narrative by 1867 in *El caballero* and, thus, points to an Atlantic position: sadistic, fatherly, modernist, and intellectual. Her work cannot be reduced to Galician language or nationalism, as most Galician literary scholars have done so far. As Moreiras-Menor points out, Castro's nationalization implies the cover-up of a nonnationalist "secret." Conversely, the marginalization of her narrative amounts to obscuring the modernist, intellectual, Atlantic position that Castro reaches across both languages. Kirkpatrick concludes:

> In 1868, a year after the novel's publication, the long-expected Glorious Revolution occurred and, in its aftermath, a new national novelistic tradition arose. But neither the revolution nor the realist canon incorporated the radical openness of structure that Castro's Muse sought to inspire.   ("Fantasy" 95)

To analyze this complex discursive positioning as Spanish would also amount to repeating the nationalist, Galician cover-up. In short, to think of Castro's work as exclusively Galician or Spanish—written exclusively in Galician or in Spanish—amounts to a nationalist reductionism against which her work, *both* in Galician and Spanish, was written.[13] Claude Poullain's suggestion that Castro's bilingualism is essential to understanding her poetry is thus even more pertinent for her entire opus in two languages (437).

The above mapping points to the fact that nationalist Galician literature constitutes itself by exiling Galician women writers from both the canon and the literary institution—a claim that can be extended to Spanish literature. The political, cultural, and historical formation of Galician literature cannot be approached from a nationalist point of view; the question of the national language cannot decide the location of the literature. On the contrary, Galician women's literature exceeds nationalism, since its exclusion constitutes the literary nation.[14] Once a geopolitical analysis is combined with a feminist biopolitical analysis, the issue of whether Galician is the sole language of Galician literature or whether Spanish must also be incorporated loses its nationalist and fetishist importance. I separate this postnationalist analysis from the neonationalist theory that claims to be postnationalist (Habermas); my analysis aims precisely to problematize the borders and limits of any nationalist literary theory and history. A postnationalist feminist approach reveals the different geopolitical and biopolitical articulations that nationalism disavows in order to uphold its hegemony.

Almost a hundred years after Castro's death, the nationalist question of literary languages and identities hides the biopolitical problem that still haunts Galician literature: the complete marginalization of women writers in a hegemonic conception of poetry as feminine is complemented by the almost exclusive monopoly of male writers over narrative and literary recognition (Noia). This situation is not new or accidental: it begins in the nineteenth century with Castro and, thus, calls for a new postnational history of Galician literature, one that exceeds its nationalist ideology and pays attention to its biopolitics.

Notes

1. In her introduction to *Cantares gallegos*, she is fully aware that the political, economic, and cultural hegemonic regime is European. Thus, when situating Galicia vis-à-vis Spain, she compares this relation of subjugation with the one that Spain holds with France (*Obras* 2: 266). We might compare her Atlanticist position with the European position of Emilia Pardo Bazán (see Gabilondo, "Towards a Postnational History").

2. Castro's conflict was not limited to Galician nationalism; it also encompassed the conservative sectors of Galician society, which were Spanish-nationalist. Yet, the conflict becomes central in the case of Galician nationalism, precisely because she had shared its political agenda and Galician nationalism had claimed her as one of its most important voices.

3. Although it would require a separate study, it is important to hypothesize that Hispanic modernism cannot be defined along nationalist lines as Spanish, Nicaraguan, Cuban, or Latin American, but rather as an Atlantic phenomenon: an arch that encompasses Latin American, Galician, and Catalan modernisms. Ultimately, it would have to be defined as an Atlantic formation that reacts against centralist-nationalist organizations of literature. Davies states, "It is no coincidence that Juan Ramón Jimenez, in a lecture on modernism (17 February 1953), should propose an outline for the history of nineteenth-century modern poetry which began with Curros Enríquez, Vicente Median, and Rosalía, and ended with Silva and Darío, all poets (often from the provinces or colonies) who rejected the stranglehold of official culture and conventional literary expression" ("Rosalía Castro's Later Poetry" 616).

4. Following Lacan and Deleuze, I define *masochism* and *sadism* not as sexual perversions but as biopolitical discursive structures by which the nationalist-patriarchal order is questioned. This questioning or critique is effected by projecting the order into either a subject of power that performs it (sadism) or a powerless subject on which it

is performed (masochism). Sadomasochist discourse requires an identification with and critique of both positions of power(lessness). The repression that the patriarchal-nationalist order exerts does not permit a direct critique---hence the recourse to other subjects to articulate it.

5. Mayoral observes that this masochist female position is important in Castro's poetry: "A lo largo del libro encontramos abundantes muestras de las fatales consecuencias que tiene para la mujer este 'amor sin medida': 'Espantada o avismo veso,' 'Para a vida e para a morte,' '!Valor que aunque eres como baranda cera!,' '!Nin as escuras!' son ejemplos de poemas en los que vemos a la mujer víctima de la pasión amorosa" (*Rosalía* 83; "Throughout the book we find abundant proof of the fatal consequences that this 'love without measure' has for women; 'Frightened I Plow the Abyss,' 'For Life and for Death,' 'Valor although You Are as Slippery Wax', 'Nor in the Dark' are examples of poems is which we see the woman as victim of amorous passion").

6. It is not clear if Castro refers to Latin American countries that gained independence earlier in the century (Argentina, Uruguay, etc.) and, thus, are postcolonial, or to actual colonies of the Spanish empire (Cuba and Puerto Rico). I decided to resort to parenthesis (post) in order to capture this ambiguity.

7. Only Pablo del Barco notes the importance of the Atlantic component, when he emphasizes the Romantic, clichéd origin of "aparición del indiano" (512).

8. Germán Gullón writes, "'[E]l libro de los libros,' acaba comiéndose al grande, el contenido (el librito) al contenedor (*El caballero*), con lo que estructuralmente los episodios protagonizados por el escritor-duque se convierten en una enorme burbuja, que estalla en el último capítulo: supone la deconstrucción de todos los capítulos precedentes" (490; "'The book of books' ends up swallowing the big one, the content [the little book] swallows the container [*El caballero*], thus, structurally, the episodes in which the duke-writer is the protagonist become a big bubble that explodes in the last chapter; it represents the deconstruction of all the previous chapters").

9. Castro's rewriting of previous literature does not reach simply *folletín* literature but also Romantic literature. One of the novels rewritten by Castro is Alexandre Dumas père's *The Count of Monte Cristo* (1844–46).

10. Mayoral finds a clear stylistic continuity between Castro's poetry and prose. Some of the same narrative strategies are found in both genres ("Voz" 364–65). Critics have also underscored the importance of the evocation of both the countryside and rural life as an announcement of what the poetry of the Generation of 98 will become (Cardwell: Suelto de Sáenz).

11. As Feldman explains, "Dandyism exists in the field of force between two opposing, irreconcilable notions about gender. First, the (male) dandy defines himself by attacking women. Second, so crucial are female characteristics to the dandy's self-creation that he defines himself by embracing women, appropriating their characteristics. . . . Rather these writers both reject and pursue women because they engage in that most self-diving of activities: living within dominant cultural forms while imagining new forms taking shape in some unspecifiable 'beyond.' Cultural change may certainly be

charted as the result of social, economic, and religious phenomena as they impinge on the collective imagination of a society. Yet such change may, on the contrary, begin within those individuals in a culture who happen to see things in a new (and often illogical or even crazy-seeming) way" (6–7).

12. Castro is aware of the reality of Galician emigration and of its results. She pays special attention to the returning *indiano* ("emigrant"), whom she criticizes in a short story entitled "El cadiceño" (1: 660–68; "The Gaditan"). This story also deals with clothing and, thus, represents the symmetrical antithesis of *El caballero*. J. M. González Herrán misses the critical element of this story when he equates Castro's critique of the *indiano* with a general critique of migration (446–47).

13. Still in 1986, Kathleen N. March noted that "segue ausente o concepto dunha Rosalía forte; a imaxe das poetas galegas non se distancia moito, ao menos nunha primeira ollada, da que lle conceden os críticos clásicos dentro e fora da Galiza" (289; "the idea of a strong Rosalía remains absent; the image of Galician women poets is not very far, at least at first glance, from the image of her circulated by traditional critics within and beyond Galicia").

14. Elizabeth J. Ordoñez suggests that there are several similarities between Castro's *La hija del mar* and Pardo Bazán's *Los pazos de Ulloa* (81). Furthermore, I see similarities between Castro's *El caballero* and Pardo Bazán's *La quimera* and *Dulce Dueño*. It is a very compelling and productive hypothesis to posit Pardo Bazán as a reader of Castro. It would represent the other (counter)founding act of Galician literature.

IDENTITIES

Introduction to Part 2

The question of who has the right to speak as Galician and for Galicia—and what it means to (claim to) do so—is a thorny one. While language and territory are key markers of identity in Galicia as in many other nations, the value attributed to them in Galicia is not straightforward. Galicia's position at multiple points of intersection—geographic, linguistic, cultural—means that Galician practitioners and individuals are highly aware of the contingent nature of location and thus of enunciation. All Galicians must be citizens of somewhere else, whether that place is Spain or, in the diaspora, Argentina, Brazil, Cuba, even Great Britain. (For those who retain their Spanish citizenship, there is also EU membership.) Furthermore, most Galicians are bilingual, in different degrees, between Galician and Castilian, and the identification of language and nation is complicated by the presence of many Galicians—not only in the diaspora—for whom Galician is not an everyday language but who still consider themselves entirely Galician. At the same time, national identification is complemented by other means of expressing identity—for example, by gender, ethnicity, or sexuality—that do not always sit easily with the established framework of the national that has developed in the twentieth century. The essays in this section explore different ways of expressing Galician identity as part of a complex network of individual, group, local, and transnational identities, in which the implications of the national are constantly being reframed and redefined.

Eugenia Romero conveys this network in spatial terms, arguing that a key consequence of the massive emigrations from Galicia to the Americas and, later, northern Europe, is that Galician national and cultural identity cannot be located only in the territory of Galicia. Romero proposes instead a concept of identity that is located between two planes: that of concrete physical space (such as the territory of Galicia) and that anchored in movement and displacement between Galicia and the places of emigration.

Galeguidade, in this framework, comes to exist as a negotiation between attachment and loss, an imagined space between here (however we define it) and there. The tension between the desire to locate Galician identity in a fixed and stable territory and the need to acknowledge the experience of emigration is, Romero argues, represented in cultural texts through absence and emptiness.

Highlighting the need to complement privileged aesthetic discourses (such as academic or literary accounts) with those created by ordinary migrants, Romero begins by analyzing two very different spaces whose focus is emigration, broadly understood: the institutional initiatives of the Xunta and a selection of Web sites created by members of the Galician diaspora. She compares the Xunta's closed, academic Arquivo da Emigración Galega with the *Fillos.org* Web site, whose motivation is primarily affective, emotional. Members of the diaspora have sought to bridge the gulf between, on the one hand, politicians and scholars and, on the other, agents of emigration through a series of political campaigns to establish their rights in relation to Galicia. Romero analyzes two literary texts that attempt to bridge this gap by providing more critical accounts of the emigration experience that subvert the elite literary-academic discourse, which has tended to dominate institutional debates: Antón Risco's *Memorias dun emigrante* (1987; "Memoirs of an Emigrant") and Manuel Rivas's *A man dos paíños* (2000; "The Hand with the Storm Petrels"). For Romero, the narrative strategies employed by these two authors place a special emphasis not only on the experiences of migration but also on the way that these experiences are told (or not told). She focuses on fantasy as a discursive and narrative tool of emigration, arguing that only by embracing the impossibility of speaking about the experience of dislocation and loss can Galicians begin to imagine alternative ways of expressing that experience and thus reclaim it from the dominating institutional discourse of the Xunta and the Arquivo.

Jaine Beswick develops Romero's proposal that movement is a foundational aspect of Galician identity to examine the intersection between ethnic (Galician) and state (Spanish, British) allegiances. Beswick is interested in how the role of language choice as a marker of Galician identity is transformed in this particular setting. The Galician diaspora in the United Kingdom is relatively recently established: although a small number of civil war exiles settled in the UK during the 1930s and 1940s, most Galicians now resident in the UK arrived in the 1960s and 1970s. This community has received much less scholarly attention, or indeed public recognition, than the longer-established and far more numerous Galician communities in South America. Beswick attributes this difference in part to a deliberate strategy of invisibility. The strategies of concealment employed by Galician migrants in the UK are strongly connected with their sense of self. She argues that the traditional, essentialized concepts of Galician identity that shaped earlier migrations to the Americas are no longer relevant for these migrants and their transnational lives. Working on the hypothesis that this change may apply also to linguistic identity, she evaluates contextual language use among a group of Galician migrants based in the suburban British town of Guildford, near London. Her research suggests that although a three-way sense of Galician-Spanish-British identity still exists in Guildford, the Galician component appears to be moving away from the question of language choice. This change might be expressed in traditional nationalist terms as a loss rather than simply a shift, but Beswick warns against the essentialist identification of language and identity, arguing instead for recognition of a range of dynamic, newly emerging forms of cultural allegiance.

John Patrick Thompson approaches the question of Galicia's multiple allegiances from a different angle, considering Galicia's location at the margins of *hispanidad* and *lusofonia*, with special reference to the ongoing controversy over the codification of standard Galician in relation to Spanish and Portuguese, known as the *conflito normativo*. Despite the importance of the Galician language as a marker of Galician identity, no standardized form of the language existed until after autonomy; the Normas da Lingua Galega ("Norms for the Galician Language") were first published by the RAG in 1982. Until then, writers were free to choose the morphological, orthographical, and lexical form of Galician most natural to them. Some wrote in a consciously *enxebre* ("purist") form of the language, mining medieval documents for authentic vocabulary and projecting morphological, phonetic, and semantic developments that would have taken place had the language not been condemned to four centuries of silence, from the fifteenth to the nineteenth century. Others looked to Portuguese for guidance; still others acknowledged the widespread influence of Castilian. Today, as Thompson explains, the conflict focuses on orthography as an identity marker; the question of whether Galician should be written using the Portuguese or Spanish graphic system has come to stand for the question of whether Galicia should be a part of *lusofonia*, the Portuguese-speaking world, or a nation independent of both Spain and Portugal. Despite their many differences, both sides are in agreement that the creeping Castilianization of Galician (particularly through the media) must be halted. Thompson expresses the hope that this agreement might provide a means to resolve a conflict which he perceives as one of the most serious obstacles to consolidation of a hegemonic Galician national movement.

Finally, Timothy McGovern picks up on the decentering of Galicia and Galician identity described by Romero and Beswick and on Thompson's demand for recognition of Galicia's minority voices. He investigates the demand for new definitions of gender and sexual identity that oppose hegemonic (and implicitly heterosexual) masculinity and femininity, arguing that this process parallels and contributes to the emergence of a new Galician identity. Building on the work of Spanish and Catalan theorists who reclaim camp in Spain as an aesthetic of resistance (thus rejecting Susan Sontag's foundational interpretation of camp as essentially apolitical), McGovern argues that the Galician poet and performance artist Antón Lopo explores in his debut novel *Ganga* the close relation between the aesthetic of camp and the queering of Galician culture to model an innovative interpretation of queer Galicianness. Lopo's unusual novel attempts to fuse the articulation of queerness and Galicianness, thus questioning the conventional view that the Galician voice is unmarked by sexuality or gender. This is not a rejection of national identity but a radical reformulation of its foundational elements, including language and territory, through a perspective marked— but not limited—by unstable categories of gender and sexuality. McGovern proposes a reading of Lopo's novel as part of a widespread reaction to the conservative government of Manuel Fraga. This reaction is most graphically conveyed by a plot in which vampires masquerade as Galician politicians to gain eternal life by sucking the blood of their constituents.

McGovern draws attention to the spatial reformulation of Iberia in the novel, which places Galicia (a postgender Galicia) at the center of world affairs, closely followed by Catalunya and Portugal. Central Spain appears to have been erased from the novel's imaginative geography. For McGovern, the centering of what is normally considered peripheral is a deliberate strategy that can be read as an enactment of the argument of the influential cultural critic Xoán González-Millán, that the artistic discourse of oppressed groups must express conflicts and discontinuities as well as a coherent national history. In other words, Galician literature and culture must be open to all, including sexual minorities, even when this disrupts the hegemonic single narrative.

All four essays in this section explore how expressions of individual identity are located in a complex network of identities in which accepted markers take on new meanings and traditional narratives must be reformulated and told anew. The Galician identity that emerges from these very different accounts is no longer monolithic or implicitly neutral but inflected by multiple markers, categories, and meanings. Only by listening carefully to every voice will we recognize the particular intersection of experiences that gives it its special quality.

The Other Galicia: Construction of National Identity through Absence

Eugenia R. Romero

When talking about identity, national, individual, or cultural, we must consider that the term is not transparent. In Galicia, notions of national community and identity have been constantly mythified and further problematized by the massive migration movements of Galicians to Europe and especially the Americas since the mid-nineteenth century. Galician national and cultural identity is framed between two planes that coexist and operate simultaneously: one rooted in a concrete physical space (A Coruña, Ourense, Santiago, Vigo, Galicia, etc.), the other anchored in the movement and displacement of emigration to and from Cuba, Argentina, Brazil, Uruguay, Mexico, Switzerland, England, and so on. Thus Galicians have long perceived themselves within the parameters of emigration.

Historically, Galicia lost more inhabitants to emigration in the search for better opportunities than any other region of Spain. The majority (about 70%) of emigrants who left during the first phase of Galician emigration in the second half of the nineteenth century never returned. This phase's characteristics were a great number of male emigrants in comparison with the rest of Spain, little female participation until 1880 (in 1859 only one Galician woman for every twenty-four men emigrated), a small number of whole families emigrating, and a migration flow mostly toward the Americas (Villares, "Idade contemporánea" 368). Subsequent waves of migration in the twentieth century, especially after the Spanish Civil War (1936–39) and during the economic transformation of the 1950s, 1960s, and 1970s, displayed different characteristics, most notably in shifting the focus from lone male migrants to young women, couples, and families. There was also greater variation in destination, especially to North America, northern Europe, and other regions of Spain.[1] In consequence of this long history of migration, most interpretations of Galicia's history (like those of Manuel Murguía; Vicente Risco [*Teoría*]; Alfonso Castelao; and Ramón Piñeiro

[*Olladas*]) show that Galicians feel incomplete if the great number of Galician emigrants around the world is not taken into consideration.[2]

In this essay, I argue that the Galician nation is constructed not only in terms of the concrete territory of Galicia but also through the experience of emigration and that the resulting tension is represented in cultural manifestations through absence or emptiness. My argument is underpinned by the flexible concept of home outlined by Angelika Bammer:

> [Home] has always occupied a particularly indeterminate space: it can mean, almost simultaneously, both the place I have left and the place I am going to, the place I have lost and the new place I have taken up, even if only temporarily. "Home" can refer to the place you grew up . . . the mythic homeland of your parents and ancestors that you yourself may never have actually seen, or the hostel where you are spending the night in transit. In other words, "home" may refer to a deeply familiar or a foreign place, or it may be no more than a passing point of reference. (vii)

According to Bammer, *Heimat* (which can refer to home or nation) is not only a mobile but also an undetermined concept that changes according to the social, political, and physical context.

In Galicia, we find a concept of *galeguidade* that exists as a virtual space of negotiation between attachment and loss; so Galician identity becomes an imagined place between here and there. My analysis shows how *galeguidade* is constructed from a concept of identity in constant tension and movement. This tension is produced, on the one hand, in a dialogic relation between Galicia and emigration (or between territorialization and deterritorialization) and, on the other, in the dichotomy between the real or concrete and the imagined or fantastic. By exploring several cultural and literary representations of Galician identity, I argue that it is impossible to localize only one Galicia. I focus on how the concrete space of a Galician territory is substituted by an imagined space, which offers, at the same time, a new territory (another Galicia) from which and in which Galician identity is created.

Emigration, as displacement, implies not only movement but also choice, as Caren Kaplan argues in *Questions of Travel* (1996). Like other concepts of displacement (tourism, nomadism, etc.), emigration depends on being able to choose when and where to emigrate (and eventually return). According to

Kaplan, it is precisely the ability to choose to migrate or not that makes the accounts of ethnographers, modernist poets, travel writers, and tourists, for example, privileged aesthetic discourses that emphasize distance and separation while "[i]mmigrants, refugees, exiles, nomads, and the homeless also move in and out of these discourses as metaphors, tropes, and symbols but rarely as historically recognized producers of critical discourses themselves" (2). The discourse of displacement thus appears to be maintained by the cultural and aesthetic production of a privileged and dominating class. But in Galicia we find several attempts to vindicate the voices of emigrants in order to recuperate a lost discourse of identity. Three of these attempts are the institutional initiatives of the Xunta de Galicia through the Arquivo da Emigración Galega ("Galician Emigration Archive") and the Internet portal *Galicia aberta* ("Open Galicia"); another virtual project that involves the emigrants themselves, the Internet site created by the cultural organization Fillos de Galicia ("Children of Galicia"); and two literary texts whose titles emphasize the need to talk about Galicia within the framework of emigration: *Memorias dun emigrante* (1988; "Memoirs of an Emigrant") by Antón Risco, and *A man dos paíños* (2000; "The Hand with Petrels"), by Manuel Rivas.[3]

The Arquivo da Emigración Galega is sponsored by the Xunta de Galicia and administered through the Consello da Cultura Galega. The Arquivo was originally part of the Sección de Cultura Galega no Exterior ("Department for Galician Culture Abroad"), initiated by Víctor F. Freixanes to promote the diffusion and study of culture in the Galician diaspora. The creation of the Arquivo in 1992 answered the need to recover "[o] patrimonio cultural galego" ("Galicia's cultural heritage") in order to "[c]onservar a memoria viva da emigración galega" ("preserve the living memory of Galician emigration") ("Obxetivos").[4] The Arquivo is a reference center of Galician migration studies that offers access to "os investigadores interesados no estudo do fenómeno migratorio" ("researchers interested in the study of the migration phenomenon" ["Investigación"]). One of the archive's ongoing projects is the compilation and digitalization of all the materials found in the *centros galegos* ("Galician Centers") around the world—they are currently working on those in Argentina, Cuba, and Uruguay—in order to facilitate access to those materials for scholars and social scientists. There is no doubt that these scholars are the Arquivo's target audience, not emigrants themselves, and so the archive's function lacks an affective or emotional motivation. This absence of emotionality places the archive and its task inside a political discourse subordinated to the institution that it serves. That is, the Arquivo is just that: a place that holds documents, letters, photographs, registry books, and so on about the emigration; it is not a place where emigrants can find information about their role in Galicia's social, cultural, and economic reality. Although there is active academic and scientific research on the subject, "there is a real though often diffuse public debate over the place of migration in the region's identity" (Núñez Seixas 233). The Arquivo is a "scientific institution" that "has collected historical sources and information concerning the past and present of Galician migration in America, Europe and other countries" (252–53). "Scientific institution" emphasizes the fact that the archive's resources available to the public are of interest only to those studying the subject from the perspective of the social sciences (sociology, economy, migration, etc.). Even though its main objective is to "[c]onservar a memoria viva da emigración galega" ("preserve the living memory of Galician emigration") the archive does not in fact take into account the biographical (and human) aspect of emigration as a cultural phenomenon in Galicia, nor does it attempt to provide access to the archive to the emigrants themselves ("Obxetivos").

In an attempt to humanize Galician emigration and to provide information directly to emigrants and their descendants, the Xunta's socialist government, through the Secretaría Xeral de Emigración ("Emigration Ministry"), created the portal *Galicia aberta* in 2005. In 2009, after regaining the presidency of the Xunta, the PP (Partido Popular) government has continued to support this initiative. The new secretary for emigration (Santiago Camba Bouzas) issued a statement recognizing the invaluable role of the Internet as a means to establish contact with the Galician diaspora. In this statement, he acknowledged that the Internet is a window

> que se abre dende a nosa querida terra galega para o mundo, quere ser o espazo común de todos, para comunicarnos e achegarnos máis.
>
> Internet permítenos acurtar tempo e distancias, axiliza as nosas xestións e mantennos máis e mellor informados. Pero de nada nos serviría senón tivésemos instrumentos e contidos actualizados, que susciten o máximo interese dos cidadáns. Ese é, precisamente, o obxectivo que nos fixamos con esta web: ofrecer unha ferramenta útil aos emigrantes, ás súas familias e en xeral a todos cantos queiran estar informados sobre o labor que o Goberno de Galicia realiza en materia de emigración. (Camba Bouzas)

that opens from our beloved Galician land to the world, it attempts to be a common space for all, to [help people] communicate and get closer.

The Internet allows us to shorten time and distance, it speeds up our negotiations, and it keeps us more and better informed. But it would not be useful if we did not keep the tools and contents up-to-date to maximize the interest of the citizens. This is precisely the objective that we set with this Web site: to offer a useful tool for emigrants, their families, and in general to all those who want to be informed about the work that the Galician government is doing in regard to emigration.

The Ministry of Emigration maintains the *Galicia aberta* portal while providing access to information about initiatives between the Galician government and the Centros Galegos no Exterior ("Galician centers abroad"). Most of these programs focus on issues such as Galician language courses and training workshops in different fields like nursing and geriatrics in certain cities with a large presence of Galicians. The site also offers access to the guidelines and application forms to different programs of financial support to return to Galicia for those qualified emigrants that would like to go home. But one of the most important contributions of *Galicia aberta* is the access to the Patrimonio dos Centros Galegos ("heritage of the Galician centers"): documents, bibliographic references, pictures, newspapers, and videos, which have not even been cataloged before, of twelve important Galician centers around the world. The journalist Perfecto Conde recognizes that "[n]unca como agora foi posíbel 'viaxar' a través do inmenso mundo da emigración galega sen erguerse da cadeira de diante do ordenador" ("it has never been as possible as now 'to travel' through the immense world of Galician emigration without having to get up from the chair in front of the computer"). This virtual site functions as a tool for emigrants and their descendants either to learn more about the other Galicia (the one in emigration) or to make a connection with *Galicia territorial* ("territorial Galicia").

The site's opening link states, "Os galegos móvemonos . . . e Galicia avanza connosco: galiciaaberta.com, o reencontro coa túa terra" ("We Galicians are on the move . . . and Galicia moves forward with us: galiciaaberta .com, the reencounter with your land" [*Galicia aberta*]). With these words and with the image of people moving through what seems to be an airport, the site dramatizes the idea that movement (emigration) is intrinsic to Galician identity as well as the fact that, despite the displacement, there is a connection between Galician emigrants and *Galicia territorial* that transcends time and space. Jessica Folkart argues, in reference to a quote by Luis Seone that expresses a similar idea, that a migrant identity "instead of indicating the place from whence one comes, . . . now implies carrying that place within oneself wherever one goes" (5). Yet there is still a sense of absence of emotion as well as absence of community. That even the "Foro" ("Forum") and the "Taboleiro" ("Message Board"), where emigrants can post comments about their experience or ask specific questions, has little or no responses posted online suggests that this virtual space does not encourage or promote the involvement of emigrants.

In contrast, *Fillos.org*, the Internet site of Fillos de Galicia, is a "comunidad virtual cuyo nexo de unión es ser *descendientes de gallegos emigrados*" (*FAQ*; "virtual community whose nexus of unity is that we are *descendants of Galician emigrants*"). The site was created in 1997 by Manuel Casal Lodeiro, the son of Galician emigrants and born in the Basque Country, as a forum for the organization Fillos de Galicia.[5] Its objectives are to

> *mantener y divulgar la cultura gallega*, la galeguidade, entre los descendientes de la diáspora gallega, así como *ampliar y fortalecer los lazos de todo tipo de la comunidad emigrante con Galicia.* (*FAQ*)

> *maintain and disseminate Galician culture*, galeguidade, among the descendants of the Galician diaspora, as well as *to broaden and strengthen bonds of all kinds between the emigrant community and Galicia.*

This site also offers the opportunity to look for relatives in Galicia or abroad and for their descendants through its "Atopadoiro" ("finding-meeting space"). The site's collaborators and users say that they have no political or partisan orientation since their only aim is to defend the rights of emigrants and to function as a virtual connection between the Galician diaspora and *Galicia territorial* (*FAQ*). However, they want to fill the void of emigrant participation in Galicia's reality through a more prominent political agenda.

In October 2001, before the elections to seats in the Galician parliament, the organization presented its first petition to representatives of every Galician political party (Beiras of the BNG, Pérez Touriño of PSdeG, and Palmou of PPdeG) as well as to other important political figures and the president of the then Consellaría da Emigración. The petition was grounded on the historical reality of Galician emigration and its social, economical, and cultural effects on Galician territory, but it also demanded recognition of the emigrants' rights and requested the possibility to participate in Galician political life through the establishment of a position for a *defensor do emigrante* ("emigrants' advocate"), who would be elected by popular vote and ensure that the initiatives proposed by the emigrants themselves were carried out ("Los hijos").

In June 2002, Fillos de Galicia presented an urgent petition to all Spanish senators and to the president of the Xunta requesting they "[no] nieguen nuestros derechos a la nacionalidad española" (Petición; "[do not] deny our right to Spanish nationality"). The petition was signed by over a thousand people through the online journal *A nosa voz* (now *Planeta galego*) and requested that the Spanish government eliminate the requirement for citizens to have their legal residence in Spain and abolish the requirement for entry visas for citizens of countries "con mayor vinculación histórica con España" ("with greater historical connection with Spain").[6] A third petition was sent to the new Galician government after the 2005 elections, requesting that the change of the Consellaría da Emigración to the Secretaría Xeral de Emigración would not mean a reduction of support for the emigrant community. The petition also requested an increase in the political participation of emigrants and their descendants. The specific demand was that emigrants in other Spanish autonomies be given the same voting rights as emigrants abroad ("Un manifesto . . . dirixido"). Whether these demands are met or not, as Kirsty Hooper has observed, the issues are highly debatable since "[u]nderpinning all of the discussion is the question of what it means to be Galician at all" ("Galicia" 171). Notwithstanding these political actions, the Internet site is charged with a deep affective tone that calls for identification between "wandering Galicians" and those who have remained in Galicia. In other words, the members of Fillos de Galicia have created a platform that offers not only the possibility to find the emigrants' relatives but also the opportunity to recognize themselves as emigrants and create a sense of unity.[7]

A main difference among *Fillos.org*, *Galicia aberta*, and the Arquivo is that in order to have access to the resources of the first two, all you need is an Internet connection and a chair in front of a computer, as Conde said, while to study the materials of the archive it is still necessary to travel to Santiago de Compostela (although they are doing a great job in digitalizing texts and giving access to them online, there is still much to consult at the archive). Another difference is the target audience of each medium: both Web sites are directed toward emigrants and their descendants, but the archive is an institutional tool only for those who are doing research and looking for statistical data.[8]

Traditionally literature has been considered a privileged discourse, which, in accordance with Kaplan, means it does not give a true voice to the agents of migration, yet two literary texts offer a more balanced analysis of the Galician emigration experience. The first, Risco's *Memorias dun emigrante* (winner of the Premio de la Crítica in 1986), explores the role of absence as a space of localization or territorialization in Galician identity. It comprises eleven fantastic short stories. Although they relate to Risco's personal experiences during his residency in the United States and Canada, memory fictionalization takes over the real, and the stories exacerbate the distance between Galicia as a localized or territorialized space and emigration as a space of displacement and deterritorialization. Risco's work argues for the impossibility of explicitly narrating the emigration experience; the stories occur not only in imagined but also in fantastic places. Risco sees the fantastic genre as that

> en que lo extranatural se enfrenta con lo natural produciendo una perturbación mental, de cierto orden, en algunos de los personajes que viven la experiencia y, en segundo término, en el lector.   (*Literatura* 139)

> in which the extranatural confronts the natural, producing a sort of mental confusion of some sort, in some of the characters who live through the experience and, subsequently, in the reader.

In other words, he agrees with Tzvetan Todorov in suggesting that fantastic literature offers a rupture from everyday reality through an extraordinary event that destabilizes characters and readers alike. Although Risco is recognized as one of Galicia's most important scholars of the fantastic genre, his literary work has not received the same critical attention.[9]

Memorias dun emigrante poses a key question: How can we interpret a fantastic text whose title implies an autobiography? In the prologue, Risco frames the short stories in the realm of his personal memories as an emigrant:

> Todas as memorias encomenzan sempre polo final. E se son as dun emigrante, nada hai máis lóxico e natural que, tomando pé e pulo nese final, encomenzar coa mesma emigración que é o feito que as xustifica.   (9)

> All memories always begin at the end. And if they are an emigrant's memories, nothing is more logical and natural than, by embracing that ending, to begin with the emigration itself, which is what justifies their existence.

Yet he defines emigration as an experience from which it is necessary to survive, relating it directly to the writing process:

> [S]e narra sempre, á forza, dende a outra beira, a definitiva, nun Alén incógnito que fica fóra do tempo e do espacio e que permite unha ollada totalizadora, absoluta, sobre o universo lembrado. (9)

> [O]ne always narrates by force, from the other shore, the definitive one, in an unknown Faraway that is outside time and space and that allows a totalizing, absolute gaze, over the remembered universe.

The connection between emigration and narration (esp. fantastic narration) is crucial to understand Risco's text. Emigration is a rupture from reality that puts the emigrant in a fantastic space and therefore in a space of constant doubt and absent memory.

The text does not distinguish between emigration and narration as discursive tools of the fantastic but rather weaves them to represent a conception of Galician emigration and identity. Like Rivas in *A man dos paíños*, Risco sees emigration as a defining characteristic of Galician identity:

> [S]er galego significa vivir nos confíns, tocando en todo tempo a beira do mundo, a derradeira marxe, e aspirando, por iso, o inquietante arrecendo do outro lado, no que se non pode saber o que hai. Así vivimos no fin da terra, nun país marxinal e marxinado por todos, feito fundamentalmente de ausencias. (*Memorias* 10)

> [B]eing Galician means living on the edge, always touching the edge of the world, the final margin, and breathing, for that reason, the unsettling smell of the other side, where it's impossible to know what's there. That's how we live at the end of the world, in a marginal country wholly marginalized, made fundamentally from absences.

It is in this absence that emigration and the act of writing meet, which suggest that such absence drives the need to create a localized space of identity. The stories of *Memorias dun emigrante* represent the quest for such a place.

In "A descuberta" ("The Discovery"), the first story, the narrator is in a plane and, landing, glimpses United States territory. Leaving Galicia behind becomes real to him only when he finds himself face to face with the new country. He reacts with surprise: "Que a América se me apareceu de súpeto, dende o avión, coma o mesmo baleiro vougo" (13; "America suddenly appeared in front of me, from the plane, like a very empty wasteland"). He knows that he is leaving his homeland but is not ready for the physicality of the new place. His voyage to the new and unknown increases his awareness of being far from the old and known. He cannot deal with reality, since the difference between old and new appears as "a dreamlike world in which the everyday suddenly transmutes into the weird" (Bourne Taylor 90). Both distance and absence are increased:

> A imaxinarme estaba nun foguete espacial que a órbita da terra abandonara para explorar un astro morto, e nos meus adentros crecía a saudade da cara tan familiar, tan amable, tan entrañable do noso planeta. Trataba eu de concentrarme e de analizar polo miúdo aquela extraña sensación completamente nova da que era obxeto e que, a título provisorio nomeaba, un pouco pedantemente (e aínda un moito), "tristura espacial" o "tristura cósmica." (A. Risco, *Memorias* 14)

> I imagined I was in a space rocket that had left earth's orbit to explore a dead star, and inside me there welled up a nostalgia for the familiar, friendly, likable face of our planet. I was trying to concentrate and analyze that strange new sensation that I was experiencing and that I called, provisionally and somewhat (or very) pedantically, "space sadness" or "cosmic sadness."

The distance between the narrator and his homeland is not great enough; his imagination intensifies the separation by making him see the new place not only as completely different from what he knows but also as an alienating or uncanny space. America represents not only the unknown but also what is impossible to know and therefore must be invented. When the plane lands for a layover in New York City, the narrator has the opportunity to explore the inhospitable territory. He and his wife take a taxi from the airport to the city, immersing themselves in the new space, which they do not want to belong to but whose existence they must verify, since earlier he wondered what would happen if New York was erased from the planet during his transatlantic flight (14).

When the taxi drops them off in front of the Empire State Building, the city becomes more concrete yet remains dehumanized, blurred by a dreamlike state that reflects the impossibility of owning the experience: "Na miña somnolenta fatiga imaxinábame un teimado rebulir activo de espectros e esqueletos a castañolar e renxer naquelas encaixoadas avenidas" (14; "In my drowsy fatigue I imagined a fearsome commotion of specters and skeletons grinding and clacking like castanets along those closed-in avenues"). The lack of contact with the locals (mostly emigrants themselves) intensifies an emotional and linguistic distance that prevents the transient Galicians from really knowing the geographic space. The absence of human contact emphasizes the absence of a collective experience and corroborates what the narrator imagined: New York is a real place but beyond his understanding.

Back in the plane and heading toward his final destination of Portland, Oregon, the narrator concludes that America will allow him to "experimentar materialmente, por primeira vez na [súa] vida, que as ideas son un puro producto da distancia" (18; "physically experience, for the first time in [his] life, that ideas are purely the product of distance"). Distance thus acquires a physicality and is presented as a space "famento, devorador, como a rapariga que collendo flores para tecerse unha cora esperta a un monstro inimaxinable que estaba alí agachado, oculto" (18; "hungry, devouring, like the girl who, when picking up flowers to make herself a crown, awakens an unimaginable monster that was crouched there, hidden"). This feeling reduces the narrator's ability to differentiate between the physical and the absent. He cannot separate his emotions from the new, unknown place and confesses being "perdido no [s]eu propio labirinto cerebral" (21; "lost in his own cerebral labyrinth"). He has "a impresión de bogar ao chou polo aire, de fundir[s]e interminablemente nel, baleiro coma un globo, ou de prospeitar o interior dun caleidoscopio" ("the sense of sailing aimlessly through the air, of mingling inextricably with it, empty as a balloon, or of looking into the inside of a kaleidoscope"), which demonstrates that when one is faced with distance and absence, one's imagination comes to the rescue (21).

While the title and first story suggest that *Memorias dun emigrante* is a biographical text, some of the stories seem to have nothing to do with emigration. They immerse the reader in spaces that overcome reality, making fantasy "unha sorte de exorcismo liberador"(24; "a sort of liberating exorcism"). Nevertheless, Risco cannot escape from his experience; in the last story of the collection, which closes the migration cycle, "Ningures" ("Nowhere"), his life as an emigrant prevails. Although "Ningures" takes place in Ourense (Risco's homeland), the emigration experience is the center of the narration. The first-person narrator gives the impression that Risco himself is talking, which connects the reader with the collection's title. "Risco" and his friend Xulio meet in Ourense after many years of not seeing each other because both had been abroad: Xulio lived in Geneva, "Risco" in Canada. Their meeting awakens their desire to remember the past (young lovers, the rain, walks in the fog, etc.). Among their memories, an excursion to "un lugar incerto que por iso chama[ban] Ningures" ("an uncertain place that was therefore called Nowhere") in inland Galicia (*Galicia territorial*) surpasses the rest (164). The desire to return to this idyllic place becomes the premise of the story. Through a retrospective lens, "Risco" describes Ningures as tiny but enchanting; at the same time, it becomes "a concreción súpeta e inexplicable" ("the sudden and explicable embodiment") of myths and of

> dos enigmas da historia, do tempo, das comunidades humans, das culturas, a atracción das Atlántidas, dos continentes o cidades sulagadas nos lagos, mares ou pasados—todo, ao fin, moi preto dese sentimento sen nome que é a saudade—como a fabulosa Antioquía que gardaba no seu fondo lamosa a xa desecada lagoa de Antela. (167)

> the enigmas of history, of time, of human communities, of cultures, the attraction of the islands of Atlantis, of continents or cities swallowed up by lakes, seas, or the past—all, in the end, very close to that nameless feeling that is *saudade*—like the fabulous Antioch that is concealed in its moldy depths by the dried-up lake of Antela.

The presence of a mythified and nostalgic past suggests that Risco believes the past is ideal yet unreachable. Both distance and emigration have buried memories, but memories are kept alive by the feeling of longing. If, as Jonathan Steinwand suggests, "[t]he vagueness of the recollection often inspires idealization of [the] past," then nostalgia "summons the imagination to supplement memory" (9).

One might extrapolate Edward Said's argument about exile to emigration. Said argues that distance or absence is "the unhealable rift forced between a human being and a native place, between the self and its true home," and therefore "its essential sadness can never be surmounted." Any narrative that talks about emigration as an idealized space is an attempt "meant to overcome the crippling sorrow of estrangement," which will always make the migration experience seem "undermined by the loss of something left behind forever" (159). In the short story, the trip Xulio and "Risco" make to find Ningures becomes one of destruction. That the two friends never make it to Ningures shows the impossibility of returning to the past—they almost die in a forest fire. The ending criticizes the desire to return to a better past. One of the two friends (it is not possible to tell who is speaking) comments:

> Hai que andar con ollo con estas cousas. Faise un mito, víveo sen darse de conta e velaí de súpeto que este se impón non se sabe como nin porqué e que pode mesmo atinguir dimensións heroicas e tráxicas. (A. Risco, *Memorias* 175)

> You have to tread carefully with these things. You turn it into a myth, you live it without realizing it, and then suddenly you find out it has taken over without your knowing how or why, and it can even reach heroic and tragic dimensions.

The allusion is clear to Galician history and culture as "producto da fábula, dunha o moitas mitoloxías" (175; "the product of a fable, or one or many mythologies"). However, as in all the other stories, the ending surprises. The two friends get lost in the fog and smoke and end up in "un lugar moi extraño, dun aspecto moi pouco galego" ("a very strange place, which didn't look at all Galician") and which neither has seen before (176).

The unstable narrative seems to suggest that, as Said argues, absence is "life led outside habitual order. It is nomadic, decentered, contrapuntal; but no sooner does one get accustomed to it then its unsettling force erupts anew" (172). That Xulio and "Risco" get lost at night and cannot see each other represents Galicia not only as unknown but also as impossible to get to know again. If this ending leaves the reader asking the unanswerable question "¿Que foi de [eles]?" (A. Risco, *Memorias* 177; "What happened to them?"), the idea of reaching "nowhere" points precisely to the absence either of a physical place to call one's own or of a collective experience of emigration for all Galicians. Galicia is transformed from a physical space into a fantastic, narrated place, and the experience of emigration is erased or suppressed. Meanwhile the need is emphasized to listen to individual accounts of emigration, since, as Kaplan argues, "[a]ll displacements are not the same" (2).

Rivas's *A man dos paíños* (or *La mano del emigrante* ["The Emigrant's Hand"] in its Spanish translation) maintains a clear and direct relation between the emigration experience and the impossibility of talking or writing about it without resorting to fictionalization. It too follows the conventions of fantastic literature. From the beginning, the book opens a space for a plurality of voices and literary genres, because it comprises a short novel, a photo album, and a journalistic account.[10] Rivas presents, on the one hand, emigration as a Galician territory and, on the other, absence as the creative or constructing motivation of Galician identity. He supports the existence of two Galicias, both because the narrative action occurs inside and outside Galician territory and because talking about *galeguidade* on these terms presupposes two poles that collapse, creating a void (or absence) of identity. Rivas recently wrote, "Non se pode entender Galicia sen América. Non se pode entender Galicia sen a emigración, para a que se inventou o eufemismo de 'residentes ausentes'" ("Proposición"; "It is not possible to understand Galicia without America. It is not possible to understand Galicia without emigration, since the euphemism 'absent residents' was invented to refer to it"). *A man dos paíños* takes emigration as a defining quality of *galeguidade*, arguing that unavoidable longing or *saudade* is a fundamental symbol of Galician identity. The relation between emigration and home is presented through its unquestionable fragmented structure and through *saudade* or *morriña* (the other Galician word for the concept). According to Cristina Moreiras-Menor, in this text Rivas

> deconstructs marks of national identity (in this case, *morriña*), giving habitation to its ghosts (its absences), and revealing the instabilities of the nation. He returns to the national past in order to narrativize the history of the absent *émigrés* who transport the frontiers of the land in their silent stories. Galicia is no longer the area bordering Portugal, Spain, and the Atlantic. Rather, it is formed through a mixture of those Galicians who depart and those who remain, all of them living with *morriña* and with multiple loss.
>
> ("Galicia" 117)

The first part of the text, from which it takes its title, is a short novel that narrates the experiences of two Galician emigrants in London in the 1980s, their close friendship, and the car accident that kills one emigrant and transforms the other. The second part is a photo album entitled "O álbum furtivo" ("Furtive Album"). Rivas explains in his introduction to the Spanish version that the photos were taken with disposable cameras and with an old broken camera that he cared for very much (*La mano* 10). In this album, he tells a story through the eyes of an emigrant, making that gaze the main character (10). The final part is a collection of journalistic essays or interviews with shipwrecked Galician fishermen, called "Os náufragos" ("The Shipwrecked Sailors"). Rivas gives voice to those who, like emigrants, find themselves constantly traveling along the border that divides the real and the fantastic, attachment and loss. He calls the weaving together of diverse narratives "el contrabando de géneros" (8; "genre contraband"). His text allows us to understand the construction of Galician identity as a similar weaving between the two Galicias, produced by the constant migrations.

"A man dos paíños" is the story of Tito Castro and the narrator, whose name we never discover.[11] They meet at Saint Thomas's Hospital in London, where they work as stretcher-bearers. One day, on their way to the airport to return to Galicia for the Christmas holiday, a car accident takes Castro's life and leaves the narrator with multiple injuries, including a severed hand (*A man* 31). At the hospital, doctors are able to reattach the hand, but the narrator wakes up from surgery believing it is his friend's. Even before the accident, the narrator was obsessed with Castro's hand: "a man de Castro exercía para min un atractivo hipnótico" (11; "Castro's hand had a hypnotic attraction for me"); "Marabíllabame a súa man" (13; "His hand astounded me"). He was attracted by Castro's tattoo of two little petrels that "[c]ando a man se pecha, ocúltanse nunha furna" ("when the hand is clenched, they hide in a crevice"). The tattoo of the petrels, "[a] derradeira compaña do mariñeiro" (14; "the sailor's last companions"), establishes a relation between emigration and the lifestyle of these birds, which "vive[n] todo o ano en mar aberto . . . voan a rentes da auga e parecen camiñar sobre ela" (9; "spend all year on the open sea . . . they fly along the water and seem to walk on it"), as it is stated in the novel's epigraphs. The petrels remain constantly close to the sea yet never seem to touch the water; they live their lives on the sea's surface or outside of the one space that constitutes their lives. That is how the text presents the emigrant lives of Castro and the narrator. The tattoo of the birds on Castro's hand symbolizes the desire for a new life as well as the land that has been abandoned. Both characters are displaced, and this condition makes them exclaim, "¡A miña patria é un hospital!" (16; "my homeland is a hospital!"), since they are away from Galicia and there is no other space they can call their own.

The text presents the emigrant's life as a perpetual state of nostalgia or *saudade*. As Roberta Rubenstein suggests, the imposition of physical distance increases the emotional detachment the emigrant suffers; nostalgia becomes "painful awareness, the expression of grief for something lost, the absence of which continues to produce significant emotional distress" (5). The pain of loss is not only the separation of something or someone but also an absence that creates a feeling of displacement. *Saudade* is the result of separation and loss that manifests as "[u]nha forma malsá de melancolía que, ás veces, cruzaba o limiar da porta do Old Crow" ("an unhealthy form of melancholy that sometimes even crosses the threshold of the Old Crow"), as the narrator says about their local bar (Rivas, *A man* 12). However, while nostalgia was "[a]lgo difícil de detectar para os demais" ("hard to see for others"), Castro and the narrator were able to recognize "co tempo . . . a chegada do pasado" (12; "in time . . . the arrival of the past").

It is thanks to the narrator's belief that his hand is actually his friend's that the reconstruction of Castro's life begins when the narrator takes his ashes back to Galicia. The hand, though separated from its owner, is a living being in itself, with its own history. It "[é] o lugar onde Castro está agora, as súas vísceras latexando, os seus ollos axexantes, as súas bocas abocando" (13; "is where Castro is now, his pumping guts, his watchful eyes, his pecking mouths"). It symbolizes not only the hidden desire to appropriate Castro's life but also the direct relation between *saudade* and Galician emigration. Rubenstein suggests that nostalgia is always associated with the physiological and psychological pain of loss. As Moreiras-Menor argues about Rivas's texts, it

> seeks to recover the sediments accumulated throughout a long experience of loss—unspeakable in the paralysis of *morriña*—in order to integrate in the present a nation which collectively forms itself from a permanently dislocated frontier.   (112)

In *saudade* there is a continued desire to recuperate what was lost, returning to an original home that exists only in an imagined place.

Confronted with Castro's death and away from Galicia, the narrator believes that his new hand allows him to remember things about his life that he had completely forgotten:

> Os daquela convalecencia foron días moi importantes na miña vida. Entre a man e a cabeza empezou a establecerse un entendemento. A man fíxome pensar na miña forma de ser. Es como un cangrexo emitán, metido na caracola, dixérame unha vez Castro. Tes que abrirte ao mundo. E niso estaba. Os paíños subían brazo arriba, polos nervos, e pairaban na cabeza. As enfermeiras que me tiñan por un túzaro, sorprendéronse co meu cambio de humor. De mozo era moi bailarín. Tamén iso mo fixo recordar a man.   (37)

> The days of my convalescence were the most important of my life. An understanding emerged between my hand and my head. The hand made me think about my way of being. You're like a hermit crab, hidden in its shell, Castro once said. You have to open yourself up to the world. And that's what was happening. The birds were flying up my arm, along the nerves, and they stopped at my head. The nurses had taken me for a troublemaker and were surprised at my changing mood. As a young man I'd been quite a dancer. The hand reminded me of that too.

As the narrator reconstructs his life in relation to Castro's, the reader forgets that the narrator is the survivor and that Castro has died. The narrator's desire to appropriate Castro's hand and life suggests the impossibility of narrating one's own life as an emigrant. Castro's hand, taking over both narrator and reader, becomes a presence of absence, in which "the absence . . . continues to occupy a palpable emotional space" (Rubenstein 5). Moreiras-Menor also argues that the fractured narrative of Rivas's novel, as the borders between past and present and between Galicia and London are erased, reveals two stories: Castro's and the narrator's (113). But I contend that it is precisely this border erasure that blurs the frontier between the two stories, presenting only one: any Galician emigrant's story.

The photo album is composed of twenty-four photographs. In the introduction to the Spanish edition, Rivas claims to tell the story of a migrating glance or look, wondering, "¿Cómo emigra una mirada? ¿Dónde deposita su afecto, su melancolía?" (*La mano* 10; "How does a gaze migrate? Where does it leave its affection, its melancholy?"). But Roland Barthes argues in *Camera Lucida*, "Whatever it grants to vision and whatever its manner, a photograph is always invisible: it is not it that we see" (6). What makes this album relevant is not the photographs themselves but what Rivas wants to tell us with them. The album functions as the *punctum*, using Barthes's term: it is the "accident" that "pricks me (but also bruises me, is poignant to me)" (27). The album-and-postcard collection that appeared in the first edition (which is a small selection of the whole album) become the elements that "[rise] from the scene [or the emigration experience], shoots out of it like an arrow, and [pierce]" the reader (26).

"O álbum furtivo" tells of a migrating gaze, yet it lacks several important elements. Even though this archive (unlike the Arquivo da Emigración Galega) intends to identify readers with the life of the emigrant, the emigrant himself is missing. As Yeon-Soo Kim argues, "[C]reating a documentary of lives of the immigrants is not the photographer's primary objective" (118). The photographs attempt to re-create a journey from Visma to London, but Rivas's gaze lacks a *punctum*; his view is erratic and depends on the novel to tell the story. That each picture has a relation, direct or indirect, to the events narrated in the novel complicates the reading of the album and prompts another reading of the novel. For instance, picture 9, "Hospital desde Ladbroke Grove" ("Hospital from Ladbrake Grove"), reminds us of the hospital where Castro and the narrator worked; picture 11, "Funeraria de Kensal Rise" ("Kensal Rise's Funeral Home"), makes us think Castro could have been in this funeral home; and picture 21, "Axencia de Viaxes de Portobello" ("Portobello's Travel Agency"), reminds us of the flight the two men booked to return to Galicia. Therefore the album "operates prosthetically to the narrative, complementing the text" (Kim 118). David Levi Strauss writes:

> Every photograph is an act amid a complex structure of choices. These choices, which extend beyond the time of the photograph, influence the photograph before, during, and after its instant. Reading photographs in context is a participation in this complex. (33)

The idea that a photograph must be read or interpreted in a particular context helps us understand that the album's narrative is dependent on the novel. Although the images refer directly to the Galician context and Galician emigrants in London, we need the story of Castro to be able to weave the photographs together into the story of a migrating gaze.

Rivas's inclusion of the word "furtive" in the title of the album problematizes the story of a migrating gaze. The reader wonders if the gaze could have focused elsewhere. We are brought back to the key question about photography, which is whether we can believe what we see (Levi Strauss 71). But in this case we do not doubt what the photographs communicate, since the album wraps them with "credibility" (74). The order of visual narration makes this collection the emigrant's album. The album could not exist without the attempt to represent the emigrant's gaze, without the story being told through the photographs. Rivas's album forces the reader to put together the pieces of the story, just as the narrator in "A man dos paíños" does with Castro's life. The gaze of the album is therefore woven and confused with the novel's narration. Furthermore, because the reader's and emigrant's gazes are woven together, it is impossible to separate the concrete experience from the fiction and consequently impossible to talk about the migration experience except in fictional terms.[12]

Because of the fictional nature of the novel and the photographic album, it is difficult to approach the last section of the text with the belief that Rivas is actually presenting us with a journalistic account. Rivas himself comments that "Os náufragos" is mostly his response to "la cuestión recurrente de lo real y de la 'verdad' en el periodismo y la literatura" (*La mano* 9; "the recurring question of reality and 'truth' in journalism and literature"). The narrative voice of this part gets lost in the first-person testimonies of Galician fishermen who suffered a shipwreck. Each of the nine protagonists is confused with the others. Usually it is impossible to distinguish whom each story is about. Testimony becomes a story, a fiction, to the point that readers cannot separate reality from fiction, their reading of the account from their role in the reconstruction of it. Just as the shipwrecked fishermen think of home at the time of the accident, readers become lost in the winding fantastic paths of anecdote and testimony. Folkart sees Rivas's strategy of weaving

> the truth of shipping tales with the fiction of his own writing by repeating motifs, sayings, and folkloric tales between the two written narratives in the book [as similar to the] intertextual reiteration of "O álbum furtivo" and "A man dos paíños," with their recurrence of images depicted first with words and then with pictures.
>
> (23)

Rivas's strategy, in which the past and the present get tangled at a critical moment for each of the shipwrecked fishermen, is similar to the organization of the stories in relation to the movement between the real and the fictional. The stories of these men and women get confused (or woven) with Castro's story and with the tale told by the migrating gaze from the album.

A man dos paíños is a text in which literary and visual genres combine, creating a hybrid space that calls for the recuperation of a collective memory that belongs to Galician identity. It allows a dialogue, albeit fragmented, between past and present and between fiction and reality. As in *Memorias dun emigrante*, Rivas's narrative strategies focus on the tension between the emigration experience and how it is told (or not). Both *Memorias dun emigrante* and *A man dos paíños* evoke a circular time in which life repeats itself and the borders between Galicia and emigration are erased through the localization of an absence that is identity. *Saudade,* implied in Risco's text and explicit in Rivas's, narrates the tangible experience of migration life while also mythifying national identity through distance. Moreiras-Menor calls these "spectral presences" that "give shape, not always through words but through traumatized texts, to a present experience colored by loss and attachment" (111). The object that originates *saudade*—Castro, the gaze, or Galicia itself—is erased and replaced by longing, which in turn emphasizes the absence of a space to call home.

The connection with a past that exists only as narration, locked into a fictional plane, is maintained through the construction of absence. It is precisely this conception of Galician identity as constant absence that allows me to speak of two Galicias. The Arquivo da Emigración Galega, the portal *Galicia aberta*, and the Internet site of Fillos de Galicia, along with the two texts analyzed in this essay, represent a *galeguidade* that moves constantly between attachment and loss, Galicia and emigration, reality and fiction, and scientific and public access to the stories of migration. In other words, the emigrants' platform through *Fillos.org, Memorias dun emigrante,* and *A man dos paíños* all restore the absent voices of Galicians in emigration, counteracting what is being done institutionally by the Consello da Cultura Galega, the Arquivo, the Secretaría Xeral de Emigración, and *Galicia aberta.* If, as we have seen, fantasy functions as the discursive and narrative tool of emigration, articulating the consequences of the desire to move between the geographic territory and the abstract emigration, then the impossibility of speaking about the experience creates the tension that appears between the territory and the emigration.

Notes

1. For more information about the different phases and characteristics of Galician migration, see Rodríguez-Galdo; Villares and Fernández Santiago; Cagiao Vila and García Domínguez; and Núñez Seixas.
2. For an analysis of Galician emigration and its role within the Galician imaginary, see my article "Amusement Parks."
3. Rivas's original Galician title was translated into Spanish as *La mano del emigrante* (2001; "The Emigrant's Hand").
4. All translations from Galician or Spanish are my own.
5. From its foundation in 1997 until February 2008, Casal Lodeiro was president of Fillos de Galicia. In 2008, he became the secretary of the organization, and Alejandro López was elected president.
6. In 2002, the Spanish Civil Code was amended to recognize the right of nationality to the children of those of Spanish origin born in Spain (including Galicians). In December 2008, a new disposition of the Ley 52/2007 or Ley de Memoria Histórica ("Law of Historical Memory") grants Spanish nationality (including the right to vote) to those whose parents (either mother or father) were of Spanish origin even though they were not born in Spain. This new law allows the grandchildren of emigrants whose children were born in another country to vote once the grandchildren turn eighteen, whether or not they live or have lived in Spain. There is one condition: in order to qualify, the parent of the grandchild applying for Spanish nationality must have been born before the grandparent renounced his or her Spanish nationality. The only ones exempt from this condition are the grandchildren of those who had to resign their Spanish nationality because of exile after the civil war (between 18 July 1936 and the end of 1955).
7. On 20 December 2006, Fillos.org updated its data, and the numbers were staggering. Over 4,000 members are registered on the site: 1,488 are children of Galician emigrants, 1,189 are grandchildren, and about 770 are Galicians still residing in Galicia.

Most of the members (about 1,450) currently reside in Argentina, about 1,030 live in Spain, about 300 are in Brazil, and about 190 live in the United States. In February 2009, Fillos.org reported that there were 6,361 registered users (Souto).

8. The future of *Fillos.org* is uncertain. In June 2010, Fillos de Galicia called for the dismantling of the Web site, partly because of economic hardship and the lack of support from governmental or civic institutions. The recently elected board of Fillos de Galicia put the site's contents up for sale after their project "Un futuro para fillos" ("A Future for Fillos") failed to find any type of support to carry on with the organization's objectives ("O desmantelamento").

9. This lack of attention may be due to his limited creative production (fifteen short stories and novels) in comparison with his literary theory and criticism (twenty books and more than one hundred articles). Also, though an emigrant himself, he had no access to the traditionally well-established migration chains between Galicians and was marginalized from the emigrant groups with political and editorial power (i.e., Galicians in Latin America). Finally, he was overshadowed by his father, Vicente Risco, a theorist and icon of Galician nationalism. For a bibliography of Risco's work, see Fariña and Troncoso.

10. The change in title from Galician to Spanish edition offers a dialogue not only between two different markets but also between two versions. The Galician title specifically describes the protagonist's hand, which has a tattoo of two *painos* (small petrels native to the Galician coast); the Spanish title, *La mano del emigrante,* alludes to the hand of any emigrant and therefore to anonymity. Along with this linguistic difference, the Spanish version has a prologue written by the author (similar to the one written by Risco), in which Rivas attempts to explain both the content and the purpose of the book. It can be argued that the author, by including this explanation, is conscious that readers who do not speak Galician need certain references to understand his text, while he assumes that Galician readers will understand everything that happens in the Galician version. Note that Risco's text has not been translated into Spanish, which brings it closer to the Arquivo's limiting view, while Rivas's text, translated, is accessible to Galicians and Spanish speakers alike. The difference is not unlike that between Fillos de Galicia and *Galicia aberta.*

11. Castro's name places the character in the context of Galician history. A *castro* is a hill fort commonly found in Galicia. It is also a "peñasco que avanza de la costa hacia el mar, o que sobresale aislado en este y próximo a aquella" ("Castro"; "rocky outcrop sticking out of the coastline toward the sea or standing isolated in the sea and close to the coast"). There is no doubt, either, of the connection with Rosalía de Castro and her works, as symbol of all that is Galician.

12. For a detailed analysis of individual photographs of the album, see Kim; Folkart.

Galician-Spanish-British?
Migrant Identification Practices, Transnationalism, and Invisibility in Guildford, England

Jaine Beswick

In this essay I examine the potential for a hyphenated Galician-Spanish-British migrant identification strategy, combining (Galician) ethnic origins with allegiances to (Spanish and British) state contexts, with particular reference to Galicians living and working in the suburban British town of Guildford, Surrey. My empirical research was carried out over a period of four months in early 2006 and used three empirical data collection techniques: semistructured ethnographic interviews with seven Galician acquaintances and with twelve participants who work in the center of Guildford; interview field notes taken after each encounter; and direct ethnographic observations of the linguistic practices of participants in daily social and cultural activities carried out at home and at work. To begin, I offer a brief overview of historical facts relevant to the sociolinguistic manifestation of hyphenated identities, particularly in migrant contact scenarios. My focus throughout is on movement away from internal or local spaces (Galicia) toward external or global spaces (Guildford).

I frame my initial discussion by brief reference to some of the more pertinent wider debates from which the issue of migrant identification emerges, such as those about diaspora and transnationalism and their relevance to globalization and contemporary migration, as well as to the significance of multiple and hyphenated definitions of identity. I also consider the role of language as a potential symbol of identity and the consequences of attitudinal factors on sociocultural and sociolinguistic perceptions of ethnic and other identities. I then highlight the relative invisibility of Galician migrants throughout Europe and particularly in the United Kingdom, both in the media and in academic works, to develop my hypothesis that the Galicians themselves adopt concealment strategies from the outside world.

Transnational Identities

The concept of transnationalism and its relevance to the study of migrant identification strategies are essential to an understanding of the Galician context, since the issue of Galician movement away from the homeland (Romero, *Las dos Galicias* 277–78) and the very nature of the ongoing relationship between Galicians at home and abroad (Hooper, "Galicia" 172) are starting to inform contemporary debates surrounding the description of a modern, ethnic identity for Galicians. As I argue below, Galician migratory patterns may be characterized by a shift in perception of self and in the relationship between autochthonous and acquired identities.

The advent of transnationalism as a global force is a result of the increase in multiple links, interactions, and bonds among communities across borders and frontiers. As a social, political, and economic movement, it facilitates the passage of people, ideas, and goods across and between such boundaries.[1] Before the emergence of a transnational perspective, prevailing receptor-society migration discourse and policy tended to assume that migrants, by consciously breaking ties with their native soil, committed themselves to being acculturated and assimilated into a new, receptor society.[2] Achieving cultural and linguistic homogeneity was seen as necessary in order to maintain national stability. Even if this homogeneity also led to the loss of migrants' sociocultural and sociolinguistic values, the hypothesis was that ethnic division and the marginalization of minority groups would be eradicated as a result. Initial conceptualizations of diaspora theory challenged this idea; more important, they also countered the notion that migration always entailed a definitive break from the homeland (e.g., see Safran's dual territory approach). Contemporary migration and settlement patterns also often imply multidimensional transnational relations rather than the maintenance of discrete ethnic groupings.[3] Relationships and ties may be established between migrants, their places of origin and reception, and the particular receptor society in question. These relationships are subject to proactive, constant, and continual appraisal and evaluation by the migrants themselves (Kivisto). In this way, migrants may be engaged in the bidirectional process of preserving certain ethnic, sociocultural, and sociolinguistic practices while divesting themselves of others; at the same time, they may adopt alternatives from the receptor society.

Transnational lives thus obscure and even ignore the boundaries of both social and geographic space[4] and often find profound expression through the manipulation of both internal, ethnic identities and external, acquired identities, as well as through the use of and attitudes toward different social and cultural practices, customs, and languages. Our perception of who we are as individuals often focuses on recognition and appreciation of our origins, of where we come from and of what we share with our autochthonous community (Beswick, *Regional Nationalism* 32). These self-identification strategies are an important dimension of communal ethnicity, in that ethnicity refers to an individual's membership in a multidimensional social group sharing a common ancestral heritage (Padilla 115). However, identity is not just an essentialized concept, a form of inherent self (or other) awareness. As Mike Holt and Paul Gubbins (1–2) and others have maintained, it is also a socially constructed phenomenon, fluid, dynamic, and subject to change. Complex and multiple identities are the norm and can be assumed or abandoned as required, for they differ in their relative significance and import. In this way, loyalties to particular identification strategies are not necessarily divided, since inherent and borrowed qualities and traits are not mutually exclusive but may be layered or overlap each other, hence the notion of mixed or hyphenated identities. Migrants' experiences and perceptions, as well as their ancestry, define who they are and who they perceive themselves to be: identities thus may be partially inherent and partially shaped by circumstance.

Of course, such complex identities may encompass traits other than those pertaining to ethnicity and nationhood, such as gender, race, and creed. But in this essay I examine the idea that hyphenated identities typically conflate allegiances to idiosyncratic ethnic and cultural origins with those to the overarching, multicultural, multiethnic receptor nation. In this sense they tend to be double-barreled terms, pairing the ancestral epithet with that of the wider context, as in *African-American*, *Irish-American*, and *Indian-British*. For the Galician migrants under discussion here, ethnic and cultural origins are closely linked to their home territories in Galicia, to the historical and political context of the Spanish nation-state, and to the UK as adopted place of residence. I therefore contend that dislocated Galician migrants may negotiate a triple-barreled epithet—that is, a hyphenated Galician-Spanish-British identity that encompasses deeply embedded connections to ethnic origins, with allegiances to the wider framework of Spain and with the potential for an acquired sense of Britishness.

Language, Identity, and Attitude

Language choice has not always been feasible for migrants in a particular diaspora. Central to the essentialized character of nation-states, even in recent history, has been the political advancement and enforcement of a common language. Linguistic homogeneity was considered the way to minimize social and cultural differences that might engender intergroup discord; the use of a common language could thus mold and define the characterization and identification of the state within its territorial limits. Even when there is no legal requirement to learn and use the state language, often it may be pragmatic to do so, since not being able to use it in spoken interactions, at the very least, may be a barrier to employment and education in intergroup contact scenarios. However, barring severe censure or discrimination, even reasonably well integrated migrants may choose to express and reinforce their ethnic or cultural identities by the use of their autochthonous language in intragroup scenarios, such as the home, social clubs, and ethnic shops and cafés. Conversely, migrants may choose to play down such identification strategies in other contexts.[5] In either case, the selection of one language over another to fulfill a particular function is deliberate and may flout conventions regarding the notion of social and geographic space and language use in the receptor society.

A sense of solidarity in a migrant group may be achieved if most members share a positive, integrative attitude toward the use of their autochthonous language in such socialization practices (Beswick, *Regional Nationalism* 32–34, 41–43; Liebkind 144). When a language is fundamental to the group's ethnicity, it will acquire prestige as an important identifier of the group's dynamism, status, and distinctiveness. It affords meaning to a group because it connects the present with the past—through, for example, its oral traditions, literary forms, music, history, and culture. In this way, language is a core value, one of the "building blocks of the group's cultural identity" (Smolicz 67), which serves to emphasize the group's linguistic, social, or other form of differentiation. Such perceptions may reinforce aspirations of otherness, even when, for various reasons, they are implicitly rather than explicitly manifest—that is, largely unknown to the outside world. But language does not always play an important role in the conceptualization of group interfaces. Stephen May thinks that language is in most cases a contingent factor, not central to the maintenance of ethnic identity (8–9). For some migrants, it is often the sense of ethnic difference, rather than its manifestation through an autochthonous language, that remains distinctive (Cohen 16–17). Although autochthonous languages are often a viable representation of the continual negotiation of migrant group identification strategies, for Galician migrants in Guildford language is not necessarily a prerequisite for ethnic group membership.

Galician Migration: The Americas

The history of Galicia is irrevocably linked to both Portugal and Spain.[6] The autochthonous language shares its origins and early diachronic development with Portuguese, but Galicia's sociopolitical bonds are with Spain, since Galicia has been subsumed under the Spanish flag for over eight hundred years. This integration has had a significant effect on the language, not only in terms of its linguistic evolution but also in terms of its perceived status and prestige and its consequent use as a means of communication and as a viable and convincing demonstration of ethnic identity and solidarity in Galicia itself. By the nineteenth century, the hegemony of Spanish society and a Castilian linguistic identification strategy were deeply entrenched in the region's larger conurbations.[7] The emergence of *galeguismo*, a largely upper-class, culture-based movement that underlined and defended the interrelationship between ethnic, regional, and linguistic identity, together with the literary renaissance that followed, became synonymous with efforts to have Galician officially recognized as the autochthonous language. Since the focus of *galeguismo* was generally confined to the urban areas, the rural population remained largely ignorant of its aims and objectives. They continued to use Galician on a daily basis yet also maintained the acute sense of linguistic inferiority that had been fostered throughout the centuries.[8] Moreover, the economic crises that pervaded the agricultural and fishing industries in particular at this time undermine the efforts of the *galeguista* movement. The consequent exodus to the towns and cities exposed the rural migrants to the predominant and continual use of Castilian and reinforced the sense that Galician was an archaic, low-status vernacular, outmoded and inferior to Castilian. By the early twentieth century, the focus of the movement's resistance and regional nationalist activity in general had shifted to the migrant groups that were emerging outside Galicia, particularly in the Americas, as Eugenia Romero's essay in this volume demonstrates.[9]

This situation was exacerbated by the Spanish Civil War and Franco's dictatorship in the 1930s and 1940s. Although attempts were made to continue the struggle for political and social reform in Galicia, Franco's highly repressive measures almost paralyzed the *galeguista* movement and other regional nationalist activity in Spain. The imprisonment of leading academics and supporters of these movements led to the exodus of many notable political and literary intellectuals, primarily to Latin America and Brazil but also to France and eventually to the UK. Away from the threat of persecution, these hubs of political, social, and cultural activity reinforced a sense of historical conscience and political consciousness among the Galicians who settled there (Pensado 89–90). An overriding objective of the leaders of Galician regional nationalism was to nurture and maintain a sense of Galician ethnic identity, albeit somewhat essentialized in its focus, among these migrant groups. Migrants were thus encouraged to endorse and support Galician cultural activities. The transmission of the language to second- and third-generation Galicians was furthered by the introduction of language courses and by radio programs broadcast in Galician.

Galician Migration to Europe

One of the most significant forums for past and present research on Galician migration is the Arquivo da Emigración Galega ("Archive of Galician Emigration"), based in Santiago de Compostela and directed by the Consello da Cultura Galega ("Council of Galician Culture"). Since 1992, the archive has become a focus for research and inquiry into migration studies at the regional, national, and international levels. One of its principal activities is the publication of the periodical *Estudios migratorios* ("Migration Studies)," which brings together empirical studies on migration from around the world.[10] The value of such research, particularly regarding migration to the Americas, should not be underestimated, since it is a source of historical documentation and also emphasizes the continuing links between the homeland and migrant groups across the Atlantic.

To date, little of any real import has been researched, written, or otherwise documented specifically on the migration of Galicians to Europe. Although the political exodus was centered on the Americas, most economic migrants leaving Galicia during the twentieth century traveled only as far as other Spanish regions, such as Catalonia, or to other, primarily western European countries. Yet the Arquivo da Emigración Galega makes no mention of Galician migrants in Europe, and *Estudios migratorios* has so far included only three articles in this area: one on Spanish, Portuguese, and South American migration to Germany; one on the return of Galician migrants from the Americas to Galicia, and one on internal migration within the region itself (*Estudios*). Web sites and associations also focus on Galician migration to Central and South America, such as the Instituto Galego de Cooperación Iberoamericana ("Galician Institute for Iberoamerican Cooperation") and the government-sponsored site *Fundación Galicia emigración* ("Galician Emigration Foundation").

Sources of practical information for Galician migrants abroad, including data on social and cultural institutions and workers' groups, also tend to be based outside Europe; at the very least, they are more active outside Europe. Most societies have established Internet sites, with the aim of fostering a sense of a collective, global Galician community. For example, the Asociación Cultural Fillos de Galicia ("Cultural Association of the Sons and Daughters of Galicia") Web site has been designated a portal for such information, but although it lists centers in some European cities, such as Las Palmas in Gran Canaria, Brussels, Barcelona, Geneva, and London, most active and frequently visited centers are in the Americas, and there appears to be little visible transatlantic cross-communication among groups. Attempts at establishing links among diffuse Galician migrants in European cities through the use of the media, such as the creation of a Galician radio station in Geneva, have not been that successful, as far as audience numbers are concerned. Online sites dedicated to migrant blogs are becoming more popular, but it is mainly the South American migrants who are enthusiastic about recounting their stories.

Galician Migration: The United Kingdom

Little attention has been given to Galician migration to the United Kingdom over the last few decades. An interesting documentation of mid-twentieth-century migration is Antonio de Toro Santos's book on the radio programs broadcast by the BBC in the 1940s and 1950s. The series was aimed at all Spanish exiles, not just at Galicians. The BBC yearbook declared in 1948:

> Since the war, the chief demand of the Spanish audience of the BBC has been for more news and comment about Spain; one of the ways of endeavoring to meet this demand has been the introduction of a weekly series of Spanish regional programs, a different part of Spain being covered in each.

Each program was transmitted in Castilian, but there was generally a ten-to-fifteen-minute interval dedicated to broadcasts in Galician, Catalan, or Basque. The Galician programs tended to emulate the radio broadcasts in Cuba, Argentina, and Uruguay. Over a nine-year period there were eighty-three programs made in the Galician language, dealing primarily with cultural issues such as art and literature and also offering ethnographic and sociological commentary. Often, the topics selected also emphasized social and cultural links with the UK, with the principal aim appearing to be to make displaced Galicians feel at home in a foreign land. The first program, broadcast 14 April 1947, was written and read by the exiled, left-wing Galician journalist and writer Fernández Armesto and was entitled "Relacións culturais entre Inglaterra e Galiza" (A. de Toro Santos 47–51; "Cultural Relations between England and Galicia"). The main target audience of the Galician series was living in or around London at the time, but Toro Santos avers that the BBC broadcasts may have also reached the ears of many people living in Galician villages and towns (32–33), who would otherwise have no access to Galician programs on the radio.[11]

Academics have tended to subsume Galician migrant issues under the generic characterization of Spanish migration.[12] Although Francisco Durán Villa's early work *La emigración galega al Reino Unido* ("Galician Emigration to the United Kingdom") examines various Galician migrant groups established in the UK in the late twentieth century, his doctoral thesis, "La emigración española al Reino Unido" ("Spanish Emigration to the United Kingdom"), considers Spanish migrants in general, as do the works of Salvador Estebañez and of Alicia Pozo-Gutiérrez. Similarly, Cristina Mateo's "Second-Generation Spanish Immigrants in Greater London" and "Identities at a Distance" deal with Galician migrants from a sociocultural perspective, but the latter work at least presupposes that Spanish, not Galician, is the only ethnic identity in question (76, 81).[13]

However, in the last thirty years or so, migrant voices—or their heralds—have started to make themselves heard, at the very least in literary circles. Hooper's extremely enlightening article about what she has termed a *cultura galego-británica* diverts the discussion of Galician migration away from the colonial context of Latin America toward that of transnational links between Galicia and the UK. Hooper catalogs the small but illustrious body of recent literary work, written largely by authors who have had firsthand experience of such migratory patterns, such as Carlos Durán, Xelís de Toro Santos, and Xavier Queipo (176–77), and discusses in some detail two new novels on migrant experiences and identities, one by John Rutherford and one by Xesús Fraga.

Migration and Invisibility

Not all official data for Galician movement away from the homeland are subsumed under those for overall Spanish migration. For example, the Instituto Galego de Estatística (IGE; "Galician Statistical Institute") has compiled comprehensive and up-to-date statistics on Galician migratory patterns in the last thirty years. But few outward mid-twentieth-century migrations from different regions of Spain were recorded as discrete entities set apart from the overarching banner of Spanish migration. For example, between 1911 and 1964, 1,140,926 Galicians migrated to areas outside Spain, constituting a third of all Spanish migrants during this period (Fraga Iribarne 60). Even when Galician migration is treated separately in this way, the number of migrants arriving at UK destinations is still unclear. Hence it is not surprising that Galician migration to the UK is poorly documented.

As far as the media is concerned, unless there is a strong sensationalist reason not to do so, such as a racist taunt regarding an idiosyncratic set of characteristics that sets a particular migrant group apart from others, newspapers that document the migration of minority groups tend to subsume them under the national category of their country of origin. These groups are labeled not by ethnic identity or allegiance but by the all-encompassing nation-state designation. Thus, Albanian exiles from Turkey, unless there is a specific reason to emphasize their ethnicity, will be included under the label Turkish by the media. Indeed, a search of the Web sites of the *Guardian* and the *Times* sheds no light on Galician migration as a phenomenon in its own right.

There are many migrant groups in the UK—Poles, Greeks, Italians, Pakistani, Portuguese—who choose to preserve one or more traits that set them apart from both the receptor and other migrant groups, such as social, cultural, or linguistic practices. By demonstrating their idiosyncratic allegiances, they underline their particular ethnicities and thus become more visible to the receptor nation. Galician migrant groups, however, choose to conceal their ethnicity, and thus they become invisible. Invisibility relies to a great extent on such migrants' sense of self. In other words, what does it really mean to be Galician?

The traditional type of migratory pattern associated with the western Iberian Peninsula has long been movement in one direction (away from the homeland), triggered in the mid–twentieth century by the right-wing political situation (Beswick, "Portuguese Diaspora"). Until recently, Galician and Portuguese waves of migration to the Americas were generally thought to have been definitive, with the notion of geographic space between homeland and reception area paramount.[14] In many scenarios, conscious desires and determined efforts to construct a better life called for a relatively high degree of acculturation and integration with the receptor nation, learning its language, social mores, and culture. This integration—in public, at least—was often accompanied by a general disassociation with ethnic traits, despite the presence of proactive social and cultural centers.

In Europe a different kind of migrant emerged. The present research into the Galicians of Guildford, Surrey, indicates that the first wave of migration from Galicia to other European countries occurred in the 1960s and early 1970s, at a time when the regional economy was stultified and lack of work, especially in rural and semirural areas, meant that many laborers had no choice but to go abroad. This migration was part of a trend to move to western Europe; the other main receptor countries were France, Germany, and Switzerland—as in the Portuguese migration. In the UK, many Galicians settled close to London, in towns such as Guildford, Leatherhead, Woking, and Bracknell. This proximity to the largest conurbation was important for socioeconomic reasons, since it ensured that public service and public sector work could be found in hotels, hospitals, and factories, although some Galician migrants also found work as itinerant agricultural laborers. However, just as important, the strategic location of these groups acted as a strong link across the geographic divide, facilitating regular travel back to Galicia. At this time, many socioeconomic migrants were men, although it was not uncommon for married couples to leave their children with their extended families back in Galicia and come to the UK in search of work. Work permits were in short supply, but many migrants managed to earn sufficient money to be able to send some back to their relatives and amass savings with the aim one day of returning home to Galicia to retire. This pattern paralleled contemporary Portuguese migratory patterns and subsequent migrations, especially from Eastern Europe. However, unlike the Portuguese, the Galician groups that sprang up were not tightly knit, so although a few community organizations and social centers were established, these were not always popular.

With the advent of democracy in Spain in the 1990s, there was a second migratory wave of Galicians to the UK, which appears to have continued until recently. Once again, this migration occurred primarily for socioeconomic reasons and was greatly facilitated by the entry of Spain into the EU. This time, migrants were generally young, single people of both genders, many of whom were educated under the democratic system, in which Galician was the language of instruction for at least some subjects. These migrants have no need to send money back home and do not appear predisposed to return to Galicia to settle later in life, thus mirroring the pattern of first-generation migrants witnessed in earlier migrations to the Americas. On arrival in Guildford, they integrated well with other Galicians, since many already had extended family among the Galicians in the town. Work was often arranged for them in companies and factories where, typically, they shadowed other Galicians in order to familiarize themselves with a particular job and sociocultural practices that went with it.

I sought to establish whether Galician migrants in Guildford wished to remain concealed in terms of their ethnicity and, if so, why. Inherent to this question is the relationship between innate and acquired identities and the role, outlined by Hooper in particular ("Galicia" 171–72), of such migrants in the general conceptualization of what constitutes Galician identity and identification practices. Because migrants' experiences and perceptions, as well as their ancestry, define who they are, identity may be partially inherent and also partially shaped by circumstance. Hooper employs Stuart Hall's conceptualization of "being" and "becoming" to argue that traditional ways of looking at cultural identity as static and homogenous are largely irrelevant (174–75). Migrant groups who must negotiate identities that are constantly subject to revision and change, such as the Galicians in the UK, constitute an important, albeit transnational, sector of Galician society. In other words, essentialized concepts of Galician cultural identity may no longer be significant to most Galician migrants, who also have to negotiate other allegiances and identities throughout their transnational lives.

Can the same be said about linguistic identity? A main objective of my case study in Guildford was to evaluate contextual language use and determine whether it played a role, in the face of new linguistic experiences and practices, in the expression of a nonessentialized Galician ethnic identity. Through a comparative examination of these migrants, I would establish whether the use or nonuse of the Galician language could be considered an important articulation of a new sense of Galicianness and whether that sense gave rise to any overt displays of linguistic identity.

Initially, I found substantial differences in language use between the first- and second-arrived migrants. From their arrival, all first-wave migrants used Galician at home and started to learn English only out of necessity. At the present time, they appear to employ Galician with their spouses but either English or Castilian Spanish with their children. Often they will code-mix between the two; in the home setting, diglossic use is often defined more by the interlocutor than by the notion of social space. Yet these respondents hardly ever use Galician outside the home or with other first-wave Galicians. One female respondent in her fifties stated:

> Well, Galician is my language, my connection to my homeland, my identity. But I would never use it outside the home, because it is impolite to do so—I cannot speak it correctly. Castilian Spanish is a much better language to use, even with other Galicians. And my children, well, they were born here—they need to remember that they are Spanish, but I have to remember that they learn and speak English at school—so when I am talking to them, I use both. And Galician, well, they know it, but only my incorrect forms, and they really use it only with their grandparents.

Another female respondent in her late forties declared:

> I rarely use Galician outside the home, but I am Galician—and so are my children, and my grandchildren. It will be great to go home and hear Galician all the time, but well, we are Spanish too.[15]

A forty-five-year-old male respondent who worked with other Galicians in a bakery added:

> I speak poor Galician, but my children don't really speak it at all. It is a pity, but then they are still Galician; but I suppose that they are also Spanish, and a little English! I would never speak Galician at work, they would laugh at me; my workmates are all Spanish, so that is what we speak, but if the boss or someone we don't know comes in, we talk to them in English. Why? Well, I don't want to be thought of as a rude Spaniard.   (interview conducted 11 Apr. 2006)

These comments regarding language use echo similar findings from my earlier research in Galicia (Beswick, *Regional Nationalism*). The Galician language has long connoted low prestige and ignorance: many people who were raised in the region before the 1980s consider their spoken Galician dialectal and thus inferior both to Castilian Spanish and to the Galician standard. As a result, it is inadequate for interactions other than with spouses and older members of the family. Some of the respondents attached even less importance to their nonuse of Galician than the quotes above imply. A consistent theme throughout their interviews was the irrelevance of the language to feeling and being Galician and to their desire that their children recognize their ancestry and realize what it means to be Galician in sociocultural terms while at the same time calling themselves Spanish. That the language itself is rarely employed does not mean a rejection of what to them constitutes a sense of Galicianness.

Language does not always play an important role in the conceptualization of group interfaces. In this case, it may be a peripheral element in the maintenance of ethnic identification strategies. For the older respondents, the use of Galician is reserved for extremely informal, familial contexts, out of sight of the world and even from other Galicians; the dominant language is Castilian Spanish. Individuals may associate the use of Galician with the maintenance of some type of supranational Spanish identification strategy. It is Castilian Spanish and not Galician that emphasizes in-group and out-group membership in certain contexts, reinforcing adherents' distinctiveness and setting them apart from the overarching, English-speaking receptor nation. Linguistic demonstrations of Galicianness may be hidden and covert, but those of Spanishness are not; speaking Castilian Spanish outside the home is seen as acceptable practice. Indeed, Castilian Spanish is still viewed as the language of advancement by the parents, rather than English, which is simply the default language of communication for the children, hence of pragmatic importance but not relevant to their future. First-wave migrants felt that the acquisition of identification features associated with being British was simply another aspect of their hyphenated distinctiveness and one that would become irrelevant (and thus abandoned) when they returned one day to Galicia to live and work, as many in Guildford have already done. These migrants may be considered transnational, since they have not broken their ties with Galicia, have not been totally acculturated and integrated into British society, and fully recognize that they have not.[16]

Of my second-wave respondents, only a few have relatives in Guildford, but they continue to use Galician with family, Castilian Spanish with one another, and English elsewhere. Without exception, all these respondents were raised and schooled in Galicia after Franco and during the incipient stages of *normalización*. Many confirmed that Galician was taught at school and was often used as the main language of instruction, and their immersion in the Galician language at a young age may have had a positive impact on their attitudes toward its use. One respondent, a twenty-seven-year-old shop assistant, declared:

> We thought that it was a bit of a laugh, learning this old language, the one we use with our grandparents. But I understand better now why we had to do it—here, we are just another bunch of Spaniards, and that is fine. . . . But, well, I am Galician, and when I am with my relatives, I want to feel Galician, so I speak it [to them]. At first, they were shocked; they wouldn't reply . . . then I realized that they were ashamed of their Galician, which, well, no one should be. Of course, I still use Castilian Spanish with my friends; it's just, well, normal. But I need to use English at work, and I want to; it's the way forward.

A twenty-five-year-old trainee chef added:

> Personally, I love speaking Galician nowadays, it just feels right: I don't know, it feels part of me. But most of my friends have been over here since childhood, and they prefer to use Castilian Spanish.

A twenty-three-year-old waiter who has no relatives in Guildford claimed:

> I am Spanish through and through, but I am also Galician, even though I never ever use the language. It is a shame, but no one wants to speak to me in Galician . . . at work we use Castilian Spanish in the kitchens, and English everywhere else. I suppose I don't like people from here knowing that I am Spanish; I am fair-haired, so it is easy for me to blend in. But with my mates, well, I don't want them to think I am English, even though I look it, so it is important to me to speak to them in Castilian Spanish.
>
> (interviews conducted 12 Apr. 2006)

Even when these respondents do not use Galician on a regular basis, they do not abandon their sense of ethnic differentiation, so once again the overt use of Galician is not considered by younger people vital to the expression of an internalized ethnic identity. There does appear to be an intergenerational shift in perceptions surrounding the potential value of language as a manifestation of such identity. The comments of the shop assistant imply that unlike the older migrants, the younger respondents may be starting to embrace the underlying and implicit value of Galician as an identifier of their hyphenated membership of their ethnic group. But any sense of otherness in terms of group membership is always contextualized as part of an overarching Spanish identification strategy in the diaspora. Indeed, the epithet *Spanish* is often equally important to their identification practices—at least three respondents regularly called themselves a Galician Spaniard.

All second-wave migrants agreed on the main reason for acquiring English. Linguistic integration with the receptor society is seen as eminently practical and thus highly desirable as the main method of improving career prospects in the UK. Some also commented on English as a core value of British identity. Indeed, becoming British is often seen as part of the transnational experience, but not to the detriment of the Galician-Spanish facets of their complex identification strategies, which are negotiated and practiced on a daily basis according to context.

Manifestations of Galician ethnic identification strategies through sociocultural practices are rarely in evidence outside the confines of the migrant group in Guildford. Unlike their counterparts elsewhere, these migrants no longer maintain their social and cultural associations, centers, and groups that at one time would organize dances, parties, and festival celebrations. There are now no dedicated Galician shops, cafés, or restaurants in Guildford, and there are no Galician lessons supported by the Galician government. Furthermore, the linguistic reinforcement of Galician ethnic identity in sociocultural contexts does not imply the use of Galician. Even when Galicians do socialize together, such as after work in the town's bars and cafés, the language of general use is Castilian Spanish. As a consequence, there is no overt Galician sociolinguistic or sociocultural presence in the town or surrounding area. The group is invisible to the receptor society.

Just as linguistic behavior in this group conforms to the normal practice of using English in intergroup situations, the acquisition of social and cultural mores of the receptor nation may be primarily a pragmatic way of being able to get on with their lives, of fitting in with the receptor society, even if it leads to a heightened sense of Britishness for some of the second-wave respondents. Many of the migrants interviewed eat in English cafés and restaurants; they attend English football games; they go to English bars and clubs and listen to English music. Yet within the confines of the home, certain ethnic social and cultural practices may be retained. Television is seen by these migrants as a good way of acquiring English, but even second-wave migrants receive satellite broadcasts from Spain. Galician festivals and saints' days are often celebrated by the preparation of a traditional meal attended by all the family and close friends, irrespective of age.

Galician football teams are avidly supported, albeit from afar, and some of the younger respondents have started to attend the Casa Galicia events in London, such as the Galician festival held in July.

The notion of a well-established, well-articulated hyphenated Galician identity in Guildford seems somewhat tenuous. As Clare Mar-Molinero points out, the advance of globalization means that changes in the notion of social and geographic space and the greater proximity and accessibility to homelands are transforming the relation migrants have both with their receptor country and with their own perceptions of identity ("Spanish" 7). Complex, multiple identities are the norm for transnational migrants; they are assumed or abandoned as required and differ in their relative significance and import. They may also differ in their content, as a result of the ongoing experiences of the groups involved. A three-way sense of Galician-Spanish-British identity does exist in Guildford, but the nature of the Galician component may be changing. Some migrants' identification strategies may be embedded in largely essentialized concepts, such as shared history, traditions, and customs of a bygone era, but such static perceptions of ethnic identity are often outmoded in contemporary life.

Galicians living in the UK are the sum total of their experiences. The assumption of other identification strategies and the adoption of practices linked to a sense of belonging outside the Galician arena changes the dynamic of the multiple identity complex and may also change the components of what constitutes Galician identity. Older migrants insist on their ultimate return to Galicia; while resident in the UK, they are reluctant to express their Galician identity through any form of ethnic linguistic practice or do not consider the use of Galician necessary to such expression. Younger, more recent migrants may feel constrained by the conventional use of language in their autochthonous group. Although they do not associate a sense of shame with the use of Galician, they often choose to express their Spanishness instead. Of course, it could be argued that the use of Spanish is an appropriate manifestation of Galician identity: Spanish is the national language and thus official in the self-governing region of Galicia, and as a legacy of the dictatorship it is the dominant language for many of the older respondents, since the use of Galician was often censured. Regular attendance at social and cultural events hosted by the Spanish Association of Woking and Leatherhead must be seen as a way of expressing overarching Spanish identification strategies rather than a rejection of cognate Galician sociocultural identification practices, even though many of those practices are no longer observed.

We might conclude that the notion of Galician identity no longer features in the hyphenated identification strategy of these migrants. Yet allegiance to and association with a new sense of Galicianness are becoming more apparent and more significant, at least to some of the younger migrants, even though language use is not necessarily a prerequisite for ethnic group membership. It will be interesting to see what develops next.

Notes

1. Appadurai offers an excellent account of the effects of globalization on transnational movement. See also Robinson 564–90.
2. The multicultural or anti-assimilationist model was an alternative paradigm based on a differentialist discourse that pervaded in the late twentieth century and was focused on a desire to maintain social, cultural, and linguistic diversity. See, for example, Rex.
3. For the seminal framing of the transnational migration model, see Basch, Schiller, and Szanton.
4. For illuminating examples of the divergence between such spaces, see Pries.
5. In his pioneering work *Ethnic Groups and Boundaries,* Barth was the first to state that ethnic groups may embrace or discard their cultural or ethnic identity, according to the particular value it affords in a given context. See also Padilla 113–18.
6. For a detailed account of this linkage, see Beswick, *Regional Nationalism* 53–74.
7. Aspirations of minoritized groups tend to be labeled as regionalism or even separatism (Beswick, *Regional Nationalism* 32; Holt and Gubbins 6) from the state perspective but as nationalism from the ethnic group perspective (see, e.g., Gellner). In the Galician context, I prefer to adopt the term *regional nationalism*, as my intention is to represent the minoritized perspective as legitimate and viable. But the term *region* may also be politically loaded. My use of it in this article simply serves to highlight its geographic significance and does not imply any particular political ideology.
8. For accounts of the political and social history of Galicia until the twentieth century, see González López and in particular Gemie. The history of the Galician language and the emergence of Castilian as the prestigious, dominant language of Spain are covered by C. Álvarez Cáccamo; Monteagudo and Santamarina 121–23; Ferreiro; Freixeiro Mato; Gómez Sánchez and Freixeiro Mato; Penny 16–22; and Álvarez Blanco, Fernández Rei, and Santamarina.
9. For a further account of migration from Galicia to Central and South America and the repercussions for the language itself, see the Consello da Cultura Galega's recently initiated project (www.consellodacaltara.org/arguivos/cdsg/loia/).

10. See *Arquivo*. The Centro de Estudos da Poboación e Analise das Migracións (CEPAM) also collates information about international migration, but the information is not exclusively Galician (see *CEPAM*). The Consello da Cultura Galega has also developed a highly informative Web site about political and intellectual exile during and just after the Spanish Civil War (*Exiliados*).

11. Many of the older migrants in my study remembered hearing the BBC Galician radio programs as children in Galicia and commented on the emotional significance the programs had for their parents.

12. As recently as 2002, Jo Labanyi commented that little academic research into Galician communities had been carried out, even in Latin America ("Part 1" 17).

13. Other academic work is limited in its scope. A rare case study on Galicians in the UK is Francisco Armas Quintá's paper, which adopts a socioeconomic approach to the experiences of only two Galician migrants in Guildford. Xelís de Toro Santos's "Bagpipes and Digital Music" makes a brief mention of the role of bagpipes in migrant Galician identity to evoke a sense of community and the homeland (243–44) as well as the role of migrants in the Galician contemporary music scene (249–50), but it is his novel *Os saltimbanquís no paraíso* that tackles the issue of cultural identity directly.

14. In his recent work on Portuguese migrants in Venezuela, Mark Dinneen reports that third-generation members of the diaspora consider their travel to and settlement in Madeira and other areas of Portugal as return, in the sense that migration is the legacy of all subsequent generations.

15. All quotations have been directly translated from Galician or Castilian. This interview was conducted 13 April 2006.

16. Attitudinal and behavioral practices of second-generation Galicians born in the UK are outside the scope of this paper.

Portuguese or Spanish Orthography for the Galizan Language? An Analysis of the *Conflito Normativo*

John Patrick Thompson

G aliza's position as part of the Spanish state means that its relationship with the outside world has largely been mediated through Spain. However, Galiza also shares a border—and a history—with Portugal, and the relationship with its neighbors to the south has often been less than straightforward. Much of the Galizan debate over the relationship with Portugal has been played out in linguistic terms: although Galiza and Portugal have been politically separated for almost nine hundred years, the languages of these nations are so similar that some consider Galizan a variety of Portuguese. A particular focus of debate has therefore been the question of whether the graphic system to be employed in modern Galizan should be more closely modeled on Portuguese or Spanish: this debate is known as the *conflito normativo*.

The crux of the *conflito normativo* in Galiza is the lack of agreement on whether Galizan is a separate language or whether it belongs to the Portuguese family. The defenders of the first position, known as *autonomistas*, *normativistas*, or *isolacionistas*, conceive of Galiza as a nation independent from both Spain and Portugal; they use the Spanish orthographic system. On the other side of the conflict, the *lusistas* or *reintegracionistas* yearn for an integration (or reintegration) of Galiza into the Portuguese linguistic, social, and cultural spheres. For adherents of both positions, orthography has come to function as an identity marker. Synonyms of *autonomismo* are *diferencialismo*, *isolacionismo*, *oficialismo*, and *independentismo lingüístico*. The *autonomistas* consider themselves both autonomists and differentialists in that they defend their community's autonomy from Spain and Portugal as well as its difference from these two national communities. *Isolacionismo*—often used in a derogatory way by *lusistas*—is an unfair denomination because many of the adherents of *autonomismo*, although they do not promote the use of Portuguese orthography, defend Galiza's entering into the Portuguese cultural sphere. *Oficialismo* can sometimes be used in a negative way by those who wish to use the *lusista*-oriented *normativas* (or *normas*), who are usually denied access to mainstream media, government subsidies, and literary prizes controlled by those supporting the official norm.

The polarization of these two views, *autonomista* and *lusista*, and the ensuing divisions have had a detrimental effect on the advancement of a Galizan national project. Though an important step was taken in 2003 to build a bridge between the sides in conflict, those who wish to write Galizan with Portuguese orthography still occupy a relatively minor space in the public sphere. The agreement of 2003 consisted of introducing *lusista*-oriented modifications into the *normativa oficial*. However, though some of the modifications are significant, the changes were limited, so that this new *normativa*, referred to as "a normativa da concordia" ("the agreed orthographic and morphological norm"), is generally considered to be all but the same as the previous one. Moreover, "concordia" is a misnomer, given that some *lusista* groups were not invited to take part in the negotiations.

Divergence over which graphic system to employ for the Galizan language has existed since the *ilustrados* ("enlightened") of the eighteenth century,[1] but the conflict became especially heated in the early 1970s. My analysis in this essay therefore focuses on the period from the 1970s to the present. In the first section, I explore some contrasting interpretations that underlie the *conflito normativo* and provide a historical account of it since 1970. In the second part, I analyze two of the main fallacies that *autonomistas* and *lusistas* use against each other. I give an account of some of the issues arising in Galiza's current relationship with Portugal in the third section and conclude the article with three suggestions for ameliorating the *conflito normativo*.

Language Planning, *Abstand* Languages, and *Ausbau* Languages

Language planning often addresses situations of minority languages in diglossia,[2] and it is generally implemented through three broad categories: corpus planning, status planning, and acquisition planning (Mar-Molinero, *Politics* 78; see also Cooper 29–34). While the first deals with the formal aspects of languages, the second and third are preoccupied with the promotion (status) and the teaching-learning (acquisition) of languages. Corpus planning is further divided into three phases: graphization, standardization, and modernization (for an explanation, see Cooper 125). The first, according to Charles A. Ferguson, refers to the "reduction to writing"; the second to the elaboration of a norm that overrides regional and social dialects; and the third to "the development of intertranslatability with other languages in a range of topics and forms of discourse characteristic of industrialized, secularized, structurally differentiated, 'modern' societies" (qtd. in Cooper 126).

The part of corpus planning that has caused so much conflict in Galiza is graphization. Status and acquisition planning, as key components of *normalización*, have also generated heated debates since the promulgation of the Spanish constitution in 1978. To normalize a language, in the words of J. Cobarrubias, means

> [a)] to empower minority languages in order to make it possible for [them] to satisfy the communicative needs of a modern society; b) to increase the number of speakers/users and increase the communicative competence of current users, and c) expand the geographic scope of the language within a given area.
> (qtd. in Mar-Molinero, *Politics* 80)

Galiza has yet to resolve either the graphization (the object of inquiry in this essay) or the normalization of its language. Normalization has been obstructed by the laws imposing "bilingüísmo harmónico" ("harmonious bilingualism") or "bilingüísmo equilibrado" ("balanced bilingualism"), which prevailed in article 3 of the Spanish constitution; in the Decreto de Bilingüísmo ("Bilingualism Act") of 1979; in article 5 of the Estatuto de Autonomía (1981; "Statute of Autonomy"); and in the Lei de Normalización Lingüística (1983; "Language Normalization Act"), which is still in effect (García Negro 32–41). Although defended by the right-wing Partido Popular (PP) and by antinationalists on the left, harmonious bilingualism between Spanish and Galizan is impossible in practice, because diglossia is an unstable, tense situation, which inevitably moves toward the elimination of one of the two languages. Though the use of Galizan has moved into spheres that were off-limits during the Franco dictatorship, the number of Galizans who speak it as a mother tongue continues to decline (Portas 230).

To inquire further into the *conflito normativo* and the differences between the *autonomista* and *lusista* positions, let us examine the concepts of *Abstand* and *Ausbau* languages developed by Heinz Kloss, who worked as a linguist for the Third Reich. The first term—translated into Galizan as *linguas por distanciamento*—refers to those languages that can be recognized as such by virtue of their evident differentness with regard to other languages; hence, the term can be paraphrased as "languages by distance" (29). Euskara, for example, is a *lingua por distanciamento* because its phonetic, morphological, syntactic, and prosodic features differ radically from all other languages (Rodrigues Fagim 27).[3] The second term—translated as *linguas por elaboración*—is applied to those languages that, in order to be recognized as such, must be shaped, reshaped, or elaborated; all the Romance languages are therefore *Ausbau* languages. While *Abstand* language is predominantly a linguistic concept, *Ausbau* language is a sociological concept (Kloss 30). *Ausbau* "refers to languages which have deliberately been reshaped so as to become vehicles of variegated literary expression" (30). Every *lingua por elaboración*, according to Zarko Muljacic, conquers its own dialectical space "creando deste xeito a respectiva lingua por distanciamento e non á inversa" (22; "creating this way the respective *lingua por distanciamento* and not the other way around"). Therefore *Ausbau* languages are also *Abstand* languages—or, rather, they become *Abstand* languages once they have been elaborated. While *linguas por distanciamento* can attain the status of languages regardless of how they have been manipulated, *linguas por elaboración* must first be manipulated through the conscious agency of their community.[4]

Though from an official standpoint Galizan and Portuguese are different *linguas de elaboración*, will we always have to consider them separate languages, or could they some day be considered dialects (or variants, branches, categories, etc.) of the same language? This question constitutes one of the primary points of division between *autonomistas* and *lusistas*. Before attempting to provide an answer, I want to make clear that I do not use *dialect* in a way that implies inferiority with respect to language. John Lyons makes this crucial point in his *Languages and Linguistics*:

> Though the linguist uses the term "dialect" and, like the layman, relates it to the term "language" by saying that a language may be composed of several different dialects, he does not accept the implications commonly associated with the term "dialect" in everyday usage. Most important of all, he does not accept that the dialect of a particular region or a particular social class is a debased or degenerate version of the standard dialect: he knows that from a historical point of view the standard dialect—to which the layman may prefer to apply the term "language," rather than "dialect"—is, in origin, though not in its subsequent development, no different in kind from the non-standard dialects. He knows too that, as long as they serve a fairly broad range of functions in

the daily life of the locality or social class in which they operate, non-standard dialects are no less systematic than the regional or national standard.   (25)

The authors who write on the *conflito normativo*—most of them linguists and philologists—usually use *dialect* in the nonpejorative way, but some do resort to the nonspecialist connotation, especially when trying to debunk their opponents' theses. Thus *lusistas* accuse *autonomistas* of allowing Galizan to become a dialect of Spanish, while the *autonomistas* blame the *lusistas* for wanting Galizan to dissolve as a dialect into Portuguese.

Let us examine *autonomista* and *lusista* interpretations of the concept of *Ausbau* language (or *lingua por elaboración*). Henrique Monteagudo, one of the leading *autonomista* scholars, considers Galizan and Portuguese as the same *lingua por distanciamento* during the medieval period but different *linguas por elaboración* today, insofar as they have undergone (since Portugal's separation from Galiza in 1128) different processes of manipulation. Monteagudo posits that "o material de base do galego-portugués experimentou (e está a experimentar) dous procesos de elaboración sucesivos e independentes, un deles deu orixe ó portugués, o outro está dando orixe ó galego" ("Sobre a polémica" 211; "the base material of Galizan-Portuguese experienced [and still experiences] two successive, independent processes of elaboration, one turned into Portuguese and the other is turning into Galizan"). Portuguese has completed the process, but Galizan is still immersed in its process, which according to Monteagudo is not the same as that of Portuguese.

Valentim Rodrigues Fagim, one of the most high-profile *lusista* voices, argues that *linguas por elaboración* are not

> compartimentos estanque como o podem ser as línguas por distanciamento onde é doado travar uns limites medianamente precisos. Nas primeiras existe umha graduaçom imperceptível similar á das cores ou á das temperaturas.
> (31)

> separate compartments like languages by distance where it is easy to mark some fairly precise boundaries. In the former there is an imperceptible gradation like that of colors or temperatures.

He claims that a language is similar to a nation and that

> nom é umha pirámide inerte e sim tem mais a ver com umha duna, a avançar e retroceder, aparecendo e desaparecendo. . . . Unha língua é um projecto, melhor, um adjetivo.
> (39–40)

it is not an inert pyramid and has more in common with a dune, advancing and retreating, appearing and disappearing. . . . A language is a project, or better still, an adjective.

He then states that "[n]om há essencias, entes imutáveis e imiscíveis, há só existencia" (41; "there are no essences, immutable and unmixable entities, only existence"). In contrast to Monteagudo's more rigid conception of differentness between Galizan and Portuguese, this *lusista* author insists on the unstable nature of *linguas por elaboración* and argues that Galizan and Portuguese are projects of creation, which can converge or diverge, depending on the desire of the elaborators.

Rodrigues Fagim therefore rejects the existence of a legitimate law determining that Galizan and Portuguese embody two different *linguas por elaboración*. That the current respective *normativas oficiais* ("official *normativas*") of these languages are different does not mean that they cannot or should not unite some time in the future. Implicit in Monteagudo's claim, on the other hand, is the idea that the two languages have become, at this stage in history, two irreversibly separate entities. Furthermore, by claiming that both have undergone different processes of elaboration, Monteagudo ignores the existence of the contending *normativas lusistas*, which though unofficial and marginalized, are in their own right agents of elaboration of Galizan.

The *Conflito Normativo* from 1970 until the Present

Until the death of Franco, the *conflito normativo* was much less conspicuous. All conscious users of the language, states Monteagudo, defended an autonomous Galizan, even Ricardo Carvalho Calero, the first postwar professor of Galizan language and literature, who became the most influential defender of the *lusista* position in the postdictatorship years (Monteagudo, "A demanda" 65). But two different approaches in the *autonomista* side had staked out their claims by the early 1970s. In 1970 and 1971, the Real Academia Galega (RAG) published its *Normas ortográficas do idioma galego* and *Normas ortográficos e morfolóxica da idioma galego*, respectively. For its part, the Instituto da Lingua Galega (ILGA) published *Gallego 1* (1971), *Gallego 2* (1972), and *Gallego 3* (1973). While the RAG defended an orthography of *galego culto*—that is, a refined continuation of the Galizan used by the authors of the Rexurdimento and Xeración Nós ("Us Generation"), the members of the ILGA endorsed a phoneticist approach.[5] The RAG, for example, promoted the use of many words and forms that had existed in the Middle Ages (the endings in *verdade, sociedade*; plural endings: *animais, sociais*), while the ILGA defended a radical *popularista* approach of representing the spoken language exactly how it is (thus instead of *verdade, verdá*; instead of *animais, animales*). These two positions united in the latter part of the decade and published together a *normativa* proposal entitled *Bases prá unificación das normas lingüísticas do galego* (1977; "Basis for the Unification of the Linguistic Standards of Galizan"). Though the proposal was unofficial, most of the Galizan academic community, according to Monteagudo and Francisco Fernández Rei, agreed on this *normativa*. Both linguists view the *Bases* as a lost opportunity for avoiding the bitter conflict that would come (Monteagudo, "A demand" 68; Fernández Rei 186).

The *lusistas* see things differently. The *lusista* perspective began to take root after the publication of Manuel Rodrígues Lapa's seminal *lusista* essay "A recuperação literária do galego" (1973; "The Literary Revival of Galizan"). Though few endorsed this project, Carvalho Calero, a figure whose influence in the Galizan nationalist establishment was unmatched, began to create a viable *lusista* project for Galiza. Carvalho Calero was writing pro-*lusista* articles as early as 1975, and in 1980—just before the Galizan Estatuto de Autonomía was passed—the Xunta (then governed by moderate and center left parties) named him president of the newly created Comisión Lingüística. This *comisión* published in 1980 a *normativa* proposal, entitled *Normas ortográficas do idioma galego*, which was made official by the Xunta the same year. *Lusista* in orientation and intention, this *normativa* nonetheless sought to unite the two main tendencies (*lusista* and *autonomista*) and permit range of options, as its introduction makes clear.[6]

This *normativa* was soon given the name *normativa de concórdia* ("agreed *normativa*") and was practically identical to the *normativa* elaborated by the Asociación Sócio-Pedagóxica Galega (AS-PG; founded in 1978) and published in *Orientacións para a escrita do noso idioma* (1979; "Guide for the Writing of Our Language"). This book was distributed in many schools during the 1979–80 academic year and was later called the *normativa de mínimos* and adopted by the progressive nationalist party Bloque Nacionalista Galego (BNG) and its weekly newspaper *A nosa terra*, which used it until 2003, when the BNG began to employ the *normativa* of 2003. The orthography of the *normativa dos mínimos*—now almost extinct because the BNG and *A nosa terra* abandoned it—is Castilian, but the system of accentuation is Portuguese and the morphology is Portuguese for nouns and Galizan for verbs. "Mínimos" refers to the minimum use of Portuguese, as opposed to the *normativa de máximos*, which uses Portuguese to the maximum extent, while still maintaining some Galizan words and verb conjugations.

The *normativa* elaborated by Carvalho Calero and the *comisión* (the first official one in Galizan history) was short-lived because the *autonomistas* immediately denounced its provisional nature and accused the *comisión* of unrealistically attempting to reconcile the irreconcilable:

> Chegados a este punto, ou ben se admitía que o galego ía carecer dun código normativo unificado e coherente, ou ben resultaba imperioso decidirse por unha opción e desbotar a outra.   (Monteagudo, "A demanda" 69)

> Having reached this point, either we had to admit the Galizan language would lack a unified standard, or else we would have to be imperious and decide on one option, rejecting the other.

In 1982 the RAG and ILGA elaborated an *autonomista* proposal, which rejected practically all the *lusista* elements of Carvalho Calero's *normativa*. This new proposal, also entitled *Normas ortográficas e morfolóxicas do idioma galego*, was then made official by the Xunta the same year and given the acronym *NOMIG-82*. This *normativa* adopted elements that moved the written language even further away from Portuguese than had the *Bases*.[7]

The *lusistas* interpreted (and still interpret) this imposition of the *NOMIG-82* as a putsch within the Galizan nationalist establishment. If the *autonomistas* believe that the *Bases* of 1977 represent the lost precious moment of agreement in the *conflito normativo*, the *lusistas* and defenders of *mínimos* view Carvalho Calero's *normativa* as the lost golden opportunity of reconciliation. Xosé Freixeiro Mato, who has always defended Galizan as a separate language from Portuguese, remarks that most teachers and professors of Galizan believed Carvalho Calero's *normativa* was the only solution that offered the possibility of consensus (125). Many *autonomistas*, on the other hand, have always asserted that only a few specialists (teachers, linguists, etc.) and a few people of the general population have endorsed the *mínimos* and *lusista* orientations. The *lusistas* claim that their adherents are not a minority, and they criticize the *autonomistas* of the RAG and ILGA for consistently playing down the numerical significance of those Galizan nationalists in favor of linguistic and cultural approximation with the Portuguese-speaking world.

Until the passing of the *NOMIG-82*, the *lusista* orthography was the *normativa dos mínimos*, employed in Carvalho Calero's *Normas ortográficas*. However, after the implementation of the *NOMIG-82,* an important split took place within the *lusista* position. This position had been defended by the AS-PG since its foundation in 1978, but some members of the group, on seeing their hopes defeated by the *NOMIG-82,* founded the Associaçom Galega da Língua (AGAL). This association created the *normativa dos máximos*—explained and elaborated in their *Prontuário ortográfico do idioma galego* (1985; "Orthographic Manual of the Galizan Language")—which employs Portuguese orthography and morphology but maintains distinctive Galizan words, verb conjugations, and grammatical aspects.[8] Other ex-adherents of the AS-PG adopted the Portuguese Acordo Ortográfico and write directly in Portuguese. The standardizing of the *NOMIG-82*, therefore, radicalized the *lusistas* and deepened the conflict.

Since the standardization of the *NOMIG-82*, *lusistas* and endorsers of the *mínimos* have been denied, for the most part, government subsidies for publishing in their desired *normativa*. However, they received a substantial boost when in September 1999 Camilo Nogueira—at that time a European Union representative of the BNG—began to use Portuguese in his interventions in Strasbourg (see Camilo Nogueira, "O galego-portugués-brasileiro"; Villamor). Nogueira made the *conflito normativo* mainstream, and it can be argued that the momentum he generated had an impact on the negotiations, which were reinitiated in 2000 and led to the new *normativa* of 2003. After the news hit the media that he was using Portuguese so that Galizan could have recognition as an official language in the European Union (albeit under the auspices of the Portuguese language), articles of opinion on the *conflito normativo* began to inundate the press. *Lusistas*, who had rarely appeared in mainstream Galizan media, all of a sudden became known. Important public figures, such as Carlos Casares, then president of the Consello da Cultura Galega, and renowned writers like Suso de Toro, Xavier Alcalá, and Maria Xosé Queizán wrote articles or made public declarations that strongly endorsed a *lusista*-oriented *normativa* (Alcalá, "Ortografia" and "Portuñol"; Queizán; Toro, "Hai un lugar"; Villar, "Cal normativa"; Vidal, "Os escritores").[9] With a popular BNG politician touting *lusismo* and famous writers pushing for a *lusista*-oriented *normativa*, this project was not (or was no longer) the closet minority the *autonomistas* had always depicted it to be.[10]

In 1999, members of the AS-PG contacted the ILGA, and this contact led to the reopening of negotiations on the *normativa*, which began to take place in 2000. According to the *autonomista* scholar and ILGA member Xosé Luís Regueira, the main reason why the AS-PG was determined to re-negotiate the *cuestión normativa* was that the BNG had possibilities in 2001 of winning the elections of Galiza (*eleccións autonómicas*) in coalition with the Partido dos Socialistas de Galiza (PSdeG) (Message). As a party that was gaining more and more power in small and medium-sized municipalities, the BNG was not benefiting from the *conflito normativo,* given that

> [se encontraba] coa contradición de que a normativa que había que usar na administración era a oficial, mentres que nos documentos internos do partido, sindicato, etc., usaba a "de mínimos," que era a propugnada polo partido. . . . Entón o problema era evidente: tiñan que chegar á Xunta co problema normativo resolto, non podían desde a Xunta utilizar unha normativa non oficial, e non podían aceptar sen máis a normativa oficial (o que suporía claudicar).

> they found themselves in the contradiction that while they had to use the *norma oficial* for administrative purposes, the internal documents of the party, union, and so on used the *mínimos,* which was promoted by the party. . . . Thus the problem was evident: they had to resolve the *normativa* issue before they began governing in the Xunta; they could not use a nonofficial *normativa* while in the Xunta, and they could not accept the *norma oficial* [the *NOMIG-82*] (which would mean to surrender).

The BNG's objective was to replace, through negotiations with the ILGA, the *NOMIG-82* with a more *lusista*-oriented *normativa,* so that the BNG, and *A nosa terra,* could abandon their use of the *normativa dos mínimos* without alienating the constituents who defended it.

The ILGA accepted the reopening of talks on the condition that the *lusistas* who used the *normativa dos máximos* be excluded. Rosario Álvarez, a member of the ILGA, justifies the exclusion of these *lusistas* in these words: "Só se podía negociar con aqueles que tiñan unha concepción do galego como lingua de seu" ("It was possible to negotiate only with those who saw Galizan as an independent language") (see also Monteagudo, "A demanda" 110–11).[11] In the fall of 2001 an agreement was reached and presented to the RAG, which, since the passing of the Language Normalization Act in 1983, has the power to approve or reject *normativa* proposals. The RAG rejected the proposal and was heavily criticized—the press ran several articles condemning its decision (see Díaz Pardo; Fraga). According to Regueira, the RAG's negative decision was due to some of its anti-*lusista* and antinationalist members, and also to pressure from the Fraga-governed Xunta. The Partido Popular de Galiza (PPdeG) pulled all the strings it could to torpedo the agreement:

> Tratábase de poñer todos os obstáculos para que o BNG non chegase ás institucións, seguir deslexitimándoo como un partido antisistema, que non aceptaba as institucións, etc.   (Regueria, Message; see Pino)

> The objective was to create all possible obstacles so that the BNG could not govern, to continue delegitimizing [this party] as an antisystem party that did not accept the institutions.

The RAG finally yielded and approved a new proposal in July 2003. The modifications of the new *normativa* are minimal, but some are significant.[12]

Fallacies

Autonomistas often accuse *lusistas* of wanting to dissolve Galizan into Portuguese, while the *lusistas* blame *autonomistas* for allowing Galizan to become a dialect of Spanish. Given the economic and historical factors that weigh heavily against Galiza's reintegrating into Portugal, coupled by the substantial opposition in Galiza to such reintegration, it is very improbable that Galizan would dilute into Portuguese if a *normativa lusista*, or even the Portuguese Acordo Ortográfico, became the standard. On the other hand, the danger of Galizan's merging into a variant of Spanish is much more realistic, given that Spanish, the dominating language for over five centuries, is in direct contact with Galizan and is influencing (Castilianizing) the language. Some commentary has been made on the lexical and syntactic influences (or corruptions) of Spanish, but there has been little discussion, let alone analysis, of the phonetic influences.

An example of the *autonomista* fallacy that the *lusistas* want to convert Galizan into a satellite of Portuguese is expressed in Fernández Rei's "A questione della lingua galega." Fernández Rei argues:

> Nesta situación, a única concordia posible é a que se pode dar entre quen ten unha mesma concepción lingüística, entre os que consideran que o galego é lingua propia e que é necesario acabar de elaborar un modelo estándar. Outra posibilidade podería ser negarmos que existe un idioma propio, que non paga a pena esforzarse por elaborar ningún estándar para o galego porque o portugués é a nosa lingua culta e pasar a usar liturxicamente o estándar portugués creando outro tipo de diglosia.   (193)

> In this situation, the only possible conciliation is between those who share a single linguistic point of view, who see Galizan as an independent language that needs a standard form. Another possibility would be to deny it is an independent language, so there is no point in creating a standard for Galizan because Portuguese is our literary language and we should use the Portuguese standard, creating another kind of diglossia.

This claim that linguistic integration into Portugal would plunge Galizan into another diglossia requires some comment. Though the author states that reintegration would entail "another type of diglossia," in reality the message he conveys is that this diglossia would be similar to the current one and that Portuguese would be as harmful to Galizan as Castilian. He implies, in other words, that Galizan is a language equidistant between Spanish and Portuguese, when in actuality Galizan is much more similar to Portuguese regardless of whether we consider it a dialect of Portuguese or a separate language.

Antón Santamarina goes as far as to insinuate that the *lusista* agenda parallels that of the Spanish centralists (the *españolistas*), arguing that they both use similar arguments to deny the validity of Galizan (76). Though some *lusistas* do dismiss Galizan as a creole (a corrupted form of a language), it is a fallacy to categorize them as antinationalists. Moreover, Santamarina implies, like Fernández Rei, that reintegration of Galizan will be as negative to the survival of the language as the current Castilian domination. Both these authors completely overlook potentially beneficial effects of reintegration, such as the reduction of Castilian influence.[13]

Like Santamarina but the other way around, the *lusistas* consistently exploit the fallacy that the *autonomistas* operate in cahoots with the anti-Galizanist sectors of society (namely, the PP and parts of the PSdeG). It is true that some supporters of the *normativa autonomista* are antinationalist and reactionary—for instance, Francisco Vázquez, the former mayor of A Coruña,[14] and the former PP-governed Xunta. It is for this reason that, in contrast to the *normativa autonomista*, whose defenders span the spectrum from Xosé Luís Méndez Ferrín (nationalist communist) to Manuel Fraga (a far-right-winger and previous minister under Franco), the *normativa lusista* hosts almost exclusively nationalist-leftist adherents. Yet despite the reactionary and antinationalist endorsers of the *normativa autonomista*—who have not participated in the planning of the Galizan language and do not care about the Galizan language, culture, or way of life—the *autonomis-*

tas who have fought for both the *normativización* ("graphization") and the *normalización* of Galizan (such as those of the ILGA and RAG) are mostly nationalist and progressive.

The *lusista* critic Mário Herrero-Valeiro correctly warns that it is necessary to avoid "a rigid identification among linguistic ideology, nationalist ideology, and political ideology" (295), but he also makes several claims that override this warning; for example, he defends the fallacy that the sanctioning of the *normativa oficial* is

> an attempt by Spanish nationalism to control Galizan linguistic planning in order to avoid an excessive political problematisation of the linguistic issue that might politically and socially endanger the State and its national language, Spanish. (294)

Likewise, he posits that the *autonomista* position "has been legitimated since 1982–1983 by means of its legal sanction by the autonomous Galizan government (*Alianza Popular*, currently *Partido Popular*, of conservative and Spanish nationalist ideology)" (293; see also Rodrigues Fagim 253). The first claim commits the fallacy of likening those involved in language planning (the nationalist *autonomista* endorsers) to Spanish nationalists.[15] It is not that the nationalist *autonomistas*, the anti-Galizanists of the PP, and part of the PSdeG have the same agenda but that their respective agendas coincide in their mutual rejection of, and authoritarian stance against, the *lusistas*. While the PP and PSdeG of the Vázquez brand demonize the *lusistas* because they are afraid to lose their Castilian identity, the nationalist *autonomistas* ostracize the *lusistas* because they fear losing their Galizan identity.[16] Herrero-Valeiro's second claim that the *normativa oficial* was sanctioned by the PP-governed Xunta is also false, for it is the RAG, not the Xunta, that has the power to sanction or reject a *normativa* proposal. The Xunta could in theory reject a RAG verdict, but such a motion would violate the Language Normalization Act. The Xunta therefore did not sanction the *NOMIG-82* or the *norma da concordia* of 2003 but rather accepted the RAG's decision on both occasions.

Portugal: So Close, So Far

In August 2001, the Galizan political-cultural magazine *Tempos novos* published a special section exploring the problematic relations between Galiza and Portugal. On the front page of the magazine is a sketch of a tiled house with two windows side by side and a woman looking out of each window. The women appear to be neighbors, but while one woman stares at the other as if wanting to catch her attention, the other looks off to the distance unaware of, or indifferent to, her neighbor. Metaphorically, this scene captures precisely the current predicament of Galizans and Portuguese; while many Galizans desire some form of convergence with the Portuguese, this desire is not reciprocal.

Eight centuries of separation between Galiza and Portugal have not passed in vain. Different political, cultural, and linguistic trajectories and isolation from each other have created barriers between the two nations to the extent that most Portuguese do not differentiate Galiza from the rest of Spain. Rodrigues Fagim addresses this issue at the end of the prologue to his book:

> Se o apoio que recebéssemos de Portugal fosse só similar ao que flamengos, valencianos, moldávios, valdostianos, sul tiroleses recebem da Holanda, a Catalunha, a Roménia, a França e a Alemanha, os nossos objectivos seriam sem dúvida mais atingíveis. Saudaçons intraculturais! (9)

> If the support we received from Portugal were only equivalent to what the Flemish, Valencians, Moldovans, Valdostians, South Tyrolese, receive from Holland, Catalonia, Romania, France, and Germany, our objectives would no doubt be more achievable. Intracultural greetings!

For a reintegration project to be minimally successful, therefore, Galiza must overcome not only the obstacles in its own community but also the lack of enthusiasm on the other side of the Minho River (which separates Galiza and Portugal) and throughout the Portuguese-speaking world.

Spain's integration into the EU could have helped foster the creation of a Euro region that spans Galiza and northern Portugal. However, the funds provided by Brussels to create such a region, claims the *lusista* scholar Carlos Quiroga, ended up in the hands of Galiza's right-wing PPdeG, which rejects any form of Galizan integration into the lusophone world ("O galego" 12). María Márquez explains that many writers, artists, and media professionals in both Galiza and Portugal agree that cross-border relations are probably now almost nonexistent. According to Márquez, the scarce cultural exchanges that take place between Galiza and Portugal are products of personal initiatives and friendships (23). The two entities subsidized by the EU, A Comunidade de Trabalho and O Eixo Atlántico ("Work Community and Atlantic Axis"), have increased commercial exchanges between the two communities but have hardly improved cultural relations (22). Commercial exchanges have little impact on cultural relations, for the economic sector has no need to build "fraternal" connections (25). Indeed, Portuguese business people usually use Spanish to communicate with Galizans (24).

Galizanists, as well as Galizan artists and writers, often criticize Portugal's lack of interest in and ignorance of Galiza and the Galizan language. Several criticisms were voiced in the press during the "Encontro Galego no mundo, Latim en pó" ("Galizan Forum in the World, Latin in Dust"), which took place in Compostela in December 2000.[17] For example, the Galizan writer Luisa Villalta declared:

> Na Galiza existimos porque existiamos. Neste encontro somos algo que Portugal non quer recoñecer, o óvulo deste conxunto lusófono, desta família vella que agora se xunta porque somos a orixe da língua, como a muller que queda supeditada ao progreso dos fillos.
> (qtd. in Vidal, "Compostela"; see also Capeáns; Vidal and Bergantiños)

> In Galiza we exist because we existed. In this forum we are something Portugal does not want to recognize, the ovum of this lusophone ensemble, of this old family that now comes together because we are the origin of the language, like the woman who remains subordinate to the progress of her children.

The irony of Portugal's ignorance of Galiza and Galizan, as Villalta pinpoints, is that the Portuguese language originated in the kingdom of Galiza.

A criticism in the same vein was made by Antón Reixa, a Galizan film director and rock singer, who explained that the only place in the world where he saw the name of his rock group Os Resentidos Castilianized (as Los Resentidos) was in Portugal. He tried to explain to the Portuguese press (first in Galizan and then in Portuguese) that this name should be left in Galizan, but the journalists, who obstinately spoke to him in Spanish, did not understand his point of view ("Portugal"). António Medeiros, a Portuguese ethnographer, tells another illustrative story of Portuguese ignorance of Galiza. In Compostela in July 1999, a Galizan young man approached a group of Portuguese tourists on the same day the king of Spain and the president of the Portuguese Republic were in the city. The tourists seemed to be "operários de fábricas mas também estariam ligados ao trabalho na terra" (321; "factory workers, but probably also involved in agricultural work"). The young man sang with them the Portuguese *cantiga* "Laurindinha." At the end of the song the Galizan man, who had been leading the chorus, shouted "Viva Galiza ceibe! Viva Portugal!" (321; "Long live a free Galiza! Long live a free Portugal!"). The tourists, bewildered by the exclamation, asked each other "O que é que este homem quer" ("What does this man want?") and declared "parece maluco o espanholito" (322; "this little Spaniard seems crazy").

Xosé Luís Méndez Ferrín, a staunch anti-*lusista*, claims that in Portugal

> hai un consenso intelectual para ignorar a Galicia. Hai excepcións pero a no-
> ción de Galicia e da lingua galega unida á portuguesa contradí o relato nacio-
> nal de Portugal. (Interview [*Tempos*] 40)[18]

> there is an intellectual agreement to ignore Galiza. There are exceptions, but
> the notion of Galiza and the Galizan language united with Portuguese contra-
> dicts Portugal's national narrative.

João de Melo, a Portuguese writer from the Azores Islands, seconds Méndez Ferrín's claim, arguing that Portuguese writers are all focused on Madrid, since that is where they perceive literary success to be based (43). Viale Moutinho, a contemporary Portuguese writer, agrees:

> O lector portugués cre que non é capaz de ler un libro en galego. Se lle pre-
> guntas que linguas sabe, non deixará de dicir que francés, inglés e, "natural-
> mente" español. E está disposto a traducir do castelán, agora que do galego
> nin pensar. (30)

> Portuguese readers don't think they can read a book in Galizan. If you ask
> what languages they know, they will only say French, English, and "naturally"
> Spanish. And they are happy to translate from Spanish, but it wouldn't occur
> to them to do so from Galizan.

The Portuguese are not willing, for the most part, to read in the *normativa dos máximos* either, thus *lusistas* cannot market their works in the Portuguese-speaking world without translating them into Portuguese. Though the *normativa de máximos* is almost identical to Portuguese, its differences are relevant enough to make Portuguese publishers reject it. However, Pilar Vázquez emphasizes that the lack of Portuguese interest in Galizan literature stems less from unwillingness to read Galizan than from simply not knowing of the existence of Galizan literature.

While Portuguese indifference to Galiza stems mainly from historical factors, the central reason for the rejection of a reintegration project within Galiza is economic. Because Portugal is a smaller and economically weaker country than Spain, Galizans have no immediate economic incentive for converging with Portugal. N. Dorian points out that "language loyalty persists as long as the economic and social circumstances are conducive to it, but if some other language proves to have greater value, a shift to that other language begins" (qtd. in Cooper 93). Robert Cooper posits that when language shifts occur regardless of economic factors, it is because a language is tied to religion (93). Given that religion is not connected to the preservation of Galizan and that the economic factors are not favorable to reintegration, stronger linguistic and cultural ties between Portugal and Galiza will not occur spontaneously; they must be promoted at a political level in both nations.

During the bipartite government of the PSdeG and BNG (2005–09), there was some political initiative to increase awareness of Galiza's cultural and linguistic relation to Portugal. Quiroga, for example, was invited to a program every other week on the Televisión de Galicia (TVG) to talk about lusophone literature. He was also invited by the Asociación de Escritores en Lingua Galega (AELG) to foster literary exchanges between Portugal and Galiza (Message). Furthermore, this government showed some signs of tolerance toward *lusismo*. Quiroga mentions that the government purchased copies of the journal he edited, *Agália* ("O galego" 12), something the previous, Fraga government had never done. But since the unexpected victory of the PPdeG in April 2009, the political perspectives for Galizan engagement with the lusophone world are dim. When asked if there are any reasons at present to be optimistic vis-à-vis Galizan reintegration into the Portuguese-speaking world, Quiroga answered:

> O ataque final aos depauperados usos lingüísticos do galego na Galiza começou, e neste sentido o contacto com a lusofonia, que reconhecidamente em todos os tempos serviu de reforço da identidade e da galeguidade, tamém será reprimido. Por isso nom existem motivos para ser optimista. (Message)

> The final attack on the impoverished uses of Galizan in Galiza have begun, and in this sense contact with the lusophone world, which has always reinforced Galizan identity, will also be repressed. For this reason there is no cause to be optimistic.

Three Suggestions for Mitigating the Conflict

The different perceptions of group identity between *autonomistas* and *lusistas* make conciliation difficult, but I do not agree with Fernández Rei's claim that the only possible conciliation is between those with the same conception of language. Such a claim is dogmatic and deterministic, especially with the *autonomistas* in control of language planning. This kind of attitude closes the door to even partial conciliations. I agree, on the other hand, with Rafa Villar, who contends that though conciliation between the two positions is not possible from the standpoint of linguistic philosophy, an understanding can occur on a sociological level. He argues that a social consensus is needed between both ideologies, both perfectly legitimate ("Cal normative" 34), so that the status and acquisition planning of Galizan can be carried out more successfully.

One way to achieve this understanding is to include all the *lusistas* in future negotiations and to support their access to government subsidies and literary prizes. Many *lusistas* would accept the current *norma oficial* as the only form of Galizan taught in schools and used in the media and official institutions in exchange for lifting the ban on their eligibility for such subsidies and prizes. The editorial board of AGAL addresses this question:

> [A] "opçom normativa" nom é a nossa reinvindicaçom mais importante. Estám também em jogo a liberdade de expressom—sobretodo na criaçom literária—, o intercámbio bidireccional da produçom bibliográfica, o fomento das relaçons artísticas e associativas a nível galego-português e a eliminaçom de fronteiras para os meios de comunicaçom. Noutras palavras: se se suprime a censura nos prémios literários e nas ajudas á produçom editorial e se temos facilidades para nos formar con livros, revistas e meios da nossa área cultural, evidentemente estamos obrigados a mover peça.
>
> ("Reforma" 276; see also Guisán Seixas)

> The "normative option" is not our most important demand. We also take into account freedom of expression—especially in terms of literature—the two-way exchange of bibliographic production, the development of artistic and other relations between Galiza and Portugal, and the elimination of borders in the media. In other words: if censorship of literary prizes and editorial subventions is lifted and if we have the opportunity to educate ourselves with books, magazines, and other media, we will obviously be obliged to make a move.

Guaranteed (and perceived) freedom of expression for all would reduce the hostility of the conflict and help promote awareness of Galiza's linguistic and cultural proximity to Portugal, which is desired by *lusistas* and many *autonomistas* (see "Aínda").

FIG. 1. "Ready now, when I lower my arm, it's time to speak Galizan, we're going on air!" The famous Galizan cartoonist Xaquín Marín satirizes the protocol use of Galizan on Televisión de Galicia (TVG). The implication is that the Galizan spoken on this channel is heavily Castilianized.

The other two suggestions for creating sociological understanding between *lusistas* and *autonomistas* are, first, that each side reject the false accusations and fallacies described above and, second, that both groups find platforms they can embrace and advance. One issue, which both agree to be serious, is the progressive Castilianization of Galizan, which is threatening the language's differential status vis-à-vis Spanish. Some scholars have analyzed, from a grammatical and lexical point of view, the poor quality of Galizan employed by politicians and the media. Only one scholar, Regueira, has analyzed in depth the main element of Castilianization at stake, which is the phonetic assimilation of Galizan into Spanish.[19] The Galizan of native speakers, regardless of their dialect, sounds similar to Portuguese; notwithstanding, the Galizan used by the TV and radio news broadcasters, anchor people, dubbing artists, and so on resembles Spanish in pronunciation and intonation. Most announcers on TVG and on Radio Televisión Galega (RTG) are nonnative speakers of the language.

Lusistas and nationalist *autonomistas* could create a common platform to demand a non-Castilian oral standard for TVG and RTG; such a platform would fulfill each side's objective of protecting Galizan from Spanish influence.[20] This is not to say that nonnative speakers should be barred from the media and discouraged from using the language—indeed, the survival of Galizan depends to a considerable extent on these *neofalantes* (new speakers of Galizan). But if the dominant accent on television and radio remains Castilian, the language will continue to lose its distinctiveness from Spanish and become phonetically assimilated. Whether nationalist Galizans consider their language an independent language or a variant of Portuguese, it is becoming increasingly evident that the main battle for its preservation in the future will be fought not over orthography but in the oral realm.

Notes

Because the name *Galicia* is Spanish (and used in English), I prefer *Galiza*, the name used in medieval Galizan and still used in Portuguese. In my writings in the Galizan language I also use—like many other Galizan writers—*Galiza* instead of *Galicia,* which continues to be the official name in Spanish.

1. The first symptoms of what would become, two centuries later, the *conflito normativo* are apparent in the writings of Martín Sarmiento and the Cura de Fruíme. Freixeiro Mato states that while Sarmiento wrote his texts in an etymological-oriented orthography (from medieval Galizan), the Cura de Fruíme employed the Castilian orthographic system in his writings. The latter orthographic system is a precursor of the current-day *normativa autonomista* (117).

2. Diglossia occurs in a bilingual society in which one language is valued positively and used for formal (official, academic, etc.) purposes, while the other language is restricted to informal uses and spheres. Linguists use the denominations *language A* to refer to the language of prestige and power and *language B* to refer to the underdog. A language conflict occurs only when an influential group attempts to reverse the roles of languages A and B. In Galiza the language conflict became especially visible in the second half of the nineteenth century, when the group of writers that commenced the Rexurdimento began to denounce the marginalization of the Galizan language and culture. For insightful studies on diglossia, see Ferguson; Fishman, "Bilinguism" and *Handbook*; and Mauro Fernández Rodriguez.

3. It is for this reason that the graphization of Euskara, which uses the Spanish orthographic system, has not caused conflict: "O emprego destas ou daquelas coberturas gráficas nom qustiona a identidade da própria língua a respeito da língua tecto e, por suposto, nom acrescenta dificuldades ao seu aprendizado, já de per si problemático"

(Rodrigues Fagim 102; "The use of this or that graphic system does not question the identity of the language with respect to the dominant language; nor does it, of course, make learning the language, which is already problematic, more difficult").

4. See Joseph's perceptive reflexion on *Abstand* and *Ausbau* (25–27).

5. In the view of some *lusistas*, the poetry of the Rexurdimento constitutes an appendix of Spanish and is disconnected from Galiza's linguistic and literary heritage. The three main figures of this movement, Rosalía de Castro, Eduardo Pondal, and Curros Enríquez, were not acquainted with the works of the *ilustrados* ("enlightened"), nor were they familiar with Galizan medieval poetry or contemporary Portuguese. For this reason, they wrote their poetry in the only graphic system they had been taught, which was Spanish. The authors of the Xeración Nós used Spanish orthography but were *lusista*-oriented on a theoretical level. The *lusista* scholar Elias Torres Feijóo claims in his doctoral thesis that the cultural exchanges between Galiza and Portugal reached an all-time high during the period between World War I and the Spanish Civil War (*a entre Guerra*). According to this author, had fascism not triumphed, Galiza would have integrated into the Portuguese cultural system.

6. The fourth paragraph states: "Non quixemos, pois, nen seria posíbel obxectivamente, crear unha ríxida armazón de preceitos que impuxese dunha vez e de xeito autoritário solucións unívocas aos problemas que enfrentamos. A codificación que oferecemos basea-se en todos os esforzos anteriores, e mesmo na realidade empírica do desenrolo da escrita. A flexibilidade de certas normas e a posibilidade de opcións nalguns casos, non é resultado de indecisión por falta de autoridade, senón meditada política de adecuación, ás cirunstáncias prácticas, das posibilidades teóricas. Temos trazado unhas canles por onde poden correr sen violéncia as águas do idioma escrito, pretendendo axudar un movimento que vai de seu na dirección xeral, se ben non podemos deixar de rectificar no posíbel as desviacións ocasionadas por forzas alleas que se teñan interferido na deriva da língua" (12; "Therefore, we did not want, nor would it be objectively possible, to create a rigid framework of precepts that impose, once and for all and in an authoritarian fashion, one-way solutions for the problems we face. The codification we offer is based on all the previous efforts, and even on the empirical reality of the development of writing. The flexibility of certain norms and the possibility of options in some cases is not a result of indecision by lack of authority but a meditated politics of adapting theoretical possibilities to practical circumstances. We have created a path down which the waters of the written language can flow without violence. We want to help a movement that goes on its own in a general direction, but we cannot stop rectifying, when possible, the deviations caused by external forces that have interfered in the drifting of the language").

7. *NOMIG-82*, unlike the *Bases*, introduced the representation of the allomorphic article (as in *colle-lo millo*, *Ti fa-lo traballo*, and *tódalas semanas* instead of *coller o millo*, *Ti fas o traballo*, and *todas as semanas*).

8. For example, *nom*, *estivo*, and *tomou-nas* are used instead of the Portuguese *não*, *esteve*, and *tomou-as*.

9. These four writers are not *lusistas*, strictly speaking, because they write (or wrote, like Casares) in the *norma oficial.*

10. For articles that criticized Nogueira's use of Portuguese and opposed reopening debate on the *normativa* question, see Dobao, "A lingua extravagante"; Ferro Ruibal, ¿"Sereas?" and "¿Podemos?"; A. Conde, "Somos perdedores," "Cada un," and "Unha opción"; Tarrío Varela, "A ver"; and Monteagudo, "Galego." Two anti-*lusista* articles that do not criticize Nogueira but were published in the wake of his interventions in Strasbourg are C. Rodríguez; Rodríguez-Fischer, "Alonso Montero".

11. According to Regueira, it was not only the ILG but also the AS-PG who agreed on carrying out the negotiations without the *lusistas* (those *lusistas* who used the *normativa dos máximos*). He also contends that many of the *lusistas* were never willing to participate in the negotiations "porque non crían que ese acordo puidese satisfacer as súas expectativas e preferían seguir defendendo as súas posturas, aínda que comprendían o carácter político do acordo. Outros (máis inxenuos) sentíronse traizoados" (Message; "because they did not believe that that agreement [on the new *normativa*] would satisfy their expectations and they preferred to continue defending their positions, even though they understood the political nature of the agreement. Others [the more ingenuous ones] felt betrayed").

12. *Estudiar* is now the Portuguese *estudar*; the Portuguese *até* is accepted alongside *ata*; the form *ao* is preferred to *ó*; the suffix *-ábel* is preferred to *-able*. Important too is that *Galiza* is now accepted alongside *Galicia*, although the latter continues to be the official name of the nation.

13. The extreme view that a *lusista* project would open the door to Portuguese imperialism is found in Abuín de Tembra, according to whom there are groups in Portugal waiting to "troca-lo imperialismo de Madrid polo imperialismo de Lisboa. . . . Móvense por convulsións de alferecía" ("exchange the imperialism of Madrid for that of Lisbon. . . . They move with epileptic convulsions").

14. Vázquez referred to the new *normativa* proposal in 2001 as "unha estratexia de nazificación do noso país" ("¿Concordia incómoda?"; "a strategy of nazifying our country") and constituting a "tramado batasuneiro que creou o BNG" ("Paco Vázquez" 31; "A *batasuna*-style [referring to the Basque pro-ETA nationalist party] plot created by the BNG").

15. The right-wing antinationalists of the PP also utilize this fallacy but as an attack against the *lusistas*. For example, Juan José Calaza states, "Sopesando los elementos en mano, la Academia Galega no puede aceptar ningún Diktat que so capa de *concordia lingüística* nos aboque a un sometimiento cultural lusista, salvo a desvincularse deslealmente del sentir expresado por la inmensa mayoría de los gallegos en las pasadas elecciones" ("Weighing up all the elements in hand, the Galizan Academy cannot accept any dictate that under the cover of *linguistic concordance* will lead us straight to *lusista* cultural subordination, except by detaching itself disloyally from the opinion expressed by the immense majority of Galizans in previous elections").

16. In my interview of Monteagudo, he manifested his fear of losing his identity and heritage if the Galizan *normativa* ever became *lusista* (Personal interview).

17. This forum brought together, for the first time in Galiza, intellectuals and artists from all over the lusophone world: Galiza, Brazil, Portugal, Timor, and the African countries. From 11 to 15 December, activities and lectures took place on cinema, literature, music, theater, media, and the Galizan diaspora. The director of the forum, Elias Torres Feijóo, is a *lusista* scholar at the Universidade de Santiago de Compostela.

18. In another interview this author declares that the reason for this lack of interest in Galiza stems from Portuguese "self-hatred": "No fondo é autoodio, porque é lembrar-lle as súas orixes históricas" (Interview [*Faro*]; "Deep down it is self-hatred because it reminds them of their historical origins").

19. I have found through my investigations and interviews that *lusistas* tend to be more concerned than *autonomistas* about the gradual phonetic assimilation of Galizan into Spanish. Except for Regueira's impressive studies on this issue (see "Estándar oral" and "Modelos fonéticos"), the other written comments I have found come mostly from *lusistas*. Camilo Nogueira, for example, states that "os meios de comunicación autonómicos están a convertir foneticamente ao galego nunha forma dialectal do castelán" ("Unha decision"; "the media are changing Galizan phonetically into a dialect of Castilian"). Montanha observes that though standard Galizan has succeeded in removing Castilian lexical influences (largely by using Portuguese as the model), it has nonetheless endorsed Castilian pronunciation and intonation as the phonetic standard: "o galego culto tem exactamente a fonética do castelhano, e na entoação também, como se os falantes quisessem deixar claro que falam galego mas não são 'de aldeia'" ("Learned Galizan has exactly the same phonetics and intonation as Castilian, as if the speakers wanted to make clear that they speak Galizan but aren't 'from the country'"). The writings I have encountered by *autonomistas* who criticize the poor quality of Galizan on TVG and RTG are by Alonso Montero (*Informe[s]*) and Dobao ("A lingua galega"). Both critics agree on the need to promote better-quality Galizan (Dobao's analysis is much more extensive than Alonso Montero's), but they do not point to the main problem, which is the phonetic assimilation of Galizan into Spanish. Manuel Veiga also overlooks it.

20. Note that the *lusistas* do not promote Portuguese pronunciation of Galizan. Even Santamarina, who accuses the *lusistas* of wanting to convert the language into a satellite of Portuguese, admits, "Por parte dos reintegracionistas deféndese a conservación dunha pronuncia 'galega,' independente da veste gráfica" (81; "The reintegrationists defend the retention of 'Galizan' pronunciation, independent of the spelling").

Camping Up the Nation: Antón Lopo's *Ganga* and the Queering of Iberia

Timothy McGovern

> Máis que nada, propúxenme contar unha historia desde outra perspectiva, inverter os resultados, traslocar os dogmas, ler con outras claves.
> —Antón Lopo, *Xerais Online*, 2002

> More than anything, I intended to tell a story from another perspective, invert results, translocate dogmas, read through other keys.

In 1990, the United States–based Galician critic Xoan González-Millán set out his manifesto for the future of minor literatures such as Galician, arguing:

> Se a razón histórica dos pobos marxinais é, hoxe máis ca nunca, un esforzo de recuperación de perspectivas históricas perdidas ou silenciadas, redescubrir este mesmo pasado, dende unha perspectiva de reivindicación e resistencia simbólicas, implica o cuestionamiento e resistencia simbólicas, implica o cuestionamiento da perda de historicidade, é dicir, o seu proceso de despersonalización en tanto que espacio cultural específico. Non debe estrañar, pois, que o discurso étnico proxecte unha historia colectiva feita de acontecementos descontinuos, de choques, de estados conflictivos fixados no nivel do consciente e do inconsciente colectivo. ("Unha etnopoética" 343)

> If the historical project of marginalized peoples is, today more than ever, a struggle for the recuperation of lost or silenced historical perspectives, rediscovering this same past, from a perspective of symbolic justification and resistance, implies a symbolic questioning and resistance, implies the questioning of the loss of historicity—that is, the process of its depersonalization as a specific cultural space. It should not be surprising, therefore, that an ethnic discourse projects a collective history made up of discontinuous events, of clashes, of conflicts fixed at the level of the collective conscious and unconscious.

He went on to set out a scheme by which this manifesto could be carried out, proposing:

> en primeiro lugar, o cuestionamento da identificación, implícita en toda literatura *maior*, entre o principio de universalidade e os valores que proxectan os textos constitutivos do seu canon; a proxección dunha nova lectura crítica, incorporando ao paradigma crítico dimensións silenciadas polas institucións canonizadoras; e finalmente, a superación dos límites epistémicos impostos polo discurso crítico-literario das literaturas maiores, historiando en profundidade os procesos da súa constitución.   (346)

> in the first place, the questioning of the identification, implicit in every *major* literature, between the principle of universality and the values projected by the texts that make up its canon; the projection of a new form of critical reading, incorporating into the critical paradigm dimensions silenced by the canonizing institutions; and, finally, the overcoming of the epistemic limits imposed by the critical-literary discourse of the major literatures, historicizing deeply the processes of its constitution.

Radical as they sound (and indeed were), González-Millán's manifesto and defense of the peripheral go only so far. Most notably, González-Millán does not address the extent to which Galicia—as he says, a marginalized people within the Spanish state—is itself home to a host of marginalized voices. Galician culture has, since 1975, become increasingly institutionalized, but this institutionalization, which should create a possibility for multiple, equally Galician forms of culture, in fact often seems to have had the opposite effect. Galicia's own minority voices are still marginalized, perhaps none more so than the voices of its sexual minorities.

In this essay I argue for the existence of a culture that is both queer and Galician and that remains largely underground and rarely acknowledged—in fact, often simply ignored—by critics. First I offer some context, outlining Spanish and specifically marginalized Spanish uses of a camp aesthetic of resistance; then I model a particular interpretation of queer Galicianness through a close and contextualized reading of the first openly queer novel to be published in modern Galicia, Antón Lopo's *Ganga* (2001). This reading paves the way for the theorization of a close relation between camp and the queering of Galician culture.

National Camp: Queering Iberia from the Margins

The definition of the term *camp* and its relevance for queer cultures have been debated ever since Susan Sontag's essay "Notes on Camp" was published in 1964. Especially contentious has been Sontag's statement, "It goes without saying that the Camp sensibility is disengaged, depoliticized—or at least apolitical" (289), because some see camp as a potent political tool. For example, Alberto Mira proposes that camp in the Spain of the 1960s and 1970s was not only a powerful form of resistance to Franco but also a means of laying claim to a place in the new Spanish democracy:

> Durante el franquismo, la expresión camp estaba íntimamente relacionada con el silenciamiento de la experiencia homosexual. Ahora una retórica similar se utilizará con una intención provocadora: la *provocación* consistuía todo un gesto que pretendía confirmar que el franquismo estaba superado.   (526)

> Under Franco, camp expression was intimately related with the silencing of the homosexual experience. Now a similar rhetoric will be used with a provocative intention: the *provocation* constituted a gesture intended to confirm that Francoism was over.

This subversive function of camp readings, shared among homosexuals during a repressive regime, demonstrates a strategy of modern camp production that cannot be explained except through modern Spanish history. While the cause of gay liberation has made significant progress on the national level in Spain, culminating in the legalization of gay marriage in 2004, national legal recognition does not necessarily translate into local acceptance, and it translates even less in the context of Spain's marginalized cultures.

In the Catalan context, Josep-Anton Fernández has studied the impact of the early works of Terenci Moix on an emerging Catalan nationalism and its attempts to normalize Catalan culture. With regard to queerness and nation building, he examines "homosexual desire and its disturbing effects on social reproduction," presenting Moix as "undertaking an effort to rewrite the history of modern Catalonia, against both the official version of Francoism and the para-official yet subaltern version of Catalan nationalism" (6). The use of elements and images from popular films is a fixture of queer fictions (including film), and Moix takes full advantage of this fact to create a uniquely camp vocabulary in works such as *Món mascle* (1971; "My Male") and in the characters of the supernatural creature-divinity that ravages Spain's socialites in *Mujercísimas* (1995; "Intensely Women") or the gay Golem that rapes his male victims in *Chulas y famosas* (1999; "Female Show-Offs and Celebs").

In Galician literature, little or nothing has been written from an explicitly queer perspective. A model does exist in feminist studies, however, where the prevalence of a male-centered (and, of course, heterocentric) concept of Galician literature and its effect on canon formation has been analyzed by feminist critics such as Helena González Fernández. She celebrates the emerging tendency in 1990s female poets to challenge that male-centered view of literature and to reclaim their place in a literature that has been labeled Galician while in fact being used to support a particular, limited version of Galicianness:

> É a poesía da outredade, empanada na reapropiación de mitos e tópicos que só foron explotados desde o punto de vista masculino, e, sobre todo, fuxir desa poesía sentimentalista e testemuñal que pexa a tradición literaria feminina. É poesía escrita para a conciencia e a rebelión, co obxectivo de construír un discurso novo, combatente, e mesmo subversivo.   ("1914" 170)

> It is the poetry of otherness, concerned with the reappropriation of myths and commonplaces that have been exploited only from a masculine point of view, and, above all, fleeing from that sentimentalist and testimonial poetry that keeps the female literary tradition on a leash. It is poetry written for the conscience and for rebellion, with the objective of constructing a discourse that is new, combative, and even subversive.

González Fernández's account of the plight of women at the hands of patriarchal institutions can be connected with González-Millán's account of the plight of Galicians in Spain and also with that of homosexuals in a heterosexist culture.

Lopo takes the connection one stage further as, in his novel *Ganga*, he explicitly develops the theoretical connection between Galicians in Spain and homosexuals in a heterosexist world to include all sexual minorities (women, homosexuals, intersexed people). Like women in Galicia and Moix in Catalunya, Galicia's sexual minorities have often resorted to a combative stance in order to battle the forces that repress their gender and sexuality from within, and beyond, their national framework. Gay utopian texts create imaginary worlds where sexual minorities exercise power, and Lopo uses this strategy to create a Galicia that is truly at the center of world affairs.

Queer Galicia? Antón Lopo and *Ganga*

Antón Lopo is the pseudonym of Antón Rodríguez López, a Galician poet, novelist, artist, journalist, and performer (born at Monforte de Lemos in 1961) who has enjoyed significant critical success with his biography *As tres mortes de Lorenzo Varela* (2005; "The Three Deaths of Lorenzo Varela"), his reception of the prestigious Álvaro Cunqueiro Literary Award for his drama *Os homes só contan até tres* (2006; "Men Can Only Count to Three"), and the enthusiastic critical reception of *Ganga*. He is also the author of numerous collections of poetry and is considered a major figure in the promotion of Galician cutting-edge cultural production (McGovern). *Ganga* is a work that may be located neatly in the tradition of modern queer cultural production. It fuses a camp aesthetic with the goal of contributing to, and defending, a more inclusive definition of Galician culture.

It is telling that Lopo has taken an artistic stance that uses a myriad strategies to foreground and also undermine sexual and gender oppression. Even more tellingly, he has applied this aesthetic to a novel that puts Galicia at the center of a plot to take over the world. The thriller genre is a recent innovation in Galicia, and its popularity has been seen by some critics as symptomatic of a radical change in the Galician cultural system (Domínguez Alberte 90). *Ganga* as a hybrid science fiction–fantasy-spy novel is thus already distanced generically from traditional Galician narrative. Lopo puts a specifically Galician twist on the foreign genre in that the hero and villain are both Galician, while the scientific mastermind is Portuguese. The novel has a further, queer twist in that the hero of the tale is homosexual. As a literary work, the novel displaces and even erases the traditional wielders of power, heterosexual males and the Spanish government and official culture centered in Madrid. They are replaced with sexual minorities (women, gay and bisexual men) to create a new Spain composed of the historically marginalized zones of Galicia and, to a lesser degree, Catalunya.

Among critics who have studied the novel, Joaquim Pujol Guerrero pays special attention to this recentering of the normal in the work, focusing especially on the central roles of sexual minorities and the foregrounding of Spain's drug culture. With regard to the novel's extensive use of drug-related terminology, in this case a drug termed Mitsubitchi, Pujol Guerrero states:

> Éste es un fenómeno interesante. Al ignorar el punto de vista del discurso dominante (que en teoría no sabe qué son las Mitscubitchi y exige una ex-

plicación) el autor emplea la misma estrategia de este discurso dominante cuando omite voluntariamente en todo tipo de representaciones a aquéllos que desea marginar (mujeres, homosexuales, etc.). De igual manera casi todo lo que habitualmente se etiqueta de *normal* se ve barrido en la novela.

This is an interesting phenomenon. By ignoring the point of view of the dominant discourse (which in theory does not know about Mitsubitchi and requires an explanation), the author employs the same strategy as this dominant discourse when he voluntarily omits those he wishes to marginalize (women, homosexuals, etc.) from any kind of representation. In the same way, almost everything that is usually labeled as *normal* is erased from the novel.

But Pujol Guerrero overlooks one of the most glaring erasures or omissions in this work, which is when Lopo applies a traditionally queer strategy, or one focusing on sexual minorities, to the current situation of linguistic and cultural minorities.

Mateo Iglesias's review of the novel notes the creative use of geography so typical to many postmodern novels and states:

> *Ganga* é unha novela nómade, á que só se lle recoñecen ancoraxes xeográficas, porque a súa trama trepidante conduce a unha festa de xéneros, unha itinerancia de rexistros por vieiros fragmentarios e paralelos.   ("Unha novela")

> *Ganga* is a nomadic novel, in which geographic anchors are only barely recognizable, because its rollicking plot leads to a carnival of genres, to registers wandering along fragmentary and parallel paths.

I disagree with Iglesias: Lopo's playful narrative does suggest a concrete geography, but an alternative one, in which Spain is composed exclusively of the autonomous communities. No mention is ever made of Madrid, and the details of Ganga's travels between Galicia and Barcelona are characterized by a total lack of description. On the other hand, fictional versions of Galicia, Barcelona, and even India are given in vivid and wide-ranging geographic detail. In fact, the novel's representation of Galicia is one that would be expected in a realist novel; throughout the work, the narrator conscientiously provides the names of streets, plazas, towns, and other geographic features.

Ganga lives on the Rúa do Xeneral Pardiñas in the city of Santiago de Compostela (33), and his travels in Galicia are repeatedly highlighted by geographic references, such as to an evening in Santiago, when the fog "ocultaba o reloxo da Berenguela e facía remuíños nas prazas" (28; "concealed the clock on the Berenguela [clock tower] and swirled around the city squares"). When he and his friend and ally Lola travel to visit the psychic Felipe Mazas, the landscape and scenery are described in detail: "Na baixada ó val de Monforte, debuxouse no horizonte a Serra dos Sete Picos" (137; "As the road descended into the Monforte valley, the outline of the Serra dos Sete Picos [Seven Peaks Mountain Range] could be glimpsed on the horizon"). This explicit use of description is in glaring contrast to the erasure of a Spain beyond the *autonomías*. During Ganga's trips between Santiago and Barcelona, no mention is made of any lands or cultures existing between the two. In fact, his first trip to Barcelona is also his first trip outside Galicia:

> Era a primeira vez que se poñía cara a cara co exterior, a primeira vez que traspasaba as fronteiras da súa xeografía biolóxica, anque nos libros e na súa cabeza viaxara polas terras incógnitas e explorara lugares que non se recollían nos atlas. (83)

> It was the first time he had come face to face with the outside world, the first time he had crossed the frontiers of his biological geography, although in books, and in his head, he had traveled through unknown lands and explored places that didn't appear in any atlas.

Fran Alonso, in another review of the novel, recognizes Lopo's project to create a new cultural geography of Galicia through its association with a cosmopolitan, contemporary world of hybrid cultures that is far from the stereotypical representation of a traditional, rural, backward Galicia:

> O inefable personaxe, Ganga, chama por nós, desde a súa caricatura, desde a súa inmensa tenrura, desde un estupendo sentido do humor para nos mostrar todo o poderío desa mestisaxe cosmopólita, galega e contemporánea que, páxina a páxina, embebeda toda a novella. ("A viaxe astral")

> That ineffable character, Ganga, calls to us, from his caricature, from his immense tenderness, from a stupendous sense of humor, to reveal to us all the power of that cosmopolitan, Galician, contemporary *mestisaxe* [*métissage*] that page after page, intoxicates the whole novel.

The *mestisaxe* that Alonso recognizes can be seen on many levels. The plot of *Ganga* demonstrates Lopo's delight in plundering tropes and moments from pop culture from the 1960s through the 1990s, especially those of anglophone popular television and film. Ganga (whose real name is Eladio Villar López) is an enormous and inactive dreamer who spends his time at home satisfying his cravings for fatty foods and hallucinogenic drugs.[1] But when he discovers the death of his lover, Rose (whose given name was Luís Meixide Vázquez), Ganga is drawn into a bizarre plot undertaken by a secret organization, the Comunidade da Intelixencia Universal ("Universal Intelligence Community"), which is attempting to take over the world and create a race of immortal shape-shifting vampires. With the help of Lola, who is from the Galician city of Lugo, Ganga makes several trips between different points in Galicia and Barcelona in order to uncover the truth of his lover's death. He is finally sent to India to battle the supernatural masterminds of the evil plot. It is there, after he has taken on the female identity of Natalia Martínez, that it is revealed that only he has the superhuman mental powers to save the world.

The novel is clearly a queer parody of several genres of film and television programs that have been highly popular since the 1960s, many of which have been recycled by gay authors internationally. The gay tradition of fusing social criticism with science fiction and the supernatural can be traced back to William S. Burroughs's works. The kind of B-movie plots that influence *Ganga* are central to the queer-camp canon of products usurped by homosexuals for alternative readings and interpretations. In his introduction to the camp film canon, *High Camp*, Paul Roen describes the sort of plot that *Ganga* emulates, here equating science fiction with horror:

> The best definition of a horror film that I ever heard is simply this: an exercise in "controlled bad taste." That may suffice in the camp horror film; in the gay camp horror film, however, it's imperative that the bad taste be seriously out of control. To appeal to gays, in other words, a camp horror film should be not only cheap, but also sleazy and vulgar. The plot should transgress the bounds of bourgeois decency. A bizarre and grotesque sexuality should pervade the proceedings (either homo- or hetero-; it makes no difference). These are the sort of films that appall the oppressive middle-class mind. (13)

One of the first genres that *Ganga* devours and then reinterprets through a new lens that is both queer and Galician is the camp (though not originally gay) 1960s spy fantasy. A curious aspect of this still-popular genre is that apparently all supervillains and maniacal geniuses aim their plans for conquering the world either at London or the English countryside. This is part of what makes these films and television programs so easily read as camp, for their preposterous plots also foreground the truth that Britain is no longer the grand empire of the past. Andrew Ross extends the fading power of the United Kingdom as a world power in the 1960s to its role as a cultural force: "That is why the British flag, for Mods and other subcultures, and Victoriana, for the later Sergeant Pepper culture, became camp objects; precisely because of the historical association with a power that was now spent" (312).

In Lopo's Galician reinterpretation of the genre, the subversion of the genre and the inversion of gender and sociopolitical hierarchies are clear from the introduction of Maxwell, the mastermind of a nefarious drug cartel:

> El estudaba con Rose e Rose bautizárao co alcume de Maxwell Smart, anti-héroe dunha serie de televisión moi famosa na época ó que fisicamente se lle parecía. A Ganga resultáballe un home desagradable. Os labios constrinxidos para disimular as pegadas dos experimentos psicodélicos nuns dentes ós que ningún dentista lograra devolverlles a brancura.   (39)

> He studied with Rose, and Rose had christened him with the nickname Max-well Smart, a TV antihero who was very popular at the time and whom he resembled physically. Ganga found him a disagreeable man. His lips were pressed together to conceal the marks left by psychedelic experiments on a set of teeth that were beyond the help of any tooth-whitening dentist.

Maxwell's namesake creates a framework for reading the text not only in the context of the 1960s spy fantasy but also in relation to the parodies that the genre inspired. For example, the protagonist of *Get Smart* was just as bun-gling as Ganga, the hero of this narrative, and both were forced to battle a maniacally criminal organization.[2] *Ganga's* Maxwell Smart is revealed to be no more than a pawn used by his superiors (and he is eventually murdered). *Get Smart* competed in popularity with another program that parodied the supersexualized James Bond character by pairing the male spy with much more intelligent and effective female sidekicks: the highly stylized British program *The Avengers* (1961–68). But the female spy and crime fighter in *The Avengers* was an amateur, and both female leads (Honor Blackman play-ing Ms. Cathy Gale, and later Diana Rigg playing Mrs. Emma Peel) had essentially asexual relationships with their partner. Both were much more educated, more physically powerful, and more adept in areas of the occult and the supernatural than their dandy male partner, John Steed, played by Patrick Macnee.

Considering that *The Avengers* also parodied the James Bond series, except that it now placed a women as the main action character, and also utilized repeatedly the plot device of a secret society bent on taking over the world, *Ganga* most certainly plunders elements from this program as well. First, Ganga has his sidekick, Lola. In true camp form, she, like Ganga himself, is wary of heterosexual males; her cynical attitude toward most men makes her impervious to seduction. Her vast knowledge of the occult brings Ganga into contact with the resistance to the nefarious plans of the Comunidade da Intelixencia Universal. With regard to romantic love, her ideas are clearly stated, and she would even seem to personify a female James Bond in her exploitation of the opposite sex:

> Nos momentos en que quedaba enviso, ela entreteíao coas historias dos seus amantes. Unha lista interminable de homes que conquistara, "moitos con notable esforzo," presumía, e polos que nunca sentira amor. "Unha muller namorada é unha mulher enferma," aseguraba con autoridade de cátedro. "O amor non é máis ca unha propaganda. Un invento para manter a rentes a exaltación xuvenil. Se pensas no amor, non pensas na loita. O amor está ben nas mulleres dos funcionarios, que non teñen outro consolo para xustificar a súa lealdade, ou para os escritores, que inventan paixóns transcendentes onde só hai lagoas de imaxinación." (30–31)

> Whenever he was down, she would entertain him with stories about her lovers. An interminable list of men she had conquered, "many with considerable force," she boasted, and for whom she had never felt any love. "A woman in love is a sick woman," she declared with the authority of a professor. "Love is nothing more than propaganda. An invention to rein in youthful exuberance. If you're thinking about love, you aren't thinking about fighting. Love is fine for civil servants' wives, who have no other consolation to justify their loyalty, or for writers, who invent transcendent passions where there are only gaps in their imagination."

Lola's character is characteristically camp on several levels. First, she is represented as an unfeeling diva, which is one of the most common figures in gay male writing: to find examples, one need only look to almost any of Pedro Almodóvar's films or Moix's novels, not to mention the films of Almodóvar's United States influence and predecessor, John Waters, or the 1930s Hollywood director Georg Cukor, to whom Moix's *Mujercísimas* is a tribute. Definitions of the camp diva vary, but Philip Core articulates a definition that certainly applies to Lola when he discusses the actress Tallulah Bankhead:

> Whether egoism or orgasm was her motive is hard to tell today; she seems to have combined them in a manic aggression more readily comprehended

in a Don Juan. . . . She died rich—from emphysema and an addiction to prescribed drugs. These were ministered by an adoring band of homosexuals who found in her a woman who liked sex divorced from love or personality and made no bones about it. (25)

Lola and Ganga's relationship echoes that of the actress and her fans. Helping Ganga recover from the discovery of his lover's death, Lola caters to his ravenous appetites for attention, food, and drugs. To raise his spirits, she promises him a fabulous luncheon with the following menu:

> "Un bisté, un par de ovos fritidos, un gran zume de laranxa, dúas cuncas de café con leite e de sobremesa . . . ," excitouno ela engruñándose como o trasno das amanitas, "de sobremesa . . ." e tirou dos petos una caixa dourada. "Opio." (30)

> "A piece of steak, a couple of fried eggs, a huge orange juice, two mugs of milky coffee and *for dessert* . . . ," she urged him, crouching like a troll, "*for dessert* . . . ,*"* and she pulled a golden box out of her pocket. "*Opium.*"

Neither Lola nor Ganga, nor even the shape-shifting villain, Ámbar, performs a traditional gender role. Ganga himself is aware of his androgyny, revealing it when he reminisces about his childhood:

> O de andróxino debía ser pola liviandade dos seus modais, que xa de neno chamaban atención. A el non lle importaba. . . . Tippi Hedren era o seu metro patrón e, durante anos, máis da adolescencia, Tippi Hedren inspirou o seu comportamento. (90)

> The androgynous thing must have been because of his volubility, which was already attracting attention when he was a boy. It didn't matter to him. . . . Tippi Hedren was his idol and, for years, for most of his adolescence, Tippi Hedren inspired his behavior.

Throughout the novel, his gender transgressions cause no shock, nor does homosexuality or homosexual acts in general. Ganga essentially functions as a James Bond but in reverse, seducing two apparently heterosexual men, both taxi drivers, one from Galicia and the other from India. Ganga seduces the first in order to steal his taxi and escape from the scene of a murder; the second seduction is unintentional. Venú, his guide and driver in India, patiently serves Ganga in the hope that a sexual liaison may finally occur— Ganga is disguised as a woman, Natalia. When he emerges from his hotel room as a man to find Venú sleeping on the floor in his doorway as his guard, the discovery has no effect on the desire that Ganga inspires: "A Venú non lle importou aquil repentino cambio de sexo. Mirouno co mesmo feitizo do día anterior" (177; "Venú didn't care about the sudden change of sex. He looked at him with the same enchantment as the previous day").

The fictional world of the novel is practically postgender. Rose has sex with both men and women but is never considered bisexual, and Ganga provides his own definition of sexuality:

> As cuestións da orientación sexual parecíanlle un método enganoso de sometemento, unha argucia para tapar conceptos incómodos, como o desexo ou a natureza aberta do amor, que el non ligaba ó instinto biolóxico. (62)

> Questions of sexual orientation seemed to him to be a treacherous means of domination, a trick to conceal uncomfortable concepts, like desire or the open nature of love, which he did not link to biological instinct.

The only truly tender scene in the novel is when Ganga finally destroys Venú's dreams of any future sexual encounter: "'Non vai ser posible, Venú, tal vez noutra vida' e Venú levantouse e marchou mexéndose cara a escuridade" (193; "'It isn't going to happen, Venú, maybe in another life,' and Venú got up and walked away, swaying, into the darkness"). Ganga, unlike traditional male adventurers in film, appears to have established priorities (at least while trying to save the world) that do not include gratuitous sex.

Lola is written as a female Don Juan, devoid of amorous sentiment, yet she is a good friend to homosexuals and to other women. Her final evaluation of love, and the role of writers who have created it as a lie to appease women, demonstrates another camp strategy, that of denaturalizing fictions and demonstrating all fictions to be far removed from lived experience—or at least proposing that traditional fictions cannot represent the lived existence of sexual minorities. The film critic Richard Dyer proposes this process as one of the leading functions of camp readings historically:

> Art and the media don't give us life as it really is—how could they?—but only life as artists and producers think it is. Camp, by drawing attention to the artifices employed by artists, can constantly remind us that what we are seeing is only a view of life. This doesn't stop us enjoying it, but it does stop us believing what we are shown too readily. It stops us thinking that those who create the landscape of culture know more about life than we do ourselves. A camp appreciation of art and the media can keep us on our guard against them—and considering their view of gayness, and sexuality in general, that's got to be a good thing. ("It's Being" 115)

The narrator of *Ganga*, and Lopo himself, is clearly aware that literature can lie and also that cultural institutions can privilege certain works, and types of works, in order to postulate that they are truer to reality than others. What makes Lopo's work so exciting and innovative in terms of contemporary Galician cultural production is that Lopo is questioning the reality of the status quo from the position not only of the cultural minority (Galicia) but also that of the sexual minority (the homosexual male). This double aspect of his work points to new ways of expressing Galician culture. If modern Galician cultural production has sought to become normalized through depictions—whether utopian or dystopian—of Galicia, Lopo uses the same strategy but infused with a queer twist.

Camp and the Queering of Galician Culture

Ganga portrays a world in which sexual minorities have usurped the position of dominance. Lopo also proposes a utopian vision of Galicians and their homeland, in part by rearticulating the themes of nostalgia and emigration that have permeated Galician cultural production since the poetry of Rosalía de Castro in the 1860s. In the novel, Galician emigration, both in Spain and beyond, is seen as positive, for it provides a web of agents to help Ganga protect the world. When he arrives in Barcelona and must disguise himself in order to continue searching for clues concerning the distribution of the drug Cofs—Cofs will be used to create human cattle on which the immortals of the Comunidade de Intelixencia Universal feed—Ganga's first acquaintance is Óscar, a hairdresser from the small Galician coastal town of Ribadeo. The flippant humor that permeates their conversation is typical of the novel, as is Lopo's use of outrageous situations, but their interaction is also one of the many moments in which an almost secret society of Galician agents is revealed:

> O de Ribadeo saíu na conversa, comentando o aburrido que lle resultaba o mar Mediterráneo. "¡Que casualidade!" exclamou Ganga. "Eu tamén sou galego." "Barcelona está chea de galegos." "Es o primeiro que vexo." "Será porque acabas de chegar." (84)

> The Ribadeo thing came up in conversation, when [Óscar] remarked on how boring he found the Mediterranean. "What a coincidence!" exclaimed Ganga. "I'm Galician too." "Barcelona is full of Galicians." "You're the first one I've seen." "That'll be because you've only just arrived."

The battle to control the planet is centered not in a postimperial England but in a post-Francoist Galicia. When Ganga is finally captured by an agent of the Comunidade, Boris Madaraiz, the agent reveals his organization's entire mission, as villains do in the spy-fantasy medium.[3] He explains their plans for world domination and for achieving immortality and says that the resistance movement began in Galicia, led by a Portuguese scientist, Dr. Liebebrief. The doctor takes several names and forms in the novel, including that of a psychonaut, or drug-induced psychic explorer, of the name Huxley—an obvious reference to Aldous Huxley and his work *The Doors of Perception* (1954). Boris narrates his mission to Galicia thus:

> Destinárano á península a finais dos anos oitenta por unha complicada operación financeira para desacreditar o doutor Liebebrief, que se introducira a través dun grupúsculo de discípulos nas universidades galegas e nas do norte de Portugal. . . . A máis de cociñeiro de intrigas, coordinaba os trabalhos das células ibéricas. En Galicia estaba a maior actividade da área, fortemente arraizada nos medios, nas empresas e na administración. . . .   (128)

> They had sent him to the peninsula at the end of the 1980s to carry out a complicated financial operation to discredit Dr. Liebebrief, which had been introduced through a small group of disciples in the Galician universities and in those in northern Portugal. . . . As well as cooking up intrigues, he coordinated the work of the Iberian cells. The greatest activity was in Galicia, where they were well established in the media, in business, and in the administration. . . .

It is revealed that one of their political pawns is a Galician politician from the ruling (at the time) Conservative Party, "un deputado galego do partido maioritario, con evidente afán de protagonismo, Xosé Sánchez Puga" (110; "a Galician politician from the ruling party, with a clear desire to be involved, Xosé Sánchez Puga"), whose moralizing stance against drugs and overeating (a jab at Ganga's two obsessions) hides his plan to transform all Galicia into a nation of drug addicts whose infected blood will give the Comunidade eternal life.

Utopian gay texts suggest imaginary worlds where sexual minorities now exercise power. Lopo extends this strategy to create a postgender Galicia that is truly at the center of world affairs. His Galicia does not have its own embassies like the imagined Catalunya of Moix's *Chulas y famosas*; it is instead the location where major world events unfold. The plot is preposterous, in part because of the radical contrast with reality—rather as much of the humor of *The Avengers* lies in its evocation of an all but extinct British

imperial culture. If, as González-Millán proposes, the artistic discourse of
oppressed ethnic groups (I would extend his theory to oppressed sexual minorities as well) must express conflicts and discontinuities as well as a coherent national history, then Lopo's novel depicts the unconscious history and
dreams of a Galicia at the center of artistic discourse while also proposing
a Galician literature and culture that are open to all participants, including
sexual minorities ("Unha etnopoética" 343).

Ganga is the necessary hero of this novel, for his gift is the ability to
store all the dreams of humankind, including those of liberation and the
formation of a truly dynamic national identity. After one of his many drug-
induced trances in which he collects the dreams that are revealed to him by
a band of his favorite angels, the importance of this task is revealed:

> Ganga metera aquiles recordos nunha caixa hermeticamente pechada e a caixa
> só se destapaba nos momentos lustrais da acción inducida, como a propiciada
> polo Asteroide.   (71)

> Ganga had placed those memories inside a hermetically sealed box, and he
> opened the box only at shining moments of forced action, like the one caused
> by the Asteroid.

It is this capacity for collecting and consuming the dreams of others that
gives him a vision of a collective state of consciousness. He is therefore the
only possible defender of humanity against a Comunidade that functions
on a parallel, but psychic, plane.

Lopo's vision is of a new, queered Spain where the peripheries have
become central and old ways of articulating national and sexual identity
must be replaced. The marked absence of Galician texts that explicitly deal
with queer identities and experiences and the even more marked reluctance
of Galician critics to acknowledge the full import of those that do remain
a serious obstacle to cultural normalization (McGovern 135–36). Nevertheless, Lopo's novel provides a model whereby multiple forms of marginality
can be combined to reclaim a position of strength. We must hope that the
model will have influence, for in Lopo's very queer world it is no surprise to
find Galicia occupying a central position in the geopolitical landscape.

Notes

1. Ganga's physical description, that of an obese drug addict with greasy long hair,
   makes his almost universal sex appeal seem preposterous, even more so when he is

dressed as a woman. However, blurring the boundaries between the repulsive and the beautiful are common to camp-queer production. One of the best-known examples of such blurring is the United States director John Waters's selection of the enormous transvestite Divine as the heroine in his early melodramatic films. The critic Paul Roen considers this contrast to be one of the characteristics of camp as an aesthetic in his discussion of female comedians: "Marilyn Monroe and Jayne Mansfield both made some very funny, very campy movies, yet both of these women are rightfully regarded as tragic figures, victimized by straight male patriarchal attitudes which, at the time these performers flourished, were operating at their highest pitch and in a most destructive capacity. Mansfield admittedly was a willing victim, conspiring in her own degradation every step of the way. And yet it is this very grotesqueness, this obviousness, this cartoonishness in her sex appeal which ultimately won her a legion of gay male fans" (14). While I would not compare Jayne Mansfield to Ganga, it is apparently the grotesqueness of his characteristics that make him so attractive to the other characters in the novel.

2. *Get Smart* (1965–70) starred Don Adams as the bumbling spy and Barbara Feldon as his sidekick, agent 99.

3. In another tribute to 1960s parodies of secret agents saving the world, Boris Madaraiz´s (perhaps truly *mala-raíz* ["bad root"]) foreign accent and name are almost certainly patterned after the United States cartoon that poked fun at cold-war hysteria, super-scientists, and evil plots. The villain in *The Bullwinkle Show* (1961–73), a program whose protagonists could easily have been read as gay lovers as much as codefenders of world peace, was named Boris Badenoff (Bad Enough), another eastern European diabolical agent with plans for world domination.

CULTURAL PRACTICES

Introduction to Part 3

In the absence of institutions of state, cultural practices often assume an importance far greater than they do in established or—in Galician parlance—normalized societies. In Galicia, as the essays in the first part of this volume showed us, the cultural sphere has often had to act as proxy for a weakened or silenced political sphere, and the writer as a surrogate for the people (see Antón Figueroa's essay in this volume). In consequence, as María do Cebreiro Rábade Villar and Joseba Gabilondo in particular showed us, certain figures (e.g., Rosalía de Castro) and certain genres (esp. poetry and popular music) have become strongly identified with the development of an autochthonous Galician culture. Since 1975, the new pluralist character of democratic Spain and the consequent institutionalization of Galician society and culture have opened up a public space for the reconstitution of both *galeguismo* and *galeguidade*. This new public space is characterized by the development of new individual, local, national, and supranational codes of identity and by innovative cultural practices, which coexist and often interact with existing popular, elite, and traditional forms. In this way, although Galician-language poetry and folk music continue to exert a powerful influence on Galician culture at the start of the twenty-first century, they must share the stage, so to speak, with new genres—cinema, performance, storytelling, and visual arts—which sometimes embrace, sometimes reject, but always transform the received understanding of what it means to make Galician culture.

The essays on histories in part 1 of this volume and those on identities in part 2 looked at overarching narratives of culture and identity in Galicia, sometimes through the medium of specific case studies. The essays that make up this final part also combine overarching conceptual analysis with analysis of specific case studies, but the focus is intended to be weighted more toward the specific. These essays thus share the objective of reflecting on exactly how interactions between new and traditional codes of identity—local, state, and global—and cultural practices have been represented in, and have shaped, Galicia since 1975.

María Reimóndez assesses the extent to which Galician culture has been able to produce an image of itself beyond the juxtaposition of the traditional and the modern. Asking whether a reductionist view of heritage as "stones and *muiñeiras* ['traditional dances']" can ever be sufficient for a culture as conflicted as Galicia's, she analyzes the two principal concepts of heritage that have shaped cultural planning in Galician since 1975: the conservative view propagated by the Fraga regime (1989–2005) and the progressive view of the new nationalist-socialist coalition government that has been in power since 2005. For Reimóndez, it is essential to deconstruct the Fraga-supported myth of backwardness, which Fernández Prieto too critiques in the opening essay of this volume, and restore a dynamic and interactive sense of Galician identity based on memory and experience. In discussing the implications of a dual concept of culture as a site of struggle and as the material practices emerging from that struggle, Reimóndez implicitly assesses the potential of cultural studies—in the Anglo-American sense—for understanding the development of contemporary Galician culture and identity.

José F. Colmeiro picks up on the questions raised by Reimóndez in his concern with the role that cinema has played in forging images of Galician identity between old and new, local and global. Colmeiro draws on wider debates in both film studies and Galician studies, proposing cinema as a testing ground for exploring the tensions between the transnational currents of economic and cultural globalization, on the one hand, and local questions of language, cultural identity, and nation building, on the other (not to mention the equally problematic tension between the central state and the peripheral nations). The development of a Galician cinema, like the development of Galician narrative (discussed by Hooper in a subsequent essay), is widely considered a key element in the normalization of Galician culture. Like the heritage projects discussed by Reimóndez and the histories reviewed by Fernández Prieto, cinema's accessibility not only helps construct a Galician self-image but also creates a public profile farther afield. Colmeiro concludes that the project of creating a Galician cinema is less advanced than more optimistic commentators have claimed. Despite the huge advances in cultural normalization since 1975, cinema—like the Galician media, which Colmeiro also discusses—is subject to economic and material forces whose center is the Spanish state; thus it remains largely a utopian dream.

Marta Pérez Pereiro continues Colmeiro's focus on Galician visual media by discussing the Galician public television station (TVG). Following Paul Julian Smith's model for the study of television through attention to "texts, producers, and institutions," Pérez Pereiro uses the issue of programming as a lens through which to view the interconnection among these three crucial elements. She looks closely at a particular corpus of texts, arguing that TVG's television drama serials covertly convey an ideologically driven representation of Galician identity that reveals the tensions between the cultures of different generations and expresses nostalgia for a vanishing rural way of life.

Burghard Baltrusch and Laura López Fernández both pick up on the question of the new to discuss how avant-garde and experimental forms of writing have sought to align Galician cultural practices (and therefore identity) with international modern and postmodern trends. Both essays deal with avant-garde cultural practices but in different and complementary ways. Baltrusch looks at the diverse, transdisciplinary careers of the collective Rompente ("Shattering"), part of the *movida gallega* ("Galician scene") of the 1980s, and its highest-profile member, the filmmaker, musician, and author Antón Reixa, as well as the novelist and polemicist Suso de Toro. For Baltrusch, the defining characteristic of Galician avant-garde (*vangardista*) production is its cultural translation of concepts from wider cultural theory—postmodern, postcolonial, transnational, and avant-garde—for the Galician situation. This translation is manifested in the incorporation by Rompente, Reixa, and Toro of the delocalized, experimental artistic forms that are conventionally connected with avant-garde cultural production and an equally determined engagement with issues of local, national, and global significance. The often shocking reinterpretation of the traditional building blocks of Galician culture and identity had a special power in the Galicia of the 1980s and 1990s. Baltrusch concludes that *vangardista* practices may now be a vital tool in the reclamation of a space for Galicia's minority voices, such as the poets of the recent feminist boom.

López Fernández too explores the exploitation of avant-garde cultural techniques to provide a novel perspective on Galician culture and identity. Where Baltrusch articulated a conceptual critique and overview of the avant-garde in a Galician context, she takes a particular case study that demonstrates the validity of that wider argument. Focusing on visual poetry, she shows how this deceptively venerable genre not only brings together traditional and avant-garde poetic practices but, in its fusion of linguistic and supralinguistic practices, also provides a new perspective for poets to examine the consequences of the sociocultural and economic changes taking place in Galicia since 1975. For López Fernández, the global shift toward the visual, particularly through the development of new technologies, has provided a powerful foundation for a progressive internationalization of Galician visual poetry based on interaction with intercultural and visual aesthetics. Perhaps most important, she suggests, is the decentering of the verbal that has for so long been dominant in expressions of *galeguidade*, in favor of what she calls the spatialization of culture. Galician visual poets are creating new cultural and intercultural maps in which Galicia is no longer isolated on the periphery of Europe but a participant in the international artistic mainstream.

Colmeiro, Baltrusch, and López Fernández all draw attention to the dynamic, transformative juxtaposition of local and global, traditional and experimental, in their respective analyses of music, film, *vangardismo,* and visual poetry in Galicia since 1975. Kirsty Hooper takes up the question of these binaries, together with López Fernández's (and Romero's) emphasis on spatial representations of identity, and uses it to point to the problematization, in recent Galician prose fiction, of the idea of a single national space and consequently a single national narrative. Since 1975, Galician society has changed at an unprecedented rate, a consequence not only of the transition to democracy but also of the dramatic, Europe-wide sociocultural and demographic changes caused by mass migration. The conventionally homogeneous—straight, white, Galician male—voice of Galician narrative is, as Timothy McGovern demonstrates in his analysis of the works of Antón Lopo, increasingly countered by alternative voices expressing new and dynamic forms of *galeguidade*. As Hooper shows, Galician narrative at the beginning of the twenty-first century is a testing ground for new narratives of identity. How we respond to emerging narratives that relate the experience of female, queer, *alófono* (nonnative, Galician-speaking), and migrant narrators who also consider themselves Galician will affect how we organize our understanding of Galicia itself.

Silvia Bermúdez too calls on readers to exploit the transformative power of culture today. Like López-Fernández, Bermúdez is interested in the way that poetry, the canonical Galician genre par excellence, is increasingly moving beyond pure verbal expression to incorporate nonlinguistic strategies that reach out to people who might not pick up a conventionally published collection of poetry. She takes as her case studies the poetic performances of the grassroots organization Redes Escarlata ("Scarlet Webs") and the poet-performers Antón Lopo and Ana Romaní, arguing that their innovative and often shocking works are also a form of highly engaged activism. As Bermúdez demonstrates, these artists work with an understanding of identity that is not just innovative but hugely transformative, using physical space and their own bodies to bend social and gender categories and thus to demand that difference be embraced as a fundamental aspect of Galician identity. Most significant for Bermúdez is the way that these artists have deliberately shifted poetry—with all its symbolic baggage—into the public sphere, literally stamping out the traces of the externally imposed relegation of Galician-language expression, and especially of poetry, to the intimate sphere of the personal.

Bermúdez brings us full circle: her focus on action over words and on the transformative relation between individual space and civic responsibility brings together the conceptual discussions of the first part of this book and the emphasis on individual voices and practices that are the focus of the second and third parts. All the essays in part 3 deal in different ways with the binaries that have for so long structured Galician experiences and expressions of culture and identity: Galician/Spanish, local/global, traditional/innovative, self/other, ethics/aesthetics, political/cultural. The picture they present of Galician culture since 1975 is dynamic, vibrant, and often contradictory. The hierarchies that shape our understanding of Galician national space and its traditional markers of identity—language, territory, and culture—remain central to the creation, dissemination, and reception of Galician cultural practices, but there is no easy answer to be had about their future. What is essential is that they be the subject of continued, strenuous, open debate. This volume is intended to provide a window on diverse and often conflicting aspects of that debate as Galicia begins a new century.

Whose Heritage Is It, Anyway? Cultural Planning and Practice in Contemporary Galicia

María Reimóndez

> Heritage: 1. That which has been or may be inherited; any property, and esp. land, which devolves by right of inheritance. ("Heritage")
>
> Patrimonio. s.m. 1. Conxunto de bens herdados ou propios que posúe unha persoa ou entidade. . . . 2. *fig.* Conxunto de cousas materiais ou inmateriais de certa antigüidade, pertencentes a unha colectividade. ("Patrimonio"; "Heritage: m. n. Property inherited or owned by a person or entity. . . . 2. *fig.* Set of material and intangible goods of some antiquity belonging to a group.")

Whoever looks up *heritage* or *patrimonio* in a dictionary (our common agreed resource for meanings, although it is of course both changeable and questionable) will be confronted with such definitions. Both definitions are wide in their scope and therefore not of much use for a scholarly discussion of heritage in the Galician case. Still, both shed light on this concept. They emphasize inheritance, and the Galician definition points beyond land to nation. In Galicia, the nation has become an element of not just intellectual but also political debate, with clear consequences for autonomy and self-government. The second entry in the Galician definition of *patrimonio* links heritage to a cultural reality both material and intangible. Intangible in what respect? Is heritage something to do with stones and *muiñeiras* ("traditional dances"), or is it something else? Is this definition enough for a culture in conflict—if there are ever cultures not in conflict—such as Galicia's?

Cultural studies has developed a new way of thinking about culture and its various manifestations. There is a trend of "cultural policy studies," defined as "the rise in the use of cultural heritages and cultural consumption to maintain or stabilize identities by nations, ethnic groups, and individuals" (During, Introduction 26). As this essay shows, there are many contradictory views on culture and heritage. I focus on the sharp contrast between two particular and influential views of Galician heritage and culture. The topic of culture and cultural policy in Galicia became all the more interesting in the summer of 2005, when the strict, conservative regime that had governed Galicia since 1989 was finally defeated at the ballot box. This regime and its supporting doctrine were known as *fraguismo,* after its leader, Manuel Fraga, the eighty-year-old former Francoist minister. The Fraga government, representing the conservative Partido Popular de Galicia (PPdeG), imposed its stringent vision of Galician culture for sixteen years. In contrast, one of the most important characteristics of the new government, a coalition between the Partidos dos Socialistas de Galicia (PSdeG-PSOE) and the Bloque Nacionalista Galego (BNG), is its progressive approach to culture and its active search for a new definition of a *cultura do país* ("national culture"). It is still too early to assess the success of the government policies, so I limit myself to the views and approaches of different artistic groups, which have expressed diametrically opposed images of culture and heritage.

Culture, Heritage, and Galicia: Who's Who?

To speak about heritage, we must first define what we understand by *culture.* To analyze Galician heritage, I combine two apparently contradicting concepts of culture expressed by the definitions of Alan Swingewood and of Lucinda Joy Peach:

> Culture is less a way of life than sites of struggle imbricated in ideology and politics, overlaid with issues of gender, race and generation. Culture is not the expression or the representation of class, but the active articulation of complex identity. (Swingewood xiii)

> The term culture is difficult to define precisely because it encompasses so many different aspects, and has been interpreted in so many different ways. Most broadly, the term "culture" refers to the practices and products of human civilization. This encompasses images, symbols, myths, values, ideas, language, the arts, folklore, philosophy and religion. Culture constructs meanings, images, belief systems, and identities. (Peach 1)

Culture is not only a site of conflict but also the material practices stemming from such conflict. Throughout the wide range of activities and conflicts, heritage plays a role. Heritage may, of course, be defined as just museums, archives, and historic buildings—that is, as the repositories of the past and of our inheritance. But there are many other aspects of heritage. It is used in both political decision-making processes and in society at large. A distinction is commonly made, or sometimes implied, between natural heritage and cultural heritage. The terms are self-explanatory but no longer as useful as they were, for in many current initiatives the natural and the cultural are combined, as we see in the increasingly popular interpretation centers (Bouzada and Rodríguez 24). Heritage can also be understood as an intangible reality. In recent discussions, this approach has gained weight.

The use of cultural studies to define heritage in the Galician context is especially interesting. As Simon During claims, "[Cultural studies] is a discipline determined to remain active in and sensitive to the cultural flows and ruptures of the contemporary world system" (*Cultural Studies Reader* 47). Galician culture and heritage are shaped by—and, of course, themselves shape—different historical moments. They are perceived differently by different groups and cannot be reduced to monolithic definitions of a set of objects or buildings. In a different context, bell hooks said, "We return to 'identity' and 'culture' for relocation, linked to political practice—identity that is not informed by a narrow cultural nationalism masking continued fascination with the power of the white hegemonic other" (Introduction 20). Let us replace the "white hegemonic other" with the "Spanish hegemonic other," and the quotation exactly fits some recent trends in Galicia.

What is especially Galician about our culture and about our heritage? Galicia has often been cast in negative terms, as a peripheral region. But many nations relegated to the peripheries (wherever the center is for them) have become a source of creativity, transforming the margin, the border, the backyard to which they were banished and making it their new home. In doing so, they developed their own way of understanding the world and relating themselves to it. Homi Bhabha writes:

> Culture as a strategy of survival is both transnational and translational. It is transnational because contemporary postcolonial discourses are rooted in specific histories of cultural displacement. . . . Culture is translational because such spatial histories of displacement . . . make the question of how culture signifies or what is signified by *culture* a rather complex issue.
>
> ("Postcolonial" 191)

Curiously enough, the definitions that give a more static image of heritage, based on an idealized and essentialized vision of the past, have not come from nationalist movements in Galicia, as happened in many other (especially postcolonial) countries. This is perhaps the main peculiarity of the Galician situation, and it deserves special attention.

Galician culture and heritage must constantly engage with the opposing hegemonic influence of Spain, which means that they are inevitably

> a site of a continual struggle between competing discourses, each offering a particular way of looking at or speaking about the social world (or particular segments of it) and engaged in a contest for visibility and legitimacy across a range of social institutions. (Murdoch 63)

Rosa Aneiros ironically states the paradoxical situation of Galician culture, located on that unstable margin, always seeming to be on its deathbed and yet also completely alive:

> Xogando co simil, podemos cualificar o estado da cultura en Galicia de hipocondríaco—sempre vai tirando, láiase de todo e, por suposto, non fai proxectos a longo prazo porque un día destes morre definitivamente. Leva tantos anos con estertores que abraia a cantidade e calidade de iniciativas que se fixeron nos últimos anos. (65)

> Playing with the simile, we can define the state of Galician culture as hypochondriac—it is always on the edge, complaining about everything, and of course it does not make any long-term plans, as it expects to die soon. It has been giving the death rattle for so long that one is surprised to see the quantity and quality of the initiatives undertaken in recent years.

Heritage of the Past or the Past of Heritage?

By examining the way that the powerful conservative movement of *fraguismo* has portrayed Galician culture and heritage, we can better understand the cultural discourse and practice that has grown up in opposition to it. For over twelve years, culture in Galicia was developed according to the guidelines of Fraga's centralist government. In 2006, just a few months after the socialist-nationalist coalition that replaced Fraga began its term in office, the cultural magazine *Tempos novos* published a clear warning to the new government from a large group of cultural agents, in the form of a manifesto. This manifesto makes numerous recommendations and includes a remarkable summary of the cultural policy of the Fraga government, which it defines as combining two antithetical approaches to cultural policy: *autocompracencia esencialista* ("essentialist self-satisfaction") and *autoodio* ("self-hatred") (Colectivo Cívico).

By *autocompracencia esencialista*, they are referring to the Fraga government's tendency to present Galicia's cultural difference as a confirmation of the typical, of the essentialized stereotypes of Galicia that are not only common currency in Spain but also projected abroad. *Fraguista* cultural policy interpreted Galician heritage solely in terms of an existing pattern of identification that resembles the stereotypes of Ireland disseminated for so many years: rural, idyllic landscapes, bagpipes and cows, women with black scarves on their heads, and good solid peasant food. In this way, the challenging political connotations of Galicia's heritage are easily erased in favor of a static and thus more easily managed cultural focus. Galician culture was officially presented as something harmless and decorative, existing peacefully within the Spanish state.

The official *fraguista* representation of Galician culture fostered a theory and political practice of heritage as a collection of old towns and buildings with some (in some cases questionable) historical significance. The most remarkable examples of this policy are the Camiño de Santiago ("Saint James Way") pilgrimage route and the promotion of *festas gastronómicas* ("food festivals"). The Camiño de Santiago, apart from its unquestionable historical and contemporary significance for Galicia, especially as a source of tourism, became a landmark of all things Galician during Fraga's era. Its rural, historical, and monumental aspects were emphasized, with fake medieval pilgrims, *meigas* ("witches"), and *queimadas* (ceremonies where incantations are recited over a bowl of burning liquor) in a representation deliberately devoid of political significance. The case of the Camiño is a clear example of how cultural policies can shape the image of Galicia abroad. While many countries, especially in Europe, are aware of the Camiño as a tourist experience, few of them have any knowledge of the fact that its destination, the city of Santiago de Compostela, is located in a country of its own, with a language of its own and a culture of its own. This unawareness is the result of the European tourist campaigns funded by both the Xunta and the Spanish government, which deliberately never mentioned the fact of Galicia's existence.

A similar thing occurred with the Ano Xacobeo, a celebration that takes place when the festival of Santiago (Saint James's Day, July 25) falls on a Sunday. Despite its importance in Galicia, and especially in Santiago de Compostela, the Ano Xacobeo was never used to promote Galicia abroad or even to give Galician artists the chance to participate in a cultural program of their own. Instead, the celebration was used only to organize unending programs of large-scale concerts, with musicians brought from all over the world to attract tourists. That Saint James's Day is a national holiday in Galicia and celebrated every year, Ano Xacobeo or not, makes the omission of Galician performers and participants all the more painful. Galicia's own celebrations of Saint James's Day are characterized both by the cultural—public performances, *son et lumière,* and firework displays—and the political, with an annual demonstration through the streets of Santiago de Compostela. The Ano Xacobeo phenomenon is a graphic example of the division between the *fraguista* view of the Galician nation and those of other groups.

The second approach to Galician culture and heritage displayed by the Fraga government was *autoodio,* manifested in a strange attachment to all things foreign—especially but not only Spanish. In this approach, the images of others are adopted as our own, and anything Galician that does not fit into the traditional, essentialized pattern is dismissed with self-deprecation. This self-hatred is especially visible with regard to Galicia's material heritage, especially cultural spaces. Xan Bouzada and Lois Rodríguez analyze the complex panorama of material heritage existing in Galicia, in particular the failed attempts to re-create foreign ideas. They focus on the mammoth project of the Cidade da Cultura ("City of Culture"), a huge infrastructure planned by the Fraga government and initially developed by the architect Peter Eisenman. As Bouzada and Rodríguez point out, the Cidade da Culture, both as a project and as a material structure, is completely devoid of either content or social participation.

The Cidade da Cultura epitomizes the cultural policy of the conservative government in Galicia. In many interviews and public statements, both Fraga and the members of his government, especially the Galician culture minister, Xesús Pérez Varela, presented the Cidade da Cultura as a world-class cultural project with hyperbolic descriptions such as "proyecto cultural sin precedentes" ("La Xunta"; "a cultural project without precedent") and "un empeño lleno de grandeza y un proyecto llamado a perdurar más allá de su magnitud y singularidad estética" ("Frage define"; "An immense endeavor and a project that will endure beyond its aesthetic impact and uniqueness"). Such statements prompted the response from both Galicia's opposition parties that the project was, in the words of Francisco Cerviño of the Socialist Party, designed "para que perviviese a un Manuel Fraga que se creyó Carlos III" ("PSOE y BNG"; "to outlive a Manuel Fraga who believed himself Carlos III"). Another disturbing element in the Fraga government's conception of the Cidade da Cultura was its religious or, rather, Catholic connotations. Time and again, the Cidade da Cultura was described as a "pilgrimage center" ("Pérez Varela presenta"). The metaphor is obvious in connection with Santiago, but it also subtly implies a connection of Galician heritage with religion. The Cidade da Cultura followed the Guggenheim effect and the motto "aquel que o faga máis grande faino mellor" (Bouzada and Rodríguez 19; "the bigger the better"), which seemed to be enough for its supporters.

Autocompracencia esencialista and *autoodio* are also present in the context of Galicia's intangible heritage. An excellent example is *Luar* ("Moonlight"), the most successful program in the history of Galician television. It has managed to embody both approaches and even leave room for real attempts to redefine heritage. The show combines traditional Galician folk music, designed to recover a particular version of *galeguidade*, with the performances of Spanish, Latin American, and international (usually second-rank) artists. This union of the traditionally local and partially global has been the landmark of Fraga's approach to heritage: the portrayal of heritage as something static and monumental, the utopia of an old-fashioned Galicia where the elderly sing their nice songs to the accompaniment of bagpipe music, while the international artist "offers the image of 'something better' to escape into, or something we want deeply that our day-to-day lives don't provide" (Dyer, "Entertainment" 373). But in between the bagpipes and the local dance troupes, the program also offered something quite different. Cracks in the heritage model were used to introduce new concepts: interesting and informative reinterpretations of Galicia's traditional music and dance, reports about the Galician language, performances by new Galician artists in genres other than folk music. *Luar* might be described as a postmodern pastiche that escapes easy definition and thus has the ability to survive any political era. It has been on the air for over thirteen years.

During the twelve years of the Fraga government, much damage was done to Galicia's intangible heritage, through both neglect and the limited and essentialist approaches described here. The prevailing image of modernity as something Spanish or foreign left no room for the development of forms of art that would help Galician heritage and culture grow in new ways. Contemporary dance, visual arts, anything related to new technologies and the modern could not be considered Galician. The image of Galician heritage promoted abroad constantly used imaginary landscapes, which can be seen in the *hórreos* ("traditional grain stores"), *carballos* ("oak trees"),

and *brétemas* ("mists") featured in the different publicity campaigns to foster tourism in Galicia. Also used was the religious value of Santiago as a
pilgrimage center.

Fortunately, Fraga's policy did not eradicate Galicia's vibrant cultural
life, in terms of both material and intangible heritage. Galician artists
worked hard during these years to establish networks abroad, through music festivals, dance, and audiovisual production. Cultural initiatives, both
individual and collective—such as the revival of events in cafés, the opening
of art galleries and theaters in different cities and towns, and the establishment of modern dance companies—bear witness to the active involvement
of Galicia's citizens in cultural activities beyond the political diktat. A remarkable initiative made during this period is the Candidatura de Patrimonio Inmaterial Galego-Portugués ("Candidacy of the Galician-Portuguese
Immaterial Heritage"), which tried to obtain UNESCO recognition of
Galician heritage as a "masterpiece of the oral and intangible heritage of
humanity." The project was initially fostered by schools in Galicia and the
north of Portugal through the Ponte nas Ondas ("Get on the Airwaves")
initiative, with special emphasis on common music and songs, stories and
legends, and other cultural practices. The proposal was presented in Paris in
2005. Even though it was not selected, UNESCO encouraged the promot-
ers to give it another try. The initiative was largely ignored by Fraga's government and has only acquired some public recognition since 2006, with the
new government's cultural policy.

Galician cultural initiatives during the Fraga period might be considered to display the characteristics of a subculture according to Dick Hebdige's definition:

> Clearly, subcultures are not privileged forms, they do not stand outside the
> reflective circuitry of production and reproduction which links together, at
> least on a symbolic level, the separate and the fragmented pieces of the social
> totality. (449)

Subculture or no subculture, Galicia's heritage, material and intangible, has
proved resistant to restrictive policies.

A Brave New Heritage?

By the time the socialist-nationalist coalition took over in the summer of
2005, the Cidade da Cultura project was too far advanced to be thrown out

completely. Some of the buildings were almost finished. But the remaining building works were halted, and meetings were arranged to redefine the project and its aims. A consultation process was opened to look into the contents of the Casa Mundo ("World House") and Escenario Obradoiro ("Workshop Stage"). The new Galician minister for culture, Ánxela Bugallo, began the consultation with some reluctance. It turned out that most of the citizen groups and artists were primarily worried about the maintenance costs of the Cidade da Cultura once it was functional; they feared it might drain the budget at the expense of other activities. There was a general feeling that culture was to be found elsewhere. That the Cidade da Cultura has so far remained inaccessible also reflects the objection expressed by various cultural actors that it represents only an elite version of culture. The project is controversial. If one Googles "Cidade da Cultura," most of the sites found are full of bitter words for the project. Even former supporters of the Cidade are now against it, as it no longer suits their political interests. The musician and filmmaker Antón Reixa reproached them in an article in Spain's principal newspaper, *País*: "Es de una gran lástima patriótica que no hubiesen gastado la misma energía para impedir que arrancase el proyecto" ("Los detractores"; "It is a real patriotic shame that they did not spend as much energy in stopping the project from taking off in the first place").

An important element of the redefinition of the Cidade da Cultura is its role in the changing of Galicia's image abroad. Some steps have already been taken. In recent campaigns to promote tourism, there is the repetition of sea, woods, and landscape but also a new focus on words from the Galician language. The Cidade da Cultura is expected to provide a place for cultural exchange. Reixa states that it "que paganice definitivamente la tradición jacobea y una oportunidad para las industrias culturales gallegas de enseñarse y ponerse en relación con el mundo" ("Los detractores"; "should finally paganize the tradition of a religious pilgrimage to Santiago and create an opportunity for Galician cultural industries to be seen and establish links with the world").

Another sign of this new approach is the celebration of the Ano da Memoria ("Year of Memory"). The year 2006 marked the seventieth anniversary of the coup d'état that started the Spanish Civil War and heralded forty years of dictatorship. So far this part of our heritage, identity, and culture has been condemned to an obscure, biased, and intentional official oblivion. The celebrations programmed for the Ano da Memoria and continuing beyond 2006 included historical research projects, documentaries, literary works, the renovation of a steamship for use as a museum, and the development of a center on the Island of San Simón to honor the victims of the dictatorship (San Simón was a jail for political prisoners during the Franco period). Though many museums were opened during the Fraga years, as Bouzada and Rodríguez have observed, few have been capable of coming to terms with this part of our past. In James Clifford's words, "Current developments question the very status of museums as historical-cultural theatres of memory. Whose memory?" (75). The Ano da Memoria tries to answer this question. Focusing on that part of our recent past will also affect the image of Galicia abroad. Because there is great awareness in Europe about the Spanish Civil War, renewed attempts to address the topic in Galicia will foster a better understanding of our past and present. Until now, the widespread understanding of the war in Galicia, promoted by the Fraga regime, has been that there was never an open battle here, which is true, and that therefore the country simply surrendered without any attempt to rebel, which is not true. The Ano da Memoria has recuperated the memory of those men and women who were shot in a country that had no arms to defend itself from the military and of the guerrilla war that went on in the mountains. Also highlighted have been the repercussions for those who were loyal to the democratic Republican regime; exile, confiscation of property, and scorn toward their children, many of whom are still alive today. Restoring the dignity of those who were scorned not just during the dictatorship but also during Fraga's regime will restore an irreplaceable part of our heritage, both material and intangible.

The new way of thinking about Galicia is still to be defined. We can begin to see, however, that whereas the conservative government fostered the most stereotypical images of Galicia, the nationalist party (esp. through the Consellería de Cultura e Deportes) and individual artists and citizens' groups are interested in developing a flexible identity that forms links with different forces, respecting not only the living remains of the past but also the inevitabilities of the future. Intangible heritage and the recovery of the histories and herstories of those oppressed by the dictatorship (for a key aspect of this new vision is that all stories, of women too, be recuperated) and by the ensuing silence have become so far the two most important aspects of this new approach to heritage.

The members of Galicia's former subcultures are now in the spotlight and being asked to participate in shaping new policies about heritage. The challenges are many, as the stereotypes of the past continue to permeate the self-image of Galicians today. Fortunately in Galicia, as Aneiros states, "a principal fortaleza do eido cultural reside no labor creador dos artistas e no traballo arreo do asociacionismo cultural" (65; "the main strength of our cultural environment lies in the creative work of artists and the hard work of cultural associations"). Maybe the expectations of many of us for the development of a real cultural policy by any government can be summarized in the following words from Tony Bennett:

> A cultural policy that . . . would respect the specific content of the activities it would administer . . . based on a self-conscious recognition of the contradictions inherent in applying planning to a field of practice which stands opposed to planning in their innermost substance . . . must develop this awareness into a critical acknowledgement of its own limits.   (487)

The aim of this essay has been not to provide definitive answers but to raise the visibility of the questions and different forces at play in the theory and practice of Galician heritage. I have moved from general definitions to the analysis of the heritage policies of two different regimes, *fraguismo* and the socialist-nationalist coalition that followed. I have indicated the flaws of the policies fostered by *fraguismo*. Seeing heritage as monuments, food festivals, and empty buildings is no longer viable. The development of an ideology of heritage has effects on both a people's identity and their image abroad. Fortunately, the suffocating definition of Galician heritage that has obtained for so long has not crippled the efforts of the many artists who have been working in the shadows, without any support from the regional government, to defend their own definition of heritage, which includes the Galician language and a vision of Galicia as a country with a past but also with a present and a future.

Galicia needs a cultural policy that articulates and gives support to our existing vibrant cultural life. The discourse, both official and inofficial, must shift toward an acknowledgment of our position as privileged. As Bhabha writes, "The great, though unsettling, advantage of this position is that it makes you increasingly aware of the construction of culture and the invention of tradition" ("Postcolonial" 191). The only way to manage, preserve, invent, and innovate heritage is to open it up to identities that move beyond clichés and that give a voice to different sectors. Much remains to be done in Galicia, because the voices of most of its cultural world have been silent for so long, including the voices of groups that have been discriminated against. Heritage is a site of struggle. It is up to us to define it, preserve it, and reinvent it for the future.

Useful References Online

Fundación Cidade da Cultura de Galicia. Home page. Text in Galician, English, and Spanish. N.d.

"Intangible Heritage." UNESCO, 20 June 2007. Regularly updated.

"Luar." Home page. CRTVG.es, n.d.

"A outra cara do *Luar.*" Article commemorating five hundered editions of *Luar.* Culturagalega.org., 3 Mar. 2005.

"O patrimonio in material." Home page. *Candidatura de patrimonio inmaterial galego-portugués.* Information about the Galician-Portuguese candidacy for UNESCO "intangible heritage" status, 2005. Text in Galician, English, Portuguese, and Spanish. N.d.

Ponte . . . nas Ondas! Home page. Text in Galician, English, Portuguese, and Spanish. N.d.

Imagining Galician Cinema: Utopian Visions?

José Colmeiro

> Este era un mundo de tebras e agora é un mundo de luz. Era un mundo de ferro e é agora un mundo de ouro.
> —Xavier Villaverde

> This was a world of shadows, and now it is a world of light. It was a world of iron, and now it is a world of gold.

> Primeiro foi a moda, agora é o audiovisual . . .
> —"O audiovisual agora"

> First it was fashion, now it's the audiovisual. . . .

> ¿Cómo vai existir o cinema en galego cando case nin existe Galicia?
> —Marcelo Martínez

> How can a cinema in Galician exist when Galicia itself barely does?

The existence of Galician cinema has long been intensely debated, defended, celebrated, and contested by critics and film professionals alike. It is considered a glass half full for some, a glass half empty for others, depending on the degree of optimism, ideological position, and perspective of the onlooker. A large part of the debate has historically focused on the definition of the ontological status of Galician cinema—that is, what exactly that cinema is or should be. The debate is embedded in a complex web of related social and political issues about Galicia's struggle for national identity and cultural normalization. It reflects a wide spectrum of positions between culturally purist nationalist views, on the one hand, and pragmatic possibilism, on the other. More recently, economic and cultural realities have shifted the terms of the debate toward wider notions, such as "cinema made in Galicia" or even "audiovisual productions made in Galicia." Although these concepts frequently overlap, it can be productive to maintain a methodological distinction between them, from a merely analytic point of view.

In this essay I address the problematic situation of Galician film production in the larger contexts of the Galician audiovisual sector, the Spanish cinema industry, and the transnational currents of economic and cultural globalization affecting national and subnational cinemas. Galician film production is situated in quite peculiar, culturally specific circumstances, although it shares the general limitations of the Spanish film industry as a whole, struggling to compete in the global market dominated by American productions. It also faces the particular problematics arising from the marginal position of autonomous cinema produced in peripheral contexts, such as the Basque and Catalan cinemas, where questions of language, cultural identity, and nation building overlap in intricate ways. The specific contexts of Galician film production reveal a complex interweaving of adverse historical, economic, political, and sociocultural conditions that have presented some challenges to its development. The often expressed need for a Galician cinema and the enormous difficulties encountered in bringing it into existence must be analyzed against the backdrop of the Galician national struggle for cultural definition in the face of Spanish state nationalism before, after, and during Franco and in the face of the long history of cultural and political repression and uneven economic development. Furthermore, we must take into account the growing erosion of the national cinema paradigm as a conceptual tool, in the context of economic, cultural, and political transnational globalization, which explains the new conceptualization of "cinema made in Galicia."[1]

To better address these complexities, some Iberian cultural studies scholars have referred to a new postnational paradigm that would provide a more refined theoretical ground on which to analyze the decentering of Spanish cultural production, the emergence of peripheral cultures and identities, the hybridization of national cultures, and the interplay of the local and the global. They advocate a remapping that would effectively deterritorialize the traditional boundaries of the national (Colmeiro, "Peripheral Visions"; Gabilondo, "Postnationalism"; Hooper, "New Cartographies"; Richardson).[2] This new conceptualization could be an effective tool to approach more productively the question of how to redefine what Galician cinema is or could be. It could also have far-reaching implications for the redefinition of Galician studies as a field, traditionally centered around the *criterio filolóxico* ("philological criterion") borrowed from literary studies and the use of the Galician vernacular language.[3] The study of Galician cinema or cinema made in Galicia, as many critics nowadays prefer to say, problematizes the question of what constitutes Galician cultural studies and potentially offers a more encompassing alternative to traditional philological approaches.

Intellectual debates since the 1970s have highlighted the need for a Galician cinema as a nation-building project, both to create *imaxe-país*, an image of and for the nation, and to be part of the process of cultural and linguistic normalization. Today, the need to reaffirm Galician cultural identity and project an image of Galicia in the global audiovisual market is seen by many critics and professionals as a simple question of cultural survival (Acuña 5). In the last two decades, Galician officials and institutions have also started to show clear signs of interest in the development of the audiovisual field, which encompasses video, television, film, animation, and multimedia productions. The audiovisual area has been officially declared by the Xunta to be a strategic and priority sector for the economic and cultural development of Galicia, although it is fair to say that Galician official institutions have frequently been erratic and dysfunctional in the implementation of their programs.[4] While there is a wide discrepancy of opinion about what Galician cinema is or could be, there is nowadays a general consensus about the importance of the expanding Galician audiovisual industry and more specifically the steadily growing number of films made in Galicia.

Since the early 1970s, there have been a series of attempts to theorize the conditions of possibility of Galician cinema, asking, What makes a film Galician? How should this cinema be? And how should it come about?[5] The origins of the continuing debate about Galician cinema go back to the last years of the dictatorship, in particular to the foundation of a *novo cinema galego* ("new Galician cinema"), discussed at the Ourense film festival in 1973, in the aftermath of the new national film movements of the 1960s. Without a unified conceptual framework, there were many different views on what would constitute Galician cinema, such as the use of the Galician language, a Galician cast and technical crew, or a theme related to Galicia. Some defined it more abstractly, as a way of feeling or expressing Galicia in images, while attempting to avoid traditional Galician "ruralism" or "folklorism" (Acuña 77–78). What all those views had in common is that they were expressing a utopian vision of a still prospective Galician cinema—a cinema more imagined than real, a cinema that could *represent* the nation in all senses of the word. The catalog of the festival summed up the situation

with sardonic relativism, in a now well-known paradoxical statement pointing to this utopian noplace, which could be considered the degree zero of
Galician cinema: "O cine galego é a conciencia da súa nada. Xa é algo" (78;
"Galician cinema is the perception of its own nothingness. That is already
a start").[6]

Fortunately, many things have changed dramatically since then. The
end of Franco's dictatorship and the establishment of autonomy in Galicia
have propelled the reawakening of Galician culture with great force, and
cinema has been no exception to this revitalization. The intellectual debate
between the creation of an alternative autonomous and self-marginalized but
authentic Galician cinema, on the one hand, and, on the other, pragmatic
possibilism, professionalization, and the creation of an industrial infrastructure has been overwhelmingly decided in favor of the latter (Hueso 188).
The cinema industry in Galicia is now part of a much larger and complex
audiovisual field with blurred boundaries among different media formats,
outlets, and technologies, such as TV, video, multimedia, advertising, and
so on (X. Nogueira, *Cine* 342, 361). The different regimes of coproduction, with national and international companies, directors, technicians, and
cast members, have also blurred the strict defining parameters of a national
cinema.

Although Galician language remains a fundamental aspect of Galician
cultural identity, the language used in the films cannot be a meaningful
distinctive marker. Most feature films shot in Galicia, with some notable
exceptions, are filmed in Spanish and then dubbed into Galician in postproduction for their general release in Galicia, as the dubbing in Galician
is required to obtain official production subsidies and be shown on Television de Galicia (TVG).[7] The general understanding nowadays is that a
Galician production, incorporating in all or in large part a Galician artistic
cast, technical crew, and economic means of production, would be officially designated as a Galician film. As Ángel Hueso succinctly put it, "Cine
galego sería aquel que utilizase uns recursos industriais, económicos, de
produción e artísticos, propios de Galicia" (qtd. in Galán 14; "A Galician
cinema would be one that used industrial, economic, production and artistic resources from Galicia"). For Nogueira, Galician cinema, *estrictu sensu*,
would be "aquel pensado, producido e realizado en Galicia por empresas
cinematográficas galegas" (*Cine* 9; "conceptualized, produced and made in
Galicia by Galician film companies"). That both statements are in the conditional mood subtly underlines their hypothetical status.

The general consensus today has gone beyond the endlessly arguable and ultimately futile debate about the ontological status of Galician cinema or the essentialist question of what makes a film Galician. Instead of returning to the restrictive and often confusing notion of Galician cinema, many critics and film professionals in Galicia prefer to use umbrella expressions such as "cinema in Galicia" or "cinema made in Galicia" (Hueso 190; X. Nogueira, *Cine* 358). These much broader categorizations encompass all facets of cinema production in Galicia and are more attuned to postnational political contexts and transnational economic and cultural conditions of audiovisual production in Galicia.[8] In my view, these are not mutually exclusive categories but complementary and almost always overlapping. In this essay I use the term "Galician cinema" to refer to films that are rooted in Galicia and predominantly Galician in their process of production, independently of their language or other factors.[9] Cinema "made in Galicia" includes films not involving Galician production in plan or execution. Juan Luis Cuerda's remarkable film *El bosque animado* (1987; "The Living Forest") is Galician in theme and location but still technically a Spanish production "made in Galicia" (a traditional Querejeta team production). Conversely, Ángel de la Cruz and Manolo Gómez's animated feature *El bosque animado* (2001), conceived and produced in its entirety in Galicia by Galician companies, is intrinsically a Galician film. There are important symbolic and pragmatic reasons to maintain this differentiation, even though both trends are part of the cinema produced in Galicia and both should have a place in a broadly defined conception of Galician studies.[10]

The last two quotations used as epigraph for this essay, taken from the special *Vieiros* online dossier on Galician audiovisual production ("Audiovisual agora"), highlight the intense debate about the supposed boom of Galician cinema, ranging from enthusiastic celebration to Galician skepticism and resigned relativism.[11] The quotation from Xavier Villaverde's film is highly symbolic. These words are the first spoken in his urban thriller *Continental,* one of three films shown at the special premiere Cinegalicia, widely considered the official launch of contemporary Galician cinema.[12] In a film with compelling imagery, ambiguous symbolism, and abundant self-referentiality, which is clearly a proposal for the aesthetic and thematic renovation of Galician cinema, mention of a past iron age of shadows and a new golden age of light have a strong metaphoric resonance. Furthermore, these words are intertextually related to Eduardo Pondal, one of the great poets of the Rexurdimento and the writer of the lyrics of the Galician national anthem. Pondal's deathbed words referred to his founding role in constructing a modern literary Galician language: "Déchedesme unha lingua de ferro i eu douvos unha lingua de ouro" (O. Iglesias; "You gave me a language made of iron and I give you a language made of gold"). This literary connection reinforces the reading of the film, underscoring its Galicianness and strongly suggesting a utopian vision for the future of new Galician cinema.

Making Galician cinema in Galicia, with all its shadows and lights, in its journey from an iron age of the past to a golden age to come, has always been a utopian enterprise. The idea of a Galician dream factory has itself been a dream, a vision against all odds, marked by the lack of an industrial infrastructure, cultural and political marginality, and the domination of the Spanish and especially the hegemonic American film industry. The long and difficult journey of Galician cinema is perhaps best encapsulated in the odyssey of the director Chano Piñeiro, who defied all obstacles to turn his dream of making cinema in Galicia into a reality. Piñeiro was one of the first to make a feature-length Galician film in every sense of the term. His *Sempre Xonxa* (1989; "Always Xonxa") is for many the best example of the *novo cine galego* ("new Galician cinema"), for its ability to capture the emotional involvement of great numbers of Galician spectators through its representation of Galicianness. This pivotal film marks the end of traditional Galician cinema—composed mostly of works of elitist auteur craftsmanship, underfunded amateur productions, and limited to traditional rural or folkloric themes—and the beginning of a new era of progressive professionalization, economic and cultural expansion, and relative normalization.[13]

Rather than a black-and-white picture, contemporary Galician cinema is a complex puzzle, having many shades of light and shadow, and shaped by many social, political, and cultural developments. Galician cinema of the last two decades must be seen against the substantial accomplishments in the recuperation of Galician language, culture, and historical identity in the years since the restoration of democracy—particularly since the Statute of Autonomy of Galicia was approved in 1981 and the Xunta de Galicia became the autonomous government. A result of this collective cultural reawakening has been the considerable success and recognition beyond Galicia of young Galicians working in the arts, design, fashion, literature, and popular music, which started with the *movida galega* ("Galician happening") of the 1980s.[14] The growth of recent years in the audiovisual and cinema arts in

Galicia, particularly since the 1990s, is only one of the latest examples of this revitalization.

The Golden Age of Light: The Boom of the Galician Audiovisual Sector

Cinema production in Galicia is directly related to and inseparable from developments in the audiovisual sector as a whole (encompassing television, multimedia, video, cinema, and advertising). Administrative and legal measures were taken to regulate and promote film production in Galicia, thus filling a public-policy audiovisual vacuum and increasing the vitality of this sector.[15] Two important official measures enacted by the Xunta de Galicia to promote Galician cinema have been the institutionalization of subsidies for Galician film production (with changing rules and regulations but firmly established since the mid-1980s) and the creation of public television (TVG) in 1985. Together, these official programs have had a direct, palpable, and continued influence on Galician cinema and the audiovisual sector as a whole. Subsidies for the audiovisual sector have become the basic sine qua non for the establishment of a minority cinema that cannot compete against other national and international film products, especially given the hegemony of the American film industry.

The launch of TVG, with its strong support of, and indeed great demand for, Galician audiovisual productions, such as videos, TV series and movies, shorts, and feature films, has helped establish an industrial audiovisual infrastructure in Galicia. This infrastructure has resulted in the creation of a plethora of small audiovisual companies, dubbing studios, production companies, and animation companies. TVG has accelerated the process of linguistic and cultural normalization in the audiovisual sector.[16] The emergence of the audiovisual sector has also meant the slow but progressive development of the cinema industry in Galicia and its professionalization. Film production companies were recently formed—Continental, Filmanova, Filminvest—with the direct participation of major Galician financial institutions. For instance, the main investor in the last two companies is the powerful savings bank Caixanova.[17]

The foundation of new institutions that promote and support the Galician audiovisual sector has been important for its development. The creation of schools of cinema and audiovisual arts and film archive centers in Galicia have been instrumental in the training of a new generation of audiovisual professionals, both technical and artistic crews, as well as in the preservation and dissemination of knowledge about Galician audiovisual culture. The official Escola de Imaxe e Son (EIS), the first professional film school in Galicia, and the Centro Galego de Artes da Imaxe (CGAI), formed from the ashes of the defunct Arquivo da Imaxe, were both established in Coruña in 1991.[18] Both centers opened their doors after Manuel Fraga took the presidency of the Xunta in 1990, but they were projects already planned and approved by the former tripartite socialist-nationalist coalition government in the late 1980s. The CGAI has been particularly attentive to the recuperation, restoration, and dissemination of Galician audiovisual history. This work has been achieved not only through its regular film showings to the general public and the opening of its facilities to research scholars, as in other public film archives and *filmotecas*, but also in a more innovative and far-reaching way, by an expansive loan policy and by making available a substantial number of works from its film collection for online viewing on its Web site (www.cgai.org).

Public organizations and private associations related to film production in Galicia have formed; they actively represent the interests of the community working in the audiovisual sector. Among the associations are APAG (Asociación de Profesionais do Audiovisual Galego [1983]) and AGAPI (Asociación Galega de Produtoras Independentes [1994]). Because of the great growth in the sector, a new association split off from AGAPI, the AEGA (Asociación de Empresas Galegas do Audiovisual [2001]), encompassing the major media and communication groups of Galicia. Artists and creators have also formed their profesional associations—AADTEG (Asociación de Actores, Directores, e Técnicos de Escena de Galicia [1985]), AGG (Asociación Galega de Guionistas [1997]), and CREA (Asociación Galega de Directores e Realizadores [2001]). In 2003, AGAPI formed the Clúster do Audiovisual Galego ("Galician Audiovisual Cluster"), a group of Galician companies from different sectors—film production, consulting, finance, mass media, and communications—to support the audiovisual field. This initiative was a conscious effort to counteract the tradition of individualism and thus become a more competitive industry in a globalized world. Also of recent creation are the Galicia Film Commission, which promotes and facilitates film production in Galicia at the national and international levels, and the Academia Galega do Audiovisual, which was established in 2002 in Vigo and awards the annual Mestre Mateo Prizes in the audiovisual sector.[19]

Recent years have seen a great variety of audiovisual productions made in Galicia by Galician companies and with Galician men and women, in the form of feature films, documentaries, shorts, video art, video clips, TV movies and series, multimedia, animation, among others. There has been a remarkable diversity of genres and approaches in feature films, which go beyond the traditional rural Galician setting; some of the new areas explored are the urban thriller, fantasy, comedy, adventure, and animation.[20] This heterogeneity is manifested in the films themselves and in their critical and public reception.[21] Current social issues and controversial topics are commonly explored in these films, such as illegal migrant workers (*Ilegal* ["Illegal"]), drug trafficking (*Entre bateas* ["Sea Farming"]), contemporary youth culture (*O ano da carracha* ["The Year of the Tick"]), and political violence (*Sé quien eres* ["I Know Who You Are"]). Genres and styles range from urban thrillers like *Lena* or *Arde Lume* ("Burning Light"), Dogme films like *Era outra vez* ("Once upon Another Time") and *Dias de voda* ("Wedding Days"), noir films like *Continental,* horror films like *13 badaladas* ("Thirteen Chimes") and *La promesa* ("The Promise"), to animated features like *El bosque animado* (the first 3-D film made in Europe) and *El sueño de una noche de San Juan* ("The Midsummer Dream of San Juan"). The animation sector in Galicia is growing particularly strong in recent years, with two companies (Dygra Films and Bren Animation) successfully selling their products in international markets. Miguelanxo Prado's *De profundis* (2006; "From the Sea") is the first animated film ever created from digitized oil paintings.[22]

Other encouraging developments are the discovery and recognition of Galician cinema in the form of prizes and awards in national and international competitions (for both shorts and long feature films by younger directors, like Ignacio Pardo, Jorge Coira, and Héctor Carré) and in the box office success beyond Galicia of recent Galician films—*13 badaladas, O ano da carracha,* and *O lapis do carpinteiro* ("The Carpenter's Pencil"). This has been particularly the case in the area of animation, such as Dygra's Ángel de la Cruz and Manolo Gómez's *El bosque animado,* winner of two Goya Awards in 2002 and released in some fifty countries, or *Pérez, el ratoncito de tus sueños* ("The Hairy Tooth Fairy"), the biggest domestic box office success in Spain in 2007. Also noteworthy are the established careers of Antón Reixa, performance artist and TV and film producer-director, and other directors such as Xavier Villaverde, Patricia Ferreira, Xavier Bermúdez, and

Juan Pinzás, the only director in Spain with three films carrying the official Dogme 95 seal of approval from Lars von Trier for the trilogy *Era outra vez, Días de voda,* and *El desenlace* ("The Outcome"). The Galician actors Uxía Blanco, Manuel Manquiña, Nancho Novo, Chete Lera, and Tristán Ulloa have all worked in both Galician and Spanish films. Luis Tosar won three Goya Awards for best Spanish actor and made frequent appearances in international films such as *Miami Vice* and Jim Jarmusch's *The Limits of Control.* Miguelanxo Prado was hired by Steven Spielberg as art director for the animated television series *Men in Black.* Perhaps most encouraging for Galician cinema is the arrival of a new generation of filmmakers and film professionals, many of them graduates from the new EIS. Jorge Coira and Ignacio Vilar are more adventurous and less academic than their predecessors, who frequently followed the elitist auteur cinema model of the 1960s and 1970s, and have been able to connect with considerable Galician audiences (*O ano da carrancha, Pradolongo*).

The combination of financial incentives provided by the Xunta in the form of subsidies and the progressive establishment of an industrial infrastructure with capable technical crews and support companies, and at lower costs, has made Galicia's natural scenery an attractive location for many Spanish and even international films, with Galician financial, technical, and artistic participation. Recent film productions in Galicia by well-known Spanish directors are José Luis Cuerda's *La lengua de la mariposas* ("The Butterfly's Tongue") and *Los girasoles ciegos* ("The Blind Sunflowers"), Fernando León de Aranoa's *Los lunes al sol* ("Mondays in the Sun"), Alejandro Amenábar's *Mar adentro* ("The Sea Inside"), Gracia Querejeta's *Cuando vuelvas a mi lado* ("By My Side Again"), Isabel Coixet's *A los que aman* ("To Those Who Love"), as well as films by foreign directors such as Adolfo Aristarain's *La ley de la frontera* ("The Law of the Frontier"), Bent Hamer's *Water Easy Reach,* Stuart Gordon's *Dagon,* and Roman Polanski's *Death and the Maiden.* [23]

In 2002 Galicia was the autonomous community in Spain with the third greatest expansion and volume of its audiovisual sector (*Libro branco de cinematografía* 163). Galician cinema has going for it a developing infrastructure that is modestly adequate in its basic components—institutional, industrial, economic, educational; a slow but regular and varied stream of films, especially since the 1990s, with increasing budgets and cinematographic values; the public acceptance of Galician audiovisual products, especially through TVG; and the recent discovery of Galicia by film audiences and film companies beyond Galicia's borders. There is room for improvement, but definitely "xa é algo" ("it's a start").[24]

Utopian Visions: Not All That Glitters Is Gold

On the other side of the coin, there are shortcomings in the field of Galician audiovisual and cinema arts that cannot be overlooked and are cause for concern. They are the result of particular political, economic, and sociocultural realities that also affect other areas of Galician cultural production. Most are structural problems difficult to circumvent. The official report *Audiovisual galego 2003* stated that the audiovisual sector in Galicia "se caracteriza por ter unha estructura fragmentada e atomizada" (*Libro branco de cinematografía* 18; "is characterized by a fragmented and atomized structure"). This challenge corresponds to what I call the Galician *minifundio cinema* infrastructure, a chronic atomization of the audiovisual industry sector that is parallel to the economic, geographic, and cultural *minifundismo* prevalent in many areas of Galician society. The small-scale filming industry is composed mainly of independent companies that often do not have the financial resources or equipment to operate in a stable and continued manner. (Significantly, two of the biggest production companies involved in Galician cinema are Barcelona-based Filmax and Madrid-based Continental, both run by relocated Galician migrants, which points out another historical reality, that of the economic Galician diaspora.) Therefore other audiovisual institutions and complex coproduction schemes must be relied on. In 2003, there were 226 companies in the audiovisual sector registered in Galicia, of which 150 were dedicated to production (15). These numbers may seem high, but many of these companies are one-person operations established around a single project. The total amount of business sales generated by production companies in the sector for the year 2001 was 51 million euros, equivalent to the average budget of one Hollywood studio movie (162).[25]

In recent years, there has been a noticeable trend toward higher specialization and greater capital expansion by audiovisual companies operating in Galicia. Still, to this day, there are few professional film laboratories in Galicia, and therefore most of the developing as well as restoration and conservation of film materials must be done elsewhere. Although audiovisual company associations and clusters are steps in the right direction, the atomization of the sector, the shortage of strong and stable companies, and poor access to equipment and financial resources make the task of creating audiovisual works professionally in Galicia still a challenging proposition.

Another major challenge is the excessive dependence on official subsidies and commissioned works, which relates to other chronic patterns of Galician society—political *caciquismo* ("local boss politics") and economic paternalism almost to the point of servitude. Galician film production is put at the mercy of arbitrary selection committees, of changing official policies, and of political parties in power. Galician filmmakers resort to a number of sources of finance for their productions—local governments, public and private television companies from Europe and Latin America. They also turn to Spain's Ministry of Culture, the ICAA, the European Union, or the strictly one-off subsidies from the Quinto Centenario or the Xacobeo celebrations. But most of the money comes from two sources, the official subventions from the Xunta de Galicia's Consellería de Cultura and the advance payments from TVG for television showing rights.[26] Dependence on public funding only aggravates the *caciquismo* syndrome in Galician film production; it also fosters conformity and conservative choices, both aesthetic and ideological, and not formal experimentation or dissidence on the part of the film directors. Hence the conspicuous absence of overtly political Galician films and films that defy gender or sexual normativity.[27] For example, the treatment of homosexual characters in *Era outra vez* and *Días de voda* is mostly anecdotal and sensationalist, and the discourse on sexual orientation in *O ano da carracha* is ultimately reactionary.[28] Such work reveals the negative consequences of accommodation to the socioeconomic realities of the status quo.[29]

The paternalism of official institutions can also exert its influence in perverse ways. Although official subsidy guidelines often state their preference that films be shot in Galician, this preference has rarely been respected by the institutions or exercised by the filmmakers. To obtain an official subvention and sell broadcasting rights to TVG or make coproductions with TVG, it is enough for a film to have a dual language track, in Galician and Spanish, which allows its commercialization in both languages and its broadcasting on TVG in Galician. In reality, few feature-length fiction films are originally shot in Galician (*Sempre Xonxa*, *Urxa*, *A metade da vida*, *Pradolongo*, and Pinzás's first two Dogme films come to mind). Most rely on the conventional practice of dubbing into Galician in postproduction (endorsed by TVG) for the sake of economic viability outside Galicia. Casts are often headed by recognizable non-Galician Spanish actors (Carmen Maura,

Fernando Guillén, Angela Molina, Jorge Sanz), who are dubbed by Galician actors (Javier Bardem is unusual: he learned Galician for parts of his role in *Mar adentro*). Films dubbed in Galician typically sound affected, artificial. A number of problems surface: the noticeable traces of translation, the overpowering of the vocal track over the background sound, the recourse to the same limited group of actors' voices, the prosody and vocal patterning inherited from Spanish.[30]

It could be argued that at least this dubbing practice assists in the linguistic normalization of Galician. In fact, it promotes conformity to a Galician standard that is the product of TVG's linguistic department rather than of Galician social reality and customs (with a varied linguistic map, subregional and social class varieties, linguistic code-switching, and diglossia).[31] The dubbing of foreign language films is an accepted practice in the Spanish film market, instead of the use of subtitles, as in other countries; but it is a questionable practice on purely aesthetic grounds—and it is another legacy of Francoism's cultural and ideological manipulation.[32] It is particularly distressing, for that reason, to see the Galician authorities, and TVG in particular, follow the hegemonic Spanish model. And if the practice of dubbing remains dominant in Spain and Galicia, why are Galician films not shot in Galician and then dubbed into Spanish or another language in postproduction?

The dubbing situation points to the lack of a coherent vision from the Xunta. Official policies regarding the audiovisual arts are not consistent, shifting with the political wind. Consider the great ideological divide between TVG, whose official leaders were appointed by the conservative Partido Popular (PP) in power between 1990 and 2005, and the impulse behind its original foundation. This divide was sharply criticized by Manuel González, the EIS director (Acuña 98). TVG, developing into a populist entity with an institutionalized folkloric view of Galician culture, has earned the ironic name of "telegaita" ("bagpipe TV").[33]

The centrality of Santiago-based TVG in the Galician audiovisual panorama points to other issues, such as the lack of a real alternative in Galicia, because local television stations have limited resources to create original programming. A paradoxical situation arises, which I would call peripheral centralism: the accumulation of political power by the Xunta. This paradox is manifested in the disconnect between reality and institutional planning, in that most official audiovisual institutions such as TVG, CGAI, and EIS are in northern Galicia, in the cities of Coruña and Santiago, the traditional recipients of government investment. In contrast, the city of Vigo, which is Galicia's industrial and commercial capital and as such the most important and dynamic urban area of Galicia, has had to rely on itself. New production companies and film schools have principally been established in Vigo as private enterprises, without official government support (Acuña 160–61).

A final, serious challenge to Galician cinema is the lack of a support system of distribution and exhibition, a system that remains largely in the hands of subsidiaries of American companies. Galician cinema shares this problem with Spanish cinema, where many national films never make it to the theater screen, and with all cinemas whose distribution system is controlled by the de facto Hollywood monopoly. The problem is particularly acute in Galicia, located at the periphery of the periphery. Aside from showings on TVG, relatively few Galician films are made available to the public at large or go on general commercial release.[34] As a result many Galician films remain unseen beyond limited groups in Galicia.

The market limitations of a minority cinema within a minority national film industry create a catch-22 situation that has no easy solution. Spanish distributors, critics, and officials in control of film subsidies simply have not been very interested in Galician films. Perhaps this trend can be reversed. The new discovery of Galician cinema is a step in that direction. For all the talk about a boom, the audiovisual sector in Galicia is still developing, and the situation of Galician cinema is still far from normalized. The day may come when one can go to a video store, brick-and-mortar or more likely virtual, and browse the Galician cinema section, next to other national or postnational cinemas. Until then, the vision of Galician cinema will remain utopian.

Notes

I would like to thank Javier Viana, Isabel Salgueiro, and Carmen Becerra for their generous assistance and intelligent insights on the audiovisual industry in Galicia. All English translations from Galician in this essay are my own.

1. For a review of these issues, see Crofts; Higson.

2. On the cultural interplay of the local and the global in the contemporary redefinition of Galicia through film and music, see Colmeiro, "Camiños de Santiago."

3. Critics such as Xoán González-Millán have noted the insufficiency of this criterion in the contemporary Galician cultural context ("O criterio filolóxico"). More recent

debates in Galician studies have also approached this problematic, such as the forum and the articles in the special issue of *Journal of Spanish Cultural Studies* devoted to Galician Studies (Hooper, *New Spaces*).

4. The former president of the Xunta de Galicia, Emilio Pérez Touriño, underlined the strategic importance of cinema made in Galicia, using the expression "longametraxes con sabor galego" ("films with Galician flavor") for the Galician economy and its cultural promotion. For a summary of the legal measures for the establishment of the audiovisual sector in Galicia, see note 15.

5. For an overview of the bleak picture of Galician cinema in the 1970s, see Rabón.

6. For an overview of the beginnings of Galician cinema in the 1920s and 1930s and its slow rebirth in the 1970s after the long desert of the Franco years, see X. Nogueira, "As temáticas."

7. The main reason for this postproduction dubbing is the widespread perception that films shot in Spanish are better suited for distribution and a commercially successful run, especially in Spanish-speaking areas outside Galicia. This reason holds particularly for long feature films, which are more dependent than shorts on commercial distribution. Unusual exceptions to this rule are the Galician-language films by Chano Piñeiro, Raúl Veiga, and a few others. Even such a well-known militant supporter of Galician-language art and culture as Antón Reixa has shot his feature films in Spanish, for pragmatic reasons. His adaptation of one of the most canonical novels of modern Galician literature, Manuel Rivas's *O lápis do carpinteiro*, received harsh criticism for this "fraud" (for an overview of the controversy between the collective Redes Escarlata and Reixa, see "El lápiz"). In this context, the recent spectacular success in theaters and video stores of Ignacio Vilar's rural, youth-themed *Pradolongo* (2008), originally shot in Galician and understood by some as a sign of the normalization of Galician cinema, seems all the more remarkable for its exceptionality ("'Pradolongo'").

8. This trend can also be observed in the titles of recent books and articles on this subject (*Cen anos de cine en Galicia, O cine en Galicia, Historia do cine en Galicia, Diccionario do cine en Galicia, Libro branco de cinematografía e artes visuais en Galicia*), of TVG programs like Miguel Anxo Fernández's *Galicia no cine*, and of video collections such as the one recently launched by the journal *La voz de Galicia* as "Galicia de cine." All avoid the ambiguous expression "Cine galego." Discussions on this topic (and the even older question of what constitutes Galician literature) have repeatedly taken place in a Galician studies e-mail discussion forum in the last couple of years. For access to the archive, see www.jiscmail.ac.uk/lists/GALICIAN-STUDIES.html.

9. Although there has been considerable growth in the production of cinema in Galicia, there is not a unified set of characteristics that would establish Galician cinema as a unique national cinema, different from other cinemas, like Iranian cinema or Indian cinema ("Audiovisual agora"). The same argument, of course, could be said of other national cinemas, including the Spanish.

10. Clear-cut distinctions cannot always be made, yet categorization helps clarify different patterns in the cinema made in Galicia. Jaime Pena states that the two trends have

almost converged in recent years, citing as an example the parallels between the two film adaptations of Manuel Rivas's work set in the civil war, *La lengua de las mariposas* and *El lápiz del carpintero* (the model of production, the look and film style, the literary referent). Beyond the intellectual debate, the argument has obvious political and economic ramifications. Which films should receive the official subsidies provided by the Xunta de Galicia? Would a more restrictive subvention policy encourage more Galician productions or discourage non-Galician companies from creating cinema in Galicia?

11. The beginning of the online special dossier of *Vieiros* shows the need to put things in perspective, without exaggerated euphoria or self-defeating fatalism (neither "boom" nor "bluff"): "Primeiro foi a moda, agora é o audiovisual. . . . Falan de "boom" e amósannos un país maquillado nas estreas en pantalla grande. Ruborizámonos ao vérmonos alí, entre os focos, entre os protagonistas, non estamos afeitos. Así que saímos do mundo da ficción e tentamos pensar con sentidiño: nin hai 'boom' nin hai 'bluff,' non hai máis que unha incipiente e ilusionante industria que nos permite, por primeira vez, vernos reflectidos en caixas máxicas, xusto alí onde nunca chegaramos. O reto: contarnos historias a nós mesmos pero, sobre todo, contarnos ao resto do mundo. Velaí o inmenso potencial" ("Audiovisual agora"; "First it was fashion, now it's the audiovisual. . . . They talk about a 'boom' and show us a tarted-up country on the big screen. We blush to see ourselves there, among the spotlights, among the protagonists; we are not used to it. And so we leave the world of fiction and we try to think with some common sense: There is neither a 'boom' nor a 'bluff,' there is only an incipient and exciting industry that allows us, for the first time, to see ourselves reflected in magical boxes, right there, where we had never been. The challenge: to tell stories to ourselves, but above all to tell ourselves to the rest of the world. And that has immense potential").

12. The Cinegalicia festival was glossed by the media as the birth of the new Galician cinema. It took place in Vigo in November 1989, as the official public premiere of the first results of the Xunta de Galicia's policy of subvention for the development of Galician film, initiated only a couple of years earlier. The other two new films featured were Chano Piñeiro's *Sempre Xonxa* and Alfredo García Pinal and Carlos Piñeiro's *Urxa*, both originally shot in Galician with exclusively Galician actors. Rivas described in *El país* the audience's enthusiastic acclamation of *Sempre Xonxa* as a collective "auto de fe" (Acuña 125).

13. For an extended analysis of Chano Piñeiro's film career and its pioneering role in the vitalization of Galician cinema, see Acuña (for the production of *Sempre Xonxa*, see the section "A odisea dunha longa e complexa rodaxe"). As a vivid illustration of the lack of local infrastructure Piñeiro had to deal with, he used to tell how there were no audiovisual support companies in Galicia at the time that could provide a Galician oak tree for a prop, a crucial element in the film to represent the passage of time and the changing of the seasons. After many frustrating and costly delays, a fiberglass tree had to be ordered for that purpose from a company in Madrid, but unfortunately the resulting product did not bear much resemblance to a Galician oak tree.

14. Among some of the most notable, many with international projection, are musicians like Carlos Núñez, Milladoiro, Luar na lubre, Siniestro Total, Golpes Bajos; multimedia artists like Antón Reixa; graphic designers like Miguelanxo Prado; fashion designers like Adolfo Dominguez, Roberto Verino, and Purificación Garcia; and writers like Manuel Rivas, Suso de Toro, and Teresa Moure.

15. The official *lei do audiovisual* in Galicia, approved unanimously in 1999 by all the representatives of the four political parties in the Galician parliament, is one of the most comprehensive in Spain and clearly spells out the special status of the sector in Galicia: "Os poderes públicos de Galicia recoñecen a importancia cultural, económica e social das actividades cinematográficas e do audiovisual, do papel que poden desempeñar como creación artística, información, coñecemento e imaxe de Galicia, a prol da consecución da normalización cultural de Galicia, polo que a consideran sector estratéxico e prioritario" (Sempere 267 ["Lei 6-1999 do audiovisual de Galicia" 1.1]; "Galicia's public authorities recognize the cultural, economic, and social importance of cinema and audiovisual activities, of the role they can play in terms of artistic creation, information, knowledge, and image of Galicia, in favor of the attainment of Galicia's cultural normalization, and therefore consider them a strategic and high-priority sector").

16. The popular acceptance of Galician TV fictional series and sitcoms has had the surprising result of TVG's becoming one of the leading producers of fictional TV series in Europe (Sempere 260). In the last decade there have been some twenty-five TV fictional series made in Galicia; many lasted more than one season and were exported outside Galicia. There have been more than thirty TV films.

17. Between 1994 and 1999 there was a 296% increase in the number of audiovisual production companies, a 125% increase of employment in the sector, and a 113% increase in volume. For a summary of the spectacular expansion of the audiovisual sector, see "Audiovisual galego, as cifras."

18. Other audiovisual schools, private and public, have appeared in more recent years throughout Galicia. Aside from the EIS, new audiovisual training schools have opened: O Raio Verde (Santiago), Escola de Imaxe e Son (Vigo and Ourense), the private Escola Superior de Cinematografia (Vigo). The three public universities in Galicia have also started offering a *diplomatura* in audiovisual communication, with a specialization in film direction and screenwriting (Santiago), film production (Vigo), and 3D and multimedia (A Coruña).

19. Many information resources about the Galician audiovisual sector are available online. See the appendix to this essay.

20. The Web site *Rodado en Galicia* lists 176 films made in Galicia between 1916 and 2009. In the last twenty years, some fifty films were made in Galicia, of which maybe half could be considered Galician productions in a strict sense. For a list of films with the number of spectators and box office results between 1986 and 2003, see *Libro branco de cinematografia* (155). The most successful of the films made in Galicia during that period was *Los lunes al sol*, which grossed 7.5 million euros at the box office

in Spain alone. Among the Galician productions, *El bosque animado* (2001) was the most successful, making almost two million euros.

21. In a poll taken among critics and historians of Galician cinema by the CGAI in 2001, the best Galician films of the decade were ranked: (1) *Sé quien eres*, (2) *Fisterra* and *Arde Amor* ("Burning Love"), and (3) *Martes de Carnaval* ("Mardi Gras"), *El baile de las animas* ("Ghosts' Dance"), and *La lengua de las mariposas* (*Libro branco de cinematografía* 156). Though vastly different in genre, location, historical setting, look, and inspiration, all did well at the box office.

22. For a detailed analysis of the state of animation in Galicia, see Colmeiro, "Bosque."

23. The promotion done by Galician film commissions and the good quality-price ratio provided by Galician audiovisual companies are two reasons why so many Spanish films are now being shot in Galicia. For a comprehensive listing and extended analysis of all feature films shot in Galicia, see the official Galician Web site *Rodado en Galicia*.

24. A final reason for optimism is the increased interest in Galician cinema by academic researchers and specialists. A growing bibliography of critical and historical works has made possible the recovery and conservation of Galician film history. New journals, such as *Vértigo* and *Cielo negro*, are devoted to film studies in Galicia. In addition to the established film festivals of Ourense and Carballiño is the more radically *enxebre* ("culturally autochthonous") indie Festival de Cans (Porriño), the Galician agroglamor response to Cannes.

25. The average audiovisual production company in Galicia in 2004 was composed of three members, one of them owning almost 60% of the company, which makes it de facto a one-person business. Of all audiovisual companies in Galicia, 79% are small businesses (less than 600,000 euros generated in business), 17.7% medium companies (between 600,000 and 3 million euros), and only 2.7% large corporations (*Libro branco do andiovisual* 18, 47). Sales generated 89 million euros in 2006 ("Cadro de mando").

26. As much as 50% of the income generated by audiovisual production companies in Galicia comes directly from TVG, and in several cases it reaches practically 100% (*Libro branco de cinematografía* 18–19).

27. Low-budget shorts and documentaries have been the principal means for making politically provocative statements. Many such audiovisual productions focused on the aftermath of the *Prestige* oil spill, such as *Carcamans* (2003; "Hulks"), *Las voces del Prestige* (2005; "The Voices of *Prestige*), or Susana Rey's experimental false documentary *Cousas do Kulechov* (2007; "Kulechov's Stories"), a metaexploration of war in the media based on everyday images of Galician life.

28. Two provocative exceptions deal with the taboo topic of incest. One is the Galician-Catalan TV film *Más que hermanos* ("More than Siblings"), about a family composed of a brother, his sister, and their common daughter, based on fact. The other is Xavier Bermúdez's *León y Olvido* ("León and Olvido"), about a young woman who defies and contests traditional gender roles and her mentally retarded brother. It is

not clear, however, to what extent these films reinforce the perception of Galicia's backwardness.

29. For an extended analysis of the complex entanglement of protectionist measures and the politics of official subsidies for audiovisual production in Galicia, see Sempere.

30. This situation extends to much of the programming of TVG. A remarkable breakthrough was the hugely popular series *Mareas vivas* ("Spring Tides"), directed by Antón Reixa, which highlighted popular Galician dialectal varieties such as *seseo* and *gheada*. As a result, new Galician TV series have been more attuned to the social realities of the Galician language.

31. The Galician director Raúl Veiga (*A metade da vida* [1994; "Midlife"], *Arde amor* [1999]) insists that Galician films address these issues more directly, by incorporating the linguistic conflicts into the film narrative. He provides an overview of the linguistic issues of Galician audiovisual production.

32. The obligatory dubbing into Castilian of all films in other languages under Franco's dictatorship was a form of ideological control and censorship of foreign films, under the guise of the defense of the Spanish language.

33. The PSdG-BNG coalition government in Galicia between 2005 and 2009 made an effort to improve the public image of TVG. Admitting its populist slant, Xesús Pérez Varela, the new minister of culture, said in 2005, "Quien iba a pensar hace 20 años que la TVG iba tener más audiencia que la TVE1 en Galicia, nadie de nosotros y, al final, en mayo se ha conseguido. . . . La telegaita sigue siendo telegaita y por muchos años, pero cada vez con más prestigio" ("El Audiovisual gallego"; "Who would have thought twenty years ago that TVG would have a larger audience in Galicia than TVE1? None of us, and yet, in the end, that was accomplished in May. . . . Bagpipe TV is still bagpipe TV, and let's hope it will be for many years more, but it is gaining more prestige with every year").

34. For an in-depth study of the specific problematics of film distribution and exhibition in Galicia, see M. Fernández.

Useful References Online

Academia Galega do Audiovisual: www.academiagalegadoaudiovisual.com/
"O audiovisual agora." *Vieiros* online dossier (12 Nov. 2002): http://vello.vieiros.com/dossier/dossier.php?estxt–v_dosier4
AVG, O Soportal do Audiovisual Galego: www.culturagalega.org/avg/
Centro Galego de Artes da Imaxe (CGAI): www.cgai.org
Centro Multimedia de Galicia (CMG): www.cmg.xunta.es
Consorcio Audiovisual de Galicia (CAG): www.consorcioaudiovisualdegalicia.org/web/
Galicia Film Commission: www.galiciafc.org
As Muxicas (list of links to Galician audiovisual Web sites): www.asmuxicas.com/audiovisual_m.htm
Rodado en Galicia: http//rodadoengalicia.galiciafc.org/

Utopian Identity in Galician Television Programming: Nostalgia as Ideology in the Series Made by Televisión de Galicia

Marta Pérez Pereiro

Galicia has had its own television since 1985, when the Galician autonomous government decided to create a public radio and television corporation, the Compañía de Radio Televisión de Galicia (CRTVG). The raison d'être of CRTVG was to broadcast programs mainly, if not exclusively, in the Galician language, whose presence on broadcast media had hitherto been marginal.[1] Like any public broadcaster (*public* meaning that it operates for the public interest), CRTVG developed general guidelines regarding its contents in terms of quality and audience. Public television

> debe de responder á realidade social, cultural e económica do país. A programación ten que ser reflexo desa realidade e, como medios institucionais, cunha obriga de contribuír á transformación da mesma dende a identidade galega. (Maneiro Vila 205)

> must answer to the country's social, cultural, and economic reality. Programming must be a reflection of this reality and, as an institutional medium, its duty is to contribute to the transformation of that reality from a Galician identity position.

The explicit aim of Televisión de Galicia (TVG) was to represent Galician reality and identity on the screen, making use of the metaphor of television as a mirror, a metaphor that has been so trenchantly critiqued by John Fiske (21): a mirror of its target society and a window to the rest of the world, particularly through news programs. Furthermore, according to A. Maneiro Vila, the form of identity promoted by Galician public media should be an open process that negotiates the incorporation of Galicia into the group of developed societies (205; see also López García 52). This procedure would answer to what Sonja De Leeuw understands as addressing people as citizens, "which involves dealing with questions of identity—questions that have come to the fore because of the changing environment . . ." (93).

At the time of TVG's creation, back in the presatellite era, the only other television available in Galicia was the two Spanish public channels broadcast by Televisión Española (TVE). Catalonia and the Basque Country were also developing their own television channels—TV3 and Euskal Televista, respectively. More than two decades later, the Galician national television service offered an analogue channel and a second DTT (digital terrestrial television) channel, together with a free à la carte Internet service. The TV offering is completed with local TV stations—both digital and analogue—and with the Spanish public and commercial television companies (Antena 3, Cuatro, Telecinco, La Sexta) with their DTT channels, and Digital+, the satellite platform. Pay-per-view television, via ADSL (Imagenio and others) or cable (R, a Galician-based company) and the Internet are new competitors for conventional broadcast television.

In terms of content, this increase in offerings did not lead to an increase in Galician products; in fact it led to a decrease in Galician output as a percentage of overall output. TVG is still the most important place for Galician citizens to watch representations of themselves, and therefore of their culture and identity, on the screen. The battle over Galician identity is played out in the Galician public media, whose role both as a public institution and as a necessary point of reference for Galician culture has been a source of intensive debate since its creation. Criticism has focused on two issues: first, the ideological and political slant in TVG's news programs; second, the allegedly anachronistic depiction of social and political issues in TVG's programming, much of it aimed at the older generation, who are considered the channel's principal target audience. The second issue includes most genres but is especially interesting in relation to TVG's drama serials.

Paul Julian Smith has argued that the study of television must take into account three principal fields: "texts, producers, and institutions" (1). My essay considers each of these fields, examining them through the prism of programming or the organization of broadcast material, shaped by the interconnection of texts, producers, and institutions. First I examine issues of programming in general, with particular reference to the most successful programs and their social reception. I then turn to a consideration of Galician TV drama, from sitcoms to soap operas, which, I argue, covertly convey an ideologically driven representation of Galician identity that reveals the tensions between the cultures of different generations—particularly the tension regarding Galician identity seen as nostalgia for a vanishing rural way of life.

News and Drama: The Pillars of Galician Programming

As the "dominant leisure activity" of the population (Casey, Casey, Calvert, French, and Lewis vi), television must be analysed not simply as a container for particular programs but also as a unified output with particular characteristics. Considering that television is also an essential institution of modern states (Silverstone), the power of any channel to act as a platform for furthering ideological and political interests should not be underestimated. The analysis of television must take into account the succession of texts organized in time slots and the organization itself—that is, programming—as a tool for social control. The interweaving of programs and commercials forms what Raymond Williams famously described as a planned flow. Public service television uses this flow to conflate the public interest (through educational and news items) with economic profit. Recent changes in the way we access both television in general and individual TV programs (the enormous proliferation of satellite channels, pay-per-view, online television, and DVD box sets) have returned us to the earlier framework of distribution where programs are received as individual units. Nevertheless—and although some scholars mocked Williams for basing the flow metaphor on his personal experience of American television (Gripsrud)[2]—conventional television is still the main experience of this medium for most of the world's population, especially for those who cannot access new technologies for economic reasons. In Galicia, some scholars claim that TV consumption will experience dramatic changes in the coming years, but the fact is that access to the Internet and cable in Galicia is still underdeveloped in comparison with other countries in Europe.[3]

Traditional programming seems to be a clear, univocal flow that is also frequently self-referential, which can be explained through the need to gain (and retain) the interest of the audience through the use of cross-references to previous episodes and programs on the same channel. In this discourse, ideology is present, albeit in the background or out of focus. Furthermore, the axes—vertical and horizontal time slots—that organize content also convey a contrasting discourse that combines the three primary objectives of television: information, entertainment, and education. This scheduling structure can lead to contradiction, even paradox, because, in the interweaving of different contents, thematic organization is not important. The mixture of programming segments expresses one of the general contradictions of television, as each viewing strip tends to organize itself around a certain type of consumer in order to obtain the most profitable results. This arrangement of products fits perfectly with one of Williams's first claims about broadcasting, that the use of viewing strips is the most adequate system for organizing audiovisual content (and taste) "directly shaped by and dependent on the norms of a capitalist society . . ." (*Television* 36). Nonetheless, viewing strips have been neglected in television studies, research that has focused primarily on programming and particular products.

Each program, a particular text included in the programming megatext, contains a "wide variety of codes [that] all cohere to present a unified set of meanings" (Fiske 13). From generic conventions to general assumptions about time schedules, these codes all suggest a great variety of possible analyses. Some researchers argue that the minimum unit for analysis is not the program but the segment, which is a five-minute piece of programming that has a certain degree of coherence (Ellis 112). Even though the rhythm of television fits into these narrative units, my aim here is to analyze the general output of TVG programming and the particular set of social issues portrayed in recent drama.

The TVG schedule is conventional, following the trends of programming in general, in its dependence on a double axis—a vertical and horizontal organization—and on the themes of each season, which are globalized. Fiske presents contradiction in the scheduling of TV programs as a positive thing, revealing the forces in tension in a society. The particular contradiction revealed by Galician television relates to one of the principles that guided the creation of the channel. CRTVG was intended to promote the normalization of the Galician language, which should be the usual language employed in the broadcasting of radio and television. This vague concept of usual language has meant that the flow of Galician-language programming is repeatedly interrupted by Spanish-language advertising. Some scholars point out that the Spanish companies that sponsor programs in Galician provide the advertisements in Spanish (Portas 241). Although Galician is now being used more in advertising, this general framework points to an underlying contradiction between the two languages: Galician is devoted to public service, Spanish to economic profit. TVG reproduces the bilingual conflict in

Galicia not only in this contradiction but also in the quality of the language, which has been the subject of harshest criticism of the channel.[4]

Criticism of TVG has focused on two main issues: (1) the presence and influence of party politics on the channel; (2) the arguably anachronistic representation of Galician society and culture, which is connected with the question of TVG's target audience. In addition, critics have raised the issue of the quality of TVG programs, which a number of observers have deemed uniformly poor. In sessions of the Galician parliament, political parties have raised concerns about their representation on TVG, especially in terms of the time slots allocated to each of them in news programs. The general understanding is that in news items, the number of minutes allocated to reporting the activities of Galicia's main political parties (the PPdeG, the PSdeG, and the BNG) should be proportional to the number of MPs each has in the Galician parliament at O Hórreo in Santiago de Compostela. This issue rears its head in the months leading up to an election, when understandably the political parties want to make use of the power and influence of TVG for their own purposes. During the sixteen years when the conservative Partido Popular (PP) was first in office, with Manuel Fraga as president of the Xunta (1990–2005), the opposition parties, Partido dos Socialistas de Galicia (PSdeG) and Bloque Nacionalista Galego (BNG), focused their criticism on the fact that news bulletins were monopolized by the figure of Fraga, who was regularly depicted attending ceremonies such as the opening of new roads or the inauguration of public events and venues. The opposition parties considered that this exposure gave the PP an unfair electoral advantage. The question of political influence seems to be understood mainly in terms of the time slots each political party is allocated.

This superficial analysis ignores other, more subtle (but no less effective) ways of conveying ideological content through programming. While criticism is of TVG's political and ideological content has been dominated by party politics, the other main target of criticism is TVG's audience and how TVG represents Galician society and culture. Both the academy and other areas of the media feel the television channel is for old people, especially those living in rural parts of inland Galicia. The intended viewer is a middle-aged or elderly woman who has little education and income and lives in a village of fewer than 10,000 people (*Libro branco do audiovisual*).

Programming for the ideal Galician demographic has changed slightly in the last years in the light of political and social transformations.[5]

Many scholars saw the change of government in 2005, when the socialist-nationalist coalition replaced the rightist PP in the Xunta, as a great opportunity to transform the channel's offering. The main challenge for the new management team of the public channel became the incorporation of a young, urban target demographic that had been lost as an audience some years before (Fandiño Alonso and Dafonte Gómez).

Immersed in this task, TVG programming has retained the news, which is the backbone of the schedule and provides a close reflection of the audience, and fiction, which represents the quality provision of the channel. The schedule is completed with a third kind of program, which fills in many of the gaps: music programs have long been successful (Ledo), but in the last five years they have been gradually replaced by other entertainment programs, following global trends in programming—for example, reality shows (Fandiño Alonso and Dafonte Gómez). But music formats or miscellanea are still an important source of audience for TVG, which is reluctant to eliminate them completely. If the television news is criticized for its subservience to the party in office, music has often been seen to convey a reactionary position in that it stresses the folkloric side of Galician culture, in opposition to the channel's foundational principles, which warned against folklorization. The flagship for this kind of show is *Luar* ("Moonlight"), a live-music broadcast on Friday nights that combines traditional Galician folk music, often gathered from oral informants from small villages, with Spanish folk music. A possible reason for the spectacular success of *Luar*, which has aired continuously since September 1992, is that it takes the place of a village party. The traditional focus of *Luar* leads to recognition by the audience of their ordinary life, thus fulfilling the reflection effect of television as a medium.

Even though *Luar* has produced high audience ratings,[6] it also provoked the popular coinage of an epithet for TVG—*telegaita* ("bagpipe TV"), a reference to the fact that programming all too frequently features this traditional Galician instrument:

> Pero o alcume "telegaita" non ten un alcance simplemente denotativo, non se limita a constatar obxectivamente a abundancia gaiteira nas emisións musicais da canle autonómica. "Telegaita" expresa unha inclinación ideolóxica e unha tendencia estética. Connota un modelo de facer televisión caracterizado por un conservadorismo de matiz populista e ruralizante que se combina coa exaltación continuada, entre sentida e ritual, dos valores patrios, do "noso."
> (Villalaín 60)

The term, widely used in informal conversation, is not confined to objectively stating the abundance of bagpipes in music shows on the autonomous television channel. *Telegaita* expresses an ideological inclination and an aesthetic tendency. It connotes a model for television characterized by a conservatism based on populism and ruralization that combines a continuous exaltation of patriotic values with the sense of what is "ours."

The term points to the fact that folklore was for decades almost the only cultural reference publicly available to a Galician audience.

Criticism of the channel's quality has also been expressed regarding the lack of cultural programs[7] and their marginalization into late-night slots:

> Entre os anos 2002 e 2003 prodúcese un incremento spectacular na emisión de programas catalogados como culturais coincidindo coa celebración do Ano Santo Xacobeo. No entanto, en 2004 e 2005 os formatos culturais non veñen facendo máis ca perder notoriamente minutos de emisión na nosa televisión pública. (Fandiño Alonso and Dafonte Gómez 95)

> Between 2002 and 2003 there is a spectacular increase in the broadcasting of so-called cultural programs, which coincides with the celebration of Saint James's Day. But in 2004 and 2005, cultural formats all too clearly lose minutes in the programming of our public television.

TVG's focus on popular culture, and especially on music, has contributed to the neglect of the representational aspect of public service broadcasting, given that so many of these programs appear to address only the principal demographic. The consequence has been naturalization: the creation of a perfect match between targeted and real audience. Galician public television produces a construction of reality that emphasizes the way of life of the channel's most loyal viewers. As television "reproduces the dominant sense of reality" (Fiske 21), the programming choices in scheduling, selection of genres, and social representation of the audience have an ideological function. This is particularly relevant for public media, as the audience is constituted by potential voters. Ideological content is not restricted to news programs; it is a central issue both in programming as a whole and in any given segment of the schedule. Ideology is particularly important for a medium whose main discourse is based on realism (Fiske),[8] not only in terms of its representation of the reality we experience but also in terms of "the extent of a text's truthfulness or lifelike qualities, whether or not the story is based on a real event" (Casey, Casey, Calvert, French, and Lewis 194).

The tensions among the different social and political discourses current in any community are explicitly played out in TV programming and its contents, drama included. As television drama is all about encounters and conflicts (De Leeuw), it functions as a battleground for social forces to work out the representation of their different interests. Most recent research on TV drama in Europe has focused on the representation of minorities and cultural change, as well as on the construction of national identity through fiction:

> [W]hen discussing national identity within the context of the European integration, nations tend to turn inwards, looking for their roots. The countryside as concept can represent our past. Accordingly, in European television drama of the past decade, the countryside, representing our past, appeared as setting. (98)

In Galician television, drama series have revealed the contrast between the rural—presented as the essential, traditional form of Galician culture—and the urban, which is portrayed as foreign to the Galician culture reproduced on and by the channel. The countryside, connected with the past in much current Galician cultural discourse, is the principal location for TVG fiction. TVG tends to turn to other times in the search for identity and the identification of its viewers.

Utopian Sensibility in Galician TV Drama

The starting point for a policy of television drama production in Galicia is 1995, when TVG coproduced its first feature series with production companies based in Galicia. There had been a few unsuccessful attempts to develop products in previous years. It was only the success of serial drama on Spanish channels that brought home the idea that European television channels could produce their own series, thus avoiding the extreme dependence on American mass production that had characterized the 1980s.[9] The production of serial drama on Galician television was designed to address two needs: on the one hand, the Xunta was firmly committed to the development of a solid audiovisual industry; on the other, the creation of quality prime-time television was perceived as necessary to eradicate the negative perception of Galician programming. Although some scholars are reluctant to consider the move a success (Martínez Hermida), TVG has so far produced around twenty television series and coproduced a number of television movies with channels from other *autonomías*, something that would have been thought impossible only a few years ago. These series increased TVG's ratings by attracting new types of audiences—namely, younger viewers who were not interested in local news or in shows like *Luar*.

Galician TV drama produced a double benefit for programmers: quality production, which started to challenge the *telegaita* label, and a better balance between resources (time in the schedule, costs) and audience figures. Significantly, drama production increased its share of the TVG schedule from 19.5% of screen time in 2000 to 33.4% in 2005 (Fandiño Alonso and Dafonte Gómez 95). These programs now provide a third of the general flow of contents of the channel.

The first two feature series produced by TVG were *Pratos combinados* (1995–2006; "Mixed Grills"), which portrayed the life of Miro Pereira, who ran a bar in a Galician village along with his family, and *A familia Pita* (1996; "The Pita Family"), a comedy about a strange neighborhood. Both were sitcoms, largely because this genre is generally considered the cheapest to produce. *Pratos combinados*, the first to be broadcast,[10] became one of TVG's most successful productions and provided the channel's managers with the ultimate support they needed to pursue their new production policy. The 261 episodes, produced over ten seasons, enjoyed remarkable success, as the sitcom's ratings far surpassed the channel's average viewing figures. TVG has around 17% of the total audience share in Galicia, but the 1996–97 season of *Pratos combinados* obtained 27.9%, and even the repeats of some episodes were among TVG's top-rated programs.

In 1998 a dramedy entitled *Mareas vivas* (1998–2002; "Spring Tides") created the model for all future dramas: a series with an ensemble cast, set in a Galician village that depicted the conflicts of a small coastal fishing community in a positive light. In the main plot, the new magistrate, a man from the city of A Coruña, adapts to village life. It is an idealized life, but the series also established the boundaries of (and dangers to) that utopia in a way that would be imitated by all the most successful Galician productions. After *Mareas vivas* came *Terra de Miranda* (2001–07; "Land of Miranda"), another reproduction of the daily life of a rural inland village through the experiences of Carmela, a veterinarian recently returned from Vigo, with her sons. Other series that proved successful were *As leis da Celavella* (2003–05; "The Laws of Celavella"), a thriller-like drama set in the 1920s, in which a lawyer and his maid solve uncommon murders, and *Libro de familia* (2005– ;

"Family Record Book"), in which a rural family in the 1960s schemes against the local ruler of the village. These two dramas provided retrospective depictions of Galician life in the previous decade, and they were also set in small communities. Time and location are crucial to the definition of these series and, above all, to their relation to the society they portray. TVG's most successful series are all placed in the past and present. That the future has been largely neglected might be because projections into the future inevitably become an ideological exercise, in that the consequences of the present must be imagined or posed.

Although the future has been conspicuously absent from TVG drama production, it could be argued that the series that have been produced are in a way science fiction. They do not feature monsters or space trips but are science fiction in the way David Lowenthal understands the term: "a world that was a better place" (23). The attempt to create or re-create an idealized Galicia is explicit in dramas set in the past but can also be seen in those series set in the present, as their temporal setting is generally unclear, imprecise, blurred, a kind of present that is credible in terms of setting but not that credible in the way conflicts are presented and solved.

Regarding location, there is the widespread belief that Galician television series are always set in rural areas. The facts do not support this affirmation: of the eighteen series produced between 1988 and 2006, ten have urban settings. Yet the most successful series throughout these years have been those located in rural or semirural settings, not those located in the cities. Urban comedies such as *Cuarto sen ascensor* (2005; "Fourth Floor, No Elevator"), a sitcom about the lives of three apartment mates and their neighbors, and *A miña sogra e máis eu* (2004; "My Mother-in-Law and Me"), where an unemployed actor and his family must go live with his mother-in-law, were canceled after the tenth episode, because of low audience figures.

The audience might prefer series located in villages and the countryside because of the producer's attempt in them to create a coherent universe where all pieces fit (Ang). Series like *Mareas vivas* or *Terra de Miranda* created a fictional world in which every element made viewers feel that what was happening could happen in any Galician village. One reason for this feeling was the use of a dialectal, as opposed to standard, Galician. In *Mareas vivas*, the variety of Galician spoken along the Costa da Morte in the far west of Galicia, with its characteristic guttural *gheada* and sibilant *seseo*, encouraged viewers to identify with the characters.[11] In addition, plots and characters were carefully designed to achieve a credible representation of a maritime village. While the city in Galician television drama is often undefined and unnamed (whether with a real or fictional name), country spaces are precisely imagined and based on reality. Some of the villages represented in Galician series are a fusion of the real and the imagined. Portozás, the town where *Mareas vivas* is set, derives from Porto and Zas, both genuine Galician place-names; the Miranda of *Terra de Miranda* is taken from the fictional name that the writer Álvaro Cunqueiro gave to his home town of Mondoñedo.

In television, the success of a drama is closely connected to the fictional space in which it takes place. The generically rural settings of many of the TVG series encouraged viewers either to draw on their own experience of living in such an area or to use their familiarity with Galician cultural history to overcome any distance between them and the setting of the drama. The mixture of real and imagined in these series can be related to what some authors have described as a "blurred Galicia" (Lamas), which reflects the particular distribution of the Galician population: the proliferation of many small villages with unclear borders. Enric Castelló calls this fictional device "typical space," an imaginary space to represent a national territory in TV drama. In Galician television, it is a small village that coincides with the geography much of the channel's audience is familiar with but with the addition of a dreamy atmosphere that contributes to the blurring of frontiers.

The attempt to create a fictional universe is related to the realism of the representations. This identity realism is a portrait that uses features of national identity to meet the requirements made of Galician public media. Emotional realism, location, and language are key strategies for the portrayal of such an identity, and all are present in the most successful series. The need for viewers to identify with the protagonists of a television series is not unique to Galicia. Spanish drama usually re-creates everyday situations, taking ideas and inspiration from the news, as part of a production model characterized by the search for immediacy. Some TVG series in the last few years have started to be produced in the same way. For instance, *A vida por diante* (2006; "A Whole Life Ahead") developed subplots based on news stories, thus creating a sort of continuum with the news bulletins that punctuate the flow of programming.

Another general feature of the representational policy of television drama is its approach to the resolution of conflicts. Even considering that the time span for these conflicts is defined by the television format itself, which usually cannot exceed ninety minutes, a drama tends toward a "felicitous resolution" that clearly contrasts with the news. Marcelo Martínez Hermida writes:

> As series galegas emitidas pola TVG responden a unha axenda revisitada de problemas con solución políticamente correctas: a sida, as drogas, a emigración, o tema do caciquismo revirado en paternalismo, o ascenso da muller, a inexperiencia da mocidade . . . sería inconcibible, por exemplo, que o tratamento de política galega, cos actuais protagonistas informativos que propón a TVG, fose trasladado ó contraste das discusións que sobre un tema ou outro tivesen os personaxes dunha serie.   (242)

> The Galician series shown on TVG . . . answer to a familiar agenda of problems with politically correct solutions: AIDS, drugs, emigration, local politics that tend toward paternalism, female power, youthful inexperience. . . . It would be inconceivable, for instance, that the treatment of Galician politics with their protagonists in the news could be transferred to the dialogue between the characters in a drama.

The television series produced in the last two decades are a direct result of TVG's attempt to create a positive image in society. Their ideological nature is to be found in the character of the social portraits they provide. Real economic and social struggles are, as a rule, left out of the narratives. There is a striking absence of the working class, of blue-collar workers.[12] At the same time, the common people in fishing villages or agricultural areas are fully represented. Thus most of the characters in TVG's drama series are peasants or fishermen whose life conflicts can be considered universal but are clearly located in a rural-urban continuum. In this world, the local ruler, or cacique, as Martínez Hermida argues, is not a bad guy but someone who has problems dealing with power. In *Mareas vivas* the conflict between the political boss, who is a builder and real estate agent, and the mayor, who holds democratic power, is perfectly dramatized. The political conflict overlaps with the emotional tension between the characters, a man and a woman in their fifties. Liberal professionals and service workers also feature in Galician drama; following Aristotelian theory, they usually play the role of heroes, while comic characters normally come from the lower classes.

With the sole exception of *A vida por diante*, which is a crude depiction of five women widowed as a result of a shipwreck, Galician television drama tends to minimize violence and misfortune and shows a clear preference for the nonconflictive, positive resolution of social problems. In this sense, serial drama is devoted to what David Lusted calls "utopian sensibility,"

> through which feelings emerge not just at the representational level (in what people say or do) but also at the non-representational level (in more abstract qualities of movement, color, music, shape, line, etc.). For Dyer, the meaning of the utopian sensibility lies in its feelings of abundance, energy, transparency, intensity and community.   (181)

Television drama offers content designed to please the viewer by means of an affective relocation of the private in a process that confirms the identity of the subject in his or her social position (Lusted). The naturalization of ideology works through emotional empathy, identification with the characters, and the reduction of social tensions. The use of emotional realism in everyday conflicts is a mechanism for social representation that serves to fix a set of social values (what is good and evil for the community) but also has another purpose: to establish the borders of that depicted community.

While it is possible to picture the borders in Galicia as just political and administrative, the question of frontiers is not that simple in any given society. Together with the obvious social divide created by emigration, Galicia shows psychological borders between the countryside and the city, setting up an all but insurmountable division between rural and urban. The foreigner in Galician television drama comes not from overseas but from the city. On *Mareas vivas*, characters from the city speak standard Galician, in contrast with the rest of the community, who use dialect.

The inhabitants of Galician television's fictional villages inevitably succeed in convincing the "foreigners" that the best place to be is this utopian dreamland: neat, pure, and innocent. The city dwellers end up recognizing the virtues and advantages of rural life. In *Mareas vivas*, Berta, the Portozás doctor, comes from the major port city of Vigo; in *Terra de Miranda*, Carmela and her sons also come from Vigo—they return to Miranda after Carmela separates from her husband. These characters fundamentally change their attitudes to rural life through their experience of living in the village; their initial derogatory statements about locals and the size of the village turn into enthusiasm after they see the advantages of this new life. The migrant experience, too, is represented: in *Pratos combinados*, Miro Pereira, a kind of modern Ulysses, and his family return from Switzerland to run the Bar Suizo; Isa returns to Valderrei (2007) to recover from an unhappy marriage and to restart her job as a doctor; Carmela returns to Miranda and resumes life in the utopia with her cheerful remark in the first episode: "Everything is as I remember it. Nothing has changed." Identity is therefore explored from the perspective of the characters' past membership in the community. Galician TV drama develops this past not only in the plots but also in the aesthetics of the series. These dramas oscillate between a home-made anthropology and a documentary style in their title sequences and production values, in a mix of the fictional world with the "real Galicia" or the "real history" of the community.

Temporal and geographic location, emotional realism, and plot conflicts are all at the service of an ideology that underlies most Galician drama series. Nostalgia is the hidden message conveyed by TVG programming about Galician identity. It could be identified with what Williams calls "residual culture," a way of life that loses its impulse with regard to another, dominant way of life that is replacing it ("Base" 171). The rural, and particularly its economic system, can be considered residual in that its population and activity have spectacularly dwindled in the last couple of decades, leading to the erosion of the social power of rural communities. One explanation for the consistent appeal to the rural might be that the rural population is the channel's most faithful audience. TVG seems to address this group when planning its schedules, displaying the same nostalgia that the viewers feel for a world that is under serious threat.

There have been recent advances toward a better balance between rural and urban cultures in Galician TV drama. Some dramas moved from a village to settle another area. *Pepe o Inglés* (2005; "Pepe the Englishman") takes place in a working-class neighborhood in a Galician city. *Maridos e mulleres* (2005; "Husbands and Wives") takes place in a housing development, where a group of women try to solve local mysteries.

There has been change, too, in the depiction of conflict. *Padre Casares* (2008; "Father Casares"), a sitcom about a young priest in a maritime village, contains explicit political ideas: the communist mayor is continually arguing with the village's elderly priest. This is the first portrayal of political struggle onscreen in Galician television fiction. It does not constitute a progressive element in itself, but it does promote dialogue between discourses and so contributes to the appearance of more voices in the public media.

Nostalgia for a rural utopia is an important part of the identity of the average TVG viewer. By choosing to cater to this audience, TVG neglects other social groups, groups that could become a new audience for the channel.

True, a public channel cannot serve the whole population in an increasingly competitive market dominated by commercial values, but it would be useful to introduce debate to generate a more critical attitude about society, not only in feature programs but throughout the schedule. There is room for hope here, as in the last few years, political debate and humor, in programs such as *Hai debate* ("We Debate") and the sketch program *Air Galicia*,[13] have both featured more prominently in the TVG schedule. Change in broadcasting does not come suddenly; it proceeds through the gradual transformation of its contents. Schedule change may occur as a result of periodic elections and political polls (and as a result of the channel controllers' agendas) and in response to the demands of an audience that pays taxes in return for being represented on the screen.

Notes

1. Televisión Española (TVE) had since 1974 broadcast a small number of news bulletins and other programs in Galician, as part of its so-called regional connection.
2. Williams first experienced the flow of commercial television in a trip to Florida, as the BBC, back home in the United Kingdom, did not have advertisements in its programming. A few decades later, Gripsrud remarked that Williams must have been dizzy because of the jet lag.
3. Around 31% of Galicians were connected to ADSL lines in 2007, one of the lowest rates in Spain (López, Gago, and Pereira). The cable company R, which offers telephone, TV, and Internet services, had 509,957 subscribers by 2007, but only 40% of them had taken the TV multichannel offer (Fandiño and Dafonte).
4. The question of language in Galician public media has been an important element of discussion in Galician academia.
5. The concept of the ideal demographic was apparently developed in the United States by NBC. Originally it was composed of young women, seen as potential consumers. The concept has been contested in recent decades as channels began to focus on fragmented and specific audiences that correspond to particular age or social groups.
6. *Luar* has topped the ratings in recent years, while other programs lost viewers because of the increasing number of channels on Spanish television. In October 2008, *Luar* obtained a 24.5% share of the Galician TV audience (the percentage of sets tuned to TVG from the total of TVs turned on).
7. "Cultural programs" refers to television shows that mix cultural news in Galicia with interviews and stories about local artists. Such programs are considered public-service as they deal with matters often neglected in general news coverage.
8. Fiske takes his definition for realism from the characteristics that Williams found in eighteenth- and nineteenth-century drama. For television, realism depends on its

audience, which is socially extended; on its representation of human action in human terms; and on its approach to the contemporary. This discourse obtains not only in programs intended to reproduce actual events but also in entertainment and fiction. Proliferation of reality shows and labels for movies such as "Based on a true story" demonstrate that realism is a reference point for most television genres.

9. The sitcom *Farmacia de guardia* (1992) started comedy series in Spanish television. Based on the classic production model of American sitcoms, it incorporated local settings and humor as the keys to audience success.

10. There is an earlier drama on TVG, *Os outros feirantes* (1989), based on the tales of the great Galician novelist Álvaro Cunqueiro, but it was an exception to the normal production modes of the channel at the time.

11. *Gheada* and *seseo* are dialectal alternations of Galician that consist of the phonetic change from /g/ to /x/ and /q/ to /s/, respectively. Although they are widespread in Galicia, namely in the western part of the country, they don't appear often in media, as radio and television use the standard version of the language.

12. In the report *Renta y empleo en los sectores productivos, 1995–2005*, produced by the Econometrics Group at the University of Santiago, the last measure, taken in 2005, gave the following job results: 44 of every 1,000 inhabitants were in agriculture and fisheries, 79 worked in industry, and 236 were white-collar workers. Even though the number of employees in rural and maritime activities was double that in the rest of Spain, Galicia had a slightly higher number of blue-collar workers.

13. *Air Galicia* (2007) is the first product on TVG that could be labeled a satirical program. Humor seemed to be banned in the last two decades, in contrast with its abundance in the channel's earliest programs, like *O mellor* (1986; "The Best"), *Velaí* (1986; "Here You Are"), and *Sitio distinto* (1990; "A Different Place"). Nonetheless, *Air Galicia* does not include real politicians in its parodies, just stereotypical portrayals of Galician people who make remarks about current situations in the country. It could be claimed therefore that political humor is still excluded from TVG programming.

Useful References Online

AVG: O soportal do audiovisual Galego. Culturagalega.org., n.d.

Axencia Audiovisual Galega. n.d.

CRTVG. Compañía de Radio Televisión de Galicia, n.d.

Observatorio Audiovisual Galego. Xunta de Galicia Secretaría Xeral de Medios, n.d.

Observatorio do Audiovisual Galego. U de Santiago de Compostela, Facultade de Ciencias da Comunicación, n.d.

The Postmodern Avant-Gardes in Post-1975 Galician Literature: Rompente, Antón Reixa, and Suso de Toro

Burghard Baltrusch

Aviso: un fantasma recorre Galicia
—Rompente, *Silabario da turbina*

Warning: A ghost is haunting Galicia

In 1975, the first recital of the Grupo de Resistencia Poética ("Poetic Resistance Group") took place; the group would be active until 1983 under the name Rompente, Grupo de Comunicación Poética ("Poetic Communication Group"). The project's collaborators were the instigators of what I call postmodern *vangardismo* in Galicia.[1] Three decades have passed since then, with many great achievements made in the fields of fine art, music, performance, and literature. The means of creating and expressing identity that emerged during these years often contrast strongly with those we might superficially characterize as traditionalist, folkloric, or lyrical, which have monopolized the Galician literary canon.

I argue here that the creators of this *vangardista* movement introduced Galicia into Western postmodernity[2] and that they initiated an unprecedented diversification of artistic forms in the Galician cultural field during the last quarter of the twentieth century. In reference to the nineteenth-century Rexurdimento and the first Galician Statute of Autonomy in 1936, I propose to speak in cultural terms of a second Rexurdimento, whose emergence coincides with the second Galician Statute of Autonomy in 1981. The poetic boom that has occurred since the 1990s also brought new *vangardista* tendencies, only recently classified (H. González, *Elas*). The proliferation of experimental and *vangardista* production since 1975 suggests, on the one hand, that there were strong systemic influences from other cultural fields. On the other hand, it demonstrates to us the existence of a pronounced political desire for progress and innovation in the Galician cultural poly-system. This Galicianizing impulse, predominantly nationalist in character, sought to overcome the impediments of diglossia, the inferiority complex created by Francoism, and a negative collective memory based on a history of poverty and emigration. Although a large proportion of these *vangardista* works are still not included in the literary and artistic canon and although they are very heterogeneous in character, they have had important and diverse repercussions. Some creative artists achieved considerable success; others remained relatively unknown or were temporarily silenced. The mechanisms of reception, too, and their understanding of aesthetics (determined by both political and economic interests) decided who would enjoy what kind of dissemination.

The *vangardista* works use traditional forms alongside generic transgressions, multimedia forms, theoretical reflection, and performance. Taking into account the great diversity of styles, genres, and themes that characterized *vangardista* creative artists, academic readers and critics are confronted with a series of fundamental challenges. How should we describe and define the notion of *avant-garde*—or, in its Galician context, *vangardismo*—in the Galician cultural field in relation to the established concepts of modernism, postmodernism, and translation?[3] How should we evaluate the principal *vangardista* lines of thought and practice in Galicia since 1975 from the perspective of a transcultural dynamic between the symbolic composites of local and national, European and Western, and global and intercultural, which characterize our present situation? Why contribute to the inclusion of antisystem texts in the literary canon? I can only offer partial responses here, starting with the hypothesis that a large part of the twentieth-century Galician cultural polysystem, in this particular case its literature and aesthetic thought, need to be analyzed in terms of postcolonialism, postmodernism, and cultural translation. In this context, it is essential to relocate the old questions: What do we mean by *vangardismo* in Galicia? What function did it have in twentieth-century Galician culture?

As a concept, avant-garde is naturally vague and heterogeneous; the concept of modernism, in its anglophone or lusophone uses, is equally problematic, since it is not generally used in Galician literature and criticism. For this reason, I have chosen to define *avant-garde* as rupture and provocation, which emerges periodically in the history of particular cultures with contextual specificities like a constant alternation of modernism and postmodernism (Lyotard). Almost all the postmodern *vangardismos* that can be seen in post-Franco Galicia engage in a critical revision of history and its metanarratives, driven by the clear desire to fuse more or less rupturist ethical and aesthetic motivations. These aesthetic-political impulses relegate the formal characteristics of postmodernism—such as hybridity, carnival, self-reflexivity, and irony—to the background.

The postmodern avant-garde in the widest senses consists of all attempts to think of and represent Galician present reality beyond current stereotypical hegemonic discourses and discourses of power: for example, forms of literary representation, the institutionalized canon, traditionalist nationalism, purely lyrical styles, conventional literary bases, mythical symbolism, the patriarchy, and sometimes culturalism itself. In a narrower sense, the literary *vangarda* would be primarily what is formally most novel, the most attention-grabbing, what offers most resistance to the institutionalized culture, which it attempts to subvert or replace. The texts of this *vangarda* are often unintelligible or untranslatable (whether intraculturally or interculturally), a fact that contributes to the fascination it evokes, and even more so when it touches on what is prohibited or taboo. This *vangardismo*, for ethico-political reasons, strongly supports and contributes to the construction of an autonomous Galician art through radical methods. In Galicia, this understanding of *vangarda* assumes a fundamental importance, when we take into account the relative weakness, the isolation, and the lack of influence of experimental tendencies in the literary field before 1975, something that has hindered linguistic and cultural normalization in Galicia. After 1975, it became necessary to turn to the postmodern perspective to describe, for example, the ironic way in which different types of performance related to Galician nationalism and to the language, and how the Galician literary field has been recovering modernist aspects and incorporating postmodern values at the same time.

Another important component of the concept of *vangardismo* is the aesthetic question. Since 1975, the criteria for understanding beauty and the sublime in the Galician literary system have become more flexible. The canonizing influence of paratexts (Genette) is also beginning slowly to be taken into account, together with the introduction of ideological values into the aesthetic-ethical process. This is not the place for an exhaustive discussion of the semiotic complexity of beauty, the sublime, and the translational contexts of their relation with the *vangardas*. But at least from the earliest time until the post-1975 period, it is evident that innovative aesthetics in the Galician cultural field has always been dependent on the immediate political demands of nationalist ideology, which traditionally used popular or ethnic symbols and values.

At the beginning of the twentieth century, when the European avant-gardes were emerging and expanding, Galicia was in a peculiar situation.[4] The natural reaction to being a historical nation subordinated to a centralizing state was to exalt Galician language and culture. Detailed studies were made of the authors of the Rexurdimento, and of Galician folklore and ethnography, creating publications that echoed these discoveries and creating assemblies, later to become political parties, which would be capable of defending and reevaluating the autochthonous in comparison with the foreign. Thus, the objective of the Xeración Nós ("Us Generation") in the 1920s—of Daniel Castelao, Vicente Risco, and Ramón Otero Pedrayo—was to restore dignity to a people that had lost it, demonstrating that the Galician language was as valid as Castilian for scientific, philosophical, religious, or literary discourse. This is the only way to understand the specific nature of the *vangarda pactada* (X. Pena 192; "avant-garde pact") in this period, which did not manage to break with the past, because that action would have left the nationalist arguments without a basis. The timid formal renewal of already explored genres and themes comes to be known as *hilozoísmo* and *neotrobadorismo*.[5] But a real avant-garde is also born in this context, embodied in the single figure of Manuel Antonio (1900–30). In collaboration with the painter Álvaro Cebreiro and with Antón Vilar Ponte, he wrote the manifesto "¡Máis alá!" (1922; "Further Still!"), followed by his only collection of poetry published during his lifetime, *De catro a catro* (1928; "From Four O'Clock till Four O'Clock"). The collection is characterized by a hitherto unknown vision of the sea from the sea itself, constructed with the powerful force of surrealist and cubist images. His premature death is also the death of the early-twentieth-century Galician avant-garde; its traces remain, faintly, only in Álvaro Cunqueiro's early poetry and some letters and a small number of poems by Vicente Risco.

Rompente

The civil war strangled avant-garde creative possibilities, and during the subsequent dictatorship the Galician language itself was silenced (literary work carried out in exile deserves to be considered separately). When publications in Galician begin again, they are traditional in style, and only with the death of Franco in 1975 do innovative works begin to reappear, with poetry such as *Mesteres*, by Arcadio López Casanova (1976; "Professions"); Alfonso

Pexegueiro's *Seraogna* (1976); and Xosé Luis Méndez Ferrín's *Con pólvora e magnolias* (1976; "With Dust and Magnolias")—the latter two connected with the poetry group Rompente.[6] These poetry collections were the revolt necessary to modify a poetic tradition, and with it a whole literature, that had become trapped in the idealist social realism represented, especially since the 1960s, by Celso Emilio Ferreiro, but also in the focus on the rural and the bucolic. For Rompente, this "realism non é realista" (Reixa, "Con Edoardo Sanguinetti"; "realism is not realistic"), because it focuses aesthetic reception on a dialectic of classes and values that is too restricted and marginal from a poetic and artistic point of view. Social realism never managed to represent the other contradictions of reality (Cochón and González 1079), nor did it produce a cultural and ideological translation of the events that changed the paradigms of Western culture.

Against the stagnation of an inherited, closed-off canon, Rompente sought a new form of appropriation and modernizing translation of Galician reality from 1975 to 1983, with an audaciousness that remained incomprehensible in its time. The trajectory of the group, initially comprising Alfonso Pexegueiro, Antón R. Reixa, Alberto Avendaño, and Manuel Romón, had a first phase, in which it defined itself as a group of poetic resistance (1975–77). When Pexegueiro decided to leave the group, a second phase began, in which the remaining members defined themselves as a group of poetic communication (Valverde, *O grupo Rompente*).

Rompente was both the most solid (in terms of the articulation of an ethical-aesthetic theory) and the most revolutionary (in terms of formal innovation) contribution to the Galician cultural field until the beginning of the 1980s. Their multiple technical innovations (appropriating futurism, Dadaism, and pop art), the Galicianized Marxist ideology, the ludic-ironic treatment of poetic objects, among other things, stemmed from the Trotskyist-Maoist concept of artistic creation as a revolutionary act. They were conscious of the limitations of the Galician literary field in the 1980s— few possibilities for publication, few media channels for culture in Galician, political dependence on Madrid. Hence they produced and disseminated their art in a virtually autonomous way, self-publishing their work and putting on recitals, demonstrations, and performances. Multimedia performance in particular stands out as a strategy for social and political intervention (Valverde, "A *performance*") but also as an "actividade interdisciplinaria" (Valverde, "Entrevista" 101; "interdisciplinary activity").

In 1979, Reixa, Avendaño, and Romón called themselves the Tres

Tristes Tigres (after a well-known Spanish tongue twister; "Three Sad Tigers") and distributed the pamphlet *Fóra as vosas sucias mans de Manuel-Antonio!* ("Get Your Filthy Hands off Manuel-Antonio!"). This text is deliberately provocative, since Manuel Antonio had been celebrated that year as the object of the annual Día das Letras Galegas ("Galician Literature Day"), accompanied by polemical editions of the work. The Three Sad Tigers were protesting the appropriation by the system and by the academy of a *vangardista* who had fought against precisely these things (Valverde, *O grupo Rompente*). It was during this second phase that Rompente began to shift from a Maoist-Trotskyist discourse to an ever more aesthetically aware language, developing a cultural theory that was both interventionist and ludic-ironic, although they never abandoned their initial ethical drive. In 1979, in a leaflet accompanying one of their acts, Rompente defined their creative-political stance as "ownstyle" (qtd. in Valverde, "A *performance*" 56). This is precisely what postmodernism has called ethics-aesthetics—that is, innovation that is simultaneously ideological and formal, stemming from the immanently aesthetic (even idiosyncratic) character of reality. Profoundly influenced by Edoardo Sanguinetti, they attempted to practice "a actitude do creador 'in work' reflexionando, intervindo sobre a concepción xeral social da arte" (Reixa, "Con Edoardo Sanguinetti"; "the attitude of the creator 'in work' reflecting, intervening in the general social concept of art"), trying to adapt the Italian critic's concept of "polilingüísmo estilístico" ("stylistic polylingualism") to the Galician context through what Reixa redefined as "atonalidade poética, que teima no traballo interdisciplinar" ("poetic atonality, which insists on interdisciplinary work").

Rompente's contributions were transdiscursive from an ideological point of view and transcreative from an aesthetic perspective: different political and aesthetic discourses are adapted, translated for the Galician cultural context, and hybridized in multimedia artistic creation. Iris Cochón and Helena González therefore speak, correctly, of a "vangarda continua" (1078; "continuous *vangarda*"), although they warn that in peripheral systems this same *vangarda* "mantén un difícil equilibrio entre innovación e propaganda" ("maintains a difficult balance between innovation and propaganda").[7] This tightrope dance was due to the imperative to reaffirm a national and cultural identity of our own, which would be characterized, combining a modernist metaphor with a postmodernist one, as an ethical-aesthetic practice in progress.

But Rompente managed to avoid the dangers of simple propaganda in their use of cutting-edge media and literary techniques at the height of Galicia's transition from a rural to urban—or popular to elite—cultural identity. The *vangardista* identification of life and art now erupted as a vindication of modernity in Galician culture. Modernity was

> acepta-la complexidade da realidade, e non a renunciar que a actividade crea-dora se plantee a interpretación desa mesma realidade, na que, en definitiva, literatura e vida loitan por se-la mesma cousa.
>
> (Reixa, "Con Edoardo Sanguinetti")

> accepting the complexity of reality, and not rejecting it, so that creative activity focuses on interpreting the very reality where, ultimately, literature and life struggle to become the same thing.

Rompente portrayed the gradual transition to postmodernity of Galician society, the massification and democratization of technological and stylistic media—as is evident, for example, in the hybrid formats and materials and in the artistic design of the series of books published by the Three Sad Tigers.[8] Along with the strong presence of irony and parody, there is a critical revisitation and a postmodern fusion of tragedy and comedy. The result is

> unha poesía cómica, non para facer rir senón para crear unha situación de risa tola que enlace co punto climático do tráxico, coma a risa esquizoide que sentía Kafka mentres escribía *O Proceso*.

> a comic poetry, not to provoke laughter, but to create a situation of crazy laughter that connects with the climax of the tragedy, like the schizophrenic laughter Kafka felt as he was writing *The Trial*.

In terms of style, the confluence of genres, word games, and chaotic collages is the rule; in ideological terms, the dialectical hierarchies between high and low, colloquial and erudite, popular and bourgeois are abolished.

Rompente's warning in *Silabario da turbina* ("ABC of the Turbine"), published in 1978, that a ghost is haunting Galicia, beyond expressing their disagreement with some of the political positions of nationalism and the left, is also a call to an artistic revolution that will overcome the traditional concepts of literature and art. In this sense, Rompente pose an objection to identity, a characteristic aspect of modern art (Adorno), and they add with typical post-modern irony a paradoxical twist that helps avoid simple propaganda: communicate with the masses (working classes) but by means of abstract techniques that tend to negate that very communication, techniques that furthermore create dissonances that irritate the masses. Echoing the project of Bertolt Brecht's epic theater, they make extensive use of defamiliarization to avoid the simple and deceptive identification of the public with the artistic product. They try to ensure that Galician cultural and national identity no longer clings to an Aristotelian aesthetic or a simple fraternization between artist and public.

Rompente fed off models from other cultural contexts, such as the Catalan Joán Salvat-Papasseit, the Englishman Christopher Logue, the Turk Nâzım Hikmet, and the Italians Sanguinetti and Pier Paolo Pasolini. They also enriched their work with ideas from a fluctuating but omnipresent group of collaborators: writers like Farruco Sesto Novás, artists like Menchu Lamas and Antón Patiño, musicians like Julián Hernández and Enrique Macías, and dramatists like the Artello group. Many of the acts carried out by Rompente took on the characteristics of a happening, as Hernández remembers:

> A través de el [E. Macías] y con Juventudes Musicales de telón de fondo, nos conocimos todos. . . . Se trataba de montar follón. La poesía de Rompente pretendía librarse del fantasma de Rosalía de Castro, entrar en la modernidad por fin y que Galicia enterrase para siempre el Cardenal Gelmírez. Los recitales de Rompente eran algo nunca visto por allí y poco visto por otros sitios. Montábamos cintas de magnetófono con collages musicales, que sonaban mientras los tres poetas recitadores iban soltando textos a cada cual más incendiario, los escenarios los pintaba Antón Patiño y Menchu Lamas, se proyectaban diapositivas y películas de super-8. . . . Los espectáculos eran un éxito de público. Lástima: no teníamos (no existía) vídeo in ilo tempore.
> (Turrón and Babas 22; qtd. in Valverde, *O grupo Rompente* 60)

> Through [Macías] and with Juventudes Musicales ["Musical Youth"] in the background, we all got to know one another. . . . It was all about kicking up a fuss. Rompente's poetry was trying to free itself from the ghost of Rosalía de Castro, to enter modernity at last, and to make Galicia bury Cardinal Gelmírez once and for all. Rompente's recitals were something never seen before in Galicia, and rarely seen anywhere else either. We played tapes with musical collages while the three poets recited ever more incendiary texts, Antón Patiño and Menchu Lamas painted the scenery, slides and super-8 films were projected. . . . The shows were a public success. Shame we didn't have (there wasn't) such a thing as video back then.

The painter Patiño, talking about Heiner Müller's *Hamlet-maschine*, gives a synthetic definition perfectly applicable to Rompente's trajectory:

Escrita da escena nun teatro total, acontecemento que taladra os nosos senti-
dos e se instala na nosa memoria. Espectáculo en progreso a partir dunha idea
sintética (expansiva). (57)

Stage writing in a total theater, an event that drills through our senses and
remains in our memory. A spectacle in progress stemming from a synthetic
(expansive) idea.

Antón Reixa

This idea of the artistic object as a synthetic, unfinished product or work
in progress persisted after Rompente broke up in 1983, and it continued to
be applied as Galician culture experienced huge transformations toward the
end of the century. Antón Reixa, for example, had as early as 1982 begun his
career as singer for the rock group Os Resentidos, which lasted until 1994.
This group pioneered rock in Galician with ludico-critical texts that developed the synthetic ideas begun by Rompente (Reixa, *Alivio* and *Viva*). Reixa
became an authentic multimedia artist; in the mid-1980s, he directed and
introduced the program *Galicia sitio distinto* ("Galicia a Different Place"),
produced by Video-Esquimal on Televisión de Galicia (broadcast between
1990 and 1991). The series was a real nonconformist, postmodern, *vangardista* jewel, in many ways ahead of its time; it gave rise to his innovative
videopoem *Ringo Rango*, which includes contributions by Menchu Lamas
and Patiño. Reixa also published prose (*Transporte de superficie* [1991; "Surface Transport"]) and *vangardista* poetry (*Historia do Rock and Roll* [1992;
"History of Rock and Roll"]). He began the musical project Nación Reixa
(1992–97; "Reixa Nation");[9] created the first Galician soap opera, *Mareas
vivas* (1998; "High Tides"); brought out the solo poetry record *Escarnio*
(1999; "Derision"); and adapted Manuel Rivas's best-selling novel *O lapis
do carpinteiro* ("The Carpenter's Pencil") for cinema in 2003. The self-titled
"ironia do resentimento" ("irony of resentment") that Reixa had cultivated
in the time of Os Resentidos continued to aspire to a total work of art (in
avant-garde and revolutionary terms) in which life and artistic creation become confused.

Reixa renders thematic the growing aestheticization of our reality, in
which the aesthetic aura is given more value than the product itself, and he
criticizes in lyrical form that aesthetic posturing of postmodernity which,
with its characteristic playfulness, distances itself from reality. He was thus

able to avoid the ghetto culture of Galician literature, which Suso de Toro had been denouncing since the early 1990s. The metanarrative *retranca* ("irony") of his aesthetic discourse consists of the re-creation of a plural, telemediated culture, which in turn is subject to a critique as sarcastic as it is sophisticated.[10] Fragmentation and the restoration of a new function for the literary text are an opposition that his aesthetic of production tries to synthesize. Reixa's culture remains basically Galician, but his aesthetic of production has already become universalized as it turned into a critique of the aestheticization imposed on everyday life by technology and the market.

Reixa succinctly defined the point of departure of his work in an interview with the Spanish newspaper *El país* in 1995. The conclusion he draws from his interpretation of contemporary culture is that "[t]odo artista debe ser cronista do caos contemporáneo" ("Antón Reixa"; "every artist should be a chronicler of contemporary chaos"), which also implies chronicling from the perspective of a peculiarly Galician way of thinking and of expressing irony (*retranca*), as his work clearly illustrates. The literary techniques and other elements he uses (ethical impulse, ludic character, irony, fragmentation, self-reflexivity, paradox, eclectic collage) bring him closer, furthermore, to a clearly postmodern aesthetic. The flow of free association so frequent in his texts creates a kind of *esperpento* of this chaotic reality, bringing together different cultural and diastratic levels (urban vs. rural, the media vs. traditional orality, etc.).[11] His artistic interpretation-translation of the chaos of an ever more aestheticized contemporary world is characterized by movement toward a multimedia work of art. All statements become unstable, given that they consciously reflect their own contradictions. From this perspective, ironic resentment is justified by an aesthetic-political *retranquismo* ("ironizing") and by the complementary tendency of Galician thought to introduce a third perspective into traditional Western dialectics. Reixa defends his *retranquismo* as "barricada antropolóxica" ("an anthropological barricade") although he accepts, critically, an intricate and aestheticizing reality. Through this artistic reworking, the games he plays with the media could easily fall into an artistic economy devoid of ethical values. The political intention of *littérature engagée* adapts itself to the market and runs the risk of being substituted by a capitalist culture of organized chaos—a simple Dionysian game with Apollonian apolitical values.

Ringo Rango, which Reixa composed from texts and videoclips that he had already used for the series *Galicia sitio distinto*, is an outstanding example of multimedia art in Galicia, even approaching a postmodernized idea of the total work of art (*Gesamtkunstwerk*). The "bibliografía contra tagore" ("bibliography against Tagore"), which introduces this work as a kind of poetic manifesto, is paradigmatic for a postmodern ethics-aesthetics in the Galician context:

> mastigar tristeSa románica sorriso arcaico etruria contra usura prét-á-porter melancolía desposuída (as casas sindicais) e venus de villendorf con toda a coraxe brecht e catulo con escarnio esclarecido guillermo de aquitania over señoritos pedrayo *farai un vers de dreit nien* e vai catulo e pónselle *lesbianas que vos dean polo curso* e virxilio pondaliano a insistir *stetit illa tremens* que se crava vibrando e son cocoteiros de presencia lanzal verbo garrido en inhuit dialectal
>
> *os nenos rin pero ¿que fan os pais?*
> e nosoutros ás gargalladas por groenlandia arredista e din rir por foder *abadessa* oíu *dizer* frotasión nariz contra nariz e vai un esquimó e dille a outro *I don't like Ike a xusticia pola man* iglús e canastros e polígonos dormitorio *I gonna take my problem to the united nations* tristeSa é o hipérbaton do escarnio en xeral *but there is no cure for the summertime blues* e maila teima de mandar christmas en agosto as ondas ó chegaren (efecto alka seltzer): sauda-lo vello océano martín lautreamont e máis codax: o polbo eléctrico ¡a calambre! e/ou a lobotomía ó posuíresme engels style a propiedade privada safo luxemburgo *leda m'and'eu as manhanas frías* ó ir para o choio: alegría diesel / punkies altivas falan de portugal en ingles / unha canción italiana que sempre diga per che / unha cousa de nervios / problemas coa carie—o contestador automático de guillermo de aquitania: *pero dirai vos de con, cals es sa leis . . .* —e con escarnio épico dille un radio afeccionado a outro: *hanse cajar na cona que os botou* (interferencias).   (11)

masticate romanesque melanChOly archaic smile etruria against prét-á-porter usury dispossessed melancholy (the trade union houses) and the willendorf venus with all her spirit brecht and catullus with clear derision william of aquitaine over hooray henrys pedrayo *farai un vers de dreit nien* and there goes catullus and writes *lesbians take it up the course* and pondal-style virgil insisting *stetit illa tremens* which is hammered in with a tremble and they are coconut palms with elegant looks word poised in dialectal inuit

the children are laughing, but what are their parents doing?
and we in peals of laughter because of separatist greenland and they say laugh for fuck *abbess* heard *saying* rubbing nose against nose and there goes one eskimo and says to the other *I don't like Ike an eye for an eye* igloos and grain stores and dormitory towns *I gonna take my problem to the united nations*

melanChOly and the hyperbaton of derision in general *but there is no cure for the summertime blues* and then the obsession with sending christmas cards in august the waves arriving (alka seltzer effect): greet the old ocean martin lautreamont and codax too: the electric octopus electric shock! and/or lobotomy when you possess me engels style private property sappho luxemburg *leda m'and'eu as manhanas frias* on going to work: diesel happiness / proud punkies talk about portugal in english / an italian song that always says per che / a nervous thing / problems with tooth decay—william of aquitaine's answerphone: *pero dirai vos de con, cals es sa leis*—and with epic derision one radio ham says to another says to him: *they are going to shit themselves* (interference).

The allusions to seemingly disparate realities have a double objective: on the one hand, to hypercodify the narration itself to parody diverse traditions; on the other, to contextualize symbolically *est/ética galega posmoderna* "Postmodern Galician ethic/aesthetics" (Baltrusch, "Estéticas" and "Teoría"). Taken literally, the bibliography is directed against the Indian Nobel laureate Rabindranath Tagore (1861–1941), who was popular in Spanish intellectual circles in the 1970s and who had already influenced Spanish writers like Ortega y Gasset and Juan Ramón Jiménez. Tagore's desire to preserve India's national unity against the aspirations to independence of its many cultures functions here as a metaphor for a colonizing, centralizing power, against which Reixa composes a subversive bibliography of historical and literary voices. The secondary though critical and interventionist character of this bibliography works as a means of resistance as well as an ironic deconstruction of the orthodox discourse of nationalism in minorized cultures, by highlighting not only the content of its claims but also its sometimes stiff and petrified bookness.

The text is presented as a stream of consciousness interrupted by a question that alludes to responsibility for the loss of Galician culture in the twentieth century. Through a sequence of quotations, different diatopic and diastratic levels are mixed up, reproducing spoken language and structuring both the text's political-cultural and ethical intention and its aesthetic-rhythmic character.[12] The symbolic hybridity of a Galician epic poet (Pondal) and a Roman epic poet (Vergil) gains intertextual strength through the onomatopoetic allusion to the *Aeneid* (2.52). Hammered (*stetit illa tremens*) by the body of post-Franco Galician culture is a question turned into an accusation: "*os nenos rin pero ¿que fan os pais?*" ("*the children are laughing, but what are their parents doing?*"). Galician culture and identity are threatened by the Trojan horse of hegemonic Spanish culture. A cultural and linguistic transformation threatens to reduce Galician to the exotic status of a minority language in the process of extinction, like Inuit. The new generations are already experiencing this linguistic-cultural change, so that the continuation of Galician identity will depend on an education that takes its Galicianizing responsibility seriously. The many different quotations evoke historical and literary relations, political commitments, and even colloquial contexts. The ideological memory of Rompente is omnipresent, whether in the invocation of Rosalía de Castro's revolutionary poem "A xusticia pola man" (*Follas novas,* pt. 2; "An eye for an eye") or the symbolic juxtaposition of "lobotomía" ("lobotomy," an allusion to the paradoxical situation of postcolonial Galician identity) and an "Engels style" that postmodernizes historical Communism.

This bibliography positions itself, therefore, against all hegemonies, also adding a critique of usury, probably in reference to the beginning of Ezra Pound's canto 45, where usury is denounced as the root of corruption in the modern world. The colloquial "interference" that brings to an end this diversifying referencing of Galician culture in a postmodern world evokes *retranca.* The referent of *"hanse cajar na cona que os botou"* (*"they are going to shit themselves"*) is undetermined: it might be a tribute to the subversion of old and petrified cultural values and models as a critique of overconfidence in modernity (technology) and the effects it has on cultural identity. But there would be no *retranca* if there were no third intention—in this case, the possibility that cultural identity will survive thanks only to interference, linguistic and otherwise, made possible by modernity and postmodernity. An example is the fatalism of "escarnio épico" ("epic derision"). But the fatalism of epic derision is not so fatalistic in the end: melancholy is "desposuída" ("dispossessed"), an allusion to the withdrawal of trade union rights and political autonomy under Franco, and it is based on "hyperbaton"—that is, on a (revolutionary) change to the established order.

Suso de Toro

Irreverent, ironic sadness or epic derision also marks the first phase of Suso de Toro's work, which is even more cynical and self-critical than Reixa's. De Toro represents a means of recovering Manuel Antonio's legacy independently of Rompente. At the end of the manifesto "Máis Alá!" (1922), Manuel Antonio sacralized "a individualidade até o estremo de desexar que a definición de cada un de nós sexa unha verva: o seu propio nome" (qtd.

in González Gómez 207; "individuality to the extreme of desiring that each one of us be defined in a single word: our own name"), an individuality that de Toro radicalizes in a postmodern manner:

> [A] maneira de que unha literatura sexa útil socialmente e ademais sexa literatura, non catecismo, é expresando encarraxadamente ao individuo.
>
> ("En confianza")

> The way for a literature to be socially useful and remain as literature rather than catechism is by furiously expressing the individual.

Between *Caixón desastre* (1983; "Miscellany") and *Tic-Tac* (1993), the Santiago-born author admits to having followed "o programa literario do 'modernismo'" ("the literary program of 'modernism'"),[13] dedicating himself since then to what he calls "mythifications," a phase I do not discuss here because it does not fit into postmodern *vangardismo*. One of the general characteristics of the first phase of de Toro's work is self-reflexive metastructuring (Baltrusch, "Teoria"); it weaves through all his work. In the photographs that illustrate *Polaroid* and *Tic-Tac*, for example, the author-narrator, poorly disguised by stylistic fragmentation and by the multiple narrative voices, mirrors himself and reveals himself psychologically. Both *Polaroid* and *Tic-Tac* are presented as instantaneous takes on the aesthetic of production, which is commented on, illustrated, disguised, and reworked. The underlying self-irony consists above all of flirtation both with the aspiration to a total work of art and with its failure. Even in the prologue to *Polaroid*, the author confesses that "o que fago eu probablemente estao a facer mellor o Sr. Joyce" (10; "What I do, Mr. Joyce probably does better"). *Tic-Tac* repeats this relativist exhibitionism with its evident attempt to reinvent a Galician *Ulysses* through the monologues of various characters, including Nano, a recurring alter ego in the first phase of de Toro's works. But the reflexive use of irony with the aesthetic of literary production conceals another self-irony. In *Polaroid*, a chapter enumerating *retranqueira* ("ironic") responses ("Ai si, oh" [41]) is contrasted with a "Manifesto Kamikaze" (89–90). The manifesto is an attempt to break from a *retranqueira* aesthetic as a possible understanding of Galicianness, for it rebels brutally against all the images, whether positive or negative, of Galicianness. It is a *retranca* that produces an aesthetic against itself, intentionally annihilating itself—to recover freedom and create an aesthetic clean slate.

In *Tic-Tac*, de Toro produces an apologia for individualism as an attempt to overcome the incommensurable nature of the fragmented discourses of modernity through the epic self-derision of a protagonist who becomes a postmodern Galician Ulysses. De Toro reactivates James Joyce's narrative techniques to create these effects. He interweaves different literary genres, diastratic and diaphasic levels, even associating them with photographs that function as an ironic pictogramic commentary. In this staging of the cult of the ego, the narrator's relativism is expressed by existentialist melancholy, an aphoristic philosophizing disguised as *docta ignorantia*, and pseudonaturalism that fluctuates between the folkloric and the vulgar until it reaches a kind of aesthetic neoliberalism.

The ultimate formal irony in *Tic-Tac* is represented by two photographs of the author's eyes, which frame the novel, staring out at the reader. The *retranqueiro* pragmatism of this metanarrative technique presents the polyvalence and polyphony of the discourses confined in this gaze, facing simultaneously outward and inward, sending and receiving, as if happening in a single head, a single brain. The brutal consequence of this situation is the desire to experience postmodernity as the empty space of the unfounded (Vattimo) and a lack of foundationalisms that reveals itself as androcentric. The critique of androcentrism goes hand in hand with an identification of ephemeral time with the idea of the eternally cruel and dominating father, embodied in the figure of Chronos or, in the Galician version of the bogeyman, the Sacaúntos ("Fatsucker").

The leitmotiv of cruel father culminates in the penultimate chapter of *Tic-Tac*, in a single-act play with the title "Breve resume do teatro universal" ("Brief Summary of Universal Theater"). In an *esperpento* environment, the story of Hansel and Gretel and the myth of Chronos who devoured his children are fused in an acidic, mythical-religious critique (Baltrusch, "Sein"). Two characters, El ("He") and Ela ("She"), synthesize the whole range of paternal and maternal images that have emerged throughout the novel: God, Chronos, Sacaúntos, phallogocentrism, patriarchy, Mary, Galicia, the punishing, dominating, repenting mother:

(Poñéndose os dous unhas batas de casa de buatiné.)

El: Só os rapaces me coñecen, só eles me ven tal cal son. Son listos os rapaces. Si, ho, si. Só os nenos me ven e me coñecen. Se non houbese nenos . . .

Ela: (Coa vista ida, fregando as mans.) ¡Aquí, aquí anda aínda unha mancha! ¡Fóra mancha condenada! ¡Fóra che digo!

El: (Mirando para ela.) Xa empezou esta tola coas súas lerias. Boh. Pois si, ho. Se non fose polos nenos xa non sabería quen son de tanto andar disfrazado. Pero eles si que me coñecen sen dubidar. "¡O Sacaúntos, o Sacaúntos!," berran en véndome. Mesmo en soños me coñecen "¡O Sacaúntos, o Sacaúntos!"

Ela: (Ida.) ¿De que habemos de ter medo? ¿Quen vai sabelo, se o noso poder ten que dar contas a ninguén? ¿E que non vou dar limpado nunca estas miñas mans?

El: Velaí está esta louca cos seus remorsos. Merda para ela. Se non me fose de utilidade xa a tiña despachado hai ben tempo. Trosma. (Bérralle a ela, que non lle oe.) ¿Pois o que máis me gusta é comer os filliños que me dás, namais saírenche da barriga! Ben tenriños. as perniñas, os braciños. (Pon voz de neno.) "¡Non me comas, Papá Cronos, non me comas!" ¡Si que te como, si que te como! ¡Ñam, ñam! Ha, ha. Parva.

Ela: Aínda segue o cheiro do sangue. Todos os perfumes de Arabia non han abondar para limpar estas mans tan pequenas. . . .   (287)

(Both are putting on dressing gowns.)

He: Only the children recognize me, only they see me as I am. Children are clever. Oh, yes. Only the little ones see me and recognize me. If there were no children . . .

She: (Looking away, scrubbing her hands.) Here, there's still a spot here! Out, damned spot! Out, I say!

He: (Looking at her.) This crazy woman has started her raving again. Hmph. Oh, yes. If it wasn't for the children I wouldn't know myself, I'm so often disguised. But they do know me, without a doubt. "The Bogeyman, the Bogeyman!" they cry when they see me. Even in dreams they know me. "The Bogeyman, the Bogeyman!"

She: (Not quite present.) What should we be afraid of? Who could know, if our power is accountable to no one? Will I never get these hands of mine clean?

He: Just look at this madwoman, with her remorse. Bollocks to her. If she wasn't so useful to me, I'd have done away with her long ago. Fool. (He shouts at her, but she does not hear.) What I like best is to eat the little children you give me, the moment they emerge from your belly! So sweet and tender, the dear little legs, the dear little arms. (He puts on a child's voice.) "Don't eat me, Father Chronos, don't eat me!" I certainly will eat you, oh yes I will! Yum yum! Ha, ha. Idiot woman.

She: The stench of blood lingers. All the perfumes in Arabia wouldn't be enough to clean these tiny hands. . . .

While She retains some memory of morality, He is interested only in the pleasure he gets from the killing and eating of his children. She also represents a subordinated Galicia, the repenting but denaturalized mother who supplies the country's children to a sadistic, arrogant, implacable God, hyperbole for a central state that has kept Galicia, humiliated, as an exploited region throughout the centuries. For this reason, She cynically pacifies the already stupefied children at the end of the play: "Veña, non perdades tempo que é a hora de cear. Ides matar a fame" (289; "Come on, don't waste time, it's dinner time. You'll be staving off hunger").

Although some of the themes appear forced and although the characters lack a certain psychological dynamism, *Tic-Tac* makes the most of a powerful historical-mythical framework, as Joyce's *Ulysses* did years before, combining the national with the universal. The problem of a minority culture in a precarious situation that symbolizes many of the difficulties of cultural (national) identification in a period of globalization is an odyssey without a clear end point, without any real possibility of returning to a foundational house of origin. Setting the novel in a minority culture portrays the tension between reality and the memory of reality, between immanence and transcendence in the postmodern world—although the masculine perspective limits the novel's claims to universality (as was also the case with *Ulysses*).

The topos of mutilation that plays throughout *Tic-Tac* refers to the alienation of beauty and humanity in the technological era of modernity, but it also evokes the political and postcolonial situation of Galicia. In the photographs, only sterile parts of the body appear, without a specific spatial relation and never as a complete whole that could have its own aura. The photographic and literary images also negate any possible (positive) relation with the countryside—that is, with Galicia's physical-real body; they tend rather to function as a metaphor for a castrated land (Fallon 146). The paradox of the desire to achieve an autonomous (Galician) identity in the face of the centrifugal forces of globalized postmodern culture, in a still centralized and colonizing Spain, is illustrated by the protagonist's obsessive attempts to control his body, his sexuality, and the aging process.

Tic-Tac indirectly questions what Fredric Jameson evoked as the historic amnesia of postmodernity. Its narrative voices are reduced to the reality of their immediate experiences, illustrating history's loss of meaning. Nevertheless, the voices persist in critical dialogue with this history, for example when they discredit the founding myths of Santiago de Compostela and the Saint James Way. Nano rejects Benedict Anderson's definition of nationness on the basis of the supposed intentions of his forebears (the dead), countering them with a consciousness that stems from the individual in a limited local and family context. Linguistic peculiarities and popular, idiosyncratic philosophy define Nano much better. This individualist, postmodern epic invites the interpretation of decentered corporeal images of (Galician) society and the (masculine, Galician) subject as a critique and ironic *saudade* ("nostalgia") for national unity.

The kinds of epic derision cultivated by Reixa and de Toro are paradigmatic in the postmodern *vangardismo* of post-Franco Galicia, representing two ways of revisiting the traces of the classic avant-garde inaugurated by Manuel Antonio. They open up a line of postmodern *vangardismo* that begins with Rompente and with Méndez Ferrín's volume of verse, *Con pólvora e magnolias*, and continues with the individual works of the group's former members and collaborators. Reixa's literary, musical, and audiovisual work has been the most visible of these, but we should also keep in mind the artistic works of Patiño and Lamas, among others. De Toro's position with regard to the new literary space opened up by Rompente is more difficult to determine, for while he is not a direct descendant or inheritor, he cultivates very similar ideas and techniques. Today, perhaps it is Xurxo Borrazás who continues to develop de Toro's postmodern *vangardismo* in the areas of narrative and essay.

The rebellion against the canon of Galician literature that Reixa and de Toro instigated in the 1990s with their synthetic ideas of an aesthetics-ethics in progress, stemmed from the fundamental premise that postmodernity permits a description of reality only in the form of a conglomeration of short narratives that compete among themselves (Lyotard 34). When it comes to communicating ethical or postmodern messages (as Reixa does), we see the paradox of the mutual incommensurability of discourses (95).

But the intentional, reflexive use that Reixa and de Toro make of a renewed Galician literary *retranca* also corresponds to a renaissance of the attention that postmodern philosophy, revitalizing the ideas of Kant and Nietzsche, gave to the aesthetic-fictional character of knowledge.

Today, from the 1990s on, we can clearly see Rompente's influence on the Galician cultural field. One example is the magazine *Anim+l* (1990–91), edited by Francisco Macías. Another example is the Ronseltz collective, their use of parody and playfulness in an attempt to break with current trends.[14] Other initiatives inspired by Rompente and by Reixa in particular are the photographic series *Jalisia sitio distinto, Galicia terra nai* ("Jalisia [phonetic rendering of Galicia] a Different Place, Galicia Motherland"), by Xurxo Lobato (1994), and the *bravú* movement, with groups such as the Skornabois, the Rastreros, and the Diplomáticos de Monte-Alto with their agro rap, which clearly owes a debt to Os Resentidos.[15]

A second strand of postmodern *vangardismo*, not discussed in this essay, stems from the boom of women writers since the 1990s. Many of these works question premises of the classical avant-garde as well as its postmodern descendants, working through cultural, national, and gender identities together with second- and third-wave feminisms in such a way that they cannot simply be subsumed into the Rompente tradition. Furthermore, there are significant aesthetic differences between writers like Yolanda Castaño, Lupe Gómez, and Chus Pato. Gómez's libertarian anticulturalism could even be about to open up a third strand of postmodern *vangardismo* in Galicia.

We can distinguish significant differences in the Galician postmodern *vangarda*—a range of approaches to the total work of art, to an identification of art with life, and in general to the transcreation of contemporary Galician reality without the lens of traditional commonplaces and discourses of power. Aestheticist elements have always been accompanied by a strong will to revise critically and to redefine identity as foundational—that is, as an alternative model to exist on the margins of the institutionalized cultural system. These elements continue to need nationalism as the elixir of an autonomous cultural life, quite the opposite of what is proposed by those who claim the arrival of a postnational age. The achievements of the Galician cultural field in relation to the Spanish in recent decades are mirrored by the postmodern *vangardismos* in Galicia. They have revealed themselves as an individualist means for the subaltern arts, with ethics-aesthetics in progress, to access the representational modes of a different and even antiofficial cultural memory. Rompente represented an identity of resistance. Antón Reixa and Suso de Toro (and also Chus Pato, Yolanda Castaño, and Lupe Gómez) added new project identities, exerting pressure on institutionalized culture and identity. This work demonstrates the existence of a dynamic culture in a constant process of redefinition in Galicia today.

But the outside view of minority cultures tends to be that they are becoming extinct and should be protected in the name of cultural diversity, a view that complicates the status of the avant-gardes in these cultures, especially when they reveal themselves as self-critical. Continually pressured as they are to adapt to institutionalized values and perspectives, they enter the vicious circle of the special treatment conceded to minorities. The antagonism between minority cultures and mass culture (as between the avant-garde and the canon) to an extent promotes aesthetic selection based on the demands of the market. It also obliges the minority culture to produce national aesthetic innovations as strategies for survival in a contradictory present, characterized not only by traumatic change but also by countless cultural and political possibilities.

Notes

This essay was translated from Galician by Kirsty Hooper and Manuel Puga Moruxa.

1. The translators leave the original Galician terms *vangarda*, *vangardismo*, and *vangardista* rather than translate them as *avant-garde*, when reference is to the specifically Galician context. When talking about the wider Western context, they use *avant-garde*.

2. By *postmodernity* I mean a period characterized by a dynamic confluence of ethics and aesthetics (in Galician, *est/ética*), which revises and critically translates both history and the ideologies and metanarratives bequeathed us by history. For further definition of this and related concepts, see Sim.

3. For the relation between modernism and postmodernism and the concept of paratranslation, see Caneda; Baltrusch, "Sein."

4. I acknowledge María Comesaña Besteiros's contribution to the definition of the historical framework for the early-twentieth-century Galician avant-garde.

5. *Hilozoísmo* ("hylozoism") in the Galician context refers to poetry that combines traditional personification of landscape with avant-garde metaphoric strategies. *Neotrobadorismo*, a movement that emerges with *hilozoísmo* in the 1920s, reimagines the poetry of the medieval Galician-Portuguese songbooks, also using avant-garde strategies.

6. The only anthology currently available is that by Cochón and González.

7. For a detailed description of the *Follas de resistencia poética* and *Crebar as liras*, see H. González, "Rompente."

8. Reixa's *As ladillas do travesty*, Romón's *Galletas kokoschka non*, and Avendaño's *Facer pulgarcitos tres*, designed by Menchu Lamas and Antón Patiño, artists from the avantgarde group Colectivo da Imaxe, were published by Rompente S.L. in 1979.

9. Nación Reixa made two records with *vangardista* lyrics: *Alivio rápido* (1994; "Rapid Relief"; also available in Spanish) and *Safari mental* (1997; "Mental Safari").

10. *Retranca* is a uniquely Galician form of irony. Its relativism is not dialectical, because it includes a three-way rather than simply binary relation. In its use as a metanarrative and stylistic element in contemporary Galician literature, it adapts itself very easily to a postmodern aesthetic (see Baltrusch, "Teoría").

11. *Esperpento* offers a distorted depiction of society. It is a specifically Spanish literary form that originated in the work of Ramón del Valle-Inclán at the beginning of the twentieth century.

12. For an attempt to systematize the quotations from a translation studies perspective, see Montero Küpper.

13. *Polaroid* (1986), *Land Rover* (1988), *Ambulancia* (1990) and *F. M.* (1991) also belong to this phase.

14. In 1991, Colectivo Ronseltz published, as a manifesto, "Análise afortunadamente pouco documentada da poesía galega dos oitenta" ("Analysis, Fortunately Little Documented, of Galician Poetry in the 1980s") as well as the jointly authored book *Unicornio de cenorias que cabalgas aos sábados* (1994; "Carrot-Unicorn You Ride on Saturdays"). The collective broke up after this publication.

15. The literary work of Xurxo Souto, a member of Os Diplomáticos, for example, derives directly from the *bravú* concept but falls, like *bravú*, at the intersection of the ideologies of rock and rap with ethnic-popular ideologies, thus losing its initial *vangardista* impulse.

Modes of Representation in Galician Visual Poetry

Laura López Fernández

Visual poetry in Galicia had a plural and discontinuous existence in the twentieth century.[1] Its development in Galicia follows national (Spanish) and international artistic practices, while also engaging in the configuration of a local, national, and transnational Galician identity. The practice of different styles of visual poetry shows a rich line of creativity, especially in the last four decades. Their approaches coincide with socio-cultural and economic changes in Spain, such as the end of the dictatorship in 1975, the consequent normalization of the Galician language, and more recently the progressive influence of globalization. This essay considers how current Galician visual poets reconceptualize these issues in the context of an international cultural and visual aesthetics.[2]

The Rise of Visual Poetry

The increasingly technological world we live in facilitates the convergence of different cultures—oral, printed, visual, digital. As part of this cultural and artistic blend, which affects the way we interact with the word and the world, interartistic practices such as visual poetry are reemerging. These other textualities are one of the most significant artistic marks of our times, but they did not arise in a cultural vacuum; they form part of a historical antimechanistic approach to art, which in the twentieth century found expression through the spirit of the avant-gardes.[3]

When studying intermedia poetic practices such as visual poetry, we have to take into consideration that while verbal poetry, the dominant poetic genre in the printed age, requires a monolinear regime of reading (a sequential syntax, one typeface), visual poetry requires a synaesthetic reading, which means that there is a simultaneous activation of several modes—visual, audial, verbal—to decode the poem. This active reading process has formal and thematic implications, which I address in this essay. Also note that manneristic and hybrid styles emerge in periods of social unrest in which more than one scale of values prevails (Tsur). The recent popularity of this genre, in Galicia and elsewhere, is in part due to a technocultural shift. The current visual and technological culture is closing gaps in space and time; but, ironically, the speed at which we receive new information does not correspond to the time we need to digest it. The resulting anxiety of communication abandons traditional verbal, linear, and teleological poetry styles in favor of mixed modes where the visual is enhanced. In this way, the concept of generational poetic groups is not linked to a specific ideology or identity, as it was in the debates among Galician poetic groups of the 1980s and 1990s.[4]

In sociohistorical terms this new creative path reveals a shift away from a simple correlation of (linguistic and political) identity, nationality, and territory and toward more flexible, globalized, and postnational forms of identity. Galician poetry provides a microcosmic example of this shift: from the linear, verbal poetry that is intrinsically connected with the emergence and development of cultural nationalism to the intermedia forms of visual poetry that problematize those correlations. The assumption that verbal language is the chief vehicle for expression is questioned in this shift. Verbal poetry, closely identified with the survival of the nation, in the new, postnational context becomes a marginal element. This change does not mean that verbal language is not important or that it must be reduced to just one or two words in a poem. The context in which visual poets work today enhances first the visual aspect of a verbal language (and of other languages as well) and then the process of articulation. This perceptive mode of thinking is multilingual, more inclusive and complex since it activates several parts of our brain.

Galician Visual Poetry: A Brief History

The history of Galician visual poetry provides a surprising counternarrative to the historical image of Galicia in the last centuries, as an isolated region poorly industrialized and developed, seen by both central and local eyes as a diminutive other. Galician visual poets today, like their peers in the rest of the world, are multifaceted. Some multimedia artists who work in cultural and artistic spaces of constant renegotiation and challenge can work in and out of the conventional artistic scene. Galician poets have access to the same information and media technologies that other artists do. They move, more than ever before, in an interdisciplinary world where the juxtaposition of images, words, sound, and performance is an essential part of the poetic mode. This artistic environment contrasts with the prevailing narrative of historical marginalization and cultural convention. But visual poetic practices in Galicia have a long history. Pattern poems can be traced back to medieval times, when Galician-Portuguese was the language of poetry and culture in the Peninsula. Some of the first examples of visual and verbal artifices (such as acrostics and labyrinths) were created by and in the court of Alfonso X of Castile; they followed the techniques of the times. In the twentieth century, visual poetry in Galicia reemerged in the context of the international avant-gardes.

The writer and artist Daniel Alfonso R. Castelao (1886–1950), in *Cousas da vida* ("Snippets of Life") and *Cincuenta homes por dez reás* ("Fifty Men for Ten *reás*"), was a pioneer in the interartistic practice of combining verbal and graphic languages. Another extraordinary avant-garde poet was Manoel Antonio (1900–30). Although only one of his books was published during his lifetime, *De catro a catro: Follas d'un diario d'abordo* (1928; "From Four till Four: Pages from an Onboard Journal"), he is the most widely praised poet in Galicia by both traditional and experimental poets: "Probablemente non hai poeta vivo en Galicia que non (se) reinvindique (d)a poética manuelantoniana" (Casas, "Poesía" 181; "There is probably no poet alive in Galicia who has not been influenced by the poetics of Manoel Antonio").[5] His distinctive and influential work is considered visual poetry because form, space, and typography are semantic and essential components of the book. Vicente Risco (1884–1963), better known as a prose writer, was also interested in interdisciplinary poetic practices. His "U . . . ju juu . . . (Poema futurista)," a visual poem in the futurist style, was published in 1920 in the iconic nationalist magazine *A nosa terra*. Galician poets of these decades knew the international literary and artistic avant-gardes of the times. Some, like Risco, were in contact with Vicente Huidobro and other international avant-garde poets.

Galician Visual Poetry since the 1970s

A familiarity with neo-avant-garde movements informs the work of Galician visual poets today, who like their predecessors use both traditional and innovative devices. Some use them to protest against globalization, neoliberalism, the pervasive power of the mass media, the dissemination of clichés, the multimedia industry, and institutions such as the church and the military. Their rebellious art has an immediate impact on the spectator through popular icons, extralinguistic elements, and multiple artifices. These visual poets attack art as a commodity, as a product of an academic and intellectual regime, and as a museum piece. They approach art and identity issues from nonconformist cultural practices. They explore the materiality of the languages used, look for visual interactions between text and context, subordinate linear expression to experimentation. This work allows them to open up a space for new avenues of meaning without falling into an impersonal or technological determinism.

The end of the dictatorship in 1975 and the establishment of the first normalization code of the Galician language in 1982 are two factors that provided the impetus for a new visual poetry, which was politically contestatory, collective-oriented, and experimental. Its style was influenced by surrealism. The main proponents of this poetry were the members of the group Rompente (1976–83): Antón Reixa, Manuel M. Romón, Alberto Avendaño, Alfonso Pexegueiro, and Camilo Valdeorras. *Rompente* can be translated as "breaking away," an idea that embodied the group's rebellious political, literary, and intellectual aims. Its members published collectively—works such as *Silabario da turbina* (1978; "ABC of the Turbine"), the series Tres tristes tigres (1979; "Three Sad Tigers"), and *A dama que fala* (1983; "The Lady Who Speaks")—but each member also published separately. These works of poetry referred in one way or another to aspects of verbal language. This emphasis is evident in the titles themselves. In *Silabario da turbina*, "silabario" is the old-fashioned schoolbook children used to learn to read. In *A dama que fala*, "fala" refers to the act of speaking. *Tres tristes tigres* reminds us of the children's tongue twister and also the humorous and experimental novel *Tres tristes tigres* (1963), by the Cuban author Guillermo Cabrera Infante.

The myth of Galicia's Celtic origins, created by the poets of the Rexurdimento to construct Galician nationalism, was of no interest to these writers.[6] Significantly, Rompente's manifesto "Textos de resistencia e comunicación" ("Texts of Resistance and Communication") remembers the aesthetic commitment of the avant-gardes in the figure of Manuel Antonio (more focused on the visual avant-gardes) rather than the poets Rosalía de Castro and Manuel Curros Enríquez, who were more committed to the search for a Galician national identity but followed a verbal, linear, teleological tradition in their verse.

In works such as *galletas kokoshcka non* (1979; "No Kokoshcka Biscuits"), by Romón, and *Silabario da turbina, facer pulgarcitos tres* (1979; "Make Tom

Thumbs Three"), and *As ladillas do travesty* (1979; "The Transvestite's Pests"), by Reixa, verbal and sequential syntax still predominate over visual and spatial syntax. The Galician language is used as an artistic artifact but also as a cultural and political vehicle of resistance. The Rompente writers use different registers and styles—satirical, ironic, and metapoetic—to criticize the United States military and the Vietnam War. There are references to popular culture: rock and roll, radio and TV programs, and so on. Experimentation is done at literary, linguistic, spatial, and semantic levels. Examples of spatial experimentation are the use of lines in reverse order at the top of the page, white spaces, and repetition of a poem on the same page. Several languages may be present in a poem. A poem may contain translations of whole poems or fragments of poems into French, English, or Spanish. This multilingualism expresses a deconstructive and subversive attitude toward the imposition of a national culture and literacy, which produced diglossia and emphasized a monolingual and monocultural society. The formal experimentation (use of different typography, languages, translations, visual devices) gives the Galician language the literary and cultural status of any other language. Multilingualism, multimedia, irony, satire, and irrationalism point the way to further experimentation.

A dama que fala constructs an imaginary visual-verbal play of artistic codes, in which the key word *slide* and its equivalent in Spanish, *diapositiva*, are given to read the poem in a visual mode:

(diapositiva 1)   eu son efectivamente o esquimó da fotografía
(d. 2)   sen mirar para atrás unha cona lateral afurricando
                 a minería dos lagartos contra min (outra vez d. 1)
(d. 3)   mais abaixo o esquimó en tanto que esquimó
                 faise o amo da situación
                 esfrega o nariz contra o plexiglás en xeral   (71)

(slide 1)   I am indeed the eskimo of the photograph
(s. 2)   without looking back a lateral cunt fucking
                 the lizards' mining against myself (again s. 1)
(s. 3)   farther down the eskimo being an eskimo
                 becomes the master of the situation
                 rubs his nose against Plexiglas in general

The poem concludes with a political note: "(agradecemos ao exército dos estados unidos de américa as facilidades que nos brindou para tomar estas imaxes e poder contar esta historia)" ("[we thank the army of the united states of america for the facilities given to us to take these pictures and be able to tell this story]").

The end of the 1970s was a rich moment for visual poetry in Galicia. Rompente was its most popular manifestation, but there were other, more personal and self-reflexive modes of visual poetry—for example, *Poemas caligráficos* (1979; "Caligraphic Poems"), by Uxío Novoneyra (1939–99), a poet whose visual work includes *Os Eidos 2: Letanías de Galicia e outros poemas* (1974; "The Fields: Galician Litanies and Other Poems"), *Muller pra lonxe* (1955–85; "Woman in the Distance"), and *Do Caurel a Compostela* (1956–86; "From Caurel to Compostela"). Novoneyra's avant-garde poetry left a mark on Galician poets of the last three decades. In *Poemas caligráficos*, he draws on the concept of calligraphy as a spiritual and aesthetic experience, one still practiced in Asian—especially Chinese and Japanese—and Arabic cultures. He was not alone; the poetic side of calligraphy had also appealed to neo-avant-garde poets in the 1960s, such as the Uruguayan Julio Campal (who died in Spain). For Novoneyra, poetry is seen as a whole process, an act of performance that goes beyond mere writing, drawing, or reciting. In this metagraphic work, he condenses the verbal and visual in a trompe l'oeil to create an abstract and metaphysical poetry. This interartistic approach opens up a perception of art in Western tradition that has been almost forgotten since the advent of the printing press, when the visual and verbal became separate modes of communication and specialized practices. Such inclusive poetry differs from a more visible and sociocritical poetry, represented by Reixa and Rompente.

Galician Visual Poetry since the 1990s

Visual poetry in Galicia entered another productive period in the 1990s, with an interest in the republication, in a technological context, of former poetic works. Reixa continued to be prolific and versatile in this decade. His *Ringo Rango* (1992) is a book and a video. The two combine visual poetic practices of the 1970s, used by Rompente, and a humorous and satirical tone. The strong performance and musical component and the new technocultural environment add a dynamism to Reixa's poetry and provide a channel for his multiartistic interests. *Upalás* (1998), an anthology with republished poems by Rompente (Cochón Otero and González Fernández), is another example of the growing interest in and receptivity to visual poetry.

Upalás is dedicated to Joan Salvat-Papasseit, a central figure in the Catalan avant-gardes, similar to Manoel Antonio in Galicia. A year later, Reixa published *Escarnio* ("Derision"), a bilingual book in Galician and Spanish, plus a CD-ROM that contains verbal, videographic, and video performance poetry. He continues to experiment with the visual (painting, drawings, film) and verbal (poetry, drama, novel) and also parodies the conservatives who governed Galicia between 1989 and 2005. Ironically, his recent works (e.g., *Escarnio*) were partially financed by the Xunta, a new practice that is common nowadays in Galicia and elsewhere. In his poetry, it is not so much the verbal aspect that changes—language is still used as a political tool—as the integration of different technologies and formats.

The shift from verbal to visual becomes more pronounced at the turn of the twenty-first century, as poets grow more eclectic and more oriented toward graphics. Some of these authors are Lino Braxe, Claudio Rodríguez Fer, Lois Gil Magariños, Pedro Gonçalves, and Antón Risco. They tend to eliminate the verbal component in favor of a graphic and kinetic form. In many works now the only thing in words is the title. With the proliferation of new technologies and a cultural environment open to artistic experimentation, many visual poets mix different codes, techniques, and materials to compose simple but appealing poems that reach a wide audience, an audience increasingly less concerned with the topic of nationalism and more receptive to international issues, technology, and the visual.

Braxe is a visual poet, scriptwriter, playwright, essayist, and journalist. He is known outside Galicia for his participation in collective events, mail art exhibitions, and anthologies. His *Territorio: Poemas obxecto e visuais* (1999; "Territory: Object and Visual Poems") attacks institutional powers (e.g., the church) and dictatorial regimes (e.g., Nazism). He also makes verbal and visual references to artists and writers such as Manuel Rivas, Jules Verne, Edgar Allan Poe, Goethe, and John Houston. Braxe's poetry does not follow Reixa's or Novoneyra's visual practices of the 1970s; they focus on semantics and tend toward immanence, which addresses international rather than national readers.

The titles of Braxe's poems are usually ironic in relation to the visual content, a device that many visual poets use today. *Poemas obxecto e visuais* has an introduction, linear pagination, conventional page formats, and editorial information—not the normal practice among contemporary visual poets. Braxe's techniques resemble the style of Joan Brossa (1919–98), an influential poet and plastic artist of the Spanish neo-avant-gardes. Braxe's

"Europa" provides a critique of economic imperialism: an American one-dollar bill is attached to a geographic map of Europe. The bill suggests that Europe's main currency is the United States dollar, although the euro was introduced to the world financial markets in 1999—the same year Braxe's book was published—and launched as a currency in 2002. The combination of collage techniques, a composition in layers, the use of objects (the dollar, a paper clip), the title, as well as the absence of the euro create thematic tension, a visual ellipsis.

Another multifaceted artist is Claudio Rodríguez Fer. His apparently simple poem "A vida" ("Life") is highly suggestive. The blood-red tones of the word-trees allude to life, death, passion, sex, violence, prison, hate, and war. The title could refer to an individual life or to a collective experience; it also evokes political movements that use red as their symbol, like Marxism, Communism, and Maoism, so "a vida" could signify a way of life. The metallic columns suggest life in prison; the word-trees and symbolic red, creativity and art as an organic process. The interaction between visual and verbal makes us reflect on life as a continuous and dynamic process where opposites are at play. Rodríguez Fer shares with Novoneyra and Antón Risco the concept of art as a continuum and also as a metaphysical and personal expression. The graphic presentation of his theme means the poem can be understood by an international audience.

Another shift in poetic practices in recent years is the increasing manifestation of collective activities, performances, and installations. Sometimes the motivation is to react against ecological disasters, such as the sinking of the oil tanker *Prestige* off the Galician coast in 2002, or international conflicts, such as the wars in the Balkans or Iraq. At other times the aim is educational and promoted by official institutions, such as Proxecto Alfabeto 05, the visual alphabet created in the town of Caldas de Reis in 2005, or the Dadaist collective art acts by Gil Magariños, or those that took place in Vilagarcía de Arousa in 2004. These artists also produce mail art, an international form that uses the postal system as a medium or, when e-mail artists are involved, the Internet. This expression is based on anticommercial, anticanonical, and interartistic values and on the idea that everyone can produce art. Pedro Gonçalves and Gil are the main members of Corporación Semiótica Galega ("Galician Semiotic Corporation"), a group of very active and unconventional poets whose works include *Futuro: Bolsa de mareo 2004* (with the motif of the disposable bags found on airplanes; "Future: Sick Bag 2004"), *De-funcionario*, *SPOT*, *Publipoemas* (a video-art work by Quique

Otero and Manolo Cortés) and the collective project Translittera (2005), devoted to new poetic languages, such as performance.[7]

These visual repertoires encourage artists to take formal and aesthetic liberties through the use of video clips, digital techniques, photomontage, and so on. An example of a visual work by Gil that takes a graphic approach to poetry is the following vignette. This vignette shows Gil's graphic

style, which keeps the verbal to a minimum. All the images are interconnected and convey an antimilitaristic message. The words "North" and "South," side by side, alter the normal geospatial order; their being linked to empty plates suggests a critique of the hegemonic order that preserves hunger. The official construction of nations, often violent or forced, is ridiculed by a flag whose icon is a roll of toilet paper. These sociocritical messages portray a world in crisis and demonstrate an artistic shift from verbal to visual and from national to global concerns.

Another significant collective work is *Extravíos* (2001; "Misplacements"), a short collection of visual poems with only thirty-five exemplars issued, signed by their authors: Gonçalves, Gil, Baldo Ramos, and Anxo Pastor. These poets, in their homage to the traditional poetic avant-gardes, show a strong similarity to Rompente's homage to Antonio and Papasseit. Gil's "Qwerty para anxo pastor" looks like a poem from the first avant-gardes, in its futuristic style. "Qwerty" is the first six letters in the second row of the keyboard. The visual arrangement of the letters, the typography, the orthographic signs, the repetition of several characters and empty spaces help create a dynamic pattern that also carries an antimilitaristic meaning. The graphic signs and characters in italics imitate the rain, which is a key word in the poem. The syntactic line "os homes chovendo en ringleira van" ("the men go raining in a line") is reinforced with the repetition of the phoneme /i/ in italics, creating the kinetic illusion of a group of soldiers advancing on the battlefield. The evocative sound and visual referents (the rain, soldiers, the *Ç*, typing) converge at different levels—phonological, phonetic, graphic, orthographic, lexical, syntactic—to honor both experimentation in the local language (Galician) and the universal theme of antimilitarism.

O libro dos abanos (Palabras no aire) (2002; "The Book of Fans (Words in the Air)" is a collective book that resulted from an exhibition of thirty-five inscribed fans in the Santiago de Compostela art gallery, A Galería Noroeste de Xoias de Autor. This exhibition has two antecedents, as Anxo Tarrío says in the foreword to the book: the exhibition of fans in Vigo in 1922 and the exhibition of painted fans by Galician artists in 1966. The re-creation of earlier visual exhibitions is another example of the increasing interest and popularity of visual poetry in recent years. These new fans, composed by a wide variety of visual and nonvisual poets, such as Xosé M. Álvarez Cáccamo, Braxe, Darío Xohán Cabana, Arturo Casas, Yolanda Castaño, Emma Couceiro, Anxo Quintela, Xesús Rábade Paredes, Xavier Seoane, and Miro Villar, combine several literary traditions in a new expressive form.

One poem in this collection is "Haiku da primavera" ("Spring Haiku"), by Xavier Seoane:

(Primavera)

A libélula
Ascende, desce, ascende
e desaparece . . .   (88–89)

(Spring)

The dragonfly
Goes up, goes down, goes up
and disappears . . .

Seoane captures a fleeting and essential moment of springtime, imitating the haiku genre. He re-creates an animated landscape through a dragonfly and its dancing flight. There is neither thematic nor formal closure in the poem; the eternal dance is reinforced by the potential movement of the fan being waved by a hand in the warm air of spring. In its simplicity, condensation of meanings, rhythm, movement, color, and lines, this composition is both a visual and an aural poem. Its rhythms act on the senses like a mantra, capturing a moment that is part of a cyclic and primordial time of existence, in line with the haiku aesthetic and the spirit of the avant-gardes.

Another poem that reflects this graphic-visual fusion is Rodríguez Fer's "Abano público" ("Public Fan"), which constitutes a variant of "A vida":

Abano público
Variación sobre a vida
(gravado sobre corpo)
a vida   (82–83)

Public fan
Variation on life
(engraving on body)
life

The author privileges a public space to make us reflect on art and creation as an organic act—like an engraving on a body. The format for a poem goes beyond the white page. That the medium can be a fan or a human body evokes ancient practices and Asian cultures but also the popular and contemporary urban tattoo. Rodríguez Fer's poems "A vida" and "Abano público" point out the organic and inclusive character of poetry and so recall Novoneyra's attitude two decades earlier.

This book includes poems composed by women writers and poets, like Olga Novo:

eu son aberta
esta cousa vermella
(62–63)

I am open
this red thing

This short composition draws our attention to the theme of female identity, gender perception, and subjectivity ("I am"). In English the poem loses the feminine grammatical mark -*a*: "I am open / this red thing." "Thing" is still associated with the subject "I." The subject of the poem, "eu," is the fan, the object, suggesting that women are things, like fans, available ("open") to be used when it is hot. Red enhances the idea of a female identity by evoking menstruation, giving birth, and sex. There is a strong female-authored poetic tradition in Galicia, but it is new in visual poetry, which is an art form predominantly constructed by male authors. Novo's poem is thus an interesting hint of future possibilities for the genre.

A significant number of visual poetic initiatives are promoted and supported by the Xunta, by local governments, and by private financial entities. The risk here, of course, is that in their promotion of the arts these bodies may condition the message as well. The book *X: Espazo para un signo* (2005; "Space for a Sign"), which celebrates the twenty-fifth anniversary of the publishing house Xerais, has the support of the funding body Fundación Caixa Galicia. The only challenging element of this book is the letter *x*, which is distinctive to Galician (it does not exist in Spanish) and therefore is a visual expression of the uniqueness of the Galician language and its identity. Beyond these and other officially supported initiatives, more or less successful, visual poets of the 1990s are significant not so much for creating poetry with an antiverbal rhetoric as for actively enhancing a visual rhetoric. They encourage formal and aesthetic freedom, minimizing the traditional search for a national identity, and they work with a variety of international themes and techniques that connect visual images—static or kinetic—with verbal and aural components, thus conditioning readers to a hybrid perception.

Visual poetry in Galicia evolved in both form and theme during the twentieth century. Its most important periods were between the two world wars; the end of the 1970s, which coincides with the end of the Francoist regime; and the end of the 1990s, which is the time of a newly technologically aware and globalized society. Visual poems of the 1970s differ notably from today's technographic expressions. Nowadays poets privilege a shifting identity, a different order of things that blurs former fixed divisions among the local, the national, and the global. The multiple terrains Galician visual poets have mapped out since the 1970s show a new trend toward spatialization, a strong link between technology and literature, and an engagement with the materials used. We may look at this type of poetry as a consequence of the new postmodern and technological culture, as part of the spirit of the avant-gardes and neo-avant-gardes with their inclusive and antimechanistic approach to art, or as part of a recurring reaction to times of crisis. Whichever approach we choose, Galician visual poetry today demonstrates a progressive internationalization of forms and themes in the artists' modus operandi, an increasing engagement with hybrid perception and multicultural literacy, and a detachment of traditional verbal configurations of the local. All these features generate alternative avenues for further debate.

Visual poets today are interested less in working with the verbal language as a vehicle to represent identity than in utilizing space as a technique for presenting an interdependent image of Galicia, as a region that is becoming part of the cultural and international artistic mainstream. Galician visual poetry at the beginning of the twenty-first century is characterized by innovative artistic and interpretative cartographies that not only provide a new vocabulary for expressing identity but also locate Galicia as an active and dynamic player in the European and international artistic scene.

Notes

1. Visual poetry can be defined as an interartistic genre that combines at least two different languages, one verbal, the other visual. Recent trends give priority to visual syntax over verbal units. Visual poetry is one of many different modalities of experimental poetry, such as sound, performance, or hypertextual poetry. See Millán, "Las otras poesías" and "Utopia."

2. Multiple factors and spheres of artistic and political influence affected the production of visual poetry in Galicia during the twentieth century. An exhaustive interdisciplinary and comparative study of this subject is needed, but here I explore significant visual poetic trends in Galicia that mark different lines of action. Some stress cultural tensions and interactions between the national and the regional; others attend to more abstract aesthetic motifs; others echo a new technocultural context, which is stimulating new hybrid practices that recontextualize collective and subjective identity issues.

3. Visual poetry is not a new art form. Although it acquires independence as an artistic genre at the end of the nineteenth century, with Mallarmé and Apollinaire, its origins are deep-rooted, at the beginning of several civilizations, when the first impulses to combine the visual and the verbal appeared. For a world prehistory of visual poetry or pattern poetry, see Higgins. In the Western world visual poetry was always a marginal mode of expression, emerging in periods of social unrest—late medieval times, the baroque, late Romanticism. For a historical background of visual poetry in Spain, see Cózar.

4. For more about the poetic generational debates in Galicia, see R. Villar, "A poesía"; Inma López Silva qtd. in F. Alonso, *Momentos*.

5. All translations into English are mine.

6. For an introduction to nationalism in Galicia, see Cuba, Miranda, and Enríquez. Eduardo Pondal (1835–1917) used the mythic pre-Roman figure of Breogán to refer to Galicia's Celtic origins. Later, Álvaro Cunqueiro (1911–1981) employed the medieval magician Merlin in a similar way.

7. For more information on this original work and about the art of Corporación Semiótica Galega, see the Web site.

Useful References Online

CyberPoem. L'associació de performers, artistes i poetes associats, n.d. Web. 5 Dec. 2010.

Poesía visual: Experimental e arte correo. Corporacion Semiótica Galega, n.d. Web. 5 Dec. 2010.

Seara, Teresa. "A poesía galega na fin de milenio" *Ianua: Revista philologica romana* 2 (2001): 125–34. Romania Minor, n.d. Web. 22 Jan. 2010.

Remapping Galician Narrative for the Twenty-First Century

Kirsty Hooper

Early in 2005, the Asociación Galega de Editores (AGE; "Galician Publishers' Association"), after lengthy consultation and debate, released its *Plan de lectura, 2005–2010* ("Reading Plan"), which it hoped would set the agenda for the future development of Galicia's publishing industry. In addition to its evident commercial imperative, the plan is a clarion call for politicians and parents to recognize the sociopolitical importance in Galicia of reading and thus, implicitly, of narrative:

> Enténdese a lectura como un instrumento vital de inclusión e democratización, canle para acceder ao coñecemento, chave de transformación social e ferramenta para unha participación cidadá libre, consciente e crítica. . . . A realidade lingüística e cultural de Galicia confírelles un especial carácter ás intervencións no ámbito cultural: se é urxente unha intervención decidida de toda a sociedade a prol do libro e da lectura, esta non pode entenderse dentro desta sen lles prestar unha atención prioritaria ao libro e á lectura en galego.
>
> (*Plan* 1)

> Reading is understood as a vital instrument for inclusion and democratization, a channel for knowledge, a key to social transformation, and a tool for free, conscious, and critical participation of citizens. . . . Galicia's linguistic and cultural situation means that cultural acts have a special character: an intervention in favor of books and reading is urgently required at all levels of society, but this intervention cannot happen without prioritizing books and reading in the Galician language.

Admittedly, as a commercial organization, the AGE has an economic interest in encouraging Galician citizens to read, and especially to read expensive, full-length novels. Nevertheless, the points it raises, especially the idea that reading is an activity to be protected and supported for the sake of the nation's health, can be connected with wider debates about the role of literature in any culture, particularly in minority cultures. This official statement reflects often voiced concerns about the historically low profile of Galician narrative, particularly when prose is compared with the strength and health of poetry, and thus taps into a debate that has been exercising observers for some decades. Silvia Bermúdez observes:

> [S]ome cultural critics considered the "excess" of poets in the last decade of the twentieth century an "anomaly" that exposed Galicia as a nation without a solid production in the genre that seems to validate the cultural significance of any nation: the novel. ("Poetry" 124)

In this essay, I examine the current status of narrative in Galicia and, picking up on Bermúdez's timely observation, argue for the potential of this historically fragile genre not only to validate but also to transform cultural significance in Galicia.

A Brief Overview of Galician Narrative before 1975

The problematic status of narrative works in the Galician canon has long provided a sharp contrast to the privileged status enjoyed by poetry. The disparity between the two genres has shaped perceptions of Galician literature since the Rexurdimento. In the first history of Galician literature (1887), the young scholar (and future politician) Augusto Besada wrote:

> La poesía es y ha sido siempre á manera de jovenzuela más o menos bonita, rubia ó morena, alegre ó triste, pero siempre hermosa y siempre encantadora; sus travesuras labráronle en Galicia la inmortalidad y en la lenta sucesión de los tiempos vivió siempre animosa y acariciada siempre. La prosa por el contrario parece destronada matrona, reina orgullosa y pobre, que vive á solas en su retiro dignándose de vez en cuando visitar á sus deudos, si por casualidad no lo hace por tarjeta. . . . (113)[1]

> Poetry is and has always been like a young girl, more or less pretty, blonde or brunette, cheerful or melancholy, but always beautiful and always enchanting; her vivacity gave her immortality in Galicia, and she has survived the slow passage of time, always lively and always beloved. Prose on the other hand seems a dethroned matron, a proud but poor queen, who lives alone in her retreat, deigning now and again to visit her relations, if by chance she does not simply leave a card. . . .

Besada's colorful metaphor illustrates graphically how poetry (identified principally with the poet and theorist Rosalía de Castro, who died just two years earlier) was from the start almost unanimously considered the genre of prestige, while narrative was seen as less exciting, less connected, and as a result less relevant to the incipient Galician national project. Besada's evocation of poetry and prose in terms of feminine stereotypes demonstrates, too, the extent to which discourses of gender shaped the emergence of Galician literature, a conceptual framework that continues to inform our understanding of Galician narrative today.

Just a few decades after the flowering of the Rexurdimento in the 1860s, critics had come to believe Galician literature required a conscious process of virilization if it was to compete with more established literatures. This perception colored both literary production and its reception at a time when Galician literature was still very much in development: the first novel in Galician, Marcial Valladares's sentimental potboiler *Maxina ou a filla espúrea* ("Maxina; or, The Illegitimate Daughter") appeared in 1880, just seven years before Besada's study.[2] It would be another forty years before the publication of the first female-authored novel in Galician, Francisca Herrera Garrido's equally sentimental *Néveda: Historia dunha dobre seducción* (1920; "Néveda: Story of a Double Seduction"). This noteworthy occurrence, however, rarely merits more than a footnote in histories of Galician literature (Hooper, "Girl").

The four decades that separate *Maxina* and *Néveda* are paradigmatic of the fragmented, disrupted critical history of Galician narrative that has been noticed by so many critics (González-Millán, *Narrativa*; Hooper, "Girl;" Gabilondo, "Towards a Postnational History"; Rábade Villar in this volume). After *Maxina*, standard histories of literature (Carballo Calero, *Historia*; Tarrío Varela, *Literatura galega* and *Literatura gallega*; Vilavedra, *Diccionario* and *Historia*) note nothing of significance until the Xeración Nós and the narrative works of Alfonso Castelao and Ramón Otero Pedrayo in the 1920s. This fertile period is followed by another break, caused by the civil war and subsequent Francoist censorship and repression of minority languages and cultures. In the 1950s, a slight relaxation of censorship and centralization allowed for the emergence of the Xeración Galaxia, based around the publishing house Galaxia, founded in 1951. This period is widely considered the beginning of modern Galician narrative, when the novelists Eduardo Blanco Amor, Álvaro Cunqueiro, and Ánxel Fole rose to prominence. They were followed in the 1960s by a younger and more overtly political generation, whose achievements include the experimental movement known as Nova Narrativa Galega ("New Galician Narrative"). Many of those who came to prominence in the 1960s, such as Xosé Luis Méndez Ferrín, María Xosé Queizán (*A orella no buraco* [1965]), and Carlos Casares (*Vento ferido* [1967] and *Cambio en tres* [1969]), remain influential in Galician narrative today.

Galician Narrative since 1975: Theoretical Perspectives

In the decades since Franco's death in 1975, which allowed *galeguismo* to reconstitute itself openly as a national discourse, Galician-language narrative has increased in both quantity and diversity. The establishment of a commercial publishing system (especially through the two major publishing houses, Galaxia and Xerais) and the expansion of the institutional spaces of education, literary criticism, and media have made Galician-language narrative accessible to a broader readership than ever before. Nevertheless, there is still much critical debate about the place of narrative works in the Galician contemporary canon, in part because of the enormous pressure placed on the narrative genre by the continued desire for normalization, which requires it to be viable in the literary marketplace but without the loss of its ideological function (González-Millán, *Narrativa*). The situation has been further complicated as the desire for normalization comes into conflict with the new cartographies and narratives of Galician identity emerging from the works of formerly marginalized groups—women and sexual minorities, writers of languages other than standard Galician, immigrants and those in the diaspora, all of whom seek to problematize the notion of a single national space or national narrative.

The connection between nation and narration, or between the health of national identity and the health of the national literature (most frequently embodied in the novel), has been a focus for theorists of nation and culture since the nineteenth century (Bhabha, *Nation*; Brennan). The central thesis of Benedict Anderson's influential study *Imagined Communities* (1983) is that the development of the modern nation in the nineteenth century was rationalized through the contemporaneous development of the realist novel. That is, as concepts of space and time were altered by the development of the modern nation, the novels of Balzac, Dickens, or Galdós provided a means by which people were able to adjust to that new framework. Anderson implies that it is the stories we tell about who we are and where we come from, whether we are telling our national history or recounting our national myths, that help us make sense of our place in the world. While this process is so embedded in hegemonic cultures as to go almost unseen, the importance of narrative for the realization of minority cultures remains a key topic of debate in Galicia as elsewhere (Hooper, "Alternative Genealogies?"). The critical consensus in Galicia is that only once a healthy narrative genre exists will Galician culture be normalized. The Galician cultural theorist Xoán González-Millán, in his 1996 study *A narrativa galega actual* ("Contemporary Galician Narrative"), observed that the end of the Franco dictatorship in the mid-1970s brought about

> a case obsesiva prioridade das diversas institucións e colectivos por canonizar unha vontade de experimentación na escrita para acadar un determinado nivel de "normalidade" cultural. (50)

> the almost obsessive concern of different groups and institutions to canonize literary experimentation in order to reach a determined level of cultural "normality."

A quarter of a century later, the desire for normalization remains strong. In her annual report on Galician narrative in 2004, the literary critic Dolores Vilavedra contrasts the "inercia" ("inertia") characteristic of "sistemas literarios normalizados" ("normalized literary systems") with the "permanente devezo de novidades entusiasmantes que padecen os que podemos considerar, coma o noso, débiles" ("constant desire for stimulating novelty suffered by those, like our own, that we might consider weak"). In this light, she reflects on the rather quiet year that has just passed, with no distorting one-off events such as film adaptations or major literary prizes, asking, "¿Será iso un síntoma da tan desexada 'normalización'?" ("Narrativa" 144; "Could this be a symptom of the long-desired 'normalization'?").

The question raised by these debates, of course, is how we judge a healthy narrative. According to the precepts set out in the nineteenth century and studied by Anderson, Homi Bhabha, and Timothy Brennan, among others, a truly national narrative is one that enables the emerging nation (and we must still consider Galicia an emerging nation) to conceptualize itself, its history, its place in the world. Back in the 1880s, Besada refused to discuss nineteenth-century Galician prose, because, he claimed, it was not independent enough of Spanish, implying that it was thus of little help to the national project:

Cualidades, verdaderamente tiene muchas la prosa de Galicia, pero no merecen ser estudiadas, porque son comunes á las de la lengua castellana. (114–15)

Galician prose does, in truth, have many virtues, but they are not worthy of study, for they are shared with those of the Spanish language.

The desire of the regionalist (later nationalist) movement to differentiate Galicia from Spain in social and political terms is thus conflated with the desire to differentiate the two literatures in aesthetic and linguistic terms. Much current scholarship continues to work on the principle that in order to be fully realized, Galician narrative must become a "narrativa nacional" (González-Millán, *Narrativa* 29–31; "national narrative").

This apparently straightforward principle raises several thorny questions. If the nineteenth-century realist-nationalist novel developed in and for a particular historical context, does it necessarily follow that it will remain valid in a different historical (twenty-first-century) and sociopolitical (stateless nation) context? Furthermore, and more pressingly, do this historically and sociopolitically contingent genre and its related critical apparatus provide the best possible tools for resolving the dilemmas facing contemporary Galician culture? These questions point to the wider, ongoing debate between those who support the pragmatic use by minority groups of tried and tested (if no longer cutting-edge) concepts such as national literature (e.g., Hutcheon) and those who reject such a strategy as futile and complicit (e.g., Greenblatt), a debate that is long-standing and probably impossible to resolve (Hooper, "New Cartographies").

The concepts of nation and national culture are themselves clearly changing in response to a number of factors, from the changing geopolitical world situation and the massive population movements that characterized the second half of the twentieth century to the effects of technology on the consumption of literature and culture. In Spain and by extension Galicia (not to mention Catalunya and the Basque Country), these changes must be seen in the context of the shift from dictatorship to democracy that has been taking place since 1975 and the consequent raising of the tension between centripetal and centrifugal concepts of culture and identity. Established notions of nation and national identity are becoming increasingly less viable. Nation continues to be a key organizing factor in our experience of culture and identity, but its borders are being questioned, redrawn, and even dissolved.

One consequence of this shift in the Iberian context is the impetus to find new ways of theorizing the changing relation between the Spanish center and the Galician, Catalan, Basque peripheries to take into account other categories, such as class, ethnicity, gender, migration, and sexuality. These theorizations are variously described as postnational (Hooper, "New Cartographies"; Resina) or "neonational" (Gabilondo, "Historical Memory"), but however we describe them, their effect is the same: to challenge the empirical and epistemological underpinnings of nation and, in consequence, to question the continued hegemonic interpretation of the national narrative. Because of its relatively unfixed state, Galician literature provides an excellent forum in which to address these questions.

Principal Trends in Post-1975 Galician Narrative

Growing commercialization and the creation of new forums for cultural discussion and dissemination in the Galician press and in academia during the 1980s and 1990s led to the emergence of a series of star novelists whose works have become consecrated as modern classics and are regularly reprinted, studied, and commented on. The three most notable are Suso de Toro (b. 1956), Manuel Rivas (b. 1957), and Carlos G. Reigosa (b. 1948). As their dates of birth show, all are part of the generation whose literary habits were formed by the resurgence of Galician narrative in the late 1960s and 1970s. Toro is considered by many the paradigmatic Galician postmodernist novelist (Vilavedra, *Sobre narrativa* 48), with *Polaroid* (1986), *Land Rover* (1988), and *Tic-Tac* (1993), although his more recent work has moved away from the postmodern experimentation of these novels to a more conventional narrative style, which permits him to address a new range of issues. While Toro is read principally on the Iberian Peninsula, Rivas, known nationally for his regular columns in the Spanish daily newspaper *El país*, has come to international recognition thanks to the English, German, and Italian translations of his work and the film adaptations of *O lapis do carpinteiro* (*The Carpenter's Pencil*) and *A lingua das bolboretas* (*Butterfly's Tongue*). Rivas's narrative is structurally much more conventional than Toro's and focused not on edgy urban Galicia but on the lyrical and vanishing rural world. This subject matter has struck a chord with the reading public: in fact, *Lapis*, a story of personal resistance and redemption set around the civil war and first published in 1998, is one of the best-selling Galician-language novels of all time, with over 60,000 copies sold by 2002 ("Resistir").

Reigosa is quite different from Toro and Rivas. He is known as the originator of Galician-language detective fiction, with *Crime en Compostela* (1984) and a further three novels featuring the detective Nivardo Castro and the journalist Carlos Conde, who work together. In the 1980s, Reigosa's work was largely responsible for bringing popular narrative (embodied in genre fiction such as the *novela negra* or detective novel) into the public eye alongside the more conventionally literary novels, which were themselves enjoying an unprecedently broad readership. *Crime en Compostela* won the first Premio Xerais (Galicia's equivalent of the Booker Prize) and became the first Galician-language best seller, going through fourteen editions to date and selling over 35,000 copies ("Resistir"), as well as being translated into Spanish. This development was not welcomed by everybody. In the 1980s, there existed a strong current of utilitarian cultural nationalism, embodied most in the writings of the literary scholar and nationalist politician Francisco Rodríguez. For Rodríguez and critics like him, Galician literature existed purely to serve the Galician national project. In a move that unwittingly evokes Besada's rejection of the new narrative genre a century before, 1980s nationalists dismissed genre fiction, such as Reigosa's detective novels, as derivative of other (particularly Spanish) literature and thus not authentic enough to be considered part of Galician literature (63).

Despite the desire of some readers to maintain the boundary between Galician and Spanish literatures first evoked by Besada, translation into Spanish became an indication of success for Galician novelists in the 1980s and 1990s. Toro, Rivas, and Reigosa have all enjoyed success on the Spanish market, which in turn has opened their works up to international view, not only in Latin America but also in the anglophone world. Another author who has enjoyed success in Spanish translation is Cid Cabido (*Grupo abeliano* [1999], trans. 2000). That the language question remains a sensitive issue, however, can be seen in the controversy surrounding the novelist and former conselleiro de cultura ("counselor for culture") Alfredo Conde, who switched from Galician-language to Spanish-language writing after his second novel and won Spain's prestigious Premio Nadal in 1991 for his third novel (and first in Spanish), *Los otros días* ("The Other Days"). The feeling among Galician-language writers and critics was that Conde, who continues to write in Spanish, had betrayed his public duty as *conselleiro* to protect and promote Galician culture, a betrayal that was attributed to commercial pressure (Vilavedra, *Sobre narrativa* 28–30). Other writers who have inspired controversy for appearing to privilege Spanish-language writing, especially for economic or egotistical reasons, are Marina Mayoral, Luisa Castro, and Marta Rivera de la Cruz (and their gender may not be irrelevant here). The language question still exercises writers and critics, for a variety of reasons (see Hooper, "Forum"), but one issue has gone largely unremarked: the relative success of Galician authors in Spanish translation has led to the growth of a Spanish-language readership that does not always recognize (or have access to information about) the Galician cultural context of the novels that they read. In other words, Galician narrative is already functioning, for some readers, as a transnational or delocalized narrative.

The expansion of the commercial, critical, and educational fields that began in the early 1980s continued through the 1990s. At the start of the twenty-first century, Galician narrative appears to be in a good position. Six times as many books in Galician were published in 2005 as two decades earlier: according to the AGE, total publications grew from 259 in 1984 to over 1,800 in 2005. Between 1999 and 2006, nearly 10,500 books were published in Galician (*Edición*). Even so, the question remains as to how far the institutional discourse about narrative maps onto the reading habits of the population at large. Galician-language sales are still low compared with those of Spanish-language books: in 2002, only 15% of sales in Galicia were of Galician-language books ("Resistir"). There is certainly a will to change this situation: the Lei do Libro e da Lectura ("Books and Reading Law"), passed 10 January 2007, made 7.1 million euros available for investment into the different parts of the process. Significantly, this investment is also for translation both into and out of Galician and for the promotion of Galician culture outside Galicia.

New Fictional Maps in Galician Narrative

The rapid growth in sales of Galician-language books since the 1980s and the consequent proliferation of authors and topics has led to a widespread sense that the long-desired normalization of Galician narrative is within reach (e.g., Vilavedra, "Narrativa"). In structural terms, the situation is clearly better than ever before. In terms of the relation among author, text, and reader, we are beginning to see a shift away from the expectation that the narrative voice will be that of a male who is straight, white, middle-class, located in Galicia, and writing in Galician. This voice cannot for long continue to speak for a nation whose demographic makeup is changing with unprecedented speed. Other voices are emerging that narrate different kinds of fictional maps of Galicia. Although most remain on the margins of institutional spaces, publishing in minor imprints and rarely reviewed by the mainstream press, the maps they construct are built around the recognition and investigation of some of the key tensions that shape Galician cultural history and identity—for example, the tension between the public and private functions of narrative, between narrating the nation and narrating the self.

Perhaps the most visible point of tension concerns gender and sexuality. Disruption and fragmentation are defining features of the history of women's writing in Galicia. Herrera Garrido's *Néveda* appeared only in 1920. It would be another forty-five years before the next female novelist, Queizán. Since the 1970s, the situation has gradually improved: around thirty women published narrative in the last quarter of the twentieth century, although the number who published only a single work is great (Blanco; Hooper, "Girl" 109–10). In the twenty-first century, female novelists are starting to be recognized and to move into institutional spaces. The Premio Xerais has now had six female winners: Marilar Aleixandre, for *Teoría de caos* (2002; "Chaos Theory"); Inma López Silva, for *Concubinas* (2003; "Concubines"); Teresa Moure, for *Herba moura* (2005; "Black Nightshade"); Rexina Vega, for *Cardume* (2007; "Shoal"); Rosa Aneiros, for *Sol de inverno* (2009; "Winter Sun"); and Iolanda Zúñiga, for *Periferia* (2010; "Periphery"). These authors together with Queizán (*Ten o seu punto a fresca rosa* [2000; "Every Rose Has Its Thorn"], *Amantia* [1984], *¡Sentinela, alerta!* [2003; "Awake, Sentinel!"]), are now regularly published in Xerais's main list. Queizán's high-profile collection of short stories *Narradoras* (2000; "[Female] Narrators") brought together works by twenty-five female writers, of whom only a small number were already established as narrators. Most were either at the beginning of their careers or better known in other genres, notably poetry and children's literature.

Although few of the women included in *Narradoras* have gone on to publish further narrative for adults, the situation for women novelists is improving. Moure's receiving the Xerais, in particular, enabled the Galician literary establishment to expend a lot of print congratulating itself on overcoming what has always been perceived as the biggest obstacle to normalization (although, as Helena Miguélez-Carballeira observed, much of the work described as groundbreaking or feminist is really anything but ["Inaugurar"]). Very few critics have questioned the extent to which this change reflects a fundamental shift in the Galician literary system. Vilavedra is skeptical, arguing in her 2005 annual review of Galician narrative that women writers, despite their increased profile, continue to be treated as "excepcionalidades" ("exceptional") and pointing out that "converter a escrita e o triunfo das mulleres nun 'fenómeno' paréceme que implica un risco" ("Atopando" 169; "turning women's writing and its triumph into a 'phenomenon' seems to me rather dangerous"). Helena González, too, is unconvinced:

> Agora mesmo vivimos nunha moda violeta, xestionada voluntaria e con-
> scientemente por quen controla a edición.   ("Helena González")

> Right now we're experiencing a craze for pink, consciously and voluntarily managed by the people who control the publishing industry.

The danger is clear:

> "[D]emasiada" visibilidade pode producir "ruído" para a mirada hexemónica, e pénsase que unha muller que gañe un premio xa fai por sete, xa é abondo, a situación está normalizada. É outra forma de misoxinia.

> "[T]oo much" visibility can be seen by the establishment as producing "noise," and they think if one women gets a prize it's worth seven, it's enough, the situation is normalized. It's another form of misogyny.

Female novelists and short story writers are still outnumbered four to one on the main lists of Xerais; they are even more conspicuous by their absence in the lists of the more traditional Galaxia. Of the contributors to *Narradoras*, a few went on to publish full-length novels, like Eva Moreda (*O demo e o profundo mar azul* [2005; "The Devil and the Deep Blue Sea"]), Beatriz Dacosta (*Contrato temporal* [2004; "Temporary Contract"] and *Precipicios* [2003; "Precipices"]), or Dolores Ruiz, who won the Premio Blanco Amor with *Dentro da illa* (2005; "Within the Island"). Women are much more likely to publish their works in minor collections and with small or local publishing houses, such as tresCtres, which published An Alfaya's award-winning *Matei un home* (2004; "I Killed a Man"), or Francka Editora, home of Dacosta's *Precipicios*.

Even when an author is allowed access to institutional spaces, it may be on limited terms. For many years Queizán was the most canonical (i.e., the most read, reviewed, and studied) of contemporary female novelists, but note the changing pattern of publication of her novels. She is now strongly linked with Xerais, but Xerais does not publish all her works, and even those that they do publish receive differing treatment. For example, *Amor de tango* (1992) went through three editions in the main list, but in 1998 it was downgraded to Xerais's Peto ("pocket-sized") imprint. No doubt there were commercial reasons for this decision, but it sends a message, given that *Amor de tango* is so far Galicia's only female-authored contribution to the growing genre of civil war narrative. John Patrick Thompson points out that Queizán and her novel are not mentioned in most studies of Galician civil war narrative. The lack of critical attention paid to what should be a novel of interest regardless of its author's gender recalls the treatment of Herrera's *Néveda* in 1920 and suggests that the same process of *virilización* may again be in operation. Queizán's first novel, *A orella no buraco* ("The Ear in the Hole"), is her only work not concerned with gender and sexuality. It is also her only work published by Galaxia, the publishing house most closely linked with the Galician literary establishment and the post–civil war renaissance of Galician literature.

Miguélez-Carballeira notes the irony of the silence that Queizán's work continues to meet with, especially given the hullabaloo surrounding the more recent publications of Moure, which, for Miguélez-Carballeira, show little advance from the second-wave feminism that characterized the work Queizán was publishing more than thirty years ago. For Miguélez-Carballeira, this reception tells less about the quality of Moure's work than about the reluctance of the Galician literary system to face the need to talk about gender ("Inaugurar" 86–87). We might see this reluctance also in the reception of Queizán's 1988 novel *A semellanza*, which was translated into English by Ana María Spitzmesser as *The Likeness*—the only work of Queizán's so far to have appeared in English translation. *A semellanza* was published not by Galaxia or Xerais, like Queizán's previous novels, but by the independent publishing house Sotelo Blanco. This story of a young man's coming to terms with his homosexuality in a hostile society has been reprinted three times yet received little or no critical attention, even from the feminist critics who responded to Queizán's other novels.

The ignoring of *A semellanza* reflects Timothy McGovern's observation that Galician scholars and critics rarely pay attention to homosexual characters and themes in Galician narrative, even when sexuality is key to an understanding of the text (136–37). For McGovern, this silence is attributable to "the reactionary tradition of folding the voices of sexual minorities into a more universal (meaning, of course, heterosexual male) tradition" (136), a tradition that is perhaps even more marked in marginalized cultures. Antón Lopo's 2001 novel *Ganga*, the fictionalized autobiography of an obese, drug-addicted gay man, McGovern sees as "transcending its localized settings to unite with national and international queer literary strategies" (137), but its gay subject matter was rarely acknowledged by Galician critics. The narrative of Xavier Queipo features characters whose lives do not always fit the established norms of sexual identification, but his approach is the opposite of Lopo's. Where Lopo's works have an openly "activist nature" (McGovern 149), the sexuality of Queipo's characters is just another aspect of the complexity of human nature. The sense of difference in Queipo's novels and short stories is located not only in sexuality but also in exotic settings and highly technical scientific vocabulary. The protagonist of *Papaventos* (2001; "Kite") is a bisexual Galician translator living and working in the United States. One finds the same exotic quality in the dystopian *Dragona* (2007) and in the stories of *Ringside* (1993), *O ladrón de esperma* (2002; "The Sperm Thief"), and *Os ciclos de bambú* (2004; "The Bamboo Cycles").

The privileging of the national as an identity marker is clearly a factor behind the marginalization of authors working with and from alternative categories of identity such as gender and sexuality. Countering the dominant perspective with alternative experiences is clearly a vital step in any move toward normalization, but it is equally important that the category of national itself come under scrutiny (Hooper, "New Cartographies"). The universalizing move that can be seen in critical responses to women or queer writers can also be seen in relation to another category of writers who have played a central part in Galicia's self-perception as an inclusive cultural space: the *alófonos*, those for whom Galician is a second language.

As Xesús Alonso Montero has shown, *alofonía* has a long and celebrated history in Galicia (Alonso and Salgado). Perhaps the most celebrated *alófono* is Federico García Lorca, whose *Seis poemas galegos* ("Six Galician Poems") qualify him, according to the *criterio filolóxico* ("language criterion"), as a Galician writer—the criterion considers only literature written in Galician to be part of Galician literature. Today, a small but significant proportion of Galician-language novelists are writing in what is for them a second (or subsequent) language. The prolific writer and journalist Úrsula Heinze de Lorenzo, from Germany, began her literary career with *O soño perdido de Elvira M* (1982; "The Lost Dream of Elvira M.") and followed it with *Anaiansi* (1989) as well as with poetry and children's fiction. *As frechas de ouro* (2004; "The Golden Arrows"), by the Galician-identified British scholar and translator John Rutherford, is a lyrical and often humorous meditation on cultural identity, based on the desire of the narrator, a middle-aged man known only as Eu ("I") to divest himself of his English identity and become Galician (Hooper, "Galicia"). In 2001, the Galician-based Cameroonian journalist and activist Víctor Omgbá published the novel *Calella sen saída* ("Dead-End Street"), about the experiences of an African law student who comes to Spain to continue his studies but finds himself excluded by the system and forced to join Madrid's clandestine migrant society. Eventually he moves north, to Galicia. A collection of short stories, *A idade da auga* (2008; "The Age of Water") by the Scottish writer James R. Salter, was written in English for the Galician market and translated into Galician by four translators. Salter's case complicates the concept of *alofonía*, extending it to include writers who may not themselves work in Galician but whose work appears originally in that language.[3]

While Heinze rarely addresses questions of national identity in her literary prose (as she does in her poetry and journalism), both Rutherford and Omgbá directly confront the question of Galician national identity and its boundaries, focusing in particular on the extent to which identity and national affiliation can be fluid rather than assigned at birth. Interestingly, the works of all three writers are accepted without question into the contemporary Galician canon—by virtue, once again, of the *criterio filológico*. Their foreign origins are noted, approvingly, in reviews and interviews, but the question of ethnicity is largely sidestepped. In other words, the *criterio* authorizes movement into and across Galician cultural boundaries but neutralizes difference within those boundaries. That Heinze, Rutherford, and Omgbá are treated as Galician writers means that their real and productive difference disappears, and with it the opportunity to examine new perspectives on Galician identity.

Marilar Aleixandre, winner of the 2001 Premio Xerais, grew up in Madrid and learned Galician on moving to Santiago as an adult. Her case counters those of Luisa Castro and Marta Rivera: Aleixandre publishes exclusively in Galician and is considered a Galician writer; Castro and Rivera, although both Galician-born native speakers, publish largely in Castilian and are therefore excluded from Galician literature. The debates about Castro's and Rivera's position and the absence of any debate about Aleixandre's demonstrate the extent to which Galician cultural identity is so often channeled through the question of language choice (Hooper, "This Festering Wound").

Women's writing, queer writing, and the writing of *alófonos* reveal the emergence of a new fictional map of Galicia, in which authors and characters reflect its changing demographic and ideological makeup. The cartographic vocabulary I have used to frame this essay is useful as a means of talking about how we view the relation between author and text, nation and culture. But, even more, it helps us see Galician narrative in spatial or geographical terms. It also helps us rethink the contribution to Galician narrative of writers working in the diaspora that is the consequence of Galicia's long history of emigration.

Histories of Galician literature, ever since Eugenio Carré Aldao's in 1911, have included the works of Galicians based in the Americas (esp. Argentina, Brazil, and Cuba)—largely but not always on the basis of language choice. Vestiges of this approach remain today, for example in the reception of the Brazilian-based writer Nélida Piñón, who writes in Portuguese but whose novels are widely read in Galicia, most notably *A república dos sonhos* (1984; "The Republic of Dreams"), an epic tale of Galician migrants in Brazil. The role the Galician diaspora in the Americas plays in the construction of Galician identity has been well studied, most notably by Eugenia Romero in this volume. The very real political stakes involved in debates about this role came to public attention in the 2005 Galician elections (Hooper, "Galicia").

By relocating discussion of diaspora and migration outside the colonial framework and the inevitably tangled linguistic, racial, cultural, and historical ties in which Galician migration to the Americas has taken place, we can begin to remap discussions of Galician culture and identity to include groups who have hitherto fitted only partially into the national cartography. These might include Galicians living elsewhere in the world, such as the small but dynamic group of writers who are, or have been, based in the anglophone world, especially in Great Britain. The founding text in this corpus, which we might call *cultura galegobritánica*, is Carlos Durán's *Galegos de Londres* (1978; "London Galicians"), a novelized account of the experiences of a group of Galician migrants in the British capital that is notable for its lack of sentiment toward either the Galicians themselves or the British society in which they operate. If narrative can function as a means of making sense of the changing world around us, Durán's novel (now out of print and difficult to obtain), with its visceral depiction of chaotic, urban 1970s Britain, provides an essential departure point for understanding the post-1960s wave of economic migration from Galicia.

Twenty-five years later, a new generation of diaspora novelists are writing this experience from the other end, from the point of view of younger migrants traveling not away from but back to their homeland. Both the novel *Os saltimbanquis no paraíso* (1999; "Acrobats in Paradise"), by the Galician-born British-based writer Xelís de Toro, and the collection of short stories *A-Z* (2003), by the British-born, Galician-based Xesús Fraga, shift the focus from the culture shock of arriving in the United Kingdom to the trauma of returning to Galicia. In the process both, like Rutherford in *Frechas de ouro*, open the way for narrating new and dynamic formations of Galician identity that transcend citizenship, ethnic origin, residence, and even language choice.

Narrative in Galicia—or, more properly, Galician-language narrative—is experiencing a period of spectacular change. Most critics and commentators in Galicia consider the healthy development of narrative to be a prerequisite for the long-desired normalization of Galician culture. The perceived connection between a strong national novel and a strong sense of national identity is not unique to Galicia, but as in many minority communities, it has a special power there. However, the emergence of new narrative voices, from formerly marginalized groups such as women, sexual minorities, immigrants, and citizens of the diaspora, demonstrates that the concept of nation itself is—must be—open to question, for it is evident that the long-standing formula of a single, homogeneous national subject with a single national space and a single national culture is no longer adequate. The way we choose to organize or map our readings of Galician narrative, especially now at the start of the twenty-first century, can not only condition but also transform the way we organize our understanding of Galicia.

Notes

1. Besada's book was planned as the first of a multivolume set, but no further volumes ever appeared.
2. *Maxina* was completed in 1870 but not published until a decade later.
3. I am grateful to Helena Miguélez-Carballeira of Bangor University for bringing to my attention the unusual circumstances of the publication of Salter's work.

Further Reading in English

Casares, Carlos. *Wounded Wind.* Trans. Rosa Rutherford. Aberystwyth: Planet, 2004. Print. Trans. of *Vento ferido.*
Castelao, Alfonso Daniel Rodríguez de. *Things.* Trans. Kirsty Hooper, Isabel Mancebo

Portela, Craig Patterson, and Manuel Puga Moruxa. Aberystwyth: Planet, 2001. Print. Trans. of *Cousas*.

Cunqueiro, Álvaro. *Merlin and Company*. Trans. Colin Smith. London: Dent, 1996. Print. Trans. of *Merlín e familia*.

Dunne, Jonathan. "Galician Literature in English Translation." *Small Stations Press*. Smallstations.com, n.d. Web. 23 Jan. 2010.

From the Beginning of the Sea: Anthology of Contemporary Galician Short Stories. Trans. John Rutherford et al. Brighton: Foreign Demand, 2008. Print.

Méndez Ferrín, Xosé Luis. *Them and Other Stories*. Trans. John Rutherford, Xelís de Toro, et al. Aberystwyth: Planet, 1998. Print.

Queizán, María Xosé. *The Likeness*. Trans. Ana María Spitzmesser. Bern: Lang, 1999. Print. Trans. of *A semellanza*.

Rivas, Manuel. *Butterfly's Tongue*. Trans. Margaret Jull Costa and Jonathan Dunne. London: Harvill, 2000. Print. Trans. of *A lingua das bolboretas*. Filmed in 1999, by José Luis Cuerda, as *La lengua de las mariposas*.

——. *The Carpenter's Pencil*. Trans. Jonathan Dunne. London: Harvill, 2001. Print. Trans. of *O lapis do carpinteiro*.

——. *In the Wilderness*. Trans. Jonathan Dunne. London: Vintage, 2004. Print. Trans. of *En salvaxe compaña*.

——. "*Vermeer's Milkmaid*" *and Other Stories*. Trans. Jonathan Dunne and Margaret Jull Costa. London: Harvill, 2002. Print. Includes the stories published as *Butterfly's Tongue*.

Poetry and Performance: The Renewal of the Public Sphere in Present-Day Galicia

Silvia Bermúdez

Poetry, Poetic Performances, and Galicia at the Turn of the Twenty-First Century

What can be the significance of poetry in the difficult times we live in? It appears to have lost its social significance in the late twentieth century, lacking "enough muscle tone for [those] concerned with social justice" (Ronell 17), and, as one critic has observed, it is increasingly seen as "a genre widely [disassociated] from the realities of everyday existence" (Hooper, "New Spaces" 101). Is there, then, any social relevance, any validity, to the practice of poetry in twenty-first-century Galicia?

Poetry may currently appear not to have a direct impact on "the realities of everyday existence," yet it played a paradigmatic role in the consolidation of Galician national identity in literary terms during the nineteenth century (Bermúdez, "Poetry"; Gómez Montero; González Fernández, "Encrucilladas"). Indeed, the cultural process that set in motion the recovery of a Galician national identity from centuries of obscurity—the Rexurdimento—is conventionally considered to have been launched by the publication of a poetic collection entitled *Cantares gallegos* (1863; "Galician Songs"), by Rosalía de Castro (1837–85). The *Cantares gallegos* are not the only foundational poems of Galicia's renaissance; Manuel Curros Enríquez (1851–1908) and Eduardo Pondal (1835–1917) also participated in the validation of a literary language for the Galician nation through their *Aires da miña terra* (1880; "Airs from My Homeland") and *Queixumes dos pinos* (1886; "Sighs of the Pine Trees"), respectively (Vilavedra, *Historia* 126–32, 133–34). The connection between nation and poetry is a well-visited concept in nationalism. It was under the aegis of German Romanticism in the late 1700s and early 1800s that this connection was advanced, and Johann Gottfried Herder proposed to identify poetry as the emblem par excellence of the language of a nation.

A series of essays in the late 1990s highlight poetry's diminished importance in nations such as Spain, the United States, and France (Bermúdez, "Poetry" 123n2),[1] but in present-day Galicia, a vibrant poetic scene has four generations of poets simultaneously participating in the reformulation of their cultural nation (X. Álvarez Cáccamo; González Fernández, "Zapadoras"). One way in which this reformulation is enacted is through poetic performances that bring poets in direct contact with the public, thus allowing it to think and experience its relation to poetry in a most corporeal way. Against the notion that poetry cannot make a vital contribution to the public sphere, these performances contribute to the network of information and ideas used by a society.

I focus on the cultural grassroots organization Redes Escarlata ("Scarlet Webs or Nets") and the poets Antón Lopo (Antonio Rodríguez López) and Ana Romaní as emblems of how this practice of poetry is also a form of social activism. Of the young readers in the early 1990s who became interested in poetry because of its "nationalist vocation," most got acquainted with the genre through the poetic readings—one modality of poetic performance—that took place not only in conventional settings such as university campuses but also in bars and town fairs throughout Galicia (Vilavedra, *Historia* 287).

Poetic performances such as these, and others more interdisciplinary in nature, are of course promoted by poets, the group most invested in defending the validity of poetry in the Galician social context, but they are also supported by the Consello da Cultura Galega, the public institution responsible for promoting Galician culture and whose funds come from the Xunta. One of the most ambitious projects organized by the Consello to date, Translittera Xornadas de Novas Linguaxes Poéticas ("Translittera Workshops on New Poetic Languages") took poetry out of the private sphere of solitary reading and into direct contact with the public. The sessions, between 18 November and 3 December 2005 in five locations throughout Galicia (Santiago, A Coruña, Vigo, Cecebre, and Trasalba) lasted approximately three hours and had a clear objective:

> establecer un espazo referencial de indagación en novas formas de expresión poética partindo de perspectivas creativas diferentes, tentando integrar o factor interdisciplinar que rexe o noso momento histórico e procurar un achegamento entre o público e a poesía máis aló do papel impreso e mediante a interación directa.   ("Translittera")

to establish a referential space for inquiry into new forms of poetic expression from different creative perspectives, trying to integrate the interdisciplinary factor that governs our historical moment and to seek a rapprochement between public and poetry beyond the printed word and through direct interaction.

The Consello's preoccupation with aesthetic concerns—"new forms of poetic expression"—as well as with ethical ones shows how poetry is considered vital to life in Galicia. The Translittera sessions brought together poets and artists from the fields of music, video, plastic arts, theater, and film. In their performances, participants were asked by the Consello to evaluate the idea that transgression expands the limits of poetic expression and the idea that poetry is an act or action that effaces time. Well-established poets such as Lopo and Yolanda Castaño participated alongside newcomers such as María Lado, Lucía Aldao, and those associated with the Web-based group alg-a (www.alg-a.com), such as Nela Que and Roi Fernández. Poetry in performance was conceived as a communicative resource available to Galicians. By calling "special attention to and heightened awareness of the act of expression," it allowed the audience "to regard the act of expression and the performer with special intensity" (Bauman 36). To be regarded with intensity is a main objective of the joint and individual performances of Lopo, Romaní, and Redes Escarlata.

The Consello is not the only Galician public agency promoting poetic expression. The Consellería de Cultura, the Xunta's ministry of culture, supports poetic performances that pay "special attention" to and provide "heightened awareness" of identity issues. An example is the series of poetic performances organized by BOGA (Mulleres Lésbicas e Bisexuais da Galiza ["Lesbian and Bisexual Women of Galicia"]) during the month-long celebration of gay pride that took place in Santiago de Compostela in June 2006. Ten women artists, most of them poets (e.g., Romaní, Lado, Aldao, Chus Pato, María do Cebreiro), participated in performances that had a specific political purpose: "seguir traballando na visibilización e reivindicación dos dereitos do colectivo lésbico, bisexual e transexual" ("Axenda"; "to continue working for the making visible of and vindicating the rights of lesbians, bisexuals, and transsexuals").

In this active poetic landscape the performances of Redes Escarlata, Lopo, and Romaní demonstrate how Galician poetry is not "the path to a transhistorical truth" but "the key to particular historically embedded social and psychological formations" (Gallagher and Greenblatt 7). Indeed, concern with the social and psychological ills of the nation is at the heart of the many poetic performances held by Redes Escarlata throughout Galicia. By making poetry the central weaving pattern of their quest for national self-determination, they "recover cultural nationalism as a strategy of resistance to globalization's push to obliterate cultures and traditions" (Bermúdez, "Poetry" 123).

One issue currently affecting Galicia is the abandonment of entire towns and the disappearance of the traditional way of life this entails.[2] To give voice to this trauma to the social fabric, Redes Escarlata staged a poetic reading in the ghost town of Santalla Vella, in the Val do Lóuzara in June 2004 ("As Redes Escarlata"). As a public act of mourning that used the rhetorical and symbolic powers of elegy, the performance called attention to the wealth of collective heritage lost when towns and villages die. Both in symbol and in language, this performance recognized the concern of many younger and older Galicians. Similar anxieties about Galician culture were expressed by cultural commentators and practitioners in interviews with Kirsty Hooper in 2006. For example, thirty years separate Olegario Sotelo Blanco (b. 1945), the founder of the Sotelo Blanco publishing house and of the Fundación Sotelo Blanco, from Ramón Pinheiro Almuinho (b. 1975), the artistic director of Ouvirmos and professor at the Conservatorio de Música Tradicional e Folque in Lalín, but both told Hooper they felt the loss of Galicia's cultural legacies (Hooper, "Forum").

"A major part of our rich collective heritage has been irrevocably lost," said Pinheiro Almuinho, adding that what "has fortunately been preserved is known only by a tiny percentage of the population" (112). Sotelo Blanco, whose foundation created a museum of anthropology to help Galicians become acquainted with their heritage, calls for the preservation of "everything that is now in danger of disappearing" (113). In the light of these comments, the poetic performance held in Santalla Vella can be seen as part of the ongoing discussion on cultural heritage taking place in Galicia now. It clearly demonstrates how poetry is engaged with the social reality of the nation.

The Renewal of the Galician Public Sphere: Romaní and Lopo

The work of Lopo and Romaní illustrates how modalities of poetic performance connected with theater, music, and photography are used in the creation and dissemination of a Galician cultural nation that recognizes and respects all sexual and gender identities while exploring the function of poetry in the social sphere. Through the Laboratorio de Indagacións Poéticas ("Laboratory of Poetic Inquiries"), which these two poets cofounded in 1997, they have actively worked to produce gender-bending poetic performances such as *Ó outro lado do paraíso* (1997; "The Other Side of Paradise") and *Lob*s* (1999; "Wolv*s"). These, placing poetry, poets, and poetic acts in immediate contact with the public, provide evidence of the possibilities of art to work against intellectual apathy and linear thinking.[3] *A boca aberta* ("The Open Mouth"), a series of poetic performances that took place at dawn on World Poetry Day in Santiago de Compostela in March 2001, prompted the daily newspaper *O correo galego* to note the transgressive nature of the events when discussing the program:

> [É] tamén certamente transgresión o que *A boca aberta*, un espacio coordinado por Ana Romaní e Antón Lopo, propón na primeira madrugada de espectáculos poéticos. ("A boca aberta")

> What *The Open Mouth*, a space coordinated by Ana Romaní and Antón Lopo, proposes for the first early-morning poetic spectacles, is certainly transgression.

Moreover, as openly gay (Lopo) and openly lesbian (Romaní), both poets have critically evaluated, in joint projects and individual performances, how the body comes to embody specific cultural meanings in specific historical contexts. Two joint projects echo Judith Butler's articulation that gender "is an identity tenuously constituted in time—an identity instituted through a *stylized repetition of acts*" (154). It is precisely to these "stylized repetition of acts" that they called attention in the late 1990s in their two gender-bending *espectáculos poéticos* ("poetic spectacles") performed in the Teatro Galán in Santiago de Compostela: *Ó outro lado do paraíso* (1997; "The Other Side of Paradise") and *Lob*s* questioned compulsory heterosexuality by foregrounding gay and lesbian desires. The first critic to call attention to Lopo's and Romaní's queering of the Galician cultural canon, Helena González Fernández established that their *Lob*s* project and the two individual poetic collections that sustain it—Romaní's *Arden* (1998) and Lopo's *Pronomes* (1998)—is the "proxecto máis ambicioso de poesía gai e lesbiana galega" ("Tres argumentos" 89; "most ambitious project of gay and lesbian Galician poetry").

Lob's cannot be understood without first considering how *Arden* and *Pronomes* focus on, as González Fernández states, "repensar criticamente as identidades homosexuais" (89; "critically rethinking homosexual identities"). The project, grounded in the written word and in the aesthetic premises that guide each poet, puts into practice a clear premise: to promote direct communication between literary productions and readers-spectators. This directness invites reflection on how, as Butler puts it, "[g]enders can be neither true nor false, neither real nor apparent" (162). The *Lob*'s booklet makes the point visually and textually. Accompanying the performance, the booklet had on its cover a photographic montage joining and blurring the gender markers in the faces of Romaní and Lopo, clearly the face of a woman and of a man at the starting points.

As processes constituted in time, Romaní's and Lopo's poetic performances follow the specific historical paradigm of the Galician nation in the late twentieth and early twenty-first centuries. Thus we must take into account the language in which they are produced—Galician—and the notion of culture under which they are operating. González Fernández makes clear that their understanding of poetry as an art that can circulate through different media and through collective production allows them to recover

> un concepto de cultura no que esta se converte en campo de experimentación e de reflexión que aporta elementos de discusión para a intervención social.
> ("Tres argumentos" 94)

> a concept of culture in which culture is transformed into a field of experimentation and reflection that contributes elements of discussion for social intervention.

In this sense both Romaní and Lopo partake in what Xoán González-Millán has articulated as the dialogic-dialectic of "nacionalismo literario / literatura nacional" ("Do nacionalismo" and "Nacionalismo y teoría"; "literary nationalism / national literature") for a stateless nation such as Galicia where literature has had to fulfill extraliterary functions. It is in this context that poetry and the poetic performances I evaluate are produced and circulated: a web of complex relations embedded in a national project that is actively defining the notion of *galeguidade*. That *galeguidade* is a social construction requiring constant negotiation (Romero, "Amusement Parks"; Hooper, "Galicia") is not just a theoretical argument in Galicia now; it is an everyday reality—as demonstrated by the discussions that took place in the Seventh Council of Galician Communities held in Santiago de Compostela on 24 and 25 August 2006 to consider amending the *lei de galeguidade* ("Galicianness Act"). First instituted in 1983, this act was being revised so that those living beyond the geographic borders of the nation could be included as part of Galicia's social body ("Días de exame").

Emigration is a well-visited identity marker of Galicianness, and writers from all periods, like Alfredo Brañas, Alfonso Castelao, Vicente Risco, and Antón Risco, have attested to its paradigmatic importance for establishing Galician identity. Ramón Piñeiro emphasizes how Galicia is also constituted by

> outro gran núcleo, cuia importancia non é só númerica senón cualitativa, [que] vive en terras alleas e, polo xeral, distantes. Si prescindíramos deste segundo núcleo, *o corpo social galego quedaría gravemente amputado*. . . .
> (*Olladas no futuro* 83)

> another large group, whose importance is not only numerical but also qualitative, [which] lives in foreign and generally faraway lands. If we were to disregard this second group, the Galician social body would be gravely amputated.

It is in this fluctuating and still contested national project that we need to contextualize the poetic performances of Romaní and Lopo and their questioning of hegemonic modes of defining gender, sexualities, and nationality.

Romaní's Circle of Women Poets

Well-known and praised throughout Galicia for her job as the director of the daily program "Diario Cultural" ("Cultural Daily") for Radio Galega since 1990, Romaní is a cofounder of the feminist journal *Festa da palabra silenciada* ("Celebration of the Silenced Word") and the association Mulleres Galegas na Comunicación ("Galician Women in Media"). She received numerous awards for her work promoting Galician culture, for her commitment to promoting reading, for her contributions to radio journalism, and for her work in promoting theater and audiovisual projects.[4]

She is the author of the poetry collections *Palabras de mar* (1987; "Words of the Sea"), *Das últimas mareas* (1994; "The Last Tides"), *Arden* (1998; "Burn"), the *Antoloxía de Antón Avilés de Taramancos* (2003; "Antón Avilés de Taramancos Anthology"), and *Love Me Tender: 24 pezas mínimas para unha caixa de música* (2005; "Love Me Tender: Twenty-Four Pieces for a Music Box"). *Love Me Tender* was distributed with the 17 November 2005 edition of *El correo gallego* as part of their Poeta en Compostela series, which was created to promote the reading of Galician poetry.[5] She actively participates in artistic ventures that involve music and performance, including "Diario de Princesa" (2002), first posted as seven poems on the Web, all precursors to *Love Me Tender*, to denounce domestic violence. During the performances of "Diario de Princesa," Romaní slowly read the seven poems standing next to a music box that had a tiny ballerina in the center and incessantly played Elvis Presley's "Love Me Tender." Her earlier musical projects include the CD homage to Rosalía de Castro "Daquelas que cantan: Rosalía na palabra de once poetas galegas" ("Those Who Sing: Rosalía in the Words of Eleven Galician Women Poets") and the musical spectacle *Son Delas*, coordinated by the musician Uxía Senlle and featuring the most important female performers of Galician folk music.[6]

Son Delas, created to celebrate International Women's Day in March 2002, reveals one of Romaní's constant poetic concerns, the inscription of a genealogy of women poets in the Galician public sphere. Her participation in *Son Delas* was crucial to the performance since, as Senlle states in the booklet provided during the events:

> A poesía é o fío conductor deste encontro. A voz de Ana Romaní recolle as palabras das outras poetas da súa generación e tamén das devanceiras (Rosalía, María Mariño, Xohana Torres . . .) para situármonos na realidade e nas fontes da literatura de muller en Galicia.

> Poetry is the guiding thread of this encounter. Ana Romaní's voice collects the words of other women poets of her generation and also of the preceding ones (Rosalía, María Mariño, Xohana Torres . . .) to situate us within the reality and the sources of women's literature in Galicia.

Romaní's gender-inflected thinking flourishes in her solo performance "Catro poetas suicidas: Intervención poética contra a levidade" ("Four Suicidal/Suicided Poets: Poetic Intervention against Levity"). Performed in the cities of Santiago de Compostela and A Coruña in April 2002, "Catro poetas suicidas" highlights her commitment to the re-presentation and validation of a genealogy of women poets. The poems and last moments of Russian poet Marina Tsvetaeva (1892–1941), the Portuguese poet Florbela Espanca (1894–1930), and the American poets Anne Sexton (1928–74) and

Sylvia Plath (1932–63) are given voice by Romaní in Galician in an effort to use the power of the spoken word to engage the public. The poet describes her strategy:

> Ante a proposta, o público reacciona cunha sensación de pánico e de impacto, de conmoción, porque se vive a traxedia dunha maneira moi real.
>
> ("Ana Romaní")

> Faced with the proposal, the public reacts with a sense of panic and impact, of shock, because the tragedy is experienced in a very real way.

Her comments on the public's response to "Catro poetas suicidas" highlight the intersubjective processes at work in poetic performances that place individual identity alongside group identification, connecting the private to the public sphere.

The impact of "Catro poetas suicidas" on the public sphere can be better appreciated if we first turn our attention to the private sphere of reading "Camiñan descalzas polas rochas" ("They Walk Barefoot on the Rocks"), one of the first of Romaní's poems to forge symbolic bonds with a community of women poets. Published in *Das últimas mareas,* a poetic collection anchored in epigraphs by the Finnish poet Edith Södergran (1892–1923) and by Emily Dickinson (1830–86), the poem is emblematic of Romaní's commitment to the recuperation of the heritage of women poets who preceded her. The first line is a play on a verse by Södergran:

> Belas irmás, subide
> ás máis firmes rochas.
> —Edith Södergran

> Camiñan descalzas polas rochas,
> pantasmas de sal habitan as sombras,
> saben que as últimas mareas
> esqueceron na praia os restos do naufraxio.
> as mulleres recollen cada noite
> os tesouros de auga, líquidos e fráxiles,
> rebélanse contra a Historia,
> constrúen co mar as estatuas
> que nunca permanezan.
> As mulleres de sal, con argazos de sombras,
> xorden das últimas mareas

e tecen tesouros de auga cada noite
contra a Historia.
Elas, que saben que o efémero permanece.   (51)

Beautiful sisters, climb up
the firmest rocks.
—Edith Södergran

They walk barefoot on the rocks,
ghosts of salt inhabit the shadows,
they know that the last tides
forgot the remains of the shipwreck on the beach.
The women collect each night
the treasures of water, liquid and fragile,
they rebel against History,
building with seawater the statues
that may never remain.
The women of salt, with shadows of seaweed,
emerge from the last tides
and weave treasures of water each night
against History.
They, who know that the ephemeral remains (my trans.)

Clearly intending to write a herstory, the poem is sustained by an oceanic imagery that pays homage to women and the sea and draws the reader into a communal understanding of production, where women "weave treasures of water each night." In the marine landscape painted by Romaní, women creatively elaborate a sisterhood sustained by the collaborative production of countermemories—"they rebel against History"—that balance out the hegemonic and homogeneous tendencies of the metanarratives of history (Bermúdez, "*Festa*" 40). Committed to intervening in the literary discourses that obscure or obliterate women poets, Romaní has made a point of recovering for Galician culture the works of women poets from around the world and from other historical moments. She enriches the symbolic capital of Galician culture by expanding its poetic and social horizons. This is nowhere more evident than in her "Catro poetas suicidas," an epitaphic performance that haunts the audience with her enactment of life, language, and death.

Described in *O correo galego* as "a recital poético con elementos de narración oral que reclama a palabra para a traxedia en tempos de levidades, espellismos e máscaras" ("Romaní leva"; "a poetic recital with elements of oral narration that demands the use of the word for tragedy in times of lightness, illusions, and masks"), the performance lasted forty minutes and was based on the reading aloud by Romaní of the poems of Tsvetaeva, Espanca, Sexton, and Plath. Such reading asks us to consider what happens to poems when they move from writing to speech and then "into silence at the end of the reading, as all performances must" (Middleton 341). The answer, according to Peter Middleton, is that written poems, when performed in poetry readings, provide a multidimensional experience that cannot be re-created even in the most imaginative mental theater (345). Enriched by their oral circulation, the poems by Tsvetaeva, Espanca, Sexton, and Plath help Romaní disseminate the legacy of the community of women poets who have preceded her in a manner that her "Camiñan descalzas polas rochas," for all its metaphoric radiance, cannot.

Romaní's poem remains in the sphere of private reading, whereas the public reading of the poems of the four poets who committed violence against themselves represents a collective effort that has an impact on the social sphere in its temporal ephemerality. Romaní recognizes that the reading of poetry is a private affair, but she is committed to making it a public matter also, and that is why she produces poetry that can be performed, that circulates on the Web, or is distributed in the daily press. Her *Love Me Tender* attests to this endeavor: the collection was first posted on the Web, then performed with a music box—media allowing the poems to circulate more freely in the social sphere. But by having the book format be part of the Poeta en Compostela series, she further contributed to making the poems accessible to the public. This representational metamorphosis underscores that for Romaní, poetry, in the words of Jerome McGann, "is itself one form of social activity," with the ability to influence people who will resist and even transform existing structures of power (21).

Lopo's Bodily Investigation of Identity

A translator, video artist, and the coordinator of the section "Revista das letras" for *O correo galego*, Antón Lopo is a well-known cultural figure for his cutting-edge performances and highly acclaimed literary productions in all genres. The author of openly gay poetic collections such as *Sucios e desexados* (1987; "Dirty and Desired"), *Manual de masoquistas* (1990; "Masochists' Manual"), *Pronomes* (1998; "Pronouns"), and *Fálame* (2003; "Talk to Me") is also a critically acclaimed novelist—*Ganga* (2001)—and a playwright. His play *Os homes só contan até tres* (2004; "Men Only Count to Three") was awarded Galicia's prestigious Álvaro Cunqueiro Prize. Like Romaní, Lopo published in the Poeta en Compostela series, where his *Libro dos amados* was distributed with the 7 April 2005 edition. His biography *As tres mortes de Lorenzo Varela* (2005; "The Three Deaths of Lorenzo Varela") received much critical praise, as have his many performances, among which is the presentation of the oral poem "Prestidixitador" in the Teatro Galán on 26 January 2001 and the performance *O lugar* ("The Place"), which entailed his measuring the old part of the city of Santiago by using his own body as the measurement tool. Lopo explained the performance:

> "O lugar" consistía en medir a cidade (aproximadamente o perímetro urbano do casco vello) a partir do meu tamaño. É dicir: eu íame tumbando no chan (ao estilo dos peregrinos budistas) e cunha tiza sinalaba o meu tamaño no chan. Logo, poñíame onde estaba a marca e repetía a operación. Así até 985 veces.   (Message)

> *The Place* consisted of measuring the city (approximately the urban perimeter of the old town) in terms of my own size. That is to say: I would lie down on the ground (in the style of the Buddhist pilgrims) and, with a piece of chalk, mark out my size on the ground. Then I placed myself where the mark was and repeated the procedure. And so on, 985 times.

By lying down in the streets of Santiago, he literally and metaphorically called attention to the urban space he inhabited to both revere—in monk-like fashion—and undermine the established discourses about the city of Santiago, another central emblem of Galicianness.

O lugar, with its insistence on the physicality of the performer's body and of the body of the city, got the attention of everyone who crossed Lopo's path. But *O lugar* pales in comparison with what Lopo does in *Dentro* ("Inside"), which opened 19 May 2006 at the Casa da Parra in Santiago de Compostela. The exhibition of the installations had to be extended after Lopo, along with the artist Iván Prado, carried through the old town of Santiago his *O ceo a costas* ("The Sky on One's Back"), one of the two performances that supported *Dentro*. There were three spaces, the first serving as an introduction to the other two, presenting the material that documented the four years that *Dentro* was in the making. The second space exhibited the photographic and verbal results of the project. In the third, with an installation specifically constructed for the Casa da Parra, the public got to experience, by walking barefoot, the thick grass (*herbal* is the Galician term) that is the centerpiece of *Dentro*.

A controversial and complex production, *Dentro* originated in Ulloa, a place to which Lopo feels particularly close. It is here that we find Portocarreiro, where the *herbal* is located and in homage to which Lopo formulated his "Hipótese de Portocarreiro" ("The Portocarreiro Hypothesis") to investigate the nonverbal marks left in the grass by those writing poems with their bodies or other objects. Sixteen people accompanied him to Ulloa during the years the project was in the making, and all were photographed by him as they inscribed themselves as signs in the thick grass of Portocarreiro.[7]

As becomes apparent in the second space of the installation, photography is pivotal to the project, but the core of the project is poetry. As Lopo explains, *Dentro* is "unha exploración sobre o carácter literario da poesía iniciada a finais dos anos noventa" ("A lux"; "an exploration of the literary nature of poetry initiated at the end of the nineties"). His relentless investigation of different artistic avenues and other media has not separated him from his continuous reflection on poetry and its possibilities for transforming the social sphere. This point was made in the newspaper *Galicia hoxe* when the number of people who visited the installations was discussed:

> Case tres mil persoas visitaron a mostra, realizada a partir dunha proposta onde as sensacións se mesturan a través de tres instalacións arrincadas á poesía, elemento básico do traballo de Lopo.   ("Unha performance")

> Almost three thousand people visited the exhibition, which originated from a proposal where sensations are combined through three installations snatched from poetry, the basic element of Lopo's work.

O ceo a costas is a performance that literally and metaphorically reflects and refers to social experience. The imposing Cathedral of Santiago de Compostela reflects and weighs on the mirror held by Lopo; it also radiates with its ability to convey the corporeality and vitality of bodies.

The weight of Galician history, symbolized here by the reflection of the cathedral in the mirror carried by Lopo and Iván Prado, is, once again, literally and metaphorically shouldered in a representation that serves as a "metáfora sobre a realidade e os límites da liberdade, sobre as tradicións sociais e as partículas de resignación emocional" ("Antón Lopo"; "metaphor about reality and the limits of freedom, about social traditions and the particles of emotional resignation"). By walking through the streets carrying a mirror that both reflects the city and weighs on the artists, Lopo turns the ancient streets of Santiago into a stage for the exercise of critical thinking and critical play about social traditions and how resigned we have become to them. Ultimately, by making a collage of the multiple ways of understanding the city, the multiple ways of understanding poetry, Lopo makes *Dentro* a collaborative project that has an impact on the public sphere by showing possible paths for Galicia and for being Galician in the twenty-first century.

Redes Escarlata, Romaní, and Lopo are all engaged in transformative practices that recognize difference as a fundamental aspect of identity issues in Galicia, that recognize the tension between identification with Galicianness and separation from oppressive and restrictive manifestations of Galicianness. Through their poetic performances, Romaní and Lopo establish an active ideological terrain in which alternative Galician experiences can be poetically narrated, experiences that bend gender and social categories and recognize that there are many ways of being Galician. Moreover, it is through their specific cultural interventions that this genre has become an integral part of the public processes by which Galicia is allowing new civic identities to emerge. Judging by the success of their poetic performances, Romaní and Lopo have made poetry an effective means of carrying out such an enterprise—not only because of the symbolic links attached to lyric production but also, and more important, because Romaní and Lopo insist on taking the practice of poetry out of its private space and into the streets.

Notes

I would like to thank Gabriel Rei-Doval for his helpful feedback on this essay.
1. Campana shows how poetry has always been pressed to "apologize" and state its value and validity (33).
2. The gradual abandonment of small towns and villages is one of Galicia's current demographic problems. The number of uninhabited locations in early 2009 rose to 1,337, which means that between 2008 and 2009, Galicia lost 76 villages. A low birth rate and an aging population are contributing factors in the present situation ("Galicia perdió"). Let us not forget that dislocation, in the form of emigration to other regions of Spain and to and from the Americas since the mid-1800s, is a defining characteristic of Galicianness. Galician authors from all periods consider dislocation a central element of Galicia's modern identity.

3. The Laboratorio produced Romaní's individual performance "Catro poetas suicidas" and Lopo's oral poem "Prestixigitador," both in 2001.

4. Romaní was awarded the I Premio Irmandade do Libro (1992; the first "Brotherhood of the Book Prize"), the Premio Xerais á Cooperación no Eido Cultural (1999; "The Xerais Prize for Cooperation in the Cultural Field"), and the Premio San Martiño á Normalización Lingüística e Cultural (2002; "San Martiño Prize for Linguistic and Cultural Normalization"). In 2007 she received the Premio da Asociación de Escritores en Lingua Galega ("The Galician Language Writers' Association Award") and, at the state level, the Premio al Fomento de la Lectura en la Modalidad de Radio de la Federación de Gremio de Editores de España ("Prize for Promoting Reading through Radio by the Spanish Publishers Guild"). The Catalan Publishers Guild also recognized her in 2008 with the Premio Atlántida a la Periodista Radiofónica ("The Atlántida Prize for Radio Journalism"). In 2009 the board of directors of the Asociación de Actores y Actrices de Galicia (AAAG; "Association of Actors and Actresses of Galicia") granted her the honorary Marisa Soto Award at the XIII Premios de Teatro María Casares ("María Casares Theater Awards").

5. This series was a joint venture of the Grupo Correo Gallego, the Consellería da Cultura Galega de Santiago de Compostela, and the Asociación de Escritores en Lingua Galega. On roughly one Thursday a month, *El correo gallego* included with its daily edition a poetry collection that could be purchased for one euro. Twenty collections were published between January 2005 and June 2006. Among the poets published in the series were Manuel María, Salvador García-Bodaño, Xesús Rábade, María do Cebreiro, Rafa Villar, María Lado, and Helena Villar. See "Un ano."

6. *Son Delas* has a double meaning that cannot be easily captured either in Spanish or in English. The Galician term *son* simultaneously refers to "sound" and the verb "to be." *Delas*, a play on the possessive *de elas* ("of them, belonging to them"), further complicates matters. The performers were Uxía Senlle, Mercedes Peón, María Manuela, Susana Seivane, Rosa Cedrón, Guadi Galego, Sonia Lebedynski, and Uxía Pedreira. *Son Delas* was performed in Vigo (7 Apr. 2002), Santiago de Compostela (8 Mar. 2002), Lugo (9 Apr. 2002), and A Coruña (11 Apr. 2002).

7. The people involved in the project were Manolo Martínez, Chus Pato, Caetano Díaz, Cristina Varela, María Salvado, Iván Prado, Xabier Cordal, Antón Dobao, Sesé Vila, Braulio Vilariño, Mónica Góñez, Nacho Muñoz, Braulio Vilariño, Brais Fernández, Xosé Perozo, and Margarita Fernández.

Further Reading

Blanco, Carmen. *Literatura galega de muller*. Vigo: Xerais, 1991. Print.

Carlson, Marvin. "What Is Performance?" *The Performance Studies Reader*. Ed. Henry Bial. New York: Routledge, 2004. 68–73. Print.

González Fernández, Helena. "Literatura gallega de muller, unha visión sistémica." *Anuario de Estudios Galegos* 1999 (2001): 41–67. Print.

González-Millán, Xoán. *Resistencia cultural e diferencia histórica: A experiencia da subalternidade*. Santiago de Compostela: Sotelo Blanco, 2000. Print.

McGovern, Timothy. "Expressing Desire, Expressing Death: Antón Lopo's *Pronomes* and Queer Galician Poetry." *Journal of Spanish Cultural Studies* 7.2 (2006): 135–53. Print.

Tarrío, Anxo. *Literatura galega: Aportacións a unha historia crítica*. Vigo: Xerais, 1994. Print.

Vilavedra, Dolores. *Diccionario da literatura Galega*. 4 vols. Vigo: Galaxia, 1995–2004. Print.

Arquivo da Emigración Galega
Galician Emigration Archive. Set up by the Section for Galician Culture Overseas in 1992, the archive is now part of the Consello da Cultura Galega. It is responsible for collecting material pertaining to Galicia's long history of emigration and promoting research into Galician emigration.
www.consellodacultura.org/arquivos/aeg/

BNG / Bloque Nacionalista Galego
The coalition of Galician nationalist political parties. It was part of the coalition government with PSdeG between 2004 and 2009, during which time the BNG national spokesman Anxo Quintana was vice president of the Xunta.
www.bng-galiza.org

Consellería de Cultura e Turismo
A Galician government department overseeing culture and tourism.
culturae turismo.xunta.es/

Consello da Cultura Galega
Galician Culture Council. This government body, set up in 1983 to defend and promote the cultural values of the Galician people, oversees and funds cultural events, research, and other activities. It hosts archives, including the Galician Emigration Archive, the Galician Sound Archive, and the Galician Center for Sociolinguistic Documentation.
consellodacultura.org/

Estatuto de Autonomía de Galicia
Galician Statute of Autonomy. The first statute was approved by referendum in 1936, but the outbreak of civil war prevented its ratification. The current statute was ratified on 6 April 1981. It is the document that sets out the institutional basis of Galicia's self-government within the framework of Spanish constitutional democracy.
www.xunta.es/estatuto

galeguidade
What it means to be Galician—literally, "Galicianness"

galeguismo
    Love for Galicia, based on the defense and promotion of the cultural, political, and social aspects of Galician national identity; political doctrine based on these principles; literally, "Galicianism." The word can also be used to describe a linguistic feature of Galician, especially where it appears as a borrowing in another language.

galeguista
    Adjective related to *galeguismo*; A *galeguista* is an adherent to the doctrine of *galeguismo*, one who loves and defends Galicia, often in a political context.

normalización
    Normalization. Term borrowed from linguistics, referring to the process whereby a given language becomes the normal vehicle of communication. In cultural terms, *normalization* is used to refer to the development of Galician culture from a fragmented minority culture to a fully realized cultural system.

PP [de G] / Partido Popular [de Galicia]
    Nationwide Spanish center-right political party, in power under José María Aznar between 1996 and 2004. Its Galician branch was in power under Manuel Fraga between 1989 and 2004.
    www.ppdegalicia.com/

PSdeG-PSOE / Partido dos Socialistas de Galicia
    Statewide social-democratic political party, in power under José Luis Rodríguez Zapatero since 2004. Its Galician branch was part of a coalition government with BNG between 2004 and 2009, during which time the PSdeG General Secretary Emilio Pérez Touriño was president of the Xunta.
    www.psdeg-psoe.org/

RAG / Real Academia Galega
    Galician Royal Academy. Founded in 1906, it promotes the study of Galician language and culture and oversees the development and standardization of the Galician language. Its seat is in A Coruña.
    www.realacademiagalega.org

Rexurdimento
    Renaissance. The Rexurdimento, a Galician cultural revival, took place in the second half of the nineteenth century. It is analogous to the Catalan Renaixença.

Xunta de Galicia
    The Galician government. It is made up of president, vice presidents, and councillors (*conselleiros*), and its seat is in Santiago de Compostela.
    www.xunta.es

Burghard Baltrusch is a lecturer in Portuguese studies at the University of Vigo and coordinates the PhD program there in translation and para-translation studies. His publications include articles and book chapters on Portuguese literature, Galician literature, postmodernism, and translation studies.

Silvia Bermúdez is professor of Iberian and Latin American studies at the University of California, Santa Barbara. She has published on contemporary Peruvian, Spanish, and Galician culture and literature. She coedited *Spanish Popular Music Studies* (2009) and edited *Constitutional Spain: Democracy and Culture, 1978–2008* (2010). Her "Rocking the Boat: Immigration and the Imagination of Race in Contemporary Spanish Music" is forthcoming.

Jaine Beswick is program leader for Portuguese studies and lecturer in linguistics with specializations in Spanish, Galician, and Portuguese at the University of Southampton. She is author of *Regional Nationalism in Spain: Language Use and Ethnic Identity in Galicia* (2007) and "*Linguistic Ideologies in Institutional Settings: The Pronunciation of Galician in Radio Broadcasts*" (2010) and coeditor of *Portuguese-Speaking Diaspora in Great Britain and Ireland* (2010).

José Colmeiro holds the Prince of Asturias Chair in Spanish studies at the University of Auckland. He has published extensively on Hispanic cultural studies. Two of his recent works are Silvia Mistral's *Éxodo: Diario de una refugiada española* (2009) and *Galeg@s sen fronteiras: Conversas sobre a cultura galega no Século XXI.*

Lourenzo Fernández Prieto is professor of contemporary history at the Universidade de Santiago de Compostela. He served on boards for the Council of Galician Universities, the Council of the Universidade de Santiago de Compostela, the Spanish Society for Agrarian History, and the *Revista de historia agraria*. He is coordinating a project that examines the Francoist repression in Galicia during and after the civil war (www .nomesevoces.net).

Antón Figueroa teaches French literature at the Universidade de Santiago de Compostela and studies the formation, problems, and relations of the Galician literary field. He is author of *Diglosia e texto* (1988), *Lecturas alleas* (1996), and *Nacion, literatura, identidade* (2001). With Xoán González-Millán, he wrote *Communication littéraire et culture en Galice* (1997).

Joseba Gabilondo, associate professor in the Department of Spanish and Portuguese, Michigan State University, has published articles on Hollywood cinema, Spanish nationalism, postnationalism, masculinity, and queer theory. He is author, in Basque, of *Remnants of the Nation: Prolegomena to a Postnational History of Contemporary Basque Culture* (2006).

Kirsty Hooper lectures in Spanish and Galician at the University of Liverpool. She is author of *A Stranger in My Own Land: Sofía Casanova, a Spanish Voice in the European Fin de Siècle* (2008) and *Writing Galicia into the World: New Cartographies, New Poetics*. She edited *Notes on Contemporary Galician Studies: New Spaces, New Voices* (2006) and coedited *Reading Iberia: Theory, History, Identity* (2007).

Laura López Fernández is senior lecturer in Spanish at the University of Canterbury, Christchurch, New Zealand. She is coordinator of *Julio Campal Experimental Poetry Collection* and is working on launching a scholarly journal dedicated to visual poetry. She is author of *Form and Perception in Visual Poetry* (2008).

Timothy McGovern (1965–2006) was associate professor of Spanish and Portuguese at the University of California, Santa Barbara. He wrote *Dickens in Galdós* (2000), *Using Portuguese* (2003), and *Galdós beyond Realism* (2004).

Marta Pérez Pereiro is assistant professor of communication sciences at the Universidade de Santiago de Compostela. She worked as a researcher for the communication section of the Consello da Cultura Galega.

Manuel Puga Moruxa teaches translation studies at the University of Vigo. He is coauthor of *Dicionario de dúblidas da lingua galega* and *Nivel Soleira* and is preparing a monograph on translation theory.

María do Cebreiro Rábade Villar teaches literary theory at the Universidade de Santiago de Compostela. She is author of *As antoloxías de poesía en Galicia e Cataluña* (2004) and *As terceiras mulleres* (2005) and coauthor, with Fernando Cabo Aseguinolaza, of *Manual de teoría de la literatura* (2006).

María Reimóndez is a feminist translator, scholar, writer, and activist. She is working on her PhD dissertation, "Translation of Feminist and Postcolonial Texts: An Empiric Approach to Ideology." She has written poetry and novels for adults and children. A development worker since 1994, she founded and is the president of the NGO Implicadas no Desenvolvemento (www.implicadas.com).

Eugenia R. Romero is assistant professor of Spanish literatures and cultures at Ohio State University. She is author of articles about Galicia, on topics ranging from amusement parks and cemeteries to popular music to emigration. Her book "Movement, Space, and Identity: Global Considerations of Galician Contemporary Literature and Culture" is forthcoming.

John Patrick Thompson is associate professor of Spanish at Montana State University. He is author of *As novelas da memoria: Trauma e representación da historia na Galiza contemporánea* (2009), which explores memory of the Second Republic and the trauma caused by fascism through Galizan novels, contemporary politics, and a variety of theoretical fields.

Abuín de Tembra, Avelino. "Carta galega a Ferro Ruibal." *O correo galego* 24 Oct. 1999: 4. Print.

Actas do Congreso Internacional de Estudios sobre Rosalía de Castro e o seu tempo. 3 vols. Santiago de Compostela: Consello da Cultura Galega; U de Santiago de Compostela, 1986. Print.

Acuña, Xoán. *Chano Piñeiro: Unha historia do cinema galego.* Vigo: Cumio, 1999. Print.

Adorno, Theodor W. *Aesthetic Theory.* 1970. Ed. Gretel Adorno and Rolf Tiedemann. Trans. C. Lenhardt. London: Routledge, 1984. Print.

"Aínda nos queda Portugal." Editorial. *Tempos novos* 8 Jan. 1998: 4. Print.

Albornoz, Aurora de. "Rosalía de Castro, en los inicios del modernismo hispánico." *Actas do Congreso Internacional* 3: 235–44. Print.

Alcalá, Xavier. "Ortografía sensata." *El mundo* [Galicia] 22 Sept. 1999: 2. Print.

———. "Portuñol." *El mundo* [Galicia] 6 Oct. 1999: 2. Print.

Alonso, Fran. *Momentos terribles.* Centro de Documentación da Asociación de Escritores en Lingua Galega, n.d. Web. 1 Nov. 2009.

———. "A viaxe astral de Antón Lopo." *Xerais Online* 43 (2002). Xerais Online, n.d. Oct. 2009. Web. 25 June 2010.

Alonso Montero, Xesús. *Informe(s) sobre a lingua galega (presente e pasado).* Vilaboa: Cumio, 1991. Print.

Alonso Montero, Xesús, and José M. Salgado, eds. *Poetas alófonos en Lingua Galega: Actas do I Congreso: Santiago de Compostela, abril de 1993.* Vigo: Galaxia, 1994. Print.

Alonso Seoane, María José. "Ironía y sátira en *Ruinas.*" *Actas do Congreso Internacional* 2: 419–27.

Álvarez Blanco, Rosario. Personal interview by John Patrick Thompson. 21 Sept. 2004. Interview.

Álvarez Blanco, Rosario, Francisco Fernández Rei, and Antón Santamarina, eds. *A lingua galega: Historia e actualidade: Actas do I Congreso Internacional 16–20 de setembro de 1996.* Santiago de Compostela: Instituto da Lingua Galega; Consello da Cultura Galega, 2004. Print.

Álvarez Cáccamo, Celso. "Cara unha caracterización da diglósia galega: História e presente dunha dominación lingüística." *Grial* 79 (1983): 23–42. Print.

Álvarez Cáccamo, Xosé Maria. "25 anos de poesía galega: A conversa interxeracional." *A nosa terra* 29 (2003): 15–17. Print.

"Ana Romaní esculca na vida de catro poetas suicidas nun recital." *O correo galego* 15 Apr. 2002: 31. Print.

Anderson, Benedict. *Imagined Communities: Reflections on the Origin and Spread of Nationalism*. London: Verso, 1983. Print.

Aneiros, Rosa. "Contra o minifundismo cultural." *Tempos novos* 104 (2006): 65–67. Print.

Ang, Ien. *Watching Dallas: Soap Opera and the Melodramatic Imagination*. Trans. Della Couling. London: Routledge, 1985. Print.

Angueira Viturro, Anxo. "Bretaña Esmeraldina e o sistema literario galego." Diss. U de Vigo, 2006. Print.

"Un ano de poetas en Compostela." *Compostelacultura.org*. Concello de Santiago de Compostela, 15 Dec. 2005. Web. 1 Nov. 2009.

"Antón Lopo y Prado callejearon 'Co ceo á costas' por Compostela." *El correo gallego*. Grupo Correo Gallego, 16 June 2006. Web. 27 Oct. 2009.

Appadurai, Arjun. *Modernity at Large: Cultural Dimensions of Globalization*. Delhi: Oxford UP, 1997. Print.

Apter, Emily. *The Translation Zone: A New Comparative Literature*. Princeton: Princeton UP, 2006. Print.

Aranzadi, Juan, Jon Juaristi, and Patxo Unzueta. *Auto de terminación: Raza, nación y violencia en el País Vasco*. Madrid: El País; Aguilar, 1994. Print.

Armas Quintá, Francisco J. "Os galegos de Guildford: Unha aproximación dende a xeografía cultural." *Scripta nova: Revista electrónica de geografía y ciencias sociales* 94 (2001): n. pag. Web. 27 Oct. 2009.

Arquivo da emigración galega. Home page. Consello da Cultura Galega, n.d. Web. 27 Oct. 2009.

"O audiovisual agora: Pintan ouros." *Vieiros*. Vieiros, 11 Nov. 2002. Web. 27 Oct. 2009.

"Audiovisual galego, as cifras." *Vieiros*. Vieiros, 12 Nov. 2002. Web. 27 Oct. 2009.

"El audiovisual gallego, el primero en contar con su particular enciclopedia de todas las películas rodadas en Galicia." *Lukor*. Lexur, 1 June 2005. Web. 27 Oct. 2009.

Auslander, Philip, ed. *Performance: Critical Concepts in Literary and Cultural Studies*. 3 vols. New York: Routledge, 2003. Print.

"Axenda: Venres, 30 de xuño de 2006." *Compostela Cultura*. Concello de Santiago, 30 June 2006. Web. 27 Oct. 2009.

Baltrusch, Burghard. "Estéticas en combate: Apontamentos acerca dun cambio cultural e buscas de identidade na literatura galega contemporánea." *Anuario de estudos literarios galegos 1994* (1995): 117–40. Print.

———. "Galiza e lusofonía: Unha tradución entre e miraxe e a utopía." *Galicia 21* 1 (2009): 4–19. Print.

———. "Sein und Zeit des galicischen Odysseus: Suso de Toros *Tic Tac*." *Galicienmagazin* 17 (2006): 22–33. Print.

———. "Teoría e práctica sincrónica da retranca a partir do refraneiro e da literatura galega vangardista." *Anuario de estudios literarios galegos 1998* (1999): 117–40. Print.

Bal y Gay, Jesús. "O momento actual da música galega." *Nós* 29 (1926): 2–4. Print.

Bammer, Angelika. Editorial. *The Question of "Home."* Spec. issue of *New Formations* 17 (1992): vii–xi. Print.

Barreiro Fernández, Xosé Ramón, et al. *Historia de Galicia*. Coruña: Frente Cultural da A. N. P. G., 1979. Print.

Barth, Frederik, ed. *Ethnic Groups and Boundaries: The Social Organisation of Cultural Difference*. Oslo: Universiteforlaget, 1969. Print.

Barthes, Roland. *Camera Lucida: Reflections on Photography*. Trans. Richard Howard. New York: Farrar, 2000. Print.

Basch, Linda, Nina Glick Schiller, and Cristina Szanton. *Nations Unbound: Transnational Projects, Postcolonial Predicaments, and Deterritorialized Nation-States*. Amsterdam: Gordon, 1994. Print.

Bases prá unificación das normas lingüísticas do galego. Santiago de Compostela: Universidade, 1977. Print.

Bauman, Richard. "Verbal Art as Performance." Auslander 3: 32–60.

Beiras Torrado, Xosé Manuel. *O atraso económico de Galicia*. Vigo: Galaxia, 1973. Print.

Benjamin, Walter. "On the Concept of History." *Walter Benjamin: Selected Writings, 1938–1940*. Ed. Howard Eiland and Michael W. Jennings. Cambridge: Harvard UP, 2003. 389–400. Print.

Bennett, Tony. "Putting Policy into Cultural Studies." During, *Cultural Studies Reader* 480–91.

Beramendi, Xusto. *De provincia a nación*. Vigo: Xerais, 2008. Print.

Bermejo Barrera, José C., et al. *Concepcións espaciais e estratexias territoriais na historia de Galicia*. Santiago de Compostela: Asociación Galega de Historiadores, 1993. Print.

———. *Historia de Galiza*. Trans. Xosé Ramón Fandiño Veiga. Madrid: Alhambra, 1980. Print.

Bermúdez, Silvia. "*Festa da Palabra* y el canon literario gallego contemporáneo: La labor (des)mitificadora de Chus Pato y Ana Romaní." *Letras galegas en Deusto: Dez anos de estudios galegos, 1991–2001*. Ed. María Luz Suárez and Isabel Seoane. Bilbao: Cátedra de Estudios Galegos, U de Deusto, 2001. 33–44. Print.

———. "Poetry on the World Wide Web: The www.redesescarlatas.org and the Weaving of a 'New' Public Sphere in Twenty-First-Century Galicia." *Journal of Spanish Cultural Studies* 7.2 (2006): 123–33. Print.

Besada, Augusto G. *Historia crítica de la literatura gallega: Edad Antigua*. Vol. 1, pt. 1. La Coruña: La Voz de Galicia, 1887. Print.

Beswick, Jaine. "The Portuguese Diaspora in Jersey." *The Consequences of Mobility: Linguistic and Sociocultural Contact Zones*. Ed. Bent Preisler, Anne Fabricius, Hartmut Haberland, Susanne Kjaerbeck, and Karen Risager. Roskilde: Roskilde U, 2006. 93–105. Print.

———. *Regional Nationalism in Spain: Language Use and Ethnic Identity in Galicia*. Clevedon: Multilingual Matters, 2007. Print.

Bhabha, Homi, ed. *Nation and Narration*. London: Routledge, 1990. Print.

———. "The Postcolonial and the Postmodern." During, *Cultural Studies Reader* 189–208.

Blanco, Carmen. *Libros de mulleres: Para unha bibliografía de escritoras en lingua galega, 1863–1992*. Vigo: Cumio, 1993. Print.

"A boca aberta." *O correo galego* 23 Mar. 2001: 30. Print.

Bourdieu, Pierre. "Le champ littéraire." *Actes de la recherche en sciences sociales* 89 (1991): 3–46. Print.

———. *Choses dites.* Paris: Minuit, 1987. Print.

———. *Les règles de l'art.* Paris: Seuil, 1992. Print.

———. *The Rules of Art: Genesis and Structure of the Literary Field.* Trans. Susan Emanuel. Stanford: Stanford UP, 1996. Print.

Bourne Taylor, Jenny. "Re: Locations—from Bradford to Brighton." Spec. issue of *New Formations* 17 (1992): 86–94. Print.

Bouzada Fernández, Xan, and Lois Rodríguez Andrade. "Entre o territorio e os públicos." *Grial* 168 (2005): 17–25. Print.

Braxe, Lino. *Territorio: Poemas obxecto e visuais.* A Coruña: Espiral Maior, 1999. Print.

Brennan, Timothy. "The National Longing for Form." Bhabha, *Nation* 44–70.

Butler, Judith. "Performative Acts and Gender Constitution: An Essay in Phenomenology and Feminist Theory." *The Performance Studies Reader.* Ed. Henry Bial. Routledge: New York, 2004. 154–66. Print.

Cabana, Ana. "Entre a resistencia e a adaptación: A sociedade rural galega no franquismo, 1936–1960." Diss. U de Santiago de Compostela, 2006. Print.

"Cadro de mando do sector audiovisual galego." *Observatorio audiovisual galego.* Xunta de Galicia, n.d. Web. 27 Oct. 2009.

Cagiao Vila, Pilar, and Teresa García Domínguez. *Muller e emigración.* Santiago de Compostela: Xunta de Galicia, 1997. Print.

Calaza, Juan José. "La RAG, los lusistas y la voluntad popular." *La voz de Galicia* 8 Nov. 2001: 10. Print.

Camba Bouzas, Santiago. "Saúdo do secretario Xeral." *Secretaria Xeral da Emigración.* Xunta de Galicia, May 2009. Web. 25 June 2010.

Campana, Joseph. "On Not Defending Poetry: Spenser, Suffering, and the Energy of Affect." *PMLA* 120.1 (2005): 33–48. Print.

Caneda Cabrera, María Teresa. "Quen lle ten medo a James Joyce? Reflexións en torno á inminente tradución galega de *Ulysses.*" *Viceversa: Revista galega de traducción* 12 (2006): 79–91. Print.

Capeáns, Juan. "Os escritores portugueses e galegos reclaman acción editoriais conxuntas." *La voz de Galicia* 14 Dec. 2000: 24. Print.

Carballo Calero, Ricardo. *Historia da literatura galega contemporánea.* 1974. 2nd ed. Vigo: Galaxia, 1975. Print.

Cardwell, Richard. "Rosalía de Castro, ¿Precursora de 'los modernos'?" *Actas do Congreso Internacional* 2: 439–60.

Carmona Badía, Joám. *El atraso industrial de Galicia: Auge y liquidación de las manufacturas textiles, 1750–1900.* Barcelona: Ariel, 1990. Print.

Carmona Badía, Xoán, and Jordi Nadal. *El empeño industrial de Galicia: 250 años de historia, 1750–2000.* A Coruña: Fundación Pedro Barrié de la Maza, 2005. Print.

Carré Aldao, Uxío [Eugenio]. *Literatura gallega: Con extensos apéndices bibliográficas y una gran antología de 300 trabajos escogidos en prosa y verso de la mayor parte de los escritores regionales.* 2nd ed. Barcelona: Maucci, 1911. Print.

Carvalho Calero, Ricardo. *See* Carballo Calero, Ricardo.

Casas Vales, Arturo. "A cuestion xeracional." *Rafael Dieste e a sua orbra literaria en galego.* Vigo: Galaxia, 1994. 61–87. Print.

———. "A poesía galega entre 1916 e 1936." *O século XX: A literatura anterior á Guerra Civil.* Ed. Darío Villanueva and Anxo Tarrío Varela. A Coruña: Hércules, 2000. 85–213. Print. Vol. 3 of *Historia da literatura galega.*

———. "Problemas de historia comparada: La comunidad interliteraria ibérica." *Interlitteraria* 5 (2000): 56–75. Print.

———. "Sistema interliterario y planificación historiográfica a propósito del espacio geocultural ibérico." *Interlitteraria* 8 (2003): 68–97. Print.

Casey, Bernadette, Neil Casey, Ben Calvert, Liam French, and Justin Lewis. *Television Studies: The Key Concepts.* London: Routledge, 2002. Print.

Castelao, Alfonso R. *Sempre en Galiza.* 1944. Buenos Aires: As Burgas, 1961. Print.

Castelló, Enric. "Identidad cultural en las series de ficción de la televisión autonómica en España." *II Congreso Ibérico de Ciências da Comunicação.* U da Beira Interior, 2004. Web. 1 Oct. 2009.

Castells, Manuel. *The Power of Identity.* Oxford: Blackwell, 1997. Print. Vol. 2 of *The Information Age: Economy, Society, and Culture.*

"Castro." *Diccionario de la lengua.*

Castro, Rosalía de. *Cantares gallegos.* 1863. Ed. Ricardo Carballo Calero. 1974. Madrid: Cátedra, 1992. Print.

———. *Follas novas / Hojas nuevas.* 1880. Bilingual ed. 3rd ed. Madrid: Akal, 2009. Print.

———. *Obras completas.* 2 vols. Madrid: Turner, 1993. Print.

Castro, Xavier. "Problemática da 'orfandade' na obra de Rosalía de Castro." *Actas do Congreso Internacional* 1: 85–91.

CEPAM Migracións. Home page. Centro de Estudos da Poboación e Analise das Migracións, n.d. Web. 28 Oct. 2009.

Charnon-Deutsch, Lou. "Gender and Beyond: Nineteenth-Century Spanish Women Writers." *The Cambridge Companion to the Spanish Novel: From 1600 to the Present.* Ed. Harriet Turner and Adelaida López de Martínez. Cambridge: Cambridge UP, 2003. 122–37. Print.

Charnon-Deutsch, Lou, and Jo Labanyi, eds. *Culture and Gender in Nineteenth-Century Spain.* New York: Oxford UP, 1995. Print.

Cleto, Fabio, ed. *Camp: Queer Aesthetics and the Performing Subject.* Edinburgh: Edinburgh UP, 1999. Print.

Clifford, James. "On Collecting Art and Culture." During, *Cultural Studies Reader* 57–76.

Cochón Otero, Iris, and Helena González Fernández, eds. *Upalás: Rompente.* Vigo: Xerais, 1997. Print.

Cohen, Anthony P. "Of Symbols and Boundaries; or, Does Ernie's Greatcoat Hold the

Key?" *Symbolising Boundaries: Identity and Diversity in British Cultures.* Ed. Cohen. Manchester: Manchester UP, 1986. 1–19. Print.

Colectivo Cívico. "Para rachar co dirixismo: Reformular as políticas culturais." *Tempos novos* 104 (2006): 74–77. Print.

Colectivo Ronseltz. "Análise afortunadamente pouco documentada da poesía galega dos oitenta." *Trabe de ouro* 8 (1991): 637–40. Print.

Colmeiro, José F. "El bosque animado: La industria de la animación infantil/juvenil en Galicia." *Discursos visuales para un receptor infantil y/o juvenil.* Ed. Manuel Candelas and Susana Pérez Pico. Frankfurt: Lang, 2010. 73–87. Print.

———. "Camiños de Santiago: Identidade cultural, modernidade e invención da tradición." *Grial* 37 (1999): 419–27. Print.

———. "Peripheral Visions, Global Positions: Remapping Galician Culture." *Bulletin of Hispanic Studies* 86.2 (2009): 213–30. Print.

———. "Smells like Wild Spirit: Galician *Rock Bravú,* between the 'Rurban' and the 'Glocal.'" *Journal of Spanish Cultural Studies* 10.2 (2009): 225–40. Print.

"¿Concordia incómoda?" *O correo galego* 8 Sept. 2001: 31. Print.

Conde, Alfredo. "Cada un polo seu lado." *El correo gallego* 28 Sept. 1999: 4. Print.

———. "Unha opción, non unha obriga." *El correo gallego* 29 Sept. 1999: 4. Print.

———. "Somos perdedores." *El correo gallego* 27 Sept. 1999: 4. Print.

Conde, Perfecto. "Galicia aberta." *Croques.* Conde, 15 Apr. 2009. Web. 21 Apr. 2009. Blog.

Constenla Bergueiro, Gonzalo, and Luis Domíngez Castro, eds. *Tempos de sermos: Galicia nos séculos contemporáneos.* Vigo: U de Vigo, 2002. Print.

Constitución española. Congreso de los Diputados, 2003. Web. 5 Nov. 2009.

Continental. Dir. Xavier Villaverde. Cameo, 2007. DVD.

Cooper, Robert L. *Language Planning and Social Change.* Cambridge: Cambridge UP, 1989. Print.

Core, Philip. *Camp: The Lie That Tells the Truth.* New York: Delilah, 1984. Print.

Cózar, Rafael de. *Poesía e imagen: Formas difíciles de ingenio literario.* Sevilla: El carro de la nieve, 1991. Print.

Crofts, Stephen. "Reconceptualizing National Cinema/s." A. Williams 25–51.

Cuba, Xoan R., Xosé Miranda, and Lazaro Enríquez. *Diccionario dos seres míticos galegos.* Vigo: Xerais, 1999. Print.

Davies, Catherine. "A ideoloxía político-social de Rosalía: Raíz do seu pesimismo existencial." *Actas do Congreso Internacional* 1: 299–306.

———. "Rosalía de Castro: Cultural Isolation in a Colonial Context." *Recovering Spain's Feminist Tradition.* Ed. Lisa Vollendorf. New York: MLA, 2001. 176–97.

———. *Rosalía de Castro no seu tempo.* Vigo: Galaxia, 1987. Print.

———. "Rosalía de Castro's Later Poetry and Anti-regionalism in Spain." *Modern Language Review* 79.3 (1984): 609–19. Print.

del Barco, Pablo. "Caminando con el caballero azul." *Actas do Congreso Internacional* 1: 511–15.

De Leeuw, Sonja. "Television Fiction and Cultural Diversity: Strategies for Cultural Change." *European Film and Media Culture.* Ed. Lenard Højberg and Henrik Sønder-gaard. Copenhagen: Museum Tusculanum; U of Copenhagen, 2006. 91–112. Print.

Deleuze, Gilles. *Masochism: An Interpretation of Coldness and Cruelty.* New York: Zone, 1991. Print.

Deleuze, Gilles, and Félix Guattari. *Kafka: Pour une littérature mineure.* Paris: Minuit, 1975. Print.

del Valle, José, and Luis Gabriel-Stheeman, eds. *The Battle over Spanish between 1800 and 2000: Language Ideologies and Hispanic Intellectuals.* New York: Routledge, 2002. Print.

Derrida, Jacques. *Mal d'archive: Une impression freudienne.* Paris: Galilee, 1995. Print.

"O desmantelamento de Fillos de Galicia." *Fillos.org.* Fillos de Galicia, 21 June 2010. Web. 24 June 2010.

"Días de exame para a lei de galeguidade." *Galicia Hoxe.* Grupo Correo Gallego, 23 Aug. 2006. Web. 29 Oct. 2009.

Díaz Pardo, Isaac. "Retrato do presidente da R.A.G."*La voz de Galicia* 26 Nov. 2001: 17. Print.

Diccionario de la lengua española. Real Academia Española, n.d. Web. 29 Oct. 2009. 21st ed., 1992; 22nd ed., 2001.

Dinneen, Mark. "Tradiciones populares de Venezuela y sus raices Ibericas." *E patrimonio cultural: Tradiciones, educacion y turismo.* Ed. Alberto E. Martos Garcia and Eloy Martos Nunez. Badajoz: U de Extremadura, 2008. 139–49. Print. Puertas a la lectura 20–21.

Dobao, Antón. "A lingua extravagante." *A nosa terra* 21 Oct. 1999: 26. Print.

———. "A lingua galega e a TVG: Situación actual e proposta para unha nova política lingüística." *Cuadernos de lingua* 7 (1993): 27–44; 9 (1994): 27–53. Print.

Domínguez Alberte, Xoán Carlos. "A diversificación do xénero narrativo dende 1975." *Actas das I Xornadas das Letras Galegas en Lisboa.* Santiago de Compostela: Xunta de Galicia, 1998. 87–111. Print.

Domínguez Almansa, Andrés. "O desenvolvemento da cultura deportiva nunha sociedade en transformación: Galicia, 1850–1920." Diss. U de Santiago de Compostela, 2006. Print.

Durán, Carlos. *Galegos de Londres.* A Coruña: Castro, 1978. Print.

Durán Villa, Francisco R. "La emigración española al Reino Unido." Diss. U de Santiago de Compostela, 1997. Print.

———. *La emigración galega al Reino Unido.* Santiago de Compostela: Caixa Galicia, 1985. Print.

During, Simon, ed. *The Cultural Studies Reader.* London: Routledge, 2000. Print.

———. Introduction. During, *Cultural Studies Reader* 1–28.

Dyer, Richard. "Entertainment and Utopia." During, *Cultural Studies Reader* 371–81.

———. "It's Being So Camp As Keeps Us Going." Cleto 110–16.

Edición en cifras. Asociación Galega de Editores, n.d. Web. 30 Oct. 2009.

Ellis, John. *Visible Fictions: Cinema, Television, Video.* London: Routledge, 1982. Print.

O Estatuto de Autonomía de Galicia. 6 Apr. 1981. Xunta de Galicia, n.d. Web. 10 Nov. 2009.

Estebañez, Salvador. "The Spanish Speech Community." *The Older Mother Tongues and Europe.* Ed. Safder Alladina and Viv Edwards. London: Longman, 1991. 239–53. Print. Vol. 1 of *Multilingualism in the British Isles.*

Estrada, Isabel. "Subversión y conservadurismo: El discurso gótico femenino en *El caballero de las botas azules* de Rosalía de Castro." *Letras femeninas* 34.1-2 (1998): 81–94. Print.

Estudios migratorios. Arquivo da Emigración Galega, Consello da Cultura Galega, n.d. Web. 30 Oct. 2009.

Exiliados. Home page. *Culturagalega.org.* Consello da Cultura Galega, n.d. Web. 30 Oct. 2009.

Extravíos: Poesía e pintura. Galería Arcana, Vilagarcía de Arousa, 2001. Exhibit.

Fallon, Paul. "Sobre a construcción do corpo político galego en *Tic-Tac* de Suso de Toro." *Anuario de estudios literarios galegos* 1998: 141–56. Print.

Fandiño Alonso, Xaime, and Alberto Dafonte Gómez. "A televisión en Galicia: Actualidade e previsión de futuro." *Informe da comunicación en Galicia 2007.* Ed. Xosé López García. Santiago de Compostela: Concello de Cultura Galega, 2007. 91–111. Print.

FAQ: Comunidade Virtual Fillos de Galicia. Fillos de Galicia, 1997. Web. 24 June 2010.

Fariña Jamardo, Xosé, and Dolores Troncoso, eds. *Sobre literatura fantástica: Homenaxe ó profesor Antón Risco.* Vigo: U de Vigo, 2001. Print.

Feldman, Jessica R. *Gender on the Divide: The Dandy in Modernist Literature.* Ithaca: Cornell UP, 1993. Print.

Ferguson, Charles A. "Diglossia Revisited." *Southwest Journal of Linguistics* 10.1 (1991): 214–34. Print.

Fernández, Josep-Anton. *Another Country: Sexuality and National Identity in Catalan Gay Fiction.* London: Maney Publishing for the Humanities Research Assn., 2000. Print.

Fernández, Miguel Anxo. "Distribución e exhibición." *Libro branco de cinematografía* 289–300.

Fernández-Pérez San Julián, Carme. "O prólogo de *El caballero de las botas azules* ou o ensaio dunha poética nova." *Actas do Congreso Internacional* 1: 475–82.

Fernández Prieto, Lourenzo. "Os espacios do cambio: Preconceptos i estereotipos na interpretación da Galicia rural con temporánea." Bermejo Barrera et al., *Concepcións* 193–200.

———, ed. "Memoria do 36." *Grial* 170 (2006): 14–82. Print.

Fernández Rei, Francisco. "A questione della lingua galega." Monteagudo, *Estudios* 177–95.

Fernández Rodríguez, Aurea. "Esbozo dunha lectura de *Ruinas* (desdichas de tres vidas ejemplares) de Rosalía de Castro." *Actas do Congreso Internacional* 1: 413–17.

Fernández Rodríguez, Mauro. "Bilingüismo y diglosia." *Verba* 5.5 (1978): 377–91. Print.

Ferreiro, Celso Emilio. *Longa noite de pedra.* A Coruña: Voz de Galicia, 2002. Print. Biblioteca galega 120.

Ferreiro, Manuel. *Gramática histórica galega: Manual.* Santiago de Compostela: Laiovento, 1996. Print.

Ferro Ruibal, Xesús. "¿Podemos paga-lo lh e mailo nh?" *O correo galego* 18 Oct. 1999: 3. Print.

———. "¿Sereas no mar de Corcubión?" *O correo galego* 17 Nov. 1999: 3. Print.

Figueroa, Antón. *Diglosia e texto.* Vigo: Xerais, 1988. Print.

Fishman, Joshua. "Bilinguism with and without Diglossia; Diglossia with and without Bilinguism." *Journal of Social Issues* 23.2 (1967): 29–38. Print.

———, ed. *Handbook of Language and Ethnic Identity.* Oxford: Oxford UP, 1999. Print.

Fiske, John. *Television Culture.* London: Routledge, 1994. Print.

Folkart, Jessica. "Itinerant Identities: Galician Diaspora and Genre Subversion in Manuel Rivas's *A man dos paíños.*" *Anales de la literatura española contemporánea* 33.1 (2008): 5–29. Print.

Fraga, Xesús. "Sectores da cultura galega coinciden en criticar a negativa ós cambios na norma." *La voz de Galicia* 20 Nov. 2001: 30. Print.

"Fraga define la Ciudad de la Cultura como el gran proyecto del milenio." *El mundo.* 4 Apr. 2001. N. pag. Fundación Cidade da Cultura de Galicia, n.d. Web. 30 Oct. 2009.

Fraga Iribarne, Manuel. *De Galicia a Europa.* Barcelona: Planeta, 1991. Print.

Freixeiro Mato, Xosé Ramón. *Lingua galega: Normalidade e conflito.* Santiago de Compostela: Laiovento, 1997. Print.

Fundación Galicia emigración. Home page. Xunta de Galicia, n.d. Web. 31 Oct. 2009.

Gabilondo, Joseba. "Historical Memory, Neoliberal Spain, and the Latin American Postcolonial Ghost: On the Politics of Recognition, Apology, and Reparation in Contemporary Spanish Historiography." *Arizona Journal of Hispanic Cultural Studies* 7 (2003): 249–68. Print.

———. "Postnationalism, Fundamentalism, and the Global Real: Historicizing Terror/ism and the New North American / Global Ideology." *Journal of Spanish Cultural Studies* 3.1 (2002): 57–86. Print.

———. "Towards a Postnational History of Galician Literature: On Pardo Bazán's Transnational and Translational Position." *Bulletin of Hispanic Studies* 86.2 (2009): 49–69. Print.

Galán, Carlos. *O bosque inanimado: Cen anos de cine en Galicia.* A Coruña: Centro Galego de Artes da Imaxe, 1997. Print.

Galicia aberta. Secretaría Xeral da Emigración, Xunta de Galicia, n.d. Web. 31 Oct. 2009.

"Galicia perdió 76 aldeas en un solo año debido al abandono y a la crisis demográfica." *Laopinioncoruña.es.* Grupo Editorial Prensa Ibérica, 7 Feb. 2010. Web. 15 June 2010.

Gallagher, Catherine, and Stephen Greenblatt. *Practicing New Historicism.* Chicago: U of Chicago P, 2000. Print.

Gallego 1–3. (ILGA) Instituto da Lingua Galega. Santiago de Compostela: U de Compostela, 1971–73. Print.

García Negro, María Pilar. *Sempre en galego.* Santiago de Compostela: Laiovento, 1993. Print.

Gellner, Ernest. *Nations and Nationalism.* Oxford: Blackwell, 1983. Print.

Gemie, Sharif. *Galicia: A Concise History.* Cardiff: U of Wales P, 2006. Print.

Genette, Gérard. *Paratexts: Thresholds of Interpretation.* Trans. Jane E. Lewin. Introd. Richard Macksey. Cambridge: Cambridge UP, 1997. Print.

Gil Magariños, Lois. Vignette. Blogger.com, n.d. Web. 5 Dec. 2010. <photos1.blogger.com/img/91/2068/640/poemas.jpg>.

Glissant, Édouard. *Poetics of Relation.* Trans. Betsy Wing. Ann Arbor: U of Michigan P, 1997. Print.

Gómez-Montero, Javier. "O paradigma galego nunha cartografía identitaria da poesía na península Ibérica: Máis alá de minorización e normalización, entre resistencia e institucionalización." *Anuario de estudios galegos 2002* (2003): 221–40. Print.

Gómez Sánchez, Anxo, and Xosé Ramón Freixeiro Mato. *Historia da lingua galega.* 2nd ed. Vigo: A Nosa Terra, 1998. Print.

González Fernández, Helena. *Elas e o paraugas totalizador: Escritoras, xénero e nación.* Vigo: Xerais, 2005. Print.

———. "Encrucilladas identitarias: Sobre xénero, nación e literatura." *Anuario de estudios galegos 2002* (2003): 241–50. Print.

———. "Helena González: 'Vivimos nunha "moda violeta," xestionada por quen controla a edición.'" Interview by Lara Rozados. *Vieiros.* Vieiros, 10 Apr. 2007. Web. 1 Nov. 2009.

———. "1994, tempos de medrío e boa saúde na poesía." *Anuario de estudos galegos 1994* (1994): 167–72. Print.

———. "Rompente, 'poderosa pomada.'" *Anuario de estudos literarios Galegos 1997* (1998): 47–84. Print.

———. "Subxectividades críticas, narrativas identitarias: Feminismos e creación contemporánea no estado español." Fundación Luis Seoane, A Coruña. 8 Mar. 2006. Roundtable address.

———. "Tres argumentos para di/versificar as identidades de xénero: *Arden, Pronomes* e *Lob*s.*" *Lectora: Revista de dones i textualitat* 5-6 (1999–2000): 89–95. Print.

———. "Zapadoras, navegadoras, insubmisas . . . escritoras no ronsel de 'eu tamén navegar.'" *A nosa terra: Cadernos de pensamento e cultura* 29 (2003): 21–26. Print.

González Gómez, Xesús. *Manifesta Galiza: Manifestos na literatura galega do século XX.* Vigo: A Nosa Terra, 2006. Print.

González Herrán, José Manuel. "Rosalía y Pereda, costumbristas: El cadiceño y el jandalo." *Actas do Congreso Internacional* 1: 435–47.

González López, Emilio. *História de Galicia.* A Coruña: La voz de Galicia, 1980. Print. Serie Nova.

González-Millán, Xoán. "O criterio filolóxico e a configuración dunha literatura nacional: Achegas a un novo marco de reflexión." *Cadernos da lingua* 17 (1998): 5–24. Print.

———. "Unha etnopoética para unha literatura periférica." *Actas do Segundo Congreso de Estudos Galegos.* Ed. Antonio Carreño. Vigo: Galaxia, 1990. 339–47. Print.

———. "Do nacionalismo literario á literatura nacional: Hipóteses de Traballo para un estudio institucional da literatura gallega." *Anuario de estudios literarios galegos 1994* (1995): 67–81. Print.

———. *Literatura e sociedade en Galicia, 1975–1990.* Vigo: Xerais, 1994. Print.

———. "Nacionalismo y teoría del campo literario: La experiencia gallega de las últimas décadas." *From Stateless Nations to Postnational Spain / De naciones sin estado a la España postnacional.* Ed. Silvia Bermúdez et al. Boulder: Soc. of Spanish and Spanish-American Studies, 2002. 223–36. Print.

———. *A narrativa galega actual, 1975–1984.* Vigo: Xerais, 1996. Print.

Greenblatt, Stephen. "Racial Memory and Literary History." Hutcheon and Valdés 50–62.

Gripsrud, Jostein. "Television, Broadcasting, Flow: Key Metaphors in TV Theory." *The Television Studies Book.* Ed. Christine Geraghty and David Lusted. London: Arnold, 1998. 17–32. Print.

Guerra da Cal, Ernesto. Introduction. *Antologia poetica: Cancioneiro Rosaliano.* By Rosalía de Castro. Viseu: Guimarães, 1985. xi–xliv. Print.

Guisán Seixas, João. "Propostas para un diálogo." *La voz de Galicia* 27 Oct. 1999: 18. Print.

Gullón, Germán. *"El caballero de las botas azules*: Farsa de las letras decimonónicas." *Actas do Congreso Internacional* 1: 483–91.

Gumbrecht, Hans Ulrich. "Epilogue: Untenable Positions." Palumbo-Lin and Gumbrecht 249–62.

Habermas, Jürgen. *The Postnational Constellation: Political Essays.* Cambridge: Polity, 2001. Print.

Haraway, Donna. "Situated Knowledges: The Science Question in Feminism and the Privilege of Partial Perspective." *Simians, Cyborgs, and Women: The Reinvention of Nature.* New York: Routledge, 1991. 183–201. Print.

Harding, Sandra. "Rethinking Standpoint Epistemology: 'What Is Strong Objectivity?'" *Feminist Epistemologies.* Ed. Linda Alcott and Elizabeth Potter. New York: Routledge, 1993. 49–82. Print.

Hebdige, Dick. "The Function of Subculture." During, *Cultural Studies Reader* 441–50.

"Heritage." *The Oxford English Dictionary.* 2nd ed. 1989. Print.

Herrero-Valeiro, Mário. "The Discourse of Language in Galiza: Normalisation, Diglossia, and Conflict." *Estudios de sociolingüística.* Vigo: U de Vigo, 2003. 289–320. Print.

Higgins, Dick. *Pattern Poetry: Guide to an Unknown Literature.* Albany: State U of New York P, 1987. Print.

Higson, Andrew. "The Concept of National Cinema." A. Williams 52–67.

"Los hijos de los emigrantes reclaman sus derechos a los candidatos de la Xunta de Galicia." *Fillos.org.* Fillos de Galicia, 18 Oct. 2001. Web. 24 June 2010.

Holt, Mike, and Paul Gubbins, eds. *Beyond Boundaries: Language and Identity in Contemporary Europe.* Clevedon: Multilingual Matters, 2002. Print.

hooks, bell. *Yearning Race, Gender, and Cultural Politics.* Boston: South End, 1990. Print.

Hooper, Kirsty. "Alternative Genealogies? History and the Dilemma of 'Origin' in Two Recent Novels by Galician Women." *Arizona Journal of Hispanic Cultural Studies* 10 (2006): 45–58. Print.

———, ed. and trans. "Forum." Hooper, *New Spaces* 103–22.

———. "Galicia desde Londres desde Galicia: New Voices in the Twenty-First-Century Diaspora." Hooper, *New Spaces* 171–88.

———. "Girl, Interrupted: The Distinctive History of Galician Women's Narrative." *Romance Studies* 21.2 (2003): 101–14. Print.

———. "The Many Faces of Julio Iglesias: 'Un canto a Galicia,' Emigration, and the Network Society." *Journal of Spanish Cultural Studies* 10.2 (2009): 149–66. Print.

———. "New Cartographies in Galician Studies: From Literary Nationalism to Postnational Readings." *Reading Iberia: Theory, History, Identity.* Ed. Helena Buffery, Stuart Davis, and Hooper. Oxford: Lang, 2007. 123–39. Print.

———. "New Spaces, New Voices." Hooper, *New Spaces* 101–02.

———. *New Spaces, New Voices: Notes on Contemporary Galician Studies.* Spec. issue of *Journal of Spanish Cultural Studies* 7.2 (2006): 101–98 Print.

———. "This Festering Wound: Negotiating Spanishness in Galician Cultural Discourse." *Spanishness in Twentieth- and Twenty-First-Century Narrative and Film.* Ed. Cristina Sánchez-Conejero. Cambridge: Cambridge Scholars', 2007. 147–56. Print.

Hueso, Ángel Luis. "Anos de efervescencia política (desde as posturas ideolóxicas cara ó mundo industrial)." *Historia do cine en Galicia.* A Coruña: Vía Láctea, 1996. 180–93. Print.

Hunt, Lynn. *Politics, Culture and Class in the French Revolution.* London: Methuen, 1984. Print.

Hutcheon, Linda. "Rethinking the National Model." Hutcheon and Valdés 3–49.

Hutcheon, Linda, and Mario Valdés, eds. *Rethinking Literary History: A Dialogue in Theory.* Oxford: Oxford UP, 2002. Print.

Iglesias, Mateo. "Unha novela de aprendizaxe da vida e da morte." *Xerais Online* 43 (2002): n pag. Web. 31 Oct. 2009.

Iglesias, Oscar. "Os problemas dun poeta nacional." *El país* [Galicia ed.] El país, 14 Sept. 2007. Web. 31 Oct. 2009.

"Investigación." *Arquivo da emigración galega.* Consello da Cultura Galega, n.d. Web. 31 Oct. 2009.

Jameson, Fredric. "The Politics of Theory: Ideological Positions in the Postmodernism Debate." *New German Critique* 33 (1984): 53–64. Print.

———. "Third-World Literature in the Era of Multinational Capitalism." *Social Text* 15 (1986): 65–88. Print.

Johnson-Hoffman, Deanna. "The Deconstruction of Romanticism in Rosalía de Castro's

Flavio and *El caballero de las botas azules.*" *Letras peninsulares* 10.1 (1997): 151–67. Print.

Joseph, John E. *Language and Politics.* Edinburgh: Edinburgh UP, 2006. Print.

Juana López, Jesús de, and Julio Prada Rodríguez, eds. *Historia contemporánea de Galicia.* Barcelona: Ariel, 2005. Print.

———, eds. *Lo que han hecho en Galicia: Violencia, represión y exilio, 1936–1939.* Barcelona: Crítica, 2006. Print.

Jurt, Joseph. "De l'analyse immanente à l'histoire sociale de la littérature: À propos des recherches littéraires en Allemagne depuis 1945." *Actes de la recherche en sciences sociales* 78 (1989): 94–101. Print.

Kaplan, Caren. *Questions of Travel: Postmodern Discourses of Displacement.* Durham: Duke UP, 1996. Print.

Kim, Yeon-Soo. "Migrancy, Memory, and Transplantation in Manuel Rivas's *La mano del emigrante.*" *Hispanic Research Journal* 7.2 (2006): 113–26. Print.

Kirkpatrick, Susan. "Fantasy, Seduction, and the Woman Reader: Rosalía de Castro's Novels." Charnon-Deutsch and Labanyi 74–97.

———. *Mujer, modernismo y vanguardia en España, 1898–1931.* Madrid: Cátedra, 2003. Print.

Kivisto, Peter, ed. *Illuminating Social Life: Classical and Contemporary Theory Revisited.* 3rd ed. Thousand Oaks: Pine Forge, 2005. Print.

Kloss, Heinz. "'Abstand Languages' and 'Ausbau Languages.'" *Anthropological Linguistics* 9 (1967): 29–41. Print.

Labanyi, Jo, ed. *Constructing Identity in Contemporary Spain: Theoretical Debates and Cultural Practice.* Oxford: Oxford UP, 2002. Print.

———. "Part 1: Ethnicity and Migration: Editor's Introduction." Labanyi, *Constructing* 17–21.

Lacan, Jacques. "Kant with Sade." *October* 59 (1989): 55–75. Print.

Lamas, Santiago. *Galicia borrosa.* Santiago de Compostela: Seminario de Estudos Galegos, 2005. Print.

Lanero Taboas, Daniel. *Os remendos da memoria: A represión franquista no Concello de Arzúa, 1936–1950.* Arzúa: Concello de Arzúa, 2006. Print.

"El lápiz del carpintero: Denuncia dunha mentira." *Redes escarlatas* 25 Apr. 2003. Web. 31 Oct. 2009.

Ledo Andión, Margarita. "15 anos de televisión." *Estudios de comunicación* 0 (2001): 67–78. Print.

Levi Strauss, David. *Between the Eyes: Essays on Photography and Politics.* New York: Aperture Foundation, 2003. Print.

Libro branco de cinematografía e artes visuais en Galicia. Santiago de Compostela: Consello da Cultura Galega, 2004. Print.

Libro branco do audiovisual. Santiago de Compostela: Xunta de Galicia, 2005. Print.

O libro dos abanos (Palabras no aire). Santiago de Compostela: Follas Novas, 2002. Print.

Liebkind, Karmela. "Social Psychology." Fishman, *Handbook* 140–51.

Lobato, Xurxo. *Jalisia*. Pontevedra: Caixa Madrid, 1994. Print.

López Carreira, Anselmo. *O reino medieval de Galicia: Contribución á súa historia política*. Vigo: A Nosa Terra, 2005. Print.

López-Casanova, Arcadio. *Mesteres*. 1976. Santiago de Compostela: Vía Láctea, 1987. Print.

López Cortón, José Pascual. *Album de la caridad: Juegos Florales de La Coruña en 1861, seguido de un mosaíco poético de nuestros vates gallegos contemporáneos*. A Coruña: López Cortón, 1862. Print.

López García, Xosé, coord. *Tres décadas de televisión en Galicia: Cronoloxía e posicións perante o desafío dun novo modelo audiovisual*. Santiago de Compostela: Consello da Cultura Galega, 2006. Print.

López García, Xosé, Manuel Gago, and Xosé Pereira. "A internet en Galicia." *Informe da Comunicación en Galicia 2007*. Ed López. Santiago de Compostela: Consello da Cultura Galega. 145–56. Print.

Lopo, Antón. *Ganga*. Vigo: Xerais, 2001. Print.

———. *Os homes só contan até tres*. Vigo: Xerais, 2006. Print.

———. *Libro dos amados*. Santiago de Compostela: Grupo Correo Gallego-Concello de Santiago-Consellaría de Cultura, 2005. Print.

———. Message to the author. 27 July 2006. E-mail.

———. *As tres mortes de Lorenzo Varela: Biografía dun poeta*. Vigo: Galaxia, 2005. Print.

Lowenthal, David. *The Past Is a Foreign Country*. Cambridge: Cambridge UP, 1985. Print.

Lusted, David. "The Popular Culture Debate and Light Entertainment on Televisión." *The Television Studies Book*. Ed. Christine Geraghty and Lusted. London: Arnold, 1998. 175–90. Print.

"A lux xoga 'Dentro.'" *Galicia Hoxe*. Grupo Correo Gallego, 19 May 2006. Web. 1 Nov. 2009.

Lyons, John. *Languages and Linguistics: An Introduction*. Cambridge: Cambridge UP, 1981. Print.

Lyotard, Jean-François. *The Inhuman: Reflections on Time*. Trans. Rachel Bowlby and Geoffrey Bennington. Stanford: Stanford UP, 1991. Print.

Maneiro Vila, A. *Funcións da TV autonómica galega e do Centro Rexional de TVE en Galicia: Investigación sobre a razón de ser de dúas ofertas públicas de TV nunha Comunidade Autónoma*. Santiago de Compostela: Consellería de Presidencia e da Administración Pública, Xunta de Galicia, 1989. Print.

"Un manifesto de Fillos de Galicia dirixido ao novo goberno da Xunta de Galicia." *Fillos .org*. Fillos de Galicia, 1 Sept. 2005. Web. 21 Apr. 2009.

Manoel Antonio. *De catro a catro / De cuatro a cuatro*. 1928. Bilingual ed. Ed. and trans. Miguel González Garcés. Madrid: Rialp, 1979. Print.

Manuel Antonio, and Álvaro Cebreiro. "¡Mais alá!" 1922. *Manifesta Galiza: Manifestos na literatura galega do século XX*. Ed. and introd. Xesús González Gómez. Vigo: Nosa Terra, 2006. 199–207. Print.

March, Kathleen N. "Rosalía de Castro como punto de referencia ideológico-literario nas escritoras galegas." *Actas do Congreso Internacional* 1: 283–92.

Mar-Molinero, Clare. *The Politics of Language in the Spanish-Speaking World.* Routledge: London, 2000. Print.

———. "Spanish as a World Language: Language and Identity in a Global Era." *Spanish in Context* 1.1 (2004): 3–21. Print.

Márquez López, María. "De costas á historia: As relacións culturais Portugal-Galicia." *Tempos Novos* 51 (2001): 22–25. Print.

Martínez de Padín, Leopoldo. *Historia política, religiosa, y descriptiva de Galicia.* Vol. 1. Madrid: Vicente, 1849. Print.

Martínez Hermida, Marcelo. "Contexto de ficción e series de televisión en Galicia." *Grial* 154 (2002): 235–44. Print.

Marx, Karl. *Economic and Philosophical Manuscripts of 1844.* Ed. and introd. Dirk J. Struik. Trans. Martin Milligan. London: Lawrence, 1970. Print.

Mateo, Cristina. "Identities at a Distance: Markers of National Identity in the Video-Diaries of Second-Generation Spanish Migrants in London." Labanyi, *Constructing* 72–85.

———. "Second-Generation Spanish Immigrants in Greater London: The Production and Refusal of Ethnic Identity in Everyday Life." Diss. U of London, 2000. Print.

May, Stephen. *Language and Minority Rights: Ethnicity, Nationalism and the Politics of Language.* London: Longman, 2001. Print.

Mayoral, Marina. *La poesía de Rosalía de Castro.* Madrid: Gredos, 1974. Print.

———. *Rosalía de Castro.* Madrid: Fundación Juan March, Cátedra, 1986.

———. "La voz del narrador desde *La hija del mar* a *El primer loco*: Un largo camino hacia la objetividad narrativa." *Actas do Congreso Internacional* 1: 341–66.

McGann, Jerome. *The Beauty of Inflections: Literary Investigations in Historical Method and Theory.* Oxford: Clarendon; New York: Oxford UP, 1985. Print.

McGovern, Timothy. "Expressing Desire, Expressing Death: Antón Lopo's Pronomes and Queer Galician Poetry." *Journal of Spanish Cultural Studies* 7.2 (2006): 135–53. Print.

Medeiros, António. "Discurso nacionalista e imagens de Portugal na Galiza." *Etnográfica* 7.2 (2003): 321–49. Print.

Melo, João de. Interview by Víctor Freixanes. *Tempos novos* 37 (1999): 37–43. Print.

Méndez Ferrín, Xosé Luís. *Con pólvora e magnolias.* 1976. Vigo: Xerais, 2004. Print.

———. Interview. *Faro de Vigo* 24 Sept. 1991: 36. Print.

———. Interview by Manuel P. Rúa. *Tempos novos* 11 Apr. 1998: 35–40. Print.

———. *Retorno a Tagen Ata.* Vigo: Castrelos, 1971. Print.

Middleton, Peter. "Poetry's Oral Stage." *Auslander* 1: 338–70.

Miguélez-Carballeira, Helena. "Alternative Values: From the National to the Sentimental in the Redrawing of Galician Literary History." *Bulletin of Hispanic Studies* 86.2 (2009): 271–92. Print.

———. "Inaugurar, reanudar, renovar: A escrita de Teresa Moure no contexto da narrativa feminista contemporánea." *Anuario de estudos galegos 2006* (2007): 72–87. Print.

Míguez Macho, Antonio. "La construcción de la ciudadanía a través de los movimientos sociales: El movimiento obrero en Galicia, 1890–1936." Diss. U de Santiago de Compostela, 2006. Print.

Millán, Fernando. "Las otras poesías." Interview by Francisco Carpio. *Lápiz* 202 (2004): 62–75. Print.

———. "A utopia within One's Reach." *CyberPoem*. L'Associació de Performers, Artistes i Poets Associates, n.d. Web. 1 Nov. 2009.

Mira, Alberto. *De Sodoma a Chueca: Una historia cultural de la homosexualidad en España en el siglo XX.* Barcelona: Egales, 2004. Print.

Miralles, Enrique. "*El caballero de las botas azules,* un manifiesto anti-anovelado." *Actas do Congreso Internacional* 1: 457–63.

Missac, Pierre. *Walter Benjamin's Passages.* Trans. Shierry Weber Nicholsen. Cambridge: MIT P, 1995. Print.

Moix, Terenci. *Chulas y famosas.* Barcelona: Planeta, 1999. Print.

———. *Món mascle.* Barcelona: Aymá, 1971. Print.

———. *Mujercísimas.* Barcelona: Planeta, 1995. Print.

Montanha, Amaro. "Os portugueses e os galegos." *A nosa terra* 21 Oct. 1999: 13. Print.

Monteagudo, Henrique. "A demanda da norma: Avances, problemas e perspectivas no proceso de estandarización do idioma galego." *O proceso de normalización do idioma galego, 1980–2000.* Vol. 3. Ed. Monteagudo and Xan M. Bouzada Fernández. Santiago de Compostela: Consello da Cultura Galega, 2003. 37–129. Print.

———, ed. *Estudios de sociolingüística galega: Sobre a norma do galego culto.* Vigo: Galaxia, 1995. Print.

———. "Galego e portugués, ou galegos e galegos." *La voz de Galicia* 8 Oct. 1999: 18. Print.

———. Personal interview with John Patrick Thompson. 23 Sept. 2004. Interview.

———. "Sobre a polémica da normativa do galego." Monteagudo, *Estudios* 197–229.

Monteagudo, Henrique, and Antón Santamarina. "Galician and Castilian in Contact: Historical, Social and Linguistic Aspects." *Bilingualism and Linguistic Conflict in Romance.* Ed. Rebecca Posner and John N. Green. The Hague: Mouton, 1993. 117–73. Print. Vol. 5 of *Trends in Romance Linguistics and Philology.*

Montero Küpper, Silvia. "A traducción da lírica vangardista: Teoría e práctica a partir da análise dun poema de Antón Reixa vertido á alemán, II." *Anovar Anosar: Estudos de traducción en interpretación.* Ed. Alberto Álvarez Lugrís and Anxo Fernández Ocampo. Vol. 1. Vigo: U de Vigo, 2000. 287–97. Print.

Moreiras Menor, Cristina. "Galicia beyond Galicia: *A man dos paíños* and the Ends of Territoriality." *Border Interrogations: Questioning Spanish Fronteirs.* Ed. Benita Sampedro Vizcaya and Simon Doubleday. New York: Berghahn, 2008. 105–19. Print.

———. "El secreto revelado y los horizontes del nacionalismo gallego en Rosalía de Castro." *Revista hispánica moderna* 52 (1999): 322–40. Print.

Moreno Márquez, María Victoria. *Os novísimos da poesía galega.* Madrid: Akal, 1973. Print.

Moutinho, Viale. Interview with Belén Puñal. *Tempos novos* 27 (2001): 26–30. Print.

Muljacic, Zarko. "A estandarización do galego á luz de procesos análogos noutras linguas 'minorizadas' europeas." Monteagudo, *Estudios* 19–51.

Murdoch, Graham. "Cultural Studies at the Crossroads." *Back to Reality? Social Experience and Cultural Studies.* Ed. Angela McRobbie. Manchester: Manchester UP, 1997. 58–73. Print.

Murguía, Manuel. *Historia de Galicia.* Lugo: Soto Freire, 1865. Print.

Nogueira, Camilo. "Unha decisión converxente."*La voz de Galicia* 1 Feb. 2000: 16. Print.

———. "O galego-portugués-brasileiro e a política linguística na Galiza." *Agália* 62 (2000): 111–17. Print.

———. *A memoria da nación: O Reino de Gallaecia.* Vigo: Xerais, 2001. Print.

Nogueira, Xosé. *O cine en Galicia.* Vigo: A Nosa Terra, 1997. Print.

———. "As temáticas." *Libro branco de cinematografía* 71–164.

Noia Campos, María Camino. "La narrativa gallega de mujeres." *Breve historia feminista de la literatura española (en lengua catalana, gallega y vasca).* Ed. Iris M. Zavala. Barcelona: Anthropos, 2000. 237–61. Print.

Nomes e voces: Proxecto interuniversitario. Nomes e Voces, n.d. Web. 25 June 2010.

Normas ortográficas do idioma galego. A Coruña: Real Academia Galega, 1970. Print.

Normas ortográficas do idioma galego. Compostela: Comisión Linguística, Xunta de Galicia, 1980. Print.

Normas ortográficas e morfolóxicas do idioma galego. A Coruña: Real Academia Galega, 1971. Print.

Novoneyra, Uxío. *Os Eidos 2: Letanía de Galicia e outros poemas.* A Coruña: eDixital, 2002. Print.

———. *Poemas caligráficos.* Madrid: Brais Pintos, 1979. Print.

Nuñez Seixas, Xosé Manuel. "History and Collective Memories of Migration in a Land of Migrants: The Case of Iberian Galicia." *History and Memory* 14.1-2 (2002): 229–58. Print.

"Obxetivos do AEG." *Arquivo.*

Oficina del Censo Electoral. Home page. Institutó Nacional de Estadística, n.d. Web. 1 Nov. 2009.

O'Flanagan, Patrick. *Xeografía histórica de Galicia.* Vigo: Xerais, 1996. Print.

Ordóñez, Elizabeth J. "Literary Longings: *La hija del mar*; or, Anxiety of the Author as a Young Woman." *Indiana Journal of Hispanic Literatures* 2.1 (1993): 75–90. Print.

Orientacións para a escrita do noso idioma. Santiago de Compostela: Xistral; Asociación Socio-Pedagóxica Galega, 1979. Print.

Otero Pedrayo, Ramón. "Occitania e Atlántida." *Nós* 128-29 (1934): 127–31. Print.

"Paco Vázquez atribúelle a normativa de concordia a 'trama batasuneira do BNG.'" *O correo galego* 8 Sept. 2001: 1. Print.

Padilla, Armand M. "Psychology." Fishman, *Handbook* 109–21.

Palumbo-Lin, David, and Hans Ulrich Gumbrecht, eds. *Streams of Cultural Capital.* Stanford: Stanford UP, 1997. Print.

Paquot, Thierry. *L'utopie ou l'ideal piégé*. Paris: Hatier, 1996. Print.

Paraíso, Isabel. "La audacia métrica de Rosalía de Castro (En las orillas del Sar)." *Actas do Congreso Internacional* 2: 285–93. Print.

Patiño, Antón. *Xeometría líquida*. Santiago de Compostela: Positivas, 1993. Print.

"Patrimonio." *Diccionario da Real Academia Galega*. A Coruña: RAG, 1997. Xunta de Galicia, n.d. Web. 5 Dec. 2010.

Paulson, Ronald. *Representations of Revolution, 1789–1820*. New Haven: Yale UP, 1983. Print.

Peach, Lucinda Joy. Introduction. *Women in Culture: A Women's Studies Anthology*. Malden: Blackwell, 1998. 1–12. Print.

Pena, Jaimé. "A produción." *Libro branco de cinematografía* 15–30.

Pena, X. R. *Manoel Antonio e a vangarda*. Santiago de Compostela: Sotelo Blanco, 1996. Print.

Penny, Ralph. *A History of the Spanish Language*. 2nd ed. Cambridge: Cambridge UP, 2002. Print.

Pensado, José Luis. "La lexicología gallega en el siglo XVIII." *Tradición, actualidade e futuro do galego: Actas do Coloquio de Tréveris*. Ed. Dieter Kremer and Ramón Lorenzo. Santiago de Compostela: Xunta de Galicia, 1982. 85–98. Print.

Pérez Botero, Luis. "La poesía de Rosalía de Castro y sus posibles relaciones con la poesía modernista." *Actas do Congreso Internacional* 3: 229–34. Print.

Pérez Touriño, Emilio. "Presentación." *Rodado en Galicia*. Rodado en Galicia, n.d. Web. 1 Nov. 2009.

"Pérez Varela presenta en Venecia el Teatro de la Música, referente de los coliseos líricos." *ABC* 12 Oct. 2004: n. pag. *Hemeroteca*. Fundación Cidade da Cultura de Galicia, n.d. Web. 1 Nov. 2009.

"Unha performance con vacas ponlle fin a 'Dentro.'" *Galicia Hoxe*. Grupo Correo Gallego, 19 July 2006. Web. 1 Nov. 2009.

"Petición ante la Reforma del Código Civil español en materia de nacionalidad." *Planeta Galego*. Fillos de Galicia, 22 June 2002. Web. 30 Oct. 2009.

Pexegueiro, Alfonso. *Seraogna*. 1976. Ed. Luciano Fernández Martínez. Vigo: Xerais, 1997. Print.

Piñeiro, Ramón. "Cultura e Política." *Grial* 111 (1991): 377–81. Print.

———. *Olladas no futuro*. Vigo: Galaxia, 1974. Print.

———. "A saudade en Rosalía." *Filosofía da saudade*. Vigo: Galaxia, 1984. 105–21. Print.

Pino, Concha. "A Xunta di estar 'moi satisfeita' de que a Academia rexeitase a reforma do galego." *La voz de Galicia* 20 Nov. 2001: 29. Print.

Pinter, Harold. *Various Voices: Prose, Poetry, Politics, 1948–1998*. London: Faber, 1998. Print.

Plan de lectura, 2005–2010. Asociación Galega de Editores, n.d. Web. 15 Dec. 2007.

Portas, Manuel. *Lingua e sociedade na Galiza*. A Coruña: Bahia, 1991. Print.

Poullain, Claude. "Poesía gallega y poesía castellana en Rosalía de Castro." *Actas do Congreso Internacional* 2: 415–37.

Pound, Ezra. *The Cantos of Ezra Pound*. New York: New Directions, 1970. Print.

Pozo-Gutiérrez, Alicia. "Presencia española en el sur de Inglaterra: Una emigración silenciosa e invisible." *Migraciones y exilios* 4 (2003): 79–90. Print.

"'Pradolongo': O cinema normalízase." *Vieiros*. Vieiros, 14 Mar. 2008. Web. 1 Nov. 2009.

"Premio Cervantes: El Rey afirma que el castellano siempre fue lengua de encuentro." *Spanish Newswire Services* 23 Apr. 2001. Web. 1 Apr. 2003.

Pries, Ludger, ed. *Migration and Transnational Social Spaces*. Aldershot: Ashgate, 1999. Print.

Prontuário ortográfico do idioma galego. A Coruña: Associaçom Galega da Língua, 1985. Print.

"PSOE y BNG discrepan en defender la Ciudad de la Cultura como el 'gran proyecto cultural' gallego." *ABC* 22 Feb. 2006: n. pag. *Hemeroteca*. Fundación Cidade da Cultura de Galicia, n.d. Web. 1 Nov. 2009.

Pujol Guerrero, Joaquim. Rev. of *Ganga*, by Antón Lopo. *Lectora: Revista de dones i textualitat* 9 (2003). n. pag. Web. 1 Nov. 2009.

Queipo, Xavier. *Glosarios*. A Coruña: Espiral Mayor, 2004. Print.

Queizán, María Xosé. "O galego en Europa." *Faro de Vigo* 27 Sept. 1999: 14. Print.

Quiroga, Carlos. Message to John Patrick Thompson. 25 May 2009. E-mail.

———. "O galego não se dobra." Interview by Cyro Andrade. *Valor* 18–20 Aug. 2006: 12–13. Print.

Rabón, Xosé M. "A percura dun cine galego." *Grial* 40 (1973): 235–38. Print.

Rancière, Jacques. "Figuras do testemunho e democracia: Entrevista com Jacques Rancière." Interview by María-Benedita Basto. *Intervalo* 2 (2006): 177–86. Print.

"As Redes Escarlata organizan un acto poético nunha aldea abandonada de Lóuzara." *Culturagalega.org*. Consello de Cultura Galega, 11 Jun. 2004. Web. 1 Nov. 2009.

"Reforma ortográfica." *Agália* 67-68 (2001): 276–78. Print.

Regueira, Xosé Luís. "Estándar oral e variación social da lingua galega." *Cinguidos por unha arela común: Homenaxe ó profesor Xesús Alonso Montero*. Ed. Rosario Álvarez and Dolores Vilavedra. Vol. 1. Santiago de Compostela: U de Santiago de Compostela, 1999. 855–75. Print.

———. Message to John Patrick Thompson. 11 May 2009. E-mail.

———. "Modelos fonéticos e autenticidade lingüística." *Cadernos de lingua* 10 (1994): 37–60. Print.

Reixa, Antón R. *Alivio Rápido*. Discos Radiactivos Organizados, 1994. CD.

———. "Antón Reixa aspira a dar la lata y ser van guardista." Interview by Rosana Torres. *El país*. El país, 3 Feb. 1995. Web. 25 June 2010.

———. "Con Edoardo Sanguinetti en Compostela." *Escrita* 4 (1984): 4. Print.

———. "Los detractores de la Cidade da Cultura." *El país* [Galicia ed.]. El país, 2 Jan. 2007. Web. 1 Nov. 2009.

———. *Escarnio*. Madrid: 52 Promociones Musicales; El Europeo-Gora Herriak, 1999. CD.

———. *Historia do Rock and Roll (Poemas)*. Vigo: Diario 16, 1992. Print.

———. "Portugal." *La voz de Galicia* 10 Oct. 1999: 18. Print.

———. *Ringo Rango.* Vigo: Xerais, 1992. Print.

———. *Safari Mental.* Esa Ozuki-Gora Herriak, 1997. CD.

———. *Transporte de superficie.* Santiago de Compostela: Positivas, 1991. Print.

———. *Viva galicia beibe.* Santiago de Compostela: Positivas, 1994. Print.

Renta y empleo en los sectores productivos, 1995–2005. Santiago de Compostela: Equipo de Econometría de la U de Santiago, 2005. Print.

Resina, Joan Ramón. "The Scale of the Nation in a Shrinking World." *Diacritics* 33.3-4 (2003): 46–74. Print.

"Resistir é vender." *Culturagalega.org.* Consello da Cultura Galega, 23 Oct. 2002. Web. 28 Oct. 2009.

Rex, John. *Race and Ethnicity.* Milton Keynes: Open UP, 1986. Print.

Richardson, Nathan E. "Animals, Machines, and Postnational Identity in Julio Medem's *Vacas.*" *Journal of Iberian and Latin American Studies* 10.2 (2004): 191–204. Print.

Ríos-Font, Wadda. "From Romantic Irony to Romantic Grotesque: Mariano José Larra's and Rosalía de Castro's Self-Conscious Novels." *Hispanic Review* 65 (1997): 177–98. Print.

Risco, Antón. *Literatura fantástica de lengua española: Teoría y aplicaciones.* Madrid: Taurus, 1987. Print.

———. *Memorias dun emigrante.* Vigo: Galaxia, 1987. Print.

Risco, Vicente. *Teoría do nacionalismo galego.* 1920. Ed. Justo Beramendi. Santiago de Compostela: Sotelo Blanco, 2000. Print.

———. "U . . . ju juu . . . (Poema futurista)." *A nosa terra* 113 (1920): 8. Print.

Rivas, Manuel. *A man dos paínos.* Vigo: Galaxia, 2000. Print.

———. *La mano del emigrante.* Madrid: Alfaguara, 2001. Print.

———. "Proposición para refundar Galicia enteira." *El país* [Galicia ed.]. El país, 6 Mar. 2009. Web. 1 Nov. 2009.

Rivera, Olga. "Conflictos ideologicos interclasistas en *Ruinas* y *El caballero de las botas azules* de Rosalia de Castro." *Hispania* 86.3 (2003): 474–81. Print.

Robinson, William I. "Beyond Nation-State Paradigms: Globalization, Sociology, and the Challenge of Transnational Studies." *Sociological Forum* 13.4 (1998): 561–94. Print.

Rodrigues Fagim, Valentim. *O galego (im)possível.* Santiago de Compostela: Laiovento, 2001. Print.

Rodrígues Lapa, Manuel. "A recuperação literária do galego." *Grial* 41 (1973): 278–87. Print.

Rodríguez, Carlos Luís. "Lusismo ilusionista." *El correo gallego* 8 Dec. 1999: 6. Print.

Rodríguez, Francisco. *Literatura galega contemporánea: Problemas de método e interpretación.* Vigo: Cumio, 1990. Print.

Rodríguez Fer, Claudio. *A vida: Gravados sobre corpo.* Lugo: Taller de Gravado Aguatinta, 2002. Print.

Rodríguez-Fischer, Ana. "Alonso Montero aboga por el inglés como lengua oficial antes que un gallego lusista." *La voz de Galicia* 6 Dec. 1999: 84. Print.

————. Introduction. *El caballero de las botas azules.* By Rosalía de Castro. Madrid: Cátedra, 1995. 9–79. Print.

Rodríguez-Galdo, María Xosé. *Galicia, país de emigración: La emigración gallega a América hasta 1930.* Gijón: Colombres, 1993. Print.

Roen, Paul. *High Camp: A Gay Guide to Camp and Cult Films.* San Francisco: Leyland, 1994. Print.

Romaní, Ana. *Love Me Tender: 24 pezas mínimas para unha caixa de música.* Santiago de Compostela: Grupo Correo Gallego; Concello de Santiago; Consellaría de Cultura, 2005. Print.

————. *Das últimas mareas.* A Coruña: Espiral Mayor, 1994. Print.

"Romaní leva 'Catro poetas suicidas' á Casa de Rosalía." *O correo galego* 18 Apr. 2002: 36. Print.

Romero, Eugenia R. "Amusement Parks, Bagpipes, and Cemeteries: Fantastic Spaces of Galician Identity through Migration." *Journal of Spanish Cultural Studies* 7.2 (2006): 155–69. Print.

————. *Las dos Galicias: Movimientos migratorios en la construcción del imaginario literario y cultural gallego.* Diss. Emory U, 2004. Ann Arbor: ProQuest, 2004. Print.

Rompente. *A dama que fala.* Vigo: Xerais, 1983. Print.

————. *Silabario da turbina.* Vigo: Rompente, 1978. Print.

————. "Textos de resistencia e comunicación." Cochón and González 85–94.

Ronell, Avital. "On the Misery of Theory without Poetry: Heidegger's Reading of Hölderlin's 'Andenken.'" *PMLA* 120.1 (2005): 16–32. Print.

Ronseltz. *Unicornio de cenorias que cabalgan os sábados.* Santiago de Compostela: Positivas, 1994. Print.

Ross, Andrew. "Uses of Camp." Cleto 308–29.

Rubenstein, Roberta. *Home Matters: Longing and Belonging, Nostalgia and Mourning in Women's Fiction.* New York: Palgrave, 2001. Print.

Rutherford, John. *As frechas de ouro.* Vigo: Xerais, 2004. Print.

Safran, William. "Diasporas in Modern Societies: Myths of Homeland and Return." *Diaspora* 1.1 (1991): 83–99. Print.

Said, Edward. "Reflections on Exile." *Granta* 13 (1984): 157–72. Print.

Sánchez Mora, Elena. "Rosalía de Castro: Bachillera o ángel del hogar?" *Actas do Congreso Internacional* 1: 251–57.

Santamarina, Antón. "Norma e estándar." Monteagudo, *Estudios* 53–98.

Savater, Fernando. *Contra las patrias.* Barcelona: Tusquets, 1996. Print.

Seligmann–Silva, Márcio, ed. *História, memória, literature: O testemunho na era das catástrophes.* Campinas: U Estadual de Campinas, 2003. Print.

Sempere, Isabel. "O apoio da Administración á creación audiovisual." *Libro branco de cinematografía* 251–88.

Senlle, Uxía, perf. *Son Delas en concerto.* Teatro Rosalía Castro, A Coruña. 11 Apr. 2002. Performance.

Silverstone, Roger. *Television and Everyday Life.* London: Routledge, 1994. Print.

Sim, Stuart, ed. *The Routledge Companion to Postmodernism.* 1998. London: Routledge, 2005. Print.

Smith, Paul Julian. "Introduction: New Approaches to Spanish Television." *Journal of Spanish Cultural Studies* 8.1 (2007): 1–4. Print.

Smolicz, Jerzy J. "In Search of a Multicultural Nation: The Case of Australia from an International Perspective." *Cultural Democracy and Ethnic Pluralism: Multicultural and Multilingual Policies in Education.* Ed. Richard J. Watts and Smolicz. Frankfurt: Lang, 1997. 52–76. Print.

Sontag, Susan. "Notes on Camp." 1964. *The Best American Essays of the Twentieth Century.* Ed. Joyce Carol Oates. Boston: Houghton, 2000. 288–302. Print.

Soto, David. "Transformacións productivas na agricultura galega contemporánea: Da agricultura orgánica á revolución verde, 1752–1986: Unha aproximación a partir das macromagnitudes." Diss. U de Santiago de Compostela, 2003. Print.

Souto, Cris. "A ponte virtual sobre o Atlántico: A páxina web fillosdegalicia.com é 'o oitavo centro galego que hai no mundo.'" *Xornal.com.* Xornal.com, 18 Feb. 2009. Web. 1 Nov. 2009.

Steinwand, Jonathan. "The Future of Nostalgia in Friedrich Schlegel´s Gender Theory: Casting German Aesthetics beyond Ancient Greece and Modern Europe." *Narratives of Nostalgia, Gender and Nationalism.* Ed. Jean Pickering and Suzanne Kehde. London: Macmillan, 1997. 9–29. Print.

Suelto de Sáenz, Pilar G. "Rosalía de Castro, anticipación del '98.'" *Actas do Congreso Internacional* 2: 453–60.

Swingewood, Alan. *Cultural Theory and the Problem of Modernity.* New York: St. Martin's, 1998. Print.

Tarrío Varela, Anxo. "A ver se nos aclaramos." *El correo gallego* 4 Oct. 1999: 2. Print.

———. *Literatura galega: Aportacións a unha historia crítica.* Vigo: Xerais, 1994. Print.

———. *Literatura gallega.* Madrid: Taurus, 1988. Print.

Thompson, John. "A Tango of a Lost Democracy and Women's Liberation: María Xosé Queizán's Feminist Vision in *Amor de tango.*" *Bulletin of Hispanic Studies* 85.3 (2008): 343–60. Print.

Todorov, Tzvetan. *The Fantastic: A Structural Approach to a Literary Genre.* Trans. Richard Howard. New York: Cornell UP, 1975. Print.

Tolliver, Joyce. "Rosalía between Two Shores: Gender, Rewriting, and Translation." *Hispania* 85.1 (2002): 33–43. Print.

Toro, Suso de. *Caixón desastre.* Vigo: Xerais, 1983. Print.

———. "En confianza, disparamos contra nós mesmos." *A nosa terra* 5 Oct. 1995: 27. Print.

———. "Hai un lugar no mundo para nós." *La voz de Galicia* 19 Oct. 1999: 18. Print.

———. *Land Rover.* Vigo: Xerais, 1988. Print.

———. *Polaroid.* Vigo: Xerais, 1986. Print.

———. *Tic-Tac.* 1993. 2nd ed. Vigo: Xerais, 2003. Print.

Toro Santos, Antonio Raúl de. *Galicia desde Londres: Galicia, Gran Bretaña e Irlanda nos programas galegos da BBC, 1947–1956*. A Coruña: Tambre, 1994. Print.

Toro Santos, Xelís de. "Bagpipes and Digital Music: The Remixing of Galician Identity." Labanyi, *Constructing* 237–54.

———. *Os saltimbanquis no paraíso*. Santiago de Composela: Sotello Blanco, 1999. Print.

Torres Feijóo, Elias. "A Galiza em Portugal, Portugal na Galiza através das revistas literárias, 1900–1936." Diss. U of Compostela, 1996. Print.

Toury, Gideon. "Translation as a Means of Planning and the Planning of Translation: A Theoretical Framework and an Exemplary Case." Proceedings of the International Conference "Translations: (Re)shaping of Literature and Culture." Bogaziçi U, Istanbul, 2002. Ed. Saliha Paker et al. *Gideon Toury's Works*. Tel Aviv U, n.d. Web. 1 Nov. 2009.

"Translittera." *Xornadas e congresos*. Consello da Cultura Galega, 2005. Web. 1 Nov. 2009.

Trousson, Raymond. "Utopie et roman utopique." *Revue des sciences humaines* 155 (1974): 367–78. Print.

Tsur, Reuven. "Picture Poetry, Mannerism, and Sign Relationships." *Poetics Today* 21.4 (2000): 751–81. Print.

Turrón, Kike, and Kike Babas. *Tremendo delirio: Conversaciones con Julián Hernández y biografía de Siniestro Total*. Zaragoza: Libros Zona de Obras; SGAE, 2002. Print.

Ucelay da Cal, Enric. "The Nationalism of the Periphery: Culture and Politics in the Construction of National Identity." *Spanish Cultural Studies: An Introduction*. Ed. Helen Graham and Jo Labanyi. Oxford: Oxford UP, 1995. 32–39. Print.

Valverde Otero, Alberto. "Entrevista a Antón Reixa." Valverde Otero, *O grupo Rompente* 101–09.

———. *O grupo Rompente, 1975–1983: Por unha resistencia nacional e unha comunicación de vangarda*. Vigo: Facultade de Filoloxía e Tradución, 2005. Print.

———. "A *performance* en Rompente." *Anuario de estudos literarios galegos 2004* (2005): 96–106. Print.

Varela Jácome, Benito. "El discurso narrativo de *Flavio*." *Actas do Congreso Internacional* 1: 387–97.

———. *Historia de la literatura gallega*. Santiago de Compostela: Porto y Cía, 1951. Print.

Vattimo, Gianni. *Beyond Interpretation: The Meaning of Hermeneutics for Philosophy*. Palo Alto: Stanford UP, 1997. Print.

Vázquez Cuesta, Pilar. Interview by Xan Carballa. *A nosa terra* 6 June 1996: 27. Print.

Vázquez Varela, X. M, et al. *Nova historia de Galicia*. Oleiros: Tambre, 1996. Print.

Veiga, Manuel. "A castelanización da TVG no vértice da crise polo caso Xosé Antón Porto."*A nosa terra* 11 June 1998: 31. Print.

Veiga, Raúl. "A lingua do noso audiovisual." *Libro branco de cinematografía* 311–30.

Verea y Aguiar, José. *Historia de Galicia: Primera parte, que comprende los orígenes y estado de los pueblos septentroniales y occidentales de la España antes de su conquista por los romanos.* Ferrol: Nicasio Taxonera, 1838. Print.

Vicetto, Benito. *Historia de Galicia.* 7 vols. Ferrol: Nicasio Taxonera, 1865–73. Print.

Vidal, Carme. "Compostela tórnase centro da lusofonía: Latim em pó estabelece pontes entre os países do ámbito galego-portugués." *A nosa terra* 14 Dec. 2000: 18. Print.

———. "Os escritores apoian a proposta de Carlos Casares de reforma da normativa." *A nosa terra* 30 Sept. 1999: 25. Print.

Vidal, Carme, and Paula Bergantiños. "O galego abre pontes entre catro continentes." *A nosa terra* 21 Dec. 2000: 2–3. Print.

Vilavedra, Dolores. "Atopando o seu espazo: Narrativa do ano 2005." *Anuario de estudos literarios galegos 2005* (2006): 168–73. Print.

———, ed. *Diccionario da literatura galega.* 4 vols. Vigo: Galaxia, 1995–2004. Print.

———. *Historia da literatura galega.* Vigo: Galaxia, 1999. Print.

———. "Narrativa en 2004: Unha xeira de profundización." *Anuario de estudos literarios galegos 2004* (2005): 144–51. Print.

———. *Sobre narrativa galega contemporánea: Estudios e críticas.* Vigo: Galaxia, 2000. Print.

Villalaín, Damián. "O piñeirogayosismo." *Tempos novos* 74 (2003): 59–61. Print.

Villamor, Luís. "Nogueira, en portugués en Europa." *La voz de Galicia* 20 Sept. 1999: 6. Print.

Villanueva, Darío. "Los marcos de la literatura española, 1975–1990: Esbozo de un sistema." *Los nuevos nombres, 1975–1990.* Ed. Villanueva et al. Barcelona: Crítica, 1992. 3–40. Print. Vol. 9 of *Historia y crítica de la literatura española.* Gen. ed. Francisco Rico.

Villar, Rafa. "Cal normativa para o galego? Elemen tos para un debate errado." *A nosa terra* 28 Oct. 1999: 34. Print.

———. "A poesía: Impresións dixitais." *Dorna* 23 (1997): 85–92. Print.

Villares, Ramón. *Historia de Galicia.* 1984. Vigo: Faro de Vigo, 1992. Print.

———. "Idade contemporánea." *Nova historia de Galicia.* Ed. Begoña Eguizábal et al. A Coruña: Tambre, 1996. 355–447. Print.

Villares, Ramón, and Marcelino Fernández-Santiago. *Historia da emigración galega a América.* Santiago de Compostela: Xunta de Galicia, 1996. Print.

Weimann, Robert. "Value, Representation, and the Discourse of Modernization: Toward a Political Economy of Postindustrial Culture." Palumbo-Lin and Gumbrecht 221–47.

Williams, Alan, ed. *Film and Nationalism.* New Brunswick: Rutgers UP, 2002. Print.

Williams, Raymond. "Base and Superstructure in Marxist Cultural Theory." *The Raymond Williams Reader.* Ed. John Higgins. Oxford: Wiley-Blackwell, 2001. 158–78. Print.

———. *Television: Technology and Cultural Form.* London: Routledge, 1990. Print.

X: Espazo para un signo. Vigo: Xerais, 2005. Print.

"La Xunta dota con más de 2.000 millones a la Fundación Cidade de Cultura." *El mundo* 15 Apr. 2000: n. pag. *Hemeroteca.* Fundación Cidade da Cultura de Galicia, n.d. Web. 1 Nov. 2009.